I0096014

"This book reflects and reveals the emergence of an already powerful and potentially monumental development in global Pentecostalism. A growing number of Pentecostals are rediscovering their own early tradition of nonviolent peacemaking grounded in their passionate desire to follow Jesus without compromise. If even a quarter of today's 600 million Pentecostals would combine Jesus' call to nonviolent peacemaking with the explosive power of Pentecost, the demons would tremble, the Church would flourish, and the world would rejoice. This important book offers exciting clues about how that might happen."

—RON SIDER,
Founder of Evangelicals for Social Action

"*Pentecostals and Nonviolence* documents . . . and charts a way forward for pentecostal pacifism. One need not be a pacifist (I'm not) or agree with every statement in this book (I don't) to recognize the important challenge it poses to Pentecostals' all-too-easy affirmation of our nation's wars."

—GEORGE PAUL WOOD,
Director of Ministerial Resourcing, Assemblies of God

PENTECOSTALS
and NONVIOLENCE

# Pentecostals, Peacemaking, and Social Justice Series

PAUL ALEXANDER AND JAY BEAMAN, SERIES EDITORS

## Volumes in the Series:

*Pentecostal Pacifism: The Origin, Development, and Rejection of Pacific Belief among the Pentecostals*
by Jay Beaman

*A Liberating Spirit: Pentecostals and Social Action in North America*
edited by Michael Wilkinson and Steven M. Studebaker

*Forgiveness, Reconciliation, and Restoration: Mulitdisciplinary Studies from a Pentecostal Perspective*
edited by Martin W. Mittelstadt and Geoffrey W. Sutton

*The Liberating Mission of Jesus: The Message of the Gospel of Luke*
by Dario Lopez Rodriguez

*Christ at the Checkpoint: Theology in the Service of Justice and Peace*
edited by Paul Nathan Alexander

# Pentecostals and Nonviolence

## Reclaiming a Heritage

EDITED BY

PAUL ALEXANDER

FOREWORD BY

STANLEY HAUERWAS

PICKWICK *Publications* · Eugene, Oregon

PENTECOSTALS AND NONVIOLENCE
Reclaiming a Heritage

Pentecostals, Peacemaking, and Social Justice 5

Copyright © 2012 Wipf and Stock Publishers. All rights reserved. Except for brief quotations in critical publications or reviews, no part of this book may be reproduced in any manner without prior written permission from the publisher. Write: Permissions, Wipf and Stock Publishers, 199 W. 8th Ave., Suite 3, Eugene, OR 97401.

Pickwick Publications
An Imprint of Wipf and Stock Publishers
199 W. 8th Ave., Suite 3
Eugene, OR 97401

www.wipfandstock.com

ISBN 13: 978-1-60608-362-8

*Cataloging-in-Publication data:*

Pentecostals and nonviolence : reclaiming a heritage / edited by Paul Alexander ; foreword by Stanley Hauerwas.

Pentecostals, Peacemaking, and Social Justice 5

xxvi + 390 p. ; 23 cm. — Includes bibliographical references.

ISBN 13: 978-1-60608-362-8

1. Peace—Religious aspects—Pentecostal churches. 2. Pentecostal churches—Doctrines. I. Alexander, Paul, 1972–. II. Hauerwas, Stanley, 1940–. III. Title. IV. Series.

BX8765.5.Z5 P44X 2012

Manufactured in the U.S.A.

*To Nathan Bird, Kharese Shalom, and Abigail Francis Hope,*

*y todos mi amig@s en Pentecostals & Charismatics for Peace & Justice*

# Contents

List of Contributors / xi

Foreword by Stanley Hauerwas / xiii

Preface by Paul Alexander / xvii

## Part I: Early Twentieth-Century Pentecostal Pacifism

1 The Extent of Early Pentecostal Pacifism / 3
*Jay Beaman*

2 "I thank my God for the persecution": Conscientious Objection in the Church of God in Christ during World War I / 39
*Theodore Kornweibel, Jr.*

3 The Foursquare Church and Pacifism / 64
*Brian K. Pipkin*

4 "Crossing Borders": Arguments Used by Early American Pentecostals in Support of the Global Character of Pacifism / 121
*Murray W. Dempster*

5 Pentecost and the End of Patriotism: A Call for the Restoration of Pacifism Among Pentecostal Christians / 143
*Joel Shuman*

6 Prophetic "Patriotic" Pentecostal Peacemaking: Early Assemblies of God Pacifism and the Twentieth Century / 171
*Paul Alexander*

## Part II: Pentecostal Peacemaking in the Twenty-first Century

Rebuild Afghanistan: A Declaration of Faithfulness / A Transforming Initiative, September 25, 2001  /  189
*Paul Alexander*

7  Jesus-Shaped and Spirit-Empowered Peace with Justice: Toward a Christomorphic Pneumatology  /  192
*Paul Alexander*

8  What the Church Teaches about War: A COGIC Conscientious Objection Principle  /  205
*David A. Hall, Sr.*

9  Send Judah First: A Pentecostal Perspective on Peace  /  215
*Marlon Millner*

10  Toward a Pentecostal Contribution to the Just War Tradition  /  229
*Michael Beals*

11  Pastoring a Peace Church  /  250
*Jonathan Martin*

12  My Almost-Abortion: A Romance in Late Capitalism  /  266
*Erica Bryand Ramirez*

13  Preaching Christ Crucified: Sharing [in] the Spirit of God's Nonviolent Future  /  283
*Jarrod Saul McKenna*

## Part III: Emerging Anabaptist/Pentecostal Conversations

Letter to the Editor, *Waxahachie Daily Light*, January 2006  /  303
*Paul Alexander*

14  Spirit-Empowered Peacemaking as Evangelical, Ecumenical, and Pentecostal Opportunity  /  305
*Paul Alexander*

15  Scandalous Partners in Protest: A Continuing Dialogue  /  320
*Andrew S. Hamilton and Kenneth J. Archer*

16    My Life as a Menno-costal: A Personal and Theological
Narrative / 333
*Martin William Mittelstadt*

17    Thank You and Please: An Address to Mennonite Church USA,
July 4, 2007 / 352
*Paul Alexander*

Bibliography of Resources for Further Study
—Compiled by Brian K. Pipkin / 369

# Contributors

**PAUL ALEXANDER**, Professor of Theology and Ethics, Palmer Theological Seminary of Eastern University, St. Davids, Pennsylvania

**KENNETH J. ARCHER**, Associate Professor of Theology, Pentecostal Theological Seminary, Cleveland, Tennessee

**MICHAEL BEALS**, Senior Pastor, Mission Hills Community Church, Rancho Santa Margarita, California; Adjunct Faculty, Vanguard University, Costa Mesa, California

**JAY BEAMAN**, Director of Institutional Research, Lewis and Clark College, Portland, Oregon

**MURRAY W. DEMPSTER**, Distinguished Professor of Social Ethics, Southeastern University, Lakeland, Florida

**DAVID A. HALL, SR.**, Senior Pastor, Temple Church of God in Christ; CEO, Church of God in Christ Publishing House, Memphis, Tennessee

**ANDREW S. HAMILTON**, Pastor, Springfield Church of the Brethren, Akron, Ohio; Adjunct Faculty, Ashland Theological Seminary, Ashland, Ohio

**STANLEY HAUERWAS**, Gilbert T. Rowe Professor of Theology and Ethics, Duke Divinity School, Durham, North Carolina

**THEODORE KORNWEIBEL**, Jr., Professor Emeritus of African-American History, San Diego State University, San Diego, California

JONATHAN MARTIN, Pastor of Renovatus Church, Charlotte, North Carolina; M.Div. Student, Duke Divinity School, Durham, North Carolina

JAROD SAUL McKENNA, National Advisor for Youth, Faith, and Activism, World Vision Australia

MARLON MILLNER, Associate Pastor, Harold O. Davis Memorial Baptist Church, Philadelphia, Pennsylvania

MARTIN WILLIAM MITTELSTADT, Associate Professor of Biblical Studies, Evangel University, Springfield, Missouri

BRIAN K. PIPKIN, Azusa Pacific University

ERICA BRYAND RAMIREZ, PhD Student, Religion and Society, Drew University, Madison, New Jersey

JOEL SHUMAN, Professor of Theology, King's College, Wilkes-Barre, Pennsylvania

# Foreword

I am often accused of having an inadequate doctrine of the Holy Spirit. I have resisted that characterization, but I have found that my attempts to claim that I take seriously the work of the Spirit are not convincing. So I welcome this opportunity to write in support of *Pentecostals and Nonviolence*. First and foremost I welcome this opportunity because this is such a fine collection of essays. But I also am honored to be asked to write this "Foreword" because I hope that these people of the Spirit have asked me to write because they glimpse in my work the work of the Holy Spirit.

I have always thought the first indication of the work of the Holy Spirit to be the commitment to say what is true. This book surely exhibits that characteristic. Many of these essays have been written by pacifists. They, moreover, represent the diverse communities that are identified as "Pentecostals." As "Pentecostal pacifists" they tell honestly the quite ambiguous story of the relation between Pentecostals and nonviolence.

As Shuman makes clear in his essay, the early Pentecostal movements represented a restorationist ecclesiology that inclined the church toward a pacifist orientation but they often failed to know how to articulate that commitment in a manner that was sustaining. And the story Pipkin tells about Aimee Semple McPherson makes any romantic idealization of the early Pentecostal movement problematic.

Yet I find it particularly interesting that the nonviolence of the early Pentecostal movement was first and foremost understood to be an ecclesial commitment. The work of the Holy Spirit is the work of building up the unity of the church through the worship of Jesus. It is not surprising, therefore, that Pentecostals began to understand why they might be characterized as "pacifist" by recognizing that they represented a renewal movement committed to Christian unity. In reading through these essays I was particularly moved by Hamilton's and Archer's proposal of foot washing as a liturgical action of reconciliation in the hope of Christian unity.

These essays, moreover, make clear that the ecclesial and correlatively biblical focus that fostered the Pentecostal commitment to peace became the source of the quite remarkable development of social analysis by Pentecostal people. They seemed to know in their bones that a strong distinction between church and world was necessary to sustain the witness of the church to a peace that can come only through the work of the Spirit. The inter-racial character of the early Pentecostal movement surely is a testimony to the prophetic stance of the church. Indeed the very existence of a figure like Bishop Mason is sufficient to challenge those who would dismiss the Pentecostal movement as a retreat from the world.

I was also struck by how important the work of John Howard Yoder has been for helping Pentecostals recover their initial commitments of Christian nonviolence. That happy development has also seemed to make possible the mutual recognition by Pentecostals and Anabaptists that they need one another to better understand who they have been and, just as important, who they now must be. I have a hunch, moreover, that the conversation between Pentecostals and Anabaptists may invite for both recognition that they are much closer to a Catholic understanding of the church than has been acknowledged in the past.

This last observation may seem quite odd given Jonathan Martin's wonderful account of Margaret Gaines' concern to stop the violence in a Palestinian village by asking "Is there anyone small enough to stop the violence?" Christian unity, however, depends on our being a church small enough to do the everyday work necessary to make peace a reality. That kind of work I think was characteristic of the Pentecostal movement as people who were moved by the Spirit were bound together in networks of trust that turn out to be but another name for peacemaking.

I suspect one of the reasons I have been asked to write this "Foreword" is to give legitimacy to the Pentecostal story narrated as a story of peace. For whatever difference I may represent, I do hope it encourages Pentecostal people to explore their heritage and future as one committed to nonviolence. But I also hope that those who are not Pentecostals will be tempted to read this book. For I think they will find that the struggles of Pentecostals to understand what it means for them to be nonviolent is a gift to all Christians who would receive the gift of the Holy Spirit.

Stanley Hauerwas

# Preface

On July 17, 2001, exactly eight weeks before 9/11, I presented my first paper at an academic conference, "Spirit Empowered Peacemaking: Toward a Pentecostal Peace Fellowship."[1] It was the direct result of my struggle to learn how to follow Jesus after having my faith shattered in graduate school. Being a Pentecostal farm boy from southeast Kansas whose grandparents still did not have indoor plumbing, I became aware that I had plenty to be embarrassed about and had a lot to learn. I learned to be ashamed of my Pentecostal heritage, theology, and practices. I learned that I could not prove there is a God. And along with Deborah, my wife, I struggled until the early morning hours of many a night with the deep questions of God's power and love and this suffering world. I eventually quit praying (in tongues and at all), stopped believing in God, devoted myself to day trading stocks and buying real estate with borrowed money and the desire to get filthy rich, while working on a PhD in theological ethics.[2]

Yet (at least) two other significant stories intersected with mine and marked me deeply during that time and remain central to my identity and calling. I consider them gifts. First, I accidentally discovered that the Assemblies of God, the denomination of my four-generation Pentecostal heritage, had been a pacifist church. I thought this was about the dumbest

1. Presented at the 10th annual conference of the European Pentecostal Charismatic Research Association at the Catholic University of Louvain, Belgium, July 17–21, 2001.

2. I told some of my story in a sermon at the Mennonite Church USA biennial convention on July 4, 2007, in San Jose, California. A slightly revised version appears as chapter sixteen of this volume.

thing I had ever heard and continued buying Wal-Mart and Exxon-Mobil stock. Second, I took a class with John Howard Yoder in the summer of 1997. At first, I sat across the table thinking, "You mean, we don't just kill our enemies?" But around that time I developed a voracious appetite for Yoder's works, as well as those of Stanley Hauerwas. I didn't stop day trading or trying to get rich, but I started thinking differently about my nationality and regretting the way I sang "bomb, bomb, bomb . . . bomb, bomb Iraq" during the war in January, 1991. I also slowly came to the re-alization that if there is a God, and if that God is revealed most clearly in Jesus, then just about everything about me was going to have to change.

I decided to study this part of my heritage that I didn't hear people talking about much anymore and to write my dissertation on the paci-fist heritage of the Assemblies of God. Reading about the Assemblies of God's changing commitments—from being pacifist to supporting war—was a painful, identity-shattering, character-transforming process. I discovered that my own grandfather and my wife's grandfather had each been Pentecostal pacifists in World War II (mine, a conscientious objector and hers, a noncombatant). I felt betrayed that my denomina-tion had changed so much, and that I had not been told anything about it. Without any critical distance from this uncovered history, I became angry. I was angry when I finished my degree program in the summer of 2000. Reading Yoder, Hauerwas, and early Pentecostal pacifists all at the same time had shaken me to my very core and I felt like I was living in a different story than when I had started. Looking back now, I can see that my faith(fulness) was being reshaped, but at the time, I felt confusingly mad and hopeful at the same time. Needing friends to talk to, I looked around for other pentecostals who were also interested in peacemaking. I found Baptist, Orthodox, and Disciples of Christ peace fellowships. I joined the Ekklesia Project. But there was nothing for those within my particular faith tradition and I felt like there should be. Deborah and I needed a community of support for our own journey, but we had not yet met many other Pentecostal pacifists.

So in 2001, after losing interest in stocks and selling out all my posi-tions (for a net loss), I imitated other faith traditions' way of maintaining their peace witness and presented a call for a Pentecostal peace fellow-ship (part of that paper is in chapter thirteen of this book).[3] Concerned

3. The full paper from 2001 was published as "Spirit Empowered Peacemaking: Toward a Pentecostal Peace Fellowship," *Journal of the European Pentecostal Theological*

I might be headed in a wrong direction, I re-read Yoder's *The Original Revolution,* one more time, which reassured me that my ancestors in the faith had certainly been on the right track. Although my writing style and thinking have changed in the few years since then, I've decided to publish some of that essay as I presented it then, eight weeks before 9/11.

That is the nature of most of this book: most of the chapters have been presented at conferences or have appeared in journals. The works collected here reflect the struggles, joys, and arguments—spiritual, historical, theological, ecclesial—that many of us have experienced in our personal lives and in our academic scholarship. The structure of the book reflects one way that some Pentecostals have dealt with the subject of peacemaking—exploring our own history of pacifism and nonviolence, thinking theologically and pastorally about it, and envisioning how peacemaking and justice seeking can be part of the contemporary Pentecostal-Charismatic movement.

Part One, "Early Twentieth-Century Pentecostal Pacifism," presents six chapters by folks who have spent a considerable amount of time with the primary literature. Earlier versions of four of these chapters were written before I personally learned that Pentecostals had a pacifist heritage, and each one had a significant impact on me. In chapter 1, Jay Beaman offers a newly revised and expanded chapter from his landmark 1989 book, *Pentecostal Pacifism,* in which he argued that the majority of early Pentecostal denominations adopted position statements that advocated conscientious objection.[4] Beaman demonstrates the breadth of the peace witness he locates across many classical Pentecostal denominations. His chapter includes new findings based on hundreds of World War I Pentecostal draft records. In chapter 2, Ted Kornweibel, a historian at San Diego State University, presents a focused examination of conscientious objection within the early Church of God in Christ and the life of Bishop C. H. Mason. In chapter 3, Brian Pipkin presents a portion of his MA thesis on early pacifism in the International Church of the Foursquare Gospel, the denomination founded by Sister Aimee Semple McPherson. Brian studied with me at Azusa Pacific University, spend-

*Association* 22 (2002) 78–102.

4. We have published a twentieth-anniversary revised version. Jay Beaman, *Pentecostal Pacifism: The Origin, Development, and Rejection of Pacific Belief Among the Pentecostals,* Pentecostals, Peacemaking, and Social Justice Series, vol. 1 (Eugene, OR: Wipf & Stock, 2009).

ing considerable time in Foursquare archives to find previously unpublished material about this aspect of Foursquare history. Brian plans to
write his PhD dissertation on this topic so this chapter is a glimpse into
what he is discovering. In chapter 4, Murray Dempster, an Assemblies of
God social ethicist, canvasses three arguments early Pentecostals used to
support their pacifism. First, they viewed pacifism as an integral aspect
of restoring the New Testament church—a "tangible moral sign that the
Pentecostal church had recovered the eschatological character of New
Testament Christianity." Second, pacifism served as a moral critique of
the existing social and political order—"[it] critique[d] the power struc-
ture of the world order in concrete action." Third, pacifism served as a
moral affirmation of the universal scope of the value of human life – as-
serting "[a] concrete moral authenticity to the gospel." Chapter 5 is Joel
Shuman's powerful argument in favor of the restoration of pacifism among
Pentecostal Christians. Joel's article had a significant impact on me when
I first read it and has continued to inspire me ever since. After we started
Pentecostals & Charismatics for Peace & Justice (PCPJ), this article was
one we always tried to hand out at conferences. I am so thankful that
it now is available in this book. Joel argues first that Pentecostals once
again need to restore the disestablishmentarianism of early Christianity/
Pentecostalism. Second, that Pentecostals need to base their position on
war in scripture. Third, that the Assemblies of God needs to evaluate
whether their "evangelistic passion" should allow them to forsake their
pacifist heritage. Fourth, that the Assemblies of God's desire for acceptability needs to be reversed. Shuman advises that the story of Pentecost
should be central to Christian nonviolence and that Pentecostals should
be the ones to bring this back to the church. In chapter 6, employing
material I found while researching and writing my dissertation, I offer a
response to the claim that pacifism was a minority position in the early
Assemblies of God and then preliminarily present the potential of what I
was then calling prophetic, "patriotic," Pentecostal peacemaking.

  Part Two, "Pentecostal Peacemaking in the Twenty-First Century,"
offers theological, ethical, pastoral, and practical possibilities in the order
in which they appeared over the course of the last few years. The introduction to Part Two, "Rebuild Afghanistan," is a piece that I wrote on
September 25, 2001, two weeks after 9/11, when many in the U.S. were
making a case for war in Afghanistan. Chapter 7 is a paper I presented
at the Society for Pentecostal Studies conference in March, 2002, a few

months after 9/11, in which I suggest that Christology is the source and Pneumatology is the means for Pentecostal peacemaking. In chapter 8, Marlon Millner presents a letter that he authored in the fall of 2002 urging President Bush not to invade Iraq. Many Pentecostals and Charismatics endorsed this letter. Marlon shares the story of how it came about and what some of the repercussions were. In chapter 9, David Hall Sr. presents an argument for reclaiming conscientious objection in the Church of God in Christ (COGIC). It is still the official position of COGIC, and Hall argues that it should be taught consistently and openly once again and that COGIC should develop an organizational structure that supports interchurch and interfaith peacemaking. This chapter is reprinted from his book, and after reading it in 2005 (thanks to Marlon Millner and Raynard Smith recommending it) PCPJ invited Elder Hall to be the first keynote speaker at our inaugural conference in October 2005, near Dallas, Texas. In chapter 10, Michael Beals presents an argument for the just war tradition as a way of helping Pentecostals find a voice that can oppose at least some wars. In chapter 11, Jonathan Martin reflects on the difficulties, joys, and smallness of pastoring a Pentecostal church on the journey of peacemaking. Jonathan shares the stories of folks within his church and also the character-shaping testimony of Margaret Gaines, a Church of God (Cleveland, TN) missionary to Palestine who established a church and school in the village of Aboud in the West Bank. Margaret is his spiritual grandmother and she continues to disciple Jonathan as well as the church he pastors. In chapter 12, Erica Bryand Ramirez narrates her experiences of peace and peacemaking with herself, her family, and her friends in the midst of sadness, loss, death, and hope. In chapter 13, Jarrod Saul McKenna, our mate from Australia, offers an analysis of the nonviolent atonement for Charismatic and Pentecostal Christians.

Part Three, "Emerging Anabaptist/Pentecostal Conversations," presents some of the interchurch work being done together by Anabaptists and Pentecostals. Chapter 14 is my reflection on peacemaking as an opportunity for evangelical, ecumenical, and Pentecostal faithfulness that I presented at the Society for Pentecostal Studies in March, 2002. I reflected on the work of John Howard Yoder and imagined the possibilities of a Pentecostal peace fellowship. Chapter 15, by Kenneth Archer (a Pentecostal) and Andrew Hamilton (an Anabaptist), is a co-authored exploration of the similarities that Pentecostals and Anabaptists have as communities of protest and a foray into the ways they can work together and learn from one another. Ken and Andy propose a liturgy for worship that centers on feetwashing, which is one of the three ordinances ("sacraments") in the Church of God (Cleveland, TN) and a valued practice in the Church of the Brethren. Chapter 16 is Martin Mittelstadt's narrative reflection of his journey as a Mennonite-Pentecostal, a Menno-costal, from Canada who immigrated to the United States. Marty presented this paper at an Anabaptist school—Messiah College—in 2008. Chapter 17 is my "testimony" as shared at the Mennonite Church USA biennial convention in 2007 where I *thank* the Mennonites for their faithfulness to Jesus' call to peacemaking and implore them to *please* stay faithful and continue to bless the rest of the church and the world with their witness. The bibliography, compiled by Brian Pipkin, provides resources for those who would like to explore the work of Pentecostals and Charismatics as related to peacemaking and social justice. It is not an exhaustive bibliography, but it is probably one of the most complete so far and could serve as a decent starting point for research.

This book has taken several years to put together. Now that it is available, I hope it can serve as a resource for people who seek to speak and live as followers of Jesus, who seek to be faithful even when it puts them at odds with various majorities, and sometimes even with each other. The goal of promoting Christian nonviolence or peacemaking is not to be at odds for oddness' sake, but some of us are willing to live at odds because we think it's better than living evenly with those who try to "get even." If the cost of being *even* is advocating violence against enemies, then we would rather be "at odds." I hope this book can help keep conversations and arguments about peacemaking alive, for a lack of argument about violence and the practices of peacemaking probably means that we're evened up with the wrong way and at odds with the better way. One perspective and practice many people who become peacemakers learn is that makers of peace walk toward conflict, not away from it. That is exactly what God did. Our Christian stories of Jesus remind us that while we were God's enemies Christ came toward us, toward the enemies of God. So perhaps this book can stir up healthy arguments and help us all be more at odds with that in us which justifies violence, and ever more at peace with that which leads to peace.

Paul Alexander

# Acknowledgments

First, I want to acknowledge my family for putting up with me as I worked through the many issues presented in this book. Deborah was ripped out of her Texas homeland because I taught peacemaking and justice at a Pentecostal school that eventually grew weary of me. Deborah and I worked together in the precipitating actions and she was an energetic catalyst; Nathan and Kharese rode their bicycles in the MLK Day parade from the courthouse in Waxahachie, Texas, to the Baptist church where we worshipped and celebrated together. But it still deeply hurt her when she had to leave her home state. Nathan was seven and Kharese was four when we left their grandmas and grandpas, aunts, uncles, cousins, and friends because my contract didn't get renewed. Deborah, Nathan, and Kharese know there are much greater sufferings in the world than these, but I want to acknowledge their sacrifices. I also want to thank them for their contributions: we have, as a family, participated in demonstrations, protests, and marches. Nathan and Kharese have made videos advocating for the abolition of nuclear weapons and in support of Heifer International. When Nathan was six he helped work on run down rent houses owned by the university that released me. Deborah's moral courage, her commitment to speaking and acting rather than silence and passivity, enables me to continue to teach, write, and engage in direct action. I acknowledge that the process of exploring the issues in this book as a family and seeking to embody them in real life has caused my family great joy as well as great pain.

I also acknowledge that only with the support of friends and community could our family have experienced the joys and pain that we have. The students at Southwestern whom I learned so much from in the last eight years I taught there (1998–2006) brought indescribable meaning to our lives. There are too many to name, but you know who you are—the lunches, the coffees, the long conversations in my office, the moments in class. I processed so much of this in class and in conversation with you all and those were such wonderful, fulfilling, and meaningful days for me. Thank you.

Peace folk from all kinds of Christian traditions have nourished Deborah and me in such deep ways. The essays in this book reflect numerous ecumenical and interfaith conversations and work. Deborah and I have wept more than once when introducing ourselves to a group of Christian peacemakers. We've been inspired by our relationships with peacemakers who have been at it for decades, for generations, even centuries: each serves as a witness to the possibilities of sustained peaceable Christian witness. This helps us feel less alone; each new friend helped us make it another day. I must name two dear friends who have passed away recently—Gene Stoltzfus and Art Gish. Gene told me the reason I have trouble asking for money for PCPJ is that I'm too proud, that a person has to be humble to ask for money. Gene said a lot of truthful things to me and I really miss him. Art Gish told me not to rely on big foundation grants to support peace work, but to rely on the support of friends who think the work is important and believe in it. Rich Foss has consulted with us for years and given invaluable direction. Andre Gingrich-Stoner invited me to speak at an interchurch relations meeting of the Mennonite Church USA, and that opened up the opportunity for me to reflect on my journey (and that is now chapter 16 of this book). To Ann Riggs, Chuck Fager, Carol Rose, Jim Fitz, and many others—thank you.

I acknowledge that institutional resistance at Southwestern Assemblies of God University was a wonderful gift that helped me refine my thoughts on nonviolence and nationalism. The University's disapproval worked much like a refiner's fire that seems to work against the metal, it actually strengthens it. I am not advocating repression and oppression; I am only acknowledging that en la lucha (in the struggle) we sometimes find out who we really are.

I deeply appreciate the work of the members of the Society for Pentecostal Studies (SPS) and the society's openness to controversial conversations. As a young scholar I found SPS to be a welcoming place where I could criticize war and nationalism, argue for nonviolence, and engage in discussions that were not acceptable at the university where I served.

I also want to express my most sincere appreciation to Ron Sider and Chris Hall at Palmer Theological Seminary of Eastern University. To have found a community in which to work where I can live out my vocation and calling is a tremendous privilege, a privilege that relatively few get to experience. Although I have only recently arrived at Palmer, the conversations and joint projects with my colleagues and students are already enriching my life.

I offer special gratitude to Erica Bryand Ramirez, without whose editorial talents this book would not have been brought to press. I also appreciate Liesl Thorsen and Holland Prior at Azusa Pacific University for helping edit along the way. I am thankful for the great people at Wipf and Stock for envisioning the potential of a series devoted to Pentecostalism, peacemaking, and social justice and for their patience in working with me these last few years—especially Charlie Collier, Jim Tedrick, Christian Amondson, and James Stock.

Lastly, Pentecostals & Charismatics for Peace & Justice is a network of folks who do the kind of work that continually inspires me and led to the publication of this work. People who are part of PCPJ authored the majority of chapters, and I am certain it would not have come together without PCPJ. I hope these essays strengthen the work, lives, and testimonies of peacemakers and justice seekers both within and well beyond the Pentecostal charismatic movement.

# Part I

## Early Twentieth-Century Pentecostal Pacifism

# 1

# The Extent of Early Pentecostal Pacifism

## Jay Beaman

In World War I, a very small number of men were counted as religious objectors. A large proportion of these were drawn from the historic peace churches, especially the Mennonites, Amish, and Hutterites, with a large representation from the Quakers. Yet, a small new sect called Pentecostals also represented themselves to each other and to the government as pacifists to war on the basis of their interpretation of the Bible as they understood it "in the latter days." They believed that their calling was to love all people and give witness in all the world, by the power of the Spirit. Like their immediate predecessors in the holiness movement, for some Pentecostals "radical holiness" called for pacifistic abstention from combat.[1]

---

1. Dayton, *Theological Roots of Pentecostalism*, 43, 76–78. Dayton traces radicalism in the Holiness Movement to John Wesley and the anti-slavery movement. See also Dayton, "Piety and Radicalism," 31–41. Also, Dayton, "An Historical Survey of Attitudes Toward War and Peace Within the American Holiness Movement," 132–52. In *A. J. Tomlinson: Plainfolk Modernist*, 162, 273, R. G. Robbins fairly champions the term "Radical Holiness" and connects it to pacifism. See also Stephens who, in *Fire Spreads*, traces Radical Holiness to Northern Holiness missionaries spreading the anti-slavery message and later Christian pacifist ideas in the South.

Early Pentecostal leaders used a rhetoric which portrayed the whole movement as pacifist. Evidence for this can be found in most Pentecostal groups from around the time of World War I. Moreover, evidence can be found in most locations where Pentecostals were located around the United States at that time, especially in the South and Appalachia, and in European countries where Pentecostalism was evident. It is also apparent that when called to arms by their government, Pentecostals in large numbers attempted to respond to the state in ways that were informed by their unique emerging faith. There is evidence of both the fairly extensive practice of pacifism by early Pentecostals and the trouble it caused them with their governments.

While the early Pentecostal Movement did not require pacifism from its members, most early Pentecostal groups left evidence of their official pacifist beliefs. There were open differences of opinion, but pacifist belief characterized the movement. Later literary witness to such beliefs remains as tacit evidence of the support for pacifism by the key leaders in each group represented.[2] Moreover, recent availability of World War I draft registration cards gives us some idea of the actual practice of early Pentecostals at the time of World War I. Although most Pentecostal groups have altered their original pacifism, even recently, some groups retained vestiges of earlier beliefs.

Most pacifist statements originated at the time of World War I because of a need for Pentecostal men to know how to respond to the war. As a result, many groups in existence at that time formulated their beliefs in relation to World War I.

## EVIDENCES OF PACIFISM IN VARIOUS PENTECOSTAL GROUPS

On April 28th, 1917, due to the entry of the United States into World War I, the Executive and General Presbytery of the Assemblies of God passed a resolution which was to remain their "official" position on war until 1967. This detailed statement became a model after which others fashioned their statements. The text in full read:

2. This is all the more significant since, while many Pentecostals did participate in World War II, many of these did so as non-combatants. For a recent discussion of the Assemblies of God in WWII, see Alexander, *Peace to War.*

Resolution Concerning the Attitude of the General Council of
the Assemblies of God Toward any Military Service which
Involves the Actual Participation in the Destruction of
Human Life.

While recognizing Human Government as of Divine ordination
and affirming our unswerving loyalty to the Government of
the United States, nevertheless we are constrained to define
our position with reference to the taking of human life.

WHEREAS, in the Constitutional Resolution adopted at the Hot
Springs General Council, April 1–10, 1914, we plainly declare the Holy Inspired Scriptures to be the all-sufficient rule
of faith and practice, and

WHEREAS the Scriptures deal plainly with the obligations and
relations of humanity, setting forth the principles of "Peace
on earth, good will toward men" (Luke 2:14); and

WHEREAS we, as followers of the Lord Jesus Christ, the Prince
of Peace, believe in implicit obedience to the Divine commands and precepts which instruct us to "Follow peace with
all men," (Heb. 12:14); "Thou shall not kill," (Exod. 20:13);
"Resist not evil," (Matt. 5:39); "Love your enemies," (Matt.
5:44); etc. and

WHEREAS these and other Scriptures have always been accepted and interpreted by our churches as prohibiting Christians
from shedding blood or taking human life;

THEREFORE we, as a body of Christians, while purposing to
fulfill all the obligations of loyal citizenship, are nevertheless
constrained to declare we cannot conscientiously participate
in war and armed resistance which involves the actual destruction of human life, since this is contrary to our view of
the clear teachings of the inspired Word of God, which is the
sole basis of our faith.[3]

While the statement was absolute in tone, there was no attempt to
enforce it upon every member of the denomination even where there was
disagreement.[4] The Assemblies of God was the prototype of the groups
who believed in a two-staged conversion process and other groups followed. Of these, six denominations give clear evidence of pacifist history.[5]
These six are represented in Table. 1.1.

3. Welch, "Pentecostal Movement and the Conscription Law," 6.
4. Ibid.
5. Piepkorn, *Profiles in Belief,* 113–15, 119–20, 130–34, 140–41, 143.

Table 1.1: Two-Staged Conversion Process Pentecostal Denominations
with History of Pacifism

| |
|---|
| 1. Assemblies of God (Pacifist until 1967) |
| 2. Calvary Pentecostal Church |
| 3. Church of God of the Union Assembly |
| 4. Filipino Assemblies of the First-Born |
| 5. General Assembly and Church of the First Born |
| 6. Latin-American Council of Christian Churches |

Four other denominations in the two-staged group left the matter of military service to the individual's conscience. The statement in each case, and the fact that the issue of military service was directly addressed in a statement of belief, was structured in such a way that it appeared to be a replacement for an earlier pacifist statement. The change is similar to the change made by the Assemblies of God in 1967, which today allows the individual to choose. The four denominations allowing individual choice are: the Christ Faith Mission, the Full Gospel Church Association, the General Council of the Assemblies of God, the Christian Church of North America, and the Latin-American Council of the Pentecostal Church of God. The latter denomination does not allow political participation.[6]

The Church of God, Cleveland, Tennessee, was perhaps emblematic of former Holiness churches who turned Pentecostal and added a third blessing to the second, resulting in a three-stage process of conversion. In 1917, the Church of God (Cleveland, Tennessee) adopted a position "against members going to war," seventh in a list of mostly prohibitions against drinking liquor, using tobacco, wearing gold jewelry, belonging to lodges, and swearing. An official prohibition "against members going to war," complete with numerous scriptural citations, can also be found as the twenty-ninth rule in a list of official Church of God "Teachings."[7]

As early as 1915, A. J. Tomlinson had written an editorial in the *Church of God Evangel* about "The Present Situation." He noted that war normalized the very behaviors punishable in times of peace, suggesting, "If this is not vilainous [sic] then we are without expression."[8] Tomlinson described the numerous practical losses for families and homes, citing "poverty and starvation," but moved quickly to relate this to the work of

6. Piepkorn, *Profiles*, 134, 136–37, 145, 156.

7. *Church of God General Assembly Minutes* (November 1–6, 1917) 65.

8. Tomlinson, "Present Situation," 1.

Satan, through whom, "[M]illions of souls are driven by the cruel war lash in to the slaughter-pens of Hell."[9] He criticized the progressives, who ". . . yesterday . . . were boasting of their high state of civilization, holding their peace conferences and planning to step right into a state of millennial peacefulness; to-day they are plunged beneath the surface of a crimson sea and bathing themselves in the blood of uncivilized barbarism." His argument critiqued the powerful and educated, while placing the solution in identification with the poor. "While the multitudes of 'up-to-date' people are studying the war problems . . . is a good time for us to humble ourselves a little lower and go among the common people and work for the salvation of their souls."[10] For Tomlinson, the solution was in fighting another war, waged for God with the discipline and sacrifice of soldiers; a war to persuade others into salvation. He grieved that some sons of Church of God members had already joined in the wrong war, WWI, for patriotic reasons.[11] As the United States entered the War in 1917, Tomlinson moved pastorally to ready the Church of God to resist the one war and fight full-on in the other war. He painted a big picture in which war was a cosmic power, "The awful war devil is still slaying his millions."[12] He was clear about the role of members of the Church of God,

> If we are of the world so we can take part in the wars then we are not of His kingdom . . . We cannot serve God and Mammon. Matt. 6:24 . . . No doubt many of our people are wondering what to do in case our country gets into war. Shall we enlist in the governmental service and fight for our rights? Can we shoulder a gun and march out to the battle front and point our gun toward our enemy and fire into his ranks and send his soul to hell, when Jesus, our King, tells us to love our enemies? Matt. 5:44.[13]

If that had been too subtle, he counseled, "Many conscientious men have refused to carry guns under any circumstances. They felt it was contrary to the spirit of their Lord."[14] The decision was spiritual, "The war demon may try to persuade you that your first duty is to the stars and stripes, but this is a delusion. And you should never permit the spell that

9. Ibid.

10. Ibid.

11. Tomlinson, "While the Wars Rage," 1.

12. Tomlinson, "Ours is a Spiritual Warfare," 1.

13. Ibid.

14. Ibid.

catches the world to get a hold on you."[15] Again he argued members to engage in the other war, "We are short of soldiers now. We have none to give up to fight in carnal wars."[16] Tomlinson was not being theoretical. His laborer-ministers were always torn between making a living and holding evangelistic meetings.

> I hope our ministers and workers will not say in their hearts, "I'll work at my trade this year and next year I will give my time to the service of the Lord." Your service is needed this year. The battle is on now.[17]

Tomlinson continued to use the *Church of God Evangel* to counsel and advocate for young men in their opposition to the war with practical advice on how to register as a religious objector. The church paper carried numerous prayers for draftees, even those who went to prison during and after the war, as well as the report of one church member who was killed by a local sheriff for resisting the draft.[18]

Tomlinson was steadfast in these concerns. Less than six weeks before the universal draft he gave practical advice to draftees. It was not the Church of God's role to dictate specific action, and if they were forced into the military they may not be able to successfully refuse all service, but clearly they must not do more than noncombatant service as a medic, hospital worker, or preacher—while being clear they were not to carry guns.[19]

The Pentecostal Holiness Church exhibited pacifist leanings.[20] Two groups which came out of the Pentecostal Holiness Church, the

15. Ibid.

16. Ibid.

17. Ibid.

18. *Church of God Evangel*, 9 June 1917, 2; 30 June 1917, 2; 7 July 1917, 3; 13 July 1918, 2; 4 August 1917, 2–4; 25 August 1917, 1; 28 September 1918, 2; 20 October 1917, 3; 10 November 1917, 2, 4; 29 December 1917, 4; 5 January 1918, 2; 28 January 1918, 1; 16 February 1918, 2; 16 March 1918, 3; 23 March 1918, 2; 27 April 1918, 4; 29 June 1918, 2; 13 July 1918, 2; 20 July 1918, 1, 4; 5 October 1918, 4; 19 October 1918, 3; 2 November 1918, 4; 10 November 1918, 4, 3; 1 February 1919, 2; 22 February 1919, 4; 12 April 1919, 4; 24 May 1919, 3; 31 May 1919, 2; 20 December 1919, 3; 17 January 1920, 2; 17 July 1920, 2; 28 August 1920, 2; 2 April 1921, 3; 13 May 1922, 4; 21 October 1922, 2; 12 May 1923, 3.

19. Ibid.

20. Synan, *Old Time Power*, 208–1. Synan notes that in 1941 ". . . the church completely abandoned its earlier pacifism." Of all Pentecostal denominations in WWI, the

Congregational Holiness Church and the Fire Baptized Holiness Church, adopted a position against going to war.[21] The Congregational Holiness Church maintained loyalty to the government but claimed that "God's children should not take up arms against their fellowman."[22] Table 1.2 shows the Holiness Pentecostal denominations with pacifist history.

Table 1.2: Holiness Pentecostal Denominations with Pacifist History

1. Church of God, Cleveland, Tennessee (Pacifist until 1945)
2. Church of God (1957 Reformation)
3. Church of God (Mountain Assembly)
4. Church of God in Christ
5. Church of God of the Apostolic Faith
6. Church of God, Huntsville, Alabama
7. Churches of God of the Original Mountain Assembly
8. Congregational Holiness Church
9. Emmanuel Holiness Church
10. International Church of Christ
11. Original Church of God
12. Pentecostal Fire Baptized Holiness Church
13. Pentecostal Holiness Church (Isolated Pacifist influence before 1941)

The Church of God in Christ was founded by C. H. Mason (1866–1961), the son of former slaves.[23] Citing their understanding that "the shedding of human blood or taking of human life [as] . . . contrary to the teaching of our Lord and Savior," Mason's Church of God is, as a body, "adverse to war in all its various forms." This group considers themselves for available service that "will not conflict with our conscientious scruples in this respect, with love to all, with malice toward none, and with due respect to all who differ from us in our interpretation of the Scriptures."[24] Seven years after C. H. Mason's death, "Martin Luther King, Jr., preached

PHC appears to be the most implicitly pacifist, even as the exception, still giving evidence of the pacifism it held in some small way in common with the larger Pentecostal movement. See also Paul, "Religious Frontier," 141–43.

21. Piepkorn, *Profiles*, 102, 112.

22. Ibid.

23. Hollenweger, "Black Pentecostal Concept," 27–28.

24. Ibid., 33. See also Moore, "Handbook" 181.

his last sermon from Mason's pulpit—Mason Temple, headquarters of the [Church of God in Christ], [in] Memphis . . ."[25]

A smaller black Pentecostal group, Triumph, was significant in the way it distinguished itself from white churches by its pacifism. Walter J. Hollenweger quotes the following dialogue:

> Q. Was there another Church in the earth before Triumph?
>
> A. Yes. Church Militant.
>
> Q. Is there any difference between the Triumph Church and Church Militant?
>
> A. Yes. Church Militant is a Church of warfare, and Triumph is a Church of Peace.
>
> Q. What happened to Church Militant when Triumph was revealed?
>
> A. God turned it upside down and emptied His Spirit into Triumph.
>
> Q. Is Triumph just a Church only?
>
> A. No. It has a kingdom with it.[26]

The Church of God (Apostolic, 1901) is a black church which does not readily present itself as Pentecostal. For our purposes, the Church of God (Apostolic, 1901) can be fairly grouped with oneness Pentecostal denominations on the bases of its position on the trinity and practice of speaking in tongues. Notably, the Church of God (Apostolic, 1901) calls for members to live in "obedience to the laws of the land, but not in war and going to war."[27]

The Church of the Lord Jesus Christ of the Apostolic Faith, founded in 1919, holds an absolute view. It opposes both combatant and noncombatant services, and even eschews wearing military uniforms and pledging allegiance to the flag. This group is multi-racial, yet predominantly black. It is part of the oneness sector of Pentecostalism.[28]

Oneness Pentecostal groups derived from a defection from the Assemblies of God, and they took a similar stand against participation in war. The United Pentecostal Church had a statement modeled after the Assemblies of God in which they recognized the validity of human gov-

---

25. Clemmons, "Mason," 587.

26. Hollenweger, *Pentecostals*, 45–46.

27. Piepkorn, *Profiles*, 36–37.

28. Ibid., 202–3.

ernment, but on the basis of a number of scriptures took a position against "participating in combatant service in war."[29] The Pentecostal Assemblies of the World, Incorporated, believed they were not "to take up any weapon of destruction to slay another, whether in our own defense or the defense of others." Yet, they implied that it would be possible to serve in noncombatant capacity.[30] While the Church of the Little Children holds to conscientious objection, and does not allow noncombatant service, the local churches do not enforce this ruling.[31] Most oneness Pentecostal groups have a stand against going to war, yet allow noncombatant service. The Apostolic Gospel Church of Jesus Christ is more absolute, stating, "We cannot take up arms against any man or support those who do so: therefore our members do not serve in the armed forces."[32] Table 1.3 lists the Oneness Pentecostal Denominations with a history of pacifism.

Table 1.3: Oneness Pentecostal Denominations with a History of Pacifism

1. Apostolic Gospel Church of Jesus Christ (Bible Apostolic Church)
2. Assemblies of the Lord Jesus Christ
3. Associated Brotherhood of Christians
4. Church of God (Apostolic) (Black Holiness)
5. Church of Jesus Christ
6. Church of Jesus Christ Ministerial Alliance
7. Church of Jesus Christ of Georgia
8. Church of our Lord Jesus Christ of the Apostolic Faith
9. Pentecostal Assemblies of the World
10. United Pentecostal Church International

A number of unclassified Pentecostal groups also had similar statements on war. The Mt. Sinai Holy Church of America, Incorporated, "takes a strong stand against war."[33] Many other smaller groups made similar statements against going to war, with a number of them allowing for noncombatant service.[34] However, not all Pentecostal churches

29. *Manual: United Pentecostal Church International*, 27.

30. Piepkorn, *Profiles*, 199. See also Moore, "Handbook" 246–47.

31. Ibid., 199–200.

32. Ibid., 215.

33. Ibid., 100.

34. Piepkorn, *Profiles*, 105–6, 119, 122, 126, 128, 130, 132, 143, 145, 181, 190. See also *Articles of Faith: Church of God of the Apostolic Faith, Inc.*; *General Constitution and By-Laws: The Pentecostal Church of God of America*, 22; Nichol, *Pentecostalism*, 142–44;

adopted a position against participation in war. The many groups which did have a statement against going to war usually allowed members to go to war in noncombatant capacities. The rationale for this allowance becomes clear upon examination of the laws concerning conscientious objection during World War I.

The following is based upon an analysis of the belief statements of 117 Pentecostal denominations which are predominantly identified with United States, using Piepkorn's *Profiles in Belief,* supplemented when possible from historical and denominational sources. Many of the denominations give no information about their views on war. Thirty-eight of the 117 Pentecostal denominations give evidence of pacifism at some point in their history. As recently as 1979, 34 of 117 denominations, held to some remnants of pacifism. The two largest white Pentecostal denominations; The Assemblies of God, and the Church of God (Cleveland, TN) have moved away from their original pacifist teaching.

Analysis of the dates in which denominations were formed is also informative. Of the groups for which the author has information regarding their date of origin, there is a lower probability of pacifist beliefs among groups formed later than 1930. Thirteen of twenty-one, or 62 percent, of groups formed by 1917 give evidence of being pacifist at some point. Twenty-four of forty-eight, or 50 percent, of those groups formed by 1934 give evidence of pacifism. Of those groups formed after 1934, eleven of fifty-four, or 20 percent, give evidence of pacifism at some point in their history. Only three of fifteen, or 20 percent of those groups for which the author has no evidence of their date of origin, have a history of pacifism.

Further analysis of the type of pacifism adhered to by these denominations suggests a strong reliance on the original statement formulated by the Assemblies of God in 1917. Few Pentecostal groups have been abso-

---

Constitution and By-Laws: *The Filipino Assemblies of the First-Born Incorporated,* 11. The following have similar views on war: Church of God of the Mountain Assembly, Inc. (1907), Churches of God of the Original Mountain Assembly, Inc. (1946), Calvary Pentecostal Church, Inc. (1932), Church of God of the Apostolic Faith (1914), Pentecostal Church of God of America (1922), International Pentecostal Assemblies (1936), The Pentecostal Fire-Baptized Holiness Church (1918), Emmanuel Holiness Church (1953), General Assembly of the Church of the First-born, Church of God of the Union Assembly (1920), Filipino Assemblies of the First-born (1933), Olazabal's Latin-American Council of Churches, Inc. (1936), Christ Faith Mission (1939), Full Gospel Church Association (1952), and (original) Church of God, Inc. The Church of God (1957 reformation, Cleveland) allows the individual to decide. See also Moore, "Handbook," 85, 149, 181, 228, 234, 246–47, 274, 286, 300.

lute pacifists. Six groups use the term conscientious objection to describe their pacifism. Two of the latter qualify their pacifism in such a way that noncombatant service is allowed, and four appear to be absolute pacifists.

While the largest part of the text of the prototype pacifist statement by the Assemblies of God was devoted to scriptural texts which support pacifism, the portion which gave interpretation to those scriptures contained what appeared to be a formula for later statements. This formula included (1) an affirmation of the legitimacy and loyalty to government, (2) an absolute pacifist ethic based in scripture, and (3) a qualification of the absolute pacifism to allow noncombatant service in war. The Assemblies of God statement affirmed legitimacy of government and loyalty to the government in the following:

> While recognizing Human Government as of Divine ordination and affirming our unswerving loyalty to the government of the United States, nevertheless we are constrained to define our position with reference to the taking of human life.
> . . . Therefore we, as a body of Christians, while purposing to fulfill all the obligations of loyal citizenship, are nevertheless constrained to declare we cannot conscientiously participate in war . . .[35]

At least seven groups followed with statements of loyalty. The following are examples of loyalty statements:

- ready to serve the government . . .
- willingness to serve . . .
- serve country in any capacity except bear arms . . .
- willing to serve in any capacity outside taking up arms . . .
- serve country in any capacity except bear arms . . .
- loyalty to U.S. . . .
- obedience to laws, but not in war . . .
- obey government . . . except in its use of armed force . . .
- duty to obey . . . laws that do not contradict God's word . . .
- affirm civil government . . .[36]

The Assemblies of God gave a qualification of absolute pacifism in stating that their position was defined "with reference to the taking of hu-

---

35. Welch, "Pentecostal Movement and Conscription Law."
36. Piepkorn, *Profiles*, 130, 136, 141, 142, 147, 156.

man life," and "the actual destruction of human life."[37] At least 14 groups gave qualifications which allowed noncombatant services in war. Most of these used the terms noncombatant service or "against combatant service." The following are examples of this type of qualification which would be interpreted as noncombatant service:

- not take up arms . . .
- not take up arms in war . . .
- not to take up any weapon of destruction to slay another . . .
- against combatant service in war, armed insurrection, property destruction, aiding . . . destruction of human life . . .
- [against] actual destruction of human lives, but will serve in any capacity outside of taking up arms if required to do so . . .[38]

Thus, the rhetoric of pacifism was moderated in the option of noncombatant service.

## EVIDENCES OF PENTECOSTAL PACIFISM IN VARIOUS COUNTRIES

Because Pentecostalism made its first advances into Europe at the time of the European War, evidence of Pentecostal pacifism is also found in Europe and not in other areas where conscription was not an issue. Nor was evidence found in areas where conscription was not an issue at the time the Pentecostal Movement arrived.

Pacifism took hold in English Pentecostal circles early in World War I. Although there were notable detractors, it was as strong there as in America, and showed signs of outliving the American variety. The Elim Foursquare Gospel Church adopted a pacifist position which they held until World War II when it was rejected.[39] The Apostolic Church (South Wales) took a position that was "absolutely opposed to war," yet allowed members to choose whether to participate.[40]

There were expressions of pacifism in Pentecostal groups in other parts of Europe during World War I. In 1917, *The Weekly Evangel* noted the international character of the Pentecostals' belief in pacifism:

37. Welch, "Pentecostal Movement and Conscription Law."

38. Piepkorn, *Profiles,* 100, 102, 105, 106, 119, 122, 123, 126, 128, 130, 133, 136, 141, 143.

39. Wilson, *Sects and Society,* 88–89.

40. *Apostolic Church: Its Principles and Practices,* 147.

From the very beginning, the movement has been characterized
by Quaker principles. The laws of the Kingdom, laid down by
our elder brother, Jesus Christ, in His Sermon on the Mount,
have been unqualifiedly adopted, consequently the movement
has found itself opposed to the spilling of the blood of any man,
or of offering resistance to any aggression. Every branch of the
movement, whether in the United States, Canada, Great Britain
or Germany, has held to this principle. When the war first broke
out in August of 1914, our Pentecostal brethren in Germany
found themselves in a peculiar position. Some of those who were
called to the colors responded, but many were court marshaled
[*sic*] and shot because they heartily subscribed to the principles
of non-resistance. Great Britain has been more humane. Some of
our British brethren have been given noncombatant service, and
none have been shot down because of their faith.[41]

Hollenweger noted that the Swiss Pentecostal Mission has taken an absolute stand against war "as an expression of violence, which is emotional
and not godly." However, he also noted that "there are no conscientious
objectors in the Swiss Pentecostal Movement."[42]

During the Russian Revolution, the Russian Pentecostals maintained
a position of pacifism. This changed during a time of extreme persecution
from Soviet authorities in 1927 to a position of "admonishing members
to participate in military service."[43] This was no small matter with the
Assemblies of God in the United States, who were sponsoring the Russian
work, and they seriously considered withdrawing support over this issue.[44] However, pacifism could still be found among the Pentecostals in
Russia in the latter half of the Twentieth century.[45]

Canadian Pentecostals also believed in pacifism during World
War I, though they were not yet officially registered with the Canadian
Government as a denomination until after the war. Therefore, those
Pentecostals who chose to ask for exemption from the Canadian draft

41. Welch, "Pentecostal Movement and Conscription Law."

42. Hollenweger, *Pentecostals*, 401.

43. Lane, *Christian Religion*, 176.

44. Peterson, letters to Perkin (September 21, 1928; June 13, 1929; July 12, 1929);
"REEM," memorandum from the General Council of the Assemblies of God, Inc. (April
30, 1935). See also Durasoff, *Russian Protestants*, 81–82.

45. Lane, *Christian Religion*, 183–84; Hollenweger, *Pentecostals*, 281; Klippenstein,
"Free Conscience," 284–85.

had to do so as individual conscientious objectors. Elmor Morrison, a Canadian Pentecostal, registered as a conscientious objector and was sentenced to Kingston Penitentiary, and he served part of his sentence in solitary confinement. According to archivist and former Pentecostal Assemblies of Canada Pastor Douglas Rudd, "George Chambers was Elmor Morrison's pastor in Kitchener. He told me the stand Elmor took 'put the steel in his back.'" Morrison became a Pentecostal missionary to China from 1923 to 1960. "He spent some time working behind Japanese lines after they invaded China and established a Bible School that still operates in Hong Kong today. We have a number of biographical sketches of Morrison . . . one mentions briefly his time in prison for refusing to kill 'innocent enemy soldiers.'"[46] He had company. Another Canadian Pentecostal, Elder Morton, "a well-known black pastor of Detroit and Windsor," was also in Kingston Penitentiary with Elmor Morrison for his conscientious objection to WWI.[47]

The Canadian Pentecostal Assemblies of the World was not officially recognized by the Canadian Government until after WWI. With the outbreak of World War II, the Canadian Pentecostals officially registered their pacifism with the following set of resolutions:

> WHEREAS, We have accepted the Word of God as our rule of conduct and purpose to be governed by its Divine principles, and as our Assemblies for the past twelve years or more have always accepted and interpreted the New Testament teaching and principles as prohibiting Christians from shedding blood or taking human life.
>
> RESOLVED, That in time of persecution or ill-treatment at the hands of the enemy, we should not "avenge ourselves," but rather give place to wrath; for it is written, "Vengeance is mine; I will repay, saith the Lord." (Rom 12:19; Deut 32:35). Neither shall (we) take up any weapon of destruction to slay another, whether in our own defence or in defence of others, for it is written, "Do no violence to no man." (See Luke 3:14; Matt 26:52; John 18:36; 15–18, 19). We should rather suffer wrong than do wrong.

46. Marilyn Stroud, email to Jay Beaman, (August 23, 2007). Marilyn Stroud is the Archivist for the Pentecostal Assemblies of the World Archives in Canada. She shared extensive quotations from archival files created by former archivist and pastor, Douglas Rudd.

47. Ibid.

RESOLVED, That all civil magistrates are ordained of God for peace, safety, and for the welfare of the people (Rom 13:1–10). Therefore it is our duty to be in obedience to all requirements of the Law that are not contrary to the Word of God. It is our duty to honor them, pay tribute, or such taxation as may be required, without murmuring (Matt 17:24–27), and show respect to them in all lawful requirements of the Civil Government.[48]

## THE EXTENT TO WHICH PENTECOSTALS PRACTICED PACIFISM IN WORLD WAR I

It is one thing to make the case that WWI Pentecostals presented themselves as pacifist and taught their followers to observe pacifism, either thoroughgoing conscientious objection or conscientious objection followed by non-combatant service, if required. It is another thing to document that early Pentecostals practiced conscientious objection when called upon to register for the draft. Over twenty years ago when I began this project, it was nearly impossible to contemplate finding the draft registration records of early Pentecostals. Two main problems presented themselves: finding lists of Pentecostal men in order to search for what they did when called upon to register for the draft, and finding individual draft registration cards from microfilm rolls. Both tasks seemed impossible. Pentecostals found official membership lists to be the very mark of dead denominationalism which they intended to reform. Even now, most Pentecostal history is focused on great leaders in the movement, mostly preachers and organizers of denominations. Moreover, even recent histories which do much to elucidate the worldview of early Pentecostals do not provide a great deal of help in creating a list of laypeople. Finding lists of "laypeople" is very problematic, even given the great archival resources across various Pentecostal denominations. Secondly, finding individual draft cards without a previous localized grouping in a particular draft board was nearly impossible. Grant Wacker, in the context of arguing Pentecostals' complete accommodation to the WWI draft, suggested:

> The pages of AOG periodicals carried requests after request for prayer for the spiritual and physical safety of mothers' sons fighting overseas. No one requested prayer for conscientious ob-

---

48. Althouse, "Canadian Pentecostal Pacifism," 32–33.

jectors. One can only assume that they were either too few to count or that editors screened out such requests, knowing how most readers would react.[49]

Yet, two weeks after the citation of prayer requests for soldiers given by Wacker, the same Assemblies of God publication actually did just that, it counted a few conscientious objectors, asked prayer for them, and apparently did so without constituency reaction.

> Fort Riley, Kans.
>
> I am sending you my tithes. Six Dollars and Seventy cents, because they belong to God and I want you to send it where it is most needed. I am from Trenton, Mo., was drafted the 23rd of July, and I ask you to pray for us that are saved that God will keep us near unto Him, and that God will save souls. If ever there was a time that souls needed salvation, it is now, and there are thousands of souls here who would be lost if Jesus would come now. There are three boys here that belong to the Assemblies of God. As I am a believer in the Apostolic Faith I am glad that God has given us a place where we don't have to take up arms. God is able to take us through. Pray for this place.
>
> Oscar Barley, Base Hospital, Fort Riley, Kansas.[50]

The man appears to be Oscar Clinton Barley, a 28 year old farmer from Missouri who did not ask for exemption on his draft card but appears to have done so soon thereafter and gives evidence, along with three others, from the Assemblies of God of serving as a non-combatant in a base hospital.[51] Still, Wacker's assumption that the conscientious objectors were too few to count was understandable. In fact, finding them is much like finding a needle in a haystack. While it may well turn out that those attempting to register as conscientious objectors were a recognizable part of Pentecostalism, they were a really microscopic part of the approximately 24 million who registered for the WWI draft.[52] Moreover, the reason thus far that they are too few to count is more likely that the

49. Wacker, *Heaven Below*, 247.

50. Name Not Given,"Reports from the Field," *Christian Evangel*, 19 October 1918, 14.

51. Draft Registration Card, Oscar Clinton Barley.

52. Keith, *Rich Man's War*, 57.

number of Pentecostal laymen found on any denominational lists are so few from the time of WWI.

Since the U.S. government did not keep any record of conscientious objectors, denominational scholars are forced to compile their own lists. Mennonite scholars have done the most to list men who were found in the various military camps, military detention camps, and prisons.[53] More recently, the Swarthmore College Peace Collection has created an online database of conscientious objectors to WWI.[54] With the dramatic proliferation of internet resources, it is now possible to search genealogical records online through such sites as Ancestry.com. Central to these sites is the extensive indexed list of WWI Draft Registrations, and thus the time has come to compare such a list with known lists of WWI-era Pentecostal males.

## THE PENTECOSTAL WWI DEMOGRAPHIC DATABASE

An iterative and emergent methodology was needed to construct lists of early Pentecostal males from the time of WWI. Two main lists have served as the backbone of this search: the list of ordained ministers and missionaries published in the General Council of the Assemblies of God from 1914 to 1924,[55] and the list of officials including ministers (Overseers and Bishops), evangelists, deacons, and clerks of the Church of God (Cleveland, TN) from 1917 to 1925.[56] Along with both groups of names, states and cities were entered into a database. The Church of God records were supplemented with a photocopy of a hand-written list of early church members and a photocopy of a fund-raising list from an early auditorium in Cleveland, TN. In 1915 and 1925, the Iowa State (Farm) Census asked a religious affiliation question, and a modest number of Iowa Pentecostals from several groups were found in this manner. From

53. For a good example, see Mininger's *Religious C.O.'s Imprisoned at the U.S. Disciplinary Barracks, Ft. Leavenworth, Kansas.* There are many Pentecostals in this list.

54. "WWI Conscientious Objectors," online database from the Swarthmore College Peace Collection.

55. *Assemblies of God Publications Pre-WWII*, Flower Pentecostal Heritage Center.

56. David Roebuck, Director of the Hal Bernard Dixon Jr. Pentecostal Research Center, Cleveland, Tennessee, provided two extensive handwritten photocopies of the first thirty pages of the Auditorium Receipts List from about 1914 and an early Church of God membership list. He also wisely suggested the CD-ROM, *Church of God General Assembly Minutes 1906–2002.*

Sherry Sherrod DuPree's, *Biographical Dictionary of African-American, Holiness-Pentecostals 1880–1990*, I was able to find seventy-six names and demographics of males of appropriate age for WWI.[57] Various Pentecostal Histories and newspaper accounts also turned up a smaller number of names from that era. Mel Robeck, professor of church history at Fuller Theological Seminary and author of *The Azusa Street Mission and Revival*, was kind enough to share a list of Azusa Street attendees, some of whom were young enough, at Azusa, to be drafted during WWI. Finally, the online list of religious objectors collected by the Swarthmore Peace Collection contributed at least twenty names identified as Pentecostal. The database has grown to 4,560 names with more added as they are made available.[58] In time, the database will be a dynamic source of early Pentecostal demographic and biographical information.[59]

The database is biased towards available sources, and thus has 3,257 names associated with the Church of God (Cleveland, TN), 934 names from the Assemblies of God, and 146 names from a variety of other groups. One-fourth of the names are female and three-fourths male. The male names were used to search for draft cards. Of 3,481 males in the database, 1,558 (45 percent) of draft cards or census documents were found. The 55 percent of Pentecostal male names not found fall into four overlapping groups: 1) those with common names found numerous times but with no clear way to distinguish between them; 2) those whose names had two initials and a last name, which could signify many actual names; 3) those old enough that they did not have to register for the draft; and 4) those whose draft cards are simply not in the catalogued online database.

Draft cards were of three types: Type I cards are dated from June 5, 1917, with a line to register exemptions; Type II cards are dated from September 12, 1918, without an exemption line; and Type III cards have

---

57. Sherry Sherrod DuPree, *Biographical Dictionary of African-American, Holiness-Pentecostals 1880–1990* (Washington, DC: Mid Atlantic Regional, 1989).

58. Since doing this analysis and writing this chapter, I have added 711 records from the Pentecostal Assemblies of the World, including 232 draft cards found and 32 religious objectors found thus far. With the help of David Daniels, I have also found 300 COGIC related names. This brings the database total to over 5,560 names. Since these recent records are not cleaned or analyzed, they are not yet in the counts or analysis. In a forthcoming work, I will analyze these and other records I am presently working to obtain.

59. I hope in time to be able to publish the database and something more about the social class and other demographic analysis of early Pentecostalism.

little useful information. Only 681 Type I cards have been found thus far--from June 5, 1917, the earliest required registration. Type I cards are most crucial for examining religious objectors because they are the only type of card with an exemption request line. Males between the ages 21 and 31 inclusive were required to register on June 5, 1917. Thus, Type I cards are reflective of this age group, the prime group for the draft. Almost ten million men registered on June 5, 1917.[60] Vetting Type II registrations, which began on September 12, 1918, yielded 815 cards for the database. These cards did not give exemption status, but did give the name of the closest relative, usually the wife. Type III cards, which bear much less useful information, were found thirty-three times, and census documents were located about fifty times when a draft card could not be found. Of the 681 Type I cards and another nine cards with useful information, 252 or 37 percent of the Pentecostal draft registration cards where exemptions could be registered, were found to be religious objectors to WWI.

However, when all draft cards with "minister" listed under occupation are selected out, we are left with 528 Type I cards with the possibility of registering an exemption. Of the 528 Type I cards registering as "laymen," 165 or 31.3 percent asked for religious exemption. Thus, of non-ministerial Pentecostals, where the draft card allows us to know if they asked for exemption, almost one-third asked for religious conscientious objector status. In the absence of better information, it is reasonable to assume that those Pentecostal men with Type II draft cards, without exemption status on the card, would have registered as conscientious objectors in roughly the same proportion. Moreover, it seems reasonable to also assume the same for Pentecostal men for whom we have not been able to identify their draft cards. The assumption that about one-third of Pentecostal men registered religious conscientious objector status to WWI may be a conservative estimate, since there is evidence that a number of Pentecostal men seemed to have assumed that God would protect them from being drafted and hence did not attempt to claim conscientious objector status until they were actually drafted.

---

60. *Report of the Provost Marshal General,* 24.

Type I Draft Registration Card. Notice line 12 for registering an exemption request. This image reprinted by permission of Ancestry.com. To view additional family history records, please visit www.ancestry.com. Annotation is mine.

My database, The Pentecostal WWI Demographic Database, was created with the knowledge that numerous men in the database were not Pentecostals until after WWI, even though I am cataloging their draft registration status at the time of WWI. This is because I included sources up to the year 1925 in my database, which allows for up to seven years after the War, during which men could have converted and been added to the list. In the database, such men are listed as non-pacifist during WWI, though they may not have been Pentecostal at that time. Thus, the estimation of approximately one-third of Pentecostal men attempting to register as conscientious objectors to WWI is probably very conservative.[61]

Even so, when over a third of the group registered religious conscientious objection during WWI and Pentecostal denominations officially sanctioned such a stand, this was overwhelmingly unpopular. Pentecostal men were killed, tarred and feathered, imprisoned, beaten, threatened, investigated, interrogated, and maligned over their religious objection to war. One would have thought the religious objectors were single-handedly stopping the war effort. This was certainly not the case, mostly because the

---

61. The advantages of including Pentecostal list records up to 1925 are that 1) I had the potential to greatly expand the size of the database, and 2) young men who were laymen at the time of WWI or before they became ministers could be included in the database.

number of men in Christian groups who were actively resistant to taking up arms was rather small compared to the larger society; Mennonites and Quakers were relatively small groups, and the Pentecostal movement was still being born. The societal reaction to religious conscientious objectors was mostly a reaction to the symbolic nature of their resistance and the potential it had for delegitimizing the righteousness of the war effort.

## PENTECOSTAL RELIGIOUS OBJECTORS IN CONTEXT

Overall, of almost ten million registrants on June 5, 1917, less than one-third were called upon for duty, and approximately fifty percent of these draftees claimed some exemption.

> Of the claims made . . . 39 percent of persons called, or 77.86 percent of claims made, were granted . . . 81.79 percent of claims made before local boards were granted."[62]

Thus, exemptions were widely—one could even say, routinely—given. Of the 1.6 million exemptions given:

- 74 percent were for family dependency
- 20 percent were on the basis of being non-resident alien
- 6 percent were for occupation or vocation (including farming, strategic industries, and ministerial)
- 0.34 percent were for religious belief (3,887).[63]

## DEPENDENT RELATIVES EXEMPTIONS AND OTHERS

Nationwide, 48 percent of the 3.1 million men called up were married. Of these, 89 percent were given exemption to take care of family. Of all the exemptions, this must have seemed the most reasonable, fair, and culturally acceptable. Some draft boards "discharged all or virtually all married men."[64] Pentecostal registrants were also ready to ask for family exemptions. Of 681 Pentecostal men between the ages of 21 to 31 registering on June 5, 1917, 37 percent were religious objectors, 23 percent registered requests for exemption based on family dependents, 5 percent requested both religious and family exemption, and 55 percent requested one or the

---

62. *Report of the Provost Marshal General*, 24.

63. Ibid.

64. Ibid., 51.

other exemption. Fifty-seven percent of the 681 men were married and 27 percent of these were religious objectors, 35 percent requested family exemption, 5 percent requested both, and 53 percent requested one or the other exemption. Forty-three percent of the 681 men were single and 48 percent of these were religious objectors, 14 percent requested exemption to care for relatives (usually parents), 5 percent of single Pentecostals requested both religious and family exemptions, and 57 percent requested one or the other exemption. The following table summarizes this data together with national rates.[65]

Table 1.4: Requests for Family Dependent or Religious Exemption to WWI

| Exemption Request | National Registration | Pentecostals | | |
|---|---|---|---|---|
| | | Married 57 percent | Single 43 percent | All |
| Family Dependents | 37.00 percent | 35 percent | 14 percent | 23 percent |
| Religious Objectors | 0.17 percent | 27 percent | 48 percent | 37 percent |
| Both | | 5 percent | 5 percent | 5 percent |
| One or the other | 37.17 percent | 53 percent | 57 percent | 55 percent |

Several things become apparent from this table. First, in the national population, the largest group of exemption requests, 37 percent, was for family dependents. Among Pentecostals it is the second largest reason for exemption, 23 percent overall and 35 percent among married men. However, the national rate of requests for religious exemption is 0.17 percent, and among the Pentecostals at 37 percent, and among single Pentecostals 48 percent. Taking the two kinds of exemption together, Pentecostals requested exemption at 55 percent, a great deal higher than the national rate of 37.17 percent. The rate for Pentecostals was fairly stable whether or not the registrant was married, with approximately 55 percent requesting exemption. However, single Pentecostals, not having access to the family exemption as readily as married men, were almost twice as likely to register religious exemption over their married counterparts. This suggests that some Pentecostals who were not strictly religious objectors may have been able to satisfy both their religious affiliation and their government by taking the family exemption, if possible,

65. The national rates were calculated from *Report of the Provost Marshal General* by taking the rates of family exemption and religious exemption granted, 74 percent and 0.34 percent respectively, times 50 percent of all men, the rate of men who requested exemption. The rates for Pentecostals are the actual rates requested in the sample.

and that they were not so ideologically driven as practical. It may well be that once the general direction of non-participation, where possible, in active pursuit of the war was enjoined, it was not so important how the goal was achieved. Of course, the family exemption was the largest exemption nationally, but not the only one. While 50 percent of the registrants nationally requested some exemption,[66] 399 or 59 percent of the 681 Pentecostals in the sample requested some exemption, significantly higher than the nation and for different reasons.

## DENOMINATIONS REPRESENTED AMONG PENTECOSTAL RELIGIOUS OBJECTORS

Of the 252 Pentecostal religious objectors to WWI identified thus far, the majority were from the Assemblies of God and the Church of God, Cleveland, TN. The Assemblies of God were half of the group and Church of God, Cleveland, more than one-fourth. Together, these two groups comprise 75 percent of religious objectors in my database. Men from these two groups represented themselves using the two official names, Assemblies of God, or more formally, The General Council of the Assemblies of God, and Church of God as well as other designations. Individuals known to be from both the Assemblies of God and Church of God on the basis of denominational sources were self-identified in the draft registration cards as Pentecostal, Pentecostal faith, Pentecostal church, Pentecostal sect, Apostolic faith, Apostolic Assemblies, Apostolic religion, Apostolic Holiness, or just plain Holiness. At the time of WWI, some still identified with an earlier denomination, such as Church of the Brethren or even Quaker. One self-identified as Methodist Episcopal. Those identified using records outside of the Assemblies of God and Church of God, Cleveland were a smaller number and from a variety of groups including those mentioned above, as well as: the Pentecostal Assemblies of the World, Church of God in Christ, Church of God and Saints of Christ, and Church of the Living God. These draft cards are a testament to the widespread deep concern about the appropriateness of Pentecostals going to war. There is evidence that almost every Pentecostal group at the time of WWI encouraged conscientious objection and found some who heeded that call. Still, draft registrants from almost all Pentecostal groups could also be found in Type I draft cards, who left

66. Ibid., 24.

the exemption line blank or sometimes stated "none." Thus, the choice of religious exemption was not nearly universal among Pentecostals.

## WHAT FORM DID THE REQUEST FOR EXEMPTION, LINE 12 ON THE JUNE 1917 DRAFT CARD, TAKE AMONG PENTECOSTALS?

One was not required to request exemption at the time of registering for the draft card to get an exemption, but it was certainly advised. The draft registrant was given up to two weeks to complete an exemption form with the local draft board. Thus far, I have not been able to find any of these exemption cards and have concluded that they were likely destroyed after the war. Therefore, the cryptic response on line 12 becomes one of the only windows into the experience of the registrant, and that only in the case of Type I cards.

### Exemption Assumed, yet Unstated

There were likely numerous Pentecostal men who believed God would not let them be drafted, and as such they did not ask for exemptions until they were drafted. Perhaps they wished to avoid confrontation, or perhaps they hoped they would not be drafted at all. Yet, there were also men who did not request an exemption on their draft registration cards but were later found in conscientious objector barracks at military camps. Edwin Mosses Bernhard, a 28-year-old hat-presser, working in a factory in Reading, Pennsylvania, and a member of the Assemblies of God, did not claim exemption at the time of filling out his registration in June 1917. Instead, he claimed conscientious objector status in October, 1917, probably sometime after being drafted, and he was discharged for health reasons.[67] Thomas Martin Cain, a 23-year-old single machinist and member of the Church of God (Cleveland, TN), from Knoxville, Tennessee, registered on June 5, 1917, and answered "no" on the exemption line. However, in August 1917 Cain wrote a letter that was intercepted by the U.S. Postal Authorities and used by the FBI to investigate the recipient, Fred L. Ryder, a Church of God Missionary to Argentina. Ryder's correspondence suggested he was pleased he went to Argentina in May 1917 before being drafted, and he was investigated throughout the War as a

---

67. Draft Card for Edwin Mosses Bernhard, Swarthmore College Peace Collection online database Online: http://130.58.64.153/fmi/xsl/SCPC_COWW1_detail.xsl?-recid =2134.

suspected draft evader. Cain had asked Ryder for details on how to effectively avoid being drafted. Ryder pointed Cain to seek help from his denomination and its Executive, A. J. Tomlinson. For his part, Ryder stayed in Argentina for the duration, only returning to the U.S. in 1923.[68]

When Hosea Brayles Roberts, a 23-year-old single farmer, filled out his draft registration in June 1917, he stated "No Sir" on the exemption line. Then, in 1919, he was charged at Ft. Leavenworth with disloyalty and sentenced to 25 years in prison, with the sentence later reduced. Sometime between his filling out his draft registration and finishing basic training, Roberts decided he was a religious objector. No doubt he, like many other Pentecostal young men, had little clear instruction in how to register their religious objection.[69] The autonomy of local draft boards in carrying out registration must have accentuated the difficulties, since there was little uniformity in instructing young men in the details of the registration process. Ora Lee, a Church of God, Cleveland, TN, member who did not request exemption was later found in Ft. Riley along with Mennonite war resisters.[70] But many young men saw the exemption line and the instructions given as suggestive that they would be given the exemption they requested, encouraging them to list an exemption.

## Standard form Religious Objection

There were attempts to clarify the situation for religious objectors before the June 5, 1917 draft registration. About a week before registration day, newspapers began carrying instructions from the government about how to file for exemption. The publications referenced question 12 which asked, "Do you claim exemption from the draft? (specify grounds.)" In the case of religious objection, prospective registrants would be told, "If you claim to be a member of a religious sect whose creed forbids its members to participate in war in any form, simply name the sect."[71] The Government also made it clear that groups which did not hold to pacifism before the draft would not be allowed to become pacifist after the draft. In

---

68. Crews, *Church of God: A Social History*, 123. Draft Card, Thomas Martin Cain, June 5, 1917, Knoxville, TN.

69. Draft Card for Hosea Brayles Roberts. Swarthmore College Peace Collection online database. Online: http://130.58.64.153/fmi/xsl/SCPC_COWW1_detail.xsl?-recid =3380.

70. Draft Card, Ora Lee.

71. "Draft Questions," *NY Times*, 23 May 1917, 2.

its official publications, the Assemblies of God, for example, published its position against going to war and very brief instructions to young men on the process they would find at their draft boards.[72] On June 2, 1917, *The Weekly Evangel* warned that all men "age 21 to 36 inclusive . . . should be sure to register," and that there would be a place to register conscientious objection and the religious body of which one was a member that objected to taking human life.[73] It appears that the intention of the exemption line was for men who belonged to groups with religious objections to war to be able to simply list their membership in said group, effectively signaling the draft board to a pre-designated list. Thus, for example, one finds draft cards for Mennonites and Quakers, the most well known pacifist groups, which simply list the name of the group to which the registrant belonged.

In the same fashion, Pentecostals could and did simply list the group to which they belonged that disallowed participation in war. I have found at least six men who simply listed "Pentecost" or "Pentecostal" as the affiliation which warranted exemption, and a similar group listing "Apostolic Faith" for exemption—much the same way that a couple of men listed "Holiness." This suggests the possibility these men saw no need to list a specific denomination within the Pentecostal tradition, but that the movement as a whole was taken by these registrants to be pacifist. Still, among the Assemblies of God and Church of God (Cleveland, TN) registrants, numerous men simply put "Assemblies of God" or "Church of God" on the exemption line. About one-fifth of the conscientious objectors found in the Assemblies of God and nearly half in the Church of God (Cleveland, TN) simply listed the name of the denomination.

Another sizable group of Pentecostal religious objectors put the locus of decision on membership in their church, which they did not name, such as: "religious sect don't believe in war," "against my church," "my church don't believe in war," "religious creed," "Pentecostal convictions object to war," or "having membership of church that forbids taking of life." Scribal influence on the exemption line, given that some men could not write and others answered the questions orally, and the need for parsimony in a limited writing space dictated that the largest group of Pentecostal religious objectors simply made a cursory mention of "religion," "religious reasons," "religious views," "religious belief," "religious

---

72. "Resolution Concerning Actual Participation in the Destruction of Human Life."

73. Welch, "Concerning Registration," *Weekly Evangel*, 2 June 1917, 6.

grounds," or "religious scruples." A smaller group appealed to conscience by name as in "conscientious objector," "conscientious scruples," "conscientious grounds," "conscience will not permit me to kill," "conscience will not permit me to kill, even for the state." Similar appeals were made citing religious belief with slight detail: "don't believe in war," "religious views opposed to war," "religious belief forbids killing fellow man," "religious belief . . . against killing mankind," "scriptural," "Word of God," and "scripture and conscience against taking human life."

Two Pentecostals gave what would today be very unusual views. Bruno M. Berger, a 23 year old single switch-board tester from Florida, simply listed "13th Amendment" (the prohibition against slavery), and Arthur Mitchel Clark, a 22 year old Pentecostal farmer from Tennessee, simply stated "Nothing except don't want to go." The latter was still in the disciplinary barracks at Ft. Leavenworth in 1919 after the war ended, although records there indicated his reason for not wanting to go to war was indeed religious.[74]

One 20-year-old Assembly of God minister reflected theologically on his exemption entry in a way that simultaneously took advantage of his unusual name, Royal Bert Fields, writing, "Now expatriated through oath of allegiance to the Kingdom of God."[75] In this way, he attempted to make explicit on his draft card what some of the more cursory entries listed earlier may have only hinted. In doing so, Royal exemplified a potent underlying notion of the rule of God expressed in a decision which most young men of the time had become convinced they had no right to make. He felt his Pentecostal faith informed his decision to resist this most fundamental requirement of the state, expressed in the draft, and he called upon an alternative allegiance to God's rule that freed him from the requirement to take a position of enemy against the people of another state.

## GEOGRAPHICAL LOCUS OF PENTECOSTAL PACIFISM IN THE UNITED STATES

Where did conscientious objectors identified as Pentecostal come from in World War I? In records examined thus far, they have been identified mostly with the South and, to a lesser extent, the Midwest. This

74. Swarthmore College Peace Collection online database. Online: http://130.58 .64.153/fmi/xsl/SCPC_COWW1_detail.xsl?-recid=2257.

75. Royal Bert Field, Draft Card.

is a reflection of the underlying sources of the lists used to search for their draft cards. For example, in the Church of God (Cleveland, TN), the largest group I identified, hails from Tennessee. Many were found in Mississippi, Alabama, Florida, Georgia, North and South Carolina, West Virginia, Virginia, Missouri, and Arkansas. While it is not surprising that their locations reflected the initial reach of their various denominations, it is amazing to think of requesting conscientious objector status during WWI so far South, as well as in Appalachia.[76] Two-thirds of identified Pentecostal objectors came from the South, Deep South, and Appalachia, followed by seventeen percent from the Midwest, eleven percent from the West and two percent from the Northeast. Pentecostal religious objectors were also found in at least 34 states.

## ETHNIC AND RACIAL GROUPS

Like the early Pentecostal movement as a whole, Pentecostal objectors were also found among American minorities. Out of 250 Pentecostal religious objectors identified primarily in draft cards, ten (4 percent) were African Americans and two were Hispanics (1 percent). African Americans may have found it difficult to register their conscientious objection with racist draft boards. In many cases, it appears the registrant did not actually write responses on the card, but answered questions to someone else who was filling out the card. Pentecostal scholar Theodore Kornweibel documents the rumors that spread around the black Pentecostal denomination, The Church of God in Christ, and the pacifist preaching of its founder, Charles H. Mason, especially in the Mississippi delta around Holmes County.[77] One newspaper rumored that the government had published a list of 70 blacks in Holmes County who were evading the draft for religious purposes, and offered a reward for their capture.[78] However, in an exhaustive search of over six thousand draft cards from Holmes County, only one obvious religious objector was found, George Gordon Allen, a single 22 year old farmer,

---

76. Keith, *Rich Man's War*, documents the social class origins of a particularly widespread resistance to the draft among rural, hill country, southerners. In her presentation, there were two southern responses to the WWI draft: 1) merchant class, wealthy class, and media supported the draft, and 2) the working, rural, poor largely resisted the draft. I will take up these themes as they apply to southern Pentecostals in detail in a forthcoming book.

77. Kornweibel, "Investigate Everything," 149–62.

78. "Draft Evasion.

and he was listed as white. Allen requested exemption saying, "Don't want to break 6th commandment."[79] A 37 year old Holmes County preacher, from Lexington, Mississippi registered for the draft listing his occupation as a preacher with the Sanctified Church. James Lewis Lee was questioned by the Bureau of Investigation's agent in regard to his associations with C. H. Mason and the Church of God in Christ, but Lee was probably able to get a ministerial exemption.[80] Lee denied that he or Mason "preached antidraft or antiwar messages."[81] However, whether through connection to C. H. Mason and the Church of God in Christ, which taught pacifism, or through the Sanctified Church listed on his draft card, which insisted that "members should not take part in war," Lee was an African American pastor associated with pacifism.[82]

Joseph Marcel Turpin, a 30 year old black Pentecostal minister in the Pentecostal Assemblies of the World, from Baltimore, Maryland, registered as a religious objector, and for exemption simply listed "Religious."[83] His draft card gave his occupation as Minister of the Gospel, Apostolic Faith of Assembly.[84] He was more likely to have received exemption for being a minister than being a religious objector. Another Pentecostal Assemblies of the World Pastor, Elder Morton, "a well-known black pastor of Detroit and Windsor [Ontario]," was sentenced and served time in Kingston Penitentiary for his conscientious objection to WWI.[85] William Henry Robinson, a twenty-five-year-old brick layer's helper from Toledo, Ohio, and Andrew Leon Coleman, a twenty-three-year-old custodian from Indianapolis, were both members of the Pentecostal Assemblies of the World and requested religious objector status on their draft cards.

79. George Gordon Allen, Draft Card, Durant, MS, but registered in Holmes County.

80. James Lewis Lee, Draft Card, Lexington, Holmes, MS.

81. Kornweibel, "Investigate Everything," 154. After I found James Lewis Lee's draft card in a systematic search of Holmes County, MS, draft records, Kornweibel's book gave the connection to the Church of God in Christ and C.H. Mason, and Kornweibel documented the Bureau of Investigation's questioning Lee.

82. Piepkorn, *Profiles*, 33. Whether it was the Christ's Sanctified Holy Church (West Columbia, South Carolina) or more likely the Christ's Sanctified Holy Church (Jennings, Louisiana) which came out if the former in 1903 is unclear.

83. Dupree, *Biographical Dictionary*, 275.

84. Joseph Mossell Turpin Draft Card. From the handwriting, it is obvious someone else filled out the card and he gave his signature. He signed Joseph Marcel Turpin.

85. Stroud, email.

This image reprinted by permission of Ancestry.com. To view additional family history records, please visit www.ancestry.com. Annotation is mine.

Robert Russell, a black, twenty-seven-year-old laborer at the Transcontinental Compress Company, listed "Religious Convictions" when requesting exemption.[86] However, the timing of his registration, July 23, 1918, on a card designed for June 5, 1917, suggests a problem. On June 14, 1917, he was arraigned on charges of failure to register. At the time, he tried to make the case that he was a Pentecostal and believed that the command, "Thou shalt not kill," applied. When pressed further, he said he would obey God rather than man.[87] It appears that after a year in jail he was registered, asking for exemption as a religious objector. Russell's case further illustrates the possibility that more African-American Pentecostals may have opted out of registration altogether. Jeanette Keith's *Rich Man's War, Poor Man's Fight: Race, Class, and Power in the Rural South during the First World War* evinces that in the South, a large proportion of blacks did not register, and if they did register and get drafted, they did not present themselves for service.[88]

## COULD PENTECOSTALS BE DISTINGUISHED AS PACIFISTS IN WWI?

Was pacifism a part of the public persona of Pentecostals in WWI? The following example is taken from the government's attempt to show that

86. Robert Russell, Draft Card, July 23, 1918.

87. Stephens, *Fire Spreads*, 261; "Holy Roller."

88. Keith, *Rich Man's War*. I plan to use this analysis in more detail in a forthcoming work to answer the question of why I have routinely found white Pentecostal's and seldom found black Pentecostal's draft registration cards.

the public, including all religious groups, were behind the war effort. In an attempt to motivate appropriate support of the Selective Service system, the government published lists to illustrate widespread church support for the war. The following table summarizes one such list, a religious census of Camp Grant, a military camp in Rockford, Illinois taken in January 1918.[89]

Table 1.5: Camp Grant, IL. Religious Census, January 1918

| | | | |
|---|---|---|---|
| Agnostics | 21 | Mennonites | 2 |
| Apostolic | 2 | Methodists | 3610 |
| Armenians | 1 | Mission Friends | 2 |
| Atheists | 13 | Moravians | 7 |
| Baptists | 1733 | Mohammedans | 2 |
| Bethany | 1 | Mormans | 72 |
| Carmelites | 1 | New Church | 1 |
| Church of Christ [Union] | 8 | New Emmanuel | 1 |
| Church of God | 1 | New Thought | 2 |
| Church of the Nazarene | 2 | Orthodox | 2 |
| Christian Scientists | 233 | Pentecostal | 3 |
| Congregationalists | 851 | Plymouth Brethren | 2 |
| Disciples of Christ | 522 | Presbyterians | 2188 |
| Dunkards | 9 | Progressive | 3 |
| Episcopalians | 1096 | Quakers | 45 |
| Evangelical | 107 | Rationalists | 4 |
| Federated Church | 1 | Reformed | 53 |
| Free Mission | 12 | Roman Catholics | 7678 |
| Freethinkers | 112 | Saints of Christ | 1 |
| Golden Rule | 2 | Spiritualists | 3 |
| Greek Catholics | 270 | Swedish Mission | 19 |
| Holy Rollers | 2 | Theosophists | 1 |
| Infidels | 1 | Unitarians | 120 |
| Jews | 658 | United Brethren | 78 |
| Kriquorenes | 1 | Universalists | 95 |
| Lutherans | 3943 | Zionists | 8 |

Total 23605

89. "Camp Creeds.

Pentecostals can be found in this military camp, but in very small numbers. The "Apostolic" group here is probably a Mennonite-derived group found mainly in Illinois and Iowa, and not the "Apostolic Faith" Pentecostal group. Assembly of God is completely missing from this list, despite numerous Assemblies of God churches in Illinois and surrounding states. The one "Church of God" soldier could be one of several Holiness groups or the Pentecostal variety. Three "Pentecostal" and two "Holy Roller" adherents were found for a total of five who were clearly Pentecostal. Other groups known to be pacifist were found here as well; 2 Mennonites and 45 Quakers were found. It is possible that the Pentecostals, Quakers, Mennonites, and Apostolics were in fact conscientious objectors held in the military camp or non-combatant soldiers, but they could have been combatants as well. Either way, five Pentecostals in this camp out of 23,605 in the census suggests there were not many Pentecostal combatants.

Of course, the Pentecostal movement was small at the time, but these numbers are certainly more in line with what we would expect if the group maintained its pacifism in practice as well. Thus, not only were very few Pentecostals among the soldiers counted at Camp Grant, Illinois, but Pentecostals were also prominent among the religious objectors "on trial" at Camp Grant. The news stories sensationalized how "the board of inquiry on investigations of conscientious objectors arrived in camp and put army slackers through another grilling under orders from the Secretary of War Baker." The same reporter documented at length the cross-examination of a non-religious conscientious objector and briefly noted, "Other objectors represented the Moody Church, Russellites, Mennonites, Dunkards, Apostolites, Pentecostalites, and the Assembly of God."[90] Not only were the Assemblies of God not found among the soldiers at Camp Grant, the Assemblies of God and other Pentecostals were prominent among the religious objectors. Only the Moody Church—founded by D. L. Moody, himself a pacifist to the Civil War—stands out in this list as generally non-pacifist.[91] The rest were clearly pacifist churches.

90. "Allison Faces Board."

91. Ibid. A professor from Moody Bible Institute in Chicago felt it necessary to point out that this lone religious objector did not in any way reflect on Moody Bible Institute, that the Moody Church and the Bible Institute were completely separate institutions, and that this professor had written a tract justifying participation in war for students to read.

Finding Pentecostals classified in practice among the pacifist groups is completely consistent with their rhetoric at the time.[92]

Examination of the Pentecostal movement at the time of WWI—from the point of view of their beliefs, as represented by their rhetoric—shows widespread representation of the movement as pacifist to war. This is true across the movement as measured by various denominational branches, or various places where Pentecostalism had taken hold by that time. More recently, it has become possible to examine the practice of WWI-era Pentecostals, what they tried to do, in light of their rhetoric. What is now apparent is that not only was the belief fairly widespread among Pentecostals, but, consistent with their overall style, when Pentecostals believed and preached something, they were not shy about attempting to practice the same. We can now find historical evidence of the practice of Pentecostal pacifism in WWI. This is all the more astounding when we reflect on the location of so much of the movement in the Deep South and Appalachia. Early Pentecostalism, in both word and deed, purveyed much that could be aptly described as counter-cultural, even radical. Early Pentecostals shared beliefs which they used to clearly delineate their differences from their larger societies, creating for themselves a separatist ethos of radical holiness. Pacifism was both a radical commitment and separatist ethic, and made Pentecostals seem unusual, troublesome, and at odds with their larger

---

92. It is possible to look in my data for Pentecostals in Illinois, the state in which Camp Grant was located. In The Pentecostal WWI Demographic Database, there are 115 persons from Illinois, 90 of whom were men, 47 of whom I found draft registration cards, and 25 of whom were of the age 21–31 in 1917 registration. Of the 25 Type I cards, eight chose no exemption, nine were religious objectors, seven requested family dependent exemption, and one requested ministerial exemption. In the June 30th edition of the *Weekly Evangel* ("In Jail for Failure to Register," 8), the editor told of receiving a letter from a Pentecostal woman in Anna, Illinois whose husband and brother-in-law were in jail for failure to register in the June 5th, 1917, registration. The editor of the *Weekly Evangel* chided the two men for very poor judgment, admonished them to repent of their mistake, and warned others to avoid their error. "If you have objections to slaying your fellow men, there is a time and place set apart for stating those objections, which will be heard and each case judged on its own merits. If there is good cause for exemption, exemption will be granted." In fact, two Assemblies of God men from Union County, IL, John Fowler and Thurman Lee Harvick, registered 20 days late, a punishable offense, and they registered as religious objectors. Did they fail to register? I am not certain these are the two in the article, nor that they ended up in Camp Grant pleading their case as religious objectors.

societies. Pentecostal practice of pacifism would be strenuously tested at the time of World War I.

## BIBLIOGRAPHY

Alexander, Paul. *Peace to War: Shifting Allegiances in the Assemblies of God.* Telford, PA: Cascadia, 2009.

"Allison Faces Board; Pacifist Talk Cut Short." *Chicago Daily Tribune,* July 3, 1918, 7.

Althouse, Peter. "Canadian Pentecostal Pacifism." *Eastern Journal of Practical Theology* 2 (1990) 32–43.

*The Apostolic Church: Its Principles and Practices.* Gradford, Great Britain: Apostolic, 1961.

*Articles of Faith: Church of God of the Apostolic Faith, Inc.* Tulsa: n.p., 1951.

*Assemblies of God Publications Pre-WWII.* Flower Pentecostal Heritage Center (2006). No pages. Online: www.AGHeritage.org/shop.

"Camp Creeds." *Chicago Daily Tribune,* January 22, 1918, 7.

*Church of God Evangel,* June 9, 1917.

*Church of God General Assembly Minutes 1906–2002.* CD-ROM. Cleveland, TN: Dixon Pentecostal Research Center, 2006.

*Church of God in Christ Yearbook.* Memphis: Church of God in Christ, 1951.

Clemmons, Ithiel C. "Mason, Charles Harrison." In *Dictionary of Pentecostal and Charismatic Movements,* edited by Stanley M. Burgess and Gary B. McGee, 587. Grand Rapids: Zondervan, 1988.

"Concerning Registration for Military Service," *Weekly Evangel* (June 2, 1917) 6.

*Constitution and By-Laws: The Filipino Assemblies of the First-Born Incorporated.* Delano, CA: n.p., 1954.

Crews, Mickey. *The Church of God: A Social History.* Knoxville: University of Tennessee Press, 1990.

Dayton, Donald W. "Piety and Radicalism: Ante-Bellum Social Evangelicalism in the U.S." In *From the Margins: A Celebration of the Theological Work of Donald W. Dayton,* edited by Christian Collins Winn, 31–41. Eugene, OR: Pickwick, 2007.

————. *Theological Roots of Pentecostalism.* Metuchen: Scarecrow, 1987.

Dayton, Donald W., and Lucille Sider Dayton. "An Historical Survey of Attitudes Toward War and Peace With the American Holiness Movement." In *Perfect Love and War: A Dialogue on Christian Holiness and the Issues of War and Peace.* Nappanee, IN: Evangel, 1974.

"Draft Evasion in Holmes County Due to Pro-German Teachings Among Blacks," *Vicksburg Evening Post,* Vicksburg, MI, April 1, 1918, 1.

"Draft Questions and How to Answer," *NY Times,* May 23, 1917, 2.

Dupree, Sherry Sherrod. *Biographical Dictionary of African-American, Holiness-Pentecostals 1880–1990.* Washington, DC: Middle Atlantic Regional, 1989.

Durasoff, Steve. *The Russian Protestants: Evangelicals in the Soviet Union, 1944-1964.* Cranbury, NJ: Associated University Presses, 1969.

*General Constitution and By-Laws: The Pentecostal Church of God of America.* Joplin, MO: n.p., 1975.

Hollenweger, Walter J. *The Pentecostals: The Charismatic Movement in the Churches.* Minneapolis: Augsburg, 1972.

———. "Black Pentecostal Concept." *Concept Journal* 30 (1970) 27–28.

"Holy Roller Held for Failure to Register." *Dallas Morning News*, June 15, 1917, 3.

Keith, Jeanette. *Rich Man's War, Poor Man's Fight: Race, Class, and Power in the Rural South during the First World War.* Chapel Hill: University of North Carolina, 2003.

Klippenstein, Lawrence. "Exercising a Free Conscience: The Conscientious Objectors of the Soviet Union and the German Democratic Republic." *Religion in Communist Lands* 3 (Winter 1985) 284–85.

Kornweibel, Theodore, Jr. "Investigate Everything." *Federal Efforts to Compel Black Loyalty during World War I.* Bloomington: University of Indiana Press, 2002.

Lane, Christel. *Christian Religion in the Soviet Union: A Sociological Study.* London: Allen & Unwin, 1978.

*Manual: United Pentecostal Church International.* Hazlewood: MO, United Pentecostal Church International, 1974.

Mininger, Jacob D. *Religious C.O.'s Imprisoned at the U.S. Disciplinary Barracks, Ft. Leavenworth, Kansas,* 1919.

Moore, Everett LeRoy. "Handbook of Pentecostal Denominations in the United States." MA Thesis, Pasadena City College, 1954.

Nichol, John Thomas. *Pentecostalism.* New York: Harper & Row, 1966.

Paul, George H. "The Religious Frontier in Oklahoma: Dan T. Muse and the Pentecostal Holiness Church." PhD diss., University of Oklahoma, 1965.

"The Pentecostal Movement and War." *The Pentecostal Testimony* 20 (1939) 2.

Peterson, Paul B. Letter to Noel Perkin, September 21, 1928.

———. Letter to Noel Perkin, June 13, 1929.

———. Letter to Noel Perkin, July 12, 1929. Letters furnished by Jeff Henderson, Assemblies of God Graduate School, Springfield, MO.

Piepkorn, Arthur C. *Profiles in Belief: Volume III, Holiness and Pentecostal.* San Francisco: Harper & Row, 1979.

"REEM." Memorandum from the General Council of the Assemblies of God, Inc., April 30, 1935.

"Reports from the Field," *Christian Evangel* (October 19, 1918) 14.

*Report of the Provost Marshal General to the Secretary of War: On the first draft under the Selective Service Act, 1917.* Washington, DC: Government Printing Office, 1918.

"Resolution Concerning the Attitude of the General Council of the Assemblies of God Toward any Military Service which Involves the Actual Participation in the Destruction of Human Life." *Weekly Evangel* (August 4, 1917) 6.

Robbins, R. G. *A. J. Tomlinson: Plainfolk Modernist.* New York: Oxford University Press, 2004.

Stephens, Randall J. *The Fire Spreads: Holiness and Pentecostalism in the American South.* Cambridge, MA: Harvard University Press, 2008.

Stroud, Marilyn. Email to Jay Beaman, August 23, 2007

Synan, Vinson. *The Old Time Power.* Franklin Springs, GA: Advocate, 1973.

Tomlinson, A. J. "The Awful World War: The War in Which We are Engaged Is of Far More Importance, Ours is a Spiritual Warfare." *Church of God Evangel* (February 24, 1917) 1.

———. "The Present Situation." *Church of God Evangel* (March 6, 1915) 1.

———. "While the Wars Rage We Must Be on Our Battle Field." *Church of God Evangel* (July 8, 1916) 1.

Wacker, Grant. *Heaven Below: Early Pentecostals and American Culture.* Cambridge, MA: Harvard University Press, 2003.

Welch, J. W., editor. "The Pentecostal Movement and the Conscription Law." *Weekly Evangel* (August 4, 1917) 6.

Wilson, Bryan R. *Sects and Society: A Sociological Study of Three Religious Groups in Britain.* Westport, CN: Greenwood, 1961.

"WWI Conscientious Objectors." Database from the Swarthmore College Peace Collection. No pages. Online: http://130.58.64.153/fmi/xsl/SCPC_COWW1_table.xsl.

2

# "I thank my God for the persecution"

## Conscientious Objection in the Church of God in Christ during World War I*

### Theodore Kornweibel, Jr.

Alarms about "enemy aliens," "Wobbly" anti-capitalist labor agitators, fifth columnists, and unpatriotic "slackers" gripped the emotions and prejudices of an anxious American public during World War I. With such fears rampant, the arrests of obscure southern black preachers on charges of obstructing the war effort elicited few national headlines. Although grand juries ultimately vindicated accused leaders of the Church of God in Christ (COGIC), widespread efforts of vigilante mobs and government officers to compel patriotism and military service on the part of persons holding biblical convictions against war reveal troubling pressures on wartime religious expression and free speech. This episode also illustrates one of the infrequent instances during the war where the legal system resisted inflamed passions of the day and ultimately protected,

* An earlier version of this article appeared as chapter 6 of Theodore Kornweibel Jr., "Investigate Everything": Federal Efforts to Compel Black Loyalty During World War I (Bloomington: Indiana University Press, 2002).

if not guaranteed, the free exercise of religion. This is one of the most striking examples of a more assertive mood growing within Black America: Thousands of African Americans, acting on their religious convictions, stood up to the federal government by refusing to perform military service, despite broad public disapproval and the likelihood of prosecution. The Church of God in Christ, scarcely two decades old, had no established pacifist doctrine at the onset of World War I. Its founder, Charles Harrison Mason, had been born in 1866, a year after slavery's end. His parents were agricultural laborers on a succession of farms and plantations in Tennessee and Arkansas. Mason attended school only to the fourth grade, yet he did not lack for scriptural training, being taught by his Missionary Baptist parents. Even as a child he displayed unusual spiritual depth. In 1893, at age twenty-six or twenty-seven, he led a re-vival in Preston, Arkansas, where many repented of their sins. Later that year, expecting that formal education would make him a better preacher, he enrolled in Arkansas Baptist College. He left after only three weeks: "The Lord showed me that there was no salvation in schools and col-leges." Rather, salvation would be offered through the preaching of a twofold blessing: Conversion—that is, a saving knowledge of Jesus Christ through a personal relationship with him—and sanctification—that is, the believer's purification from all sin. Mason and like-minded preachers planted the seeds of a new Pentecostal church which bore fruit in 1897 in an old gin house in Lexington, Mississippi where Mason founded the first Church of God in Christ congregation.[1]

During the early years of the twentieth century, dormant spiritual embers burst into flame in widespread corners of the world. A particular-ly dramatic manifestation was the interracial "Azusa Street revival" in Los Angeles, led by black evangelist William J. Seymour. He began "preaching the new doctrine of a third blessing—baptism by the Holy Ghost and fire—which empowered saints to cast out devils, heal the sick, and speak in other tongues." Soon hundreds of persons, black and white, made pilgrimages to Seymour's renovated livery stable, seeking the anointing of the Spirit.[2] The doctrine of a third blessing provided Mason with the missing experiential and theological pieces of the holiness puzzle. Now

1. Ross, *History and Formative Years*, 14–16; Cornelius, *Pioneer*, 9–12; Clemmons, "Mason, Charles Harrison," 585–88.

2. Cornelius, *Pioneer*, 3–5, 11–13; Ross, *History and Formative Years*, 17–18; Tucker, *Black Pastors*, 88–90.

based in Memphis, he went to Los Angeles, received the gift of tongues, and returned to spread the fire of revival. All-night meetings stretching over five weeks aroused dramatic interest in the new Pentecostal worship and belief.[3]

Charles Harrison Mason was named Chief Apostle of the Church of God in Christ at its first General Assembly, in 1907. COGIC saw rapid growth in Mississippi, Tennessee, and Arkansas among both rural sharecroppers and urban mill hands.[4] Growth into Texas soon followed. By the 1910s, as black Texans migrated to the West Coast, the church established itself in southern California, under the leadership of Elder E. R. Driver. It also moved eastward, with churches planted in Norfolk, Pittsburgh, Philadelphia, Detroit, Harlem, and Brooklyn. Expansion up the Mississippi Valley led to outposts in St. Louis, Kansas City, and Chicago. Although the majority of COGIC members remained concentrated in Arkansas, Florida, Louisiana, Mississippi, Oklahoma, Tennessee, and Texas, by 1917 the burgeoning church had congregations in all the major Midwestern and Eastern cities that attracted blacks during the "Great Migration."[5] It would have remained invisible to most whites, who little noticed the growth of urban storefront or rural southern sanctified congregations, had it not been for World War I. The war brought unanticipated challenges and attention from public authorities as well as super-patriotic vigilantes. It was COGIC's time of persecution and testing.

\* \* \* \* \* \* \* \*

In the supercharged wartime atmosphere, both patriotic organizations and public officials manipulated and exacerbated prejudices against conscientious objectors, who were frequently accused of being enemy sympathizers. All but the most single-minded devotees of unpopular causes found it prudent to fall silent, comply, or both. Religious objectors to participation in war suffered much persecution, as neither the government

3. Tucker, *Black Pastors*, 91. The Church of God in Christ was the first black Pentecostal denomination, and it remains the largest. Stanley, "Churches of God," 279; Jones, "Black Pentecostals," 150.

4. Synan, *Holiness-Pentecostal Movement*, 177; Jones, "Church of God in Christ," 204–5.

5. Tucker, *Black Pastors*, 95–96. By 1926 there were seven hundred congregations and thirty thousand members, two-thirds residing in the South, with more congregations in urban areas than in country districts; see Hall, *Negroes*, 532, 538–50.

nor the public was tolerant of those who believed that God forbade them to render military service unto Caesar. Nonreligious objectors, including some blacks, faced even more hostility. Those who were jailed suffered worst: "The treatment of the imprisoned World War I resisters was barbaric." Given such an intolerant popular mood, the Church of God in Christ's leaders were fortunate to escape conviction and draconian punishment. After months of intense investigation, two grand juries in eastern Texas ultimately exercised unusual good sense in rejecting the arguments of federal agents and prosecutors.[6]

Leaders and members of COGIC drew the scrutiny of the federal government because church doctrine forbade the shedding of blood, a belief that compelled their noncompliance with the draft. The Department of Justice was responsible for enforcement of selective service regulations. United States attorneys prepared legal cases while the rapidly expanding Bureau of Investigation, as the FBI was then known, gathered evidence and apprehended non-registrants or refusers. Constitutional liberties were often trampled, the most notorious example being the 1918 "slacker raids." Though caught in the crossfire between the public's intolerance and the government's zealous enforcement of conscription, COGIC members and other religious objectors would not betray what they regarded as the dictates of Scripture. Although Bishop Mason and other church members did not articulate political or racial opposition to the war or raise challenges to the racial status quo, their willingness to stand up to the government and its (white) agents of authority is evidence of a growing black willingness to abandon Bookerite accommodation

---

6. Kohn, *Jailed for Peace*, 29. A good survey of this intolerance is H. C. Peterson and Gilbert C. Fite, *Opponents of War, 1917–1918* (Seattle: University of Washington Press, 1968). Other useful sources are Zechariah Chafee Jr., *Free Speech in the United States* (Cambridge, MA: Harvard University Press, 1941); Donald Johnson, *The Challenge to American Freedom: World War I and the Rise of the American Civil Liberties Union* (Lexington: University of Kentucky Press, 1963); Harry N. Scheiber, *The Wilson Administration and Civil Liberties, 1917–1921* (Ithaca, NY: Cornell University Press, 1960); William Preston, *Aliens and Dissenters: Federal Suppression of Radicals, 1903–1933* (Cambridge, MA: Harvard University Press, 1963); Julian E Jaffe, *Crusade against Radicalism: New York during the Red Scare, 1914–1924* (Port Washington, NY: Kennikat, 1972); Paul L. Murphy, *The Meaning of Freedom of Speech: First Amendment Freedoms from Wilson to FDR* (Westport, CT: Greenwood, 1972); and idem, *World War I and the Origin of Civil Liberties in the United States* (New York: Norton, 1979). For details on treatment of black conscientious objectors, see Kornweibel Jr., "Apathy and Dissent."

and more assertively seek racial progress.[7] By the time America entered the war in April 1917, millions had already died on the battlefields of Europe. Soldiers had to be conscripted quickly if the United States was to have a decisive combat role. Congress, in creating the draft, provided that only conscientious objectors who were members of religious bodies opposed to participation in war would be granted exemptions. President Wilson declared that members of "a well recognized religious sect or organization" that had a creed prohibiting war service were eligible for exemption from combat, but they still had to perform noncombatant military service. (That is, there was no provision for complete exemption or for alternative service under civilian direction.) Applicants had to convince local draft boards of the sincerity of their beliefs in order to obtain noncombatant status. In practice the Mennonites, Quakers, Church of the Brethren, and a few smaller long-time pacifist groups such as the Brethren in Christ were the only denominations whose pacifism was recognized without undue difficulty. And the government demanded that even they don military uniforms and work under military command and discipline.[8] Hundreds who refused to cooperate were court-martialed and sentenced to long, abusive terms at maximum-security prisons such as Alcatraz and Leavenworth. Seventeen men received death sentences, although their sentences were commuted after the war. Public opinion associated conscientious objection with Wobbly-style economic radicalism or pro-German sympathies. An assistant secretary of war noted the public's "dislike and distrust of this small minority of Americans professing conscientious objections to warfare."[9]

In addition to hostile public opinion, the administration of the draft was compromised by bias and inconsistency on the part of local draft boards. Southern boards, staffed typically by middle- and upper-class white patriots, were ill-equipped to assess sympathetically the claims of members of the Church of God in Christ for exemption on the basis of conscience. In general, blacks were much more likely to be declared fit and available for induction than were whites, and they

7. The growing black militancy to which the federal government took such strong objection is analyzed in depth in Theodore Kornweibel, "Investigate Everything": Federal Efforts to Compel Black Loyalty during World War I (Bloomington: Indiana University Press, 2002) and "Seeing Red": Federal Campaigns Against Black Militancy, 1919–1925 (Bloomington: Indiana University Press, 1998).

8. Peterson and Fite, Opponents, 121–25.

9. U.S. War Department, Statement, 7–9, 14–19.

were less likely to receive deferments for agricultural necessity or family support. Thus the proportion of black to white draft "delinquents" was more than two to one.[10] The public often made no distinction between conscientious objection and disloyalty: A refusal to bear arms was tantamount to treason. Given such attitudes and policies, Bishop Mason and members of the Church of God in Christ were guaranteed tribulation in 1917 and 1918. The southern white populace lived in fear of blacks being incited to disloyalty or revolt by German agents. Bureau of Investigation agents probed hundreds of such rumors. Not surprisingly, despite COGIC assurances of patriotism and love for country, the public misunderstood the church's stand against participation in war. To many white southerners, conditioned by ancient fears of slave revolts, black dissent of unrest could be interpreted only as the product of "outside agitators" and a desire for vengeance.

Church of God in Christ doctrine, defined during World War I, included an unambiguous prohibition against combatant military service. Jesus Christ's teaching on the virtue of brotherly love and the sinfulness of hating others was to be obeyed. "We believe the shedding of human blood or taking of human life to be contrary to the teaching of our Lord and Saviour, and as a body, we are adverse to war in all its various forms." This did not mean that church members were sympathetic to Germany, however. Addressing a large baptismal gathering on June 23, 1918, Mason preached a sermon entitled "The Kaiser in the Light of the Scriptures." The German ruler was said to be the "Beast" or Antichrist depicted in Revelation 13, a man of warfare, pillage, and suffering. Mason found scriptural approval, in Matthew 5:42, for the purchase of Liberty Bonds, and he would later claim to have raised more than $3,000 for the government. His sermon ended in prayer not only that all peoples would beat their swords into plowshares and study war no more, but also that the "German hordes" would be driven back behind their borders.[11] While delivering such patriotic assurances, however, Mason nevertheless encouraged male parishioners to seek conscientious objector status. In the eyes of many whites, this in itself was treasonable.

10. Barbeau and Henri, *Unknown Soldiers*, 35–37; U.S. Provost Marshal General's Office, *Second Report*, 459, 461.

11. Cornelius, *Pioneer*, 68; Ross, *History and Formative Years*, 25–28.

\* \* \* \* \* \* \* \*

Bishop Mason first drew federal scrutiny in September 1917 when an alarmed chancery clerk at Lexington, Mississippi warned authorities that he "openly advised against registration and made treasonable and seditious remarks against the United States government."[12] The church had many members in Holmes County, Mississippi's Delta region, where blacks constituted nearly 80 percent of the population and local whites worried not only about meeting draft quotas, but about maintaining their racial domination.

Bureau of Investigation agent M. M. Schaumburger, whose jurisdiction included rural Mississippi and Louisiana, tried to verify the allegations. Interviewing indignant whites who attended Mason's assemblies, he learned that the "negro revivalist preacher" had conducted nightly meetings with overflow crowds of two or three thousand during the first two weeks in August. Mason was said to exert as much influence over his race as did Billy Sunday among whites—and to have amassed considerable personal wealth, including a $60,000 mansion in Memphis. Informants charged that he taught opposition to war and bloodshed while informing his members they need not register for the draft. Worse, Schaumburger learned that Mason allegedly labeled the present conflict a rich man's war and a poor man's fight, in which blacks had no grudge against the Germans, a good people who treated blacks better than did other whites. Mason was said to have praised Germany so profusely that one of his fellow preachers threatened to quit the church. Schaumburger believed all this was sufficient to convict Mason of treason, obstructing the draft, and giving aid and comfort to the enemy, particularly since two church members had not reported for induction.[13]

Confident of prosecution, Schaumburger obtained sworn statements from members of both races. The affidavits of four members of the (black) Mississippi Cavalry who had attended Mason's meetings were couched, however, in such racially guarded language that they proved to be useless. Schaumburger noted ruefully, "while all the men know by reputation that Mason is a menace to the country, they are unable to furnish direct testimony."[14] Hence on its first attempt to prosecute Mason, the

12. Schaumburger, file 144128, RG65, BI, NA.
13. Schaumburger, OG64788, RG65, BI, NA. Sept. 26, 1917.
14. Schaumburger, OG64788, OG172841 RG65, BI, NA. Sept. 26, 1917 & Sept. 27,

government was stymied, possessing only hearsay evidence. Of course this failure did nothing to allay either the patriotic or the racial anxieties of local whites and federal authorities.

The next individual to come under government suspicion was Rev. E. R. Driver, overseer of COGIC churches in California and one of the denominations' founding elders. He was summoned to the Bureau office in Los Angeles in February 1918 and accused of being "pro-German and bitter toward the Government." Driver insisted on his loyalty while defending the church's opposition to taking life, but agent George T. Holman was skeptical of Driver's patriotism: "This colored minister is supposed to have considerable influence among a number of people of his race and his attitude is very aggressive with reference to this country's entrance into the war . . . It would be possible for him to be of considerable menace to the country." The agent vowed to keep Driver under observation and halt his activities should they become "pronounced."[15] Such a confrontation was typical. Bureau conscription case files are replete with records of inquisitional interviews in which agents argued with suspects, assailed them with patriotic bombast, and threatened them toward compliance with the draft.

Many southern whites suspected that blacks' loyalty had been subverted by "German gold." Such dastardly deeds were seemingly confirmed by an April 1, 1917 headline in the *Vicksburg Post* proclaiming "Draft Evasion in Holmes County [is] Due to Pro-German Teachings among Blacks." The state adjutant general's office, the paper reported, had found it "virtually impossible" to get Lexington blacks to comply because of Mason's allegedly pro-German sermons and advice to "resist" conscription. Investigators learned that three weeks earlier a mysterious foreigner, Dimitrius Giannokulion, conducted a meeting at Mason's church during which time he received a message in code. To anxious whites there was no coincidence between this information and the allegation that Mason was "suddenly wealthy," enjoying a new brick-and-stone residence in Memphis. The situation seemed all the more sinister because in the preceding two months only a small proportion of several hundred black registrants had reported for induction. In desperation the adjutant general published the names of seventy alleged Holmes County draft dodgers, offering a $50 reward for each one delivered to the nearest military

---

1917, respectively.

15. Holman, OG64788, RG65, BI, NA. Feb. 27, 1918.

post. The story linking Mason, Giannokulion, and draft resistance was picked up by the national wire services, which spread this alarming tale of German intrigue across the country. Only black newspapers like the *New York Age,* debunked the idea of enemy subversion through Mason's church. It called instead for an investigation of southern draft boards that were said to be inducting all black registrants regardless of fitness while exempting many eligible whites.[16]

These "revelations" prompted the Bureau of Investigation to open a new case on Bishop Mason. At the same time, thanks to the patriotic tip of a local U.S. Food Administration official, the military intelligence section of the War Department was alerted to this perceived threat to preparedness. Henceforth the Bureau and army officers would share information on Mason and the Church of God in Christ.[17]

Bureau agent Harry D. Gulley found matters to be somewhat different from the reports in the excited press. Local officials in Lexington told him that the number of black draft respondents was indeed alarmingly low but that part of the blame lay with the draft board's inefficiency and poor record keeping. Nothing was learned about Giannokulion, although Gulley heard new rumors of five suspicious foreigners—three Germans, an Englishman, and a Frenchman—who were believed to have some connection with Mason. Gulley interviewed alleged draft delinquents held in the local jail but only one had been to Mason's church, and he denied hearing any anti-draft propaganda. Hearsay charging Mason with supporting Germany and holding secret anti-draft meetings at 3 o'clock in the morning also surfaced. Although Gulley could substantiate nothing, he nonetheless concluded that blacks "had evidently been admonished not to talk 'war talk.'"[18]

One church member did agree to speak with Gulley, but James Lee, one of five ordained COGIC preachers in Holmes County, insisted that neither he nor Mason preached anti-draft or anti-war messages. Gulley's only success was in obtaining several church documents, including a doctrinal statement drawn up the previous August by Mason and elders W. B. Holt (white) and E. R. Driver. This piece affirmed loyalty to all God-given

16. See "Draft Evasion," "Negro Admits," "German Money Fights Draft," and "German Money."

17. Leider, PF1811-2, Apr. 2,1918; Van Deman, PF1811-3, RG165, MID, NA, Apr. 12, 1918.

18. Gulley, OG64788, RG65, BI, NA, Apr. 12, 1918.

institutions, including magistrates, civil laws, the Constitution, the president, and the flag while also stating that taking life or shedding blood was contrary to the teachings of Jesus. Church members were allowed to perform any other service that did not conflict with the no-bloodshed principle. Another earlier doctrinal statement, written decades earlier by Holt in 1895, forbidding members to shed blood or bear arms, was collected. However, the Bureau devoted their most intense interest to a blank petition, signed by Mason and addressed to draft boards, to be used by registrants seeking exemption based on church doctrine.[19]

Despite an absence of direct evidence, Gulley was convinced that church leaders had induced blacks to disobey the draft law and that doctrinal statements against war were adopted merely to increase membership. Disregarding Holt's 1895 statement, Gulley also warned that COGIC's recent association with white churches in the West could well be the result of German anti-draft activities. Recognizing the need for more concrete evidence, however, he urged the United States attorney in Jackson and Bureau agents in Memphis and Los Angeles to further investigate Mason, Holt, and Driver.[20]

Ironically, by assuring townsfolk that the "menace" was being taken seriously, Gulley's investigation gave Mason temporary protection from outraged white Lexingtonians. Events elsewhere demonstrated that when worried patriots felt no governmental action was forthcoming, vigilantism was likely to occur. One victim of such action was Rev. Jesse Payne, a COGIC pastor in Blytheville, Arkansas, who was fortunate to escape with his life on April 18, 1918. Under the headline "Negro Preacher Tarred," the *Memphis Commercial Appeal* reported that this

> pastor of the colored holly [*sic*] roller church in the southeast suburbs of this city, was given a coat of tar and feathers last night as a result of alleged seditious remarks for some months concerning the president, the war, and a white man's war.
>
> Earlier in the evening the preacher is alleged to have said something about the kaiser being as good a man as the president, and that the kaiser did not require his people to buy bonds and some one landed a solar plexus on him sending him into the ditch, from which he got up running . . . [After the tarring and feathering, Payne] repeated the soldier's oath, and promised to

19. Ibid. The church's antiwar doctrine is printed in Cornelius, *Pioneer*, 68.
20. Gulley, OG64788, RG65, BI, NA, Apr 2, 1918.

talk Liberty Bonds and Red Cross to the end of his life and the end of the war.

It is said his flock has shown no interest in the war work, while the negroes of other churches have been most liberal, $2,000 having been subscribed by the Methodist and Baptist churches Sunday night. This church is circulating literature which he says was sent to him by a brother preacher in Memphis, showing from Bible quotations that it is not right for Christians to fight. The literature is scattered broadcast over the country.

The newspaper concluded its report by editorializing that the pastor's punishment "will result in great good to demonstrate to not only blacks but some whites that it is time to get into the war work and quit talking such rot as is attributed to Payne."[21]

Bureau of Investigation personnel continued inquiries in the South and on the West Coast. Mason agreed to an interview with Memphis Special Agent in Charge W. E. McElveen in which he claimed to have advised men who became church members after passage of the draft act to register but to claim conscientious objector exemptions, explaining that church members should respect and obey current laws. Mason also said he had sent a telegram to President Wilson after the draft act was passed, explaining the church's doctrines and offering to meet with him. Regulations concerning conscientious objection had been sent to Mason, which he claimed to have followed. He likewise avowed support for Liberty Bond, war stamp, and Red Cross drives. McElveen was particularly worried about German influence in the church, but Mason denied any outside funding or pro-German preaching in COGIC pulpits. Finding nothing concrete to confirm suspicions of subversion, McElveen concluded that the Mason was less extreme than other religious objectors such as the Seventh-Day Adventists.[22]

McElveen's conclusions notwithstanding, Mason remained under surveillance. After he conducted a camp meeting in late May at E. R. Driver's Los Angeles church, local "agents" of the American Protective League (APL), a two hundred thousand member organization of "secret service" volunteers, supplied the Bureau with an excited report of dramatic increases in COGIC membership owing, it was alleged, to members getting noncombatant status. The web of suspicion went further, the

21. "Negro Preacher Tarred," 11.
22. McElveen, OG64788, RG65, BI, NA, May 2, 1918.

APL reporting that several Germans were members of Driver's church and that other wealthy "Teutons" gave generous donations. "Fine autos quite frequently stop at the above church and their occupants are of a strong German type." And the white neighbors who protested the late night revivals reported receiving threats.[23]

By now, Bureau of Investigation headquarters in Washington was keenly monitoring the case. In the opinion of Chief A. Bruce Bielaski, enough evidence had been amassed by late spring of 1918, from Mississippi, Tennessee, and California, to support Mason's prosecution. Believing there was "some special basis for complaint of pro-German activities in these sections of the country," he directed that "a strong case should be prepared in order to make a striking example of some of the alleged agitators."[24]

\* \* \* \* \* \* \* \*

At this point events overtook the Bureau, forcing it to protect the life of the man it held in suspicion. Bishop Mason returned to Lexington in early June, not realizing the depth of antipathy of local whites who blamed him for an alarming decline in draft compliance. Many black registrants had failed to appear for induction. When apprehended, they produced COGIC petitions containing religious objections to war. White residents claimed Mason had told would-be converts that "if you want to stay out of this war you must get right with God, and join my church. There is no occasion for the negroes to go to war; the Germans are the best friends the negroes have. Germany is going to whip the United States for the mistreatment accorded the negroes, if for no other reason. This is a rich man's war anyway." A lynching appeared likely, prompting the sheriff to try to protect Mason by arresting him for obstructing the draft. This action, plus news of an imminent investigation by the Bureau, momentarily quelled the mob spirit. When Bureau agent Eugene Palmer arrived in Lexington, however, he discovered local whites were un-pacified by the arrest. Fearing the worst, Palmer borrowed the sheriff's car, got Mason

23. Killick, OG64788, RG65, BI, NA, June 17, 1918 .The presence of whites in the church was not unusual, for there were many mixed Pentecostal congregations in the early twentieth century, following the interracial Azusa Street revival; see Jones, *Black Pentecostals*, 148.

24. Bielaski, OG644128, RG65, BI, NA, May 17, 1918.

out of jail, and drove him to Durant, where they caught a southbound Illinois Central Railroad train, arriving safely in Jackson. Arraigned there on draft obstruction charges, Mason pleaded not guilty, waived a preliminary hearing, and posted a $2,000 bond guaranteeing his appearance in federal court in November. Meanwhile, back in Lexington, a "large number" of black men said to have been influenced by Mason were summarily rounded up and sent to Camp Pike, Arkansas, for induction.[25]

In numerous instances during the war, alarmed southern whites found it difficult to believe that blacks could hold their own antiwar beliefs or be disenchanted with the war. It was much more comforting to believe black disaffection was the result of gullible blacks being manipulated by enemy agents. The hoary southern myth of "outside agitators" stirring up an otherwise contented black population had clearly not died with slavery. The *Jackson Daily News* hailed Mason's arrest as "an important step in countering German propaganda," holding the preacher responsible not only for the large number of Holmes County blacks who allegedly evaded the draft but also for "making false statements for the purpose of promoting the cause of Germany, and detrimental to the military welfare of the United States." When agent Palmer examined Mason's suitcase for incriminating evidence, however, he found little to establish an enemy connection other than several pieces of "anointed cloth" and a bottle of German cologne with which to perform the consecration.[26]

Meanwhile, the Military Intelligence Division, which conducted widespread investigations of civilians during the war, was mustering its own evidence against Mason. Like the Bureau of Investigation, MID developed a special focus on alleged black subversives. Any activity threatening to impair enlistments was naturally of their concern. Col. Marlborough Churchill, then head of MID, instructed intelligence officers in Los Angeles and St. Louis to investigate Elders E. R. Driver, W. B. Holt, and Randolph R. Booker to determine whether there was German influence behind the church's non-participation policy. He addressed a similar letter to Bureau Chief Bielaski recommending further investigation of COGIC leadership and its "propaganda," suggesting "the inquiry

25. Palmer, OG227347, RG65, BI, NA, Apr. 2, 1918 (quotation); "Jail Pastor." No record has been found to identify the men sent into the military or to determine whether they persisted in claiming to be conscientious objectors. Such summary "justice" obviously narrowed their options.

26. Palmer , OG227347, RG65, BI, NA, June 20, 1918; "Lexington Negro," Jackson Daily News.

concerning William B. Holt should be especially rigid." Churchill explained that Holt "is a white man, very insulting and overbearing in manner, and [that he had] traveled all the way from Los Angles to Jackson to arrange bail for Mason, putting up $2,000 in cash."[27]

Soon thereafter, the Bureau opened a case on Henry Kirvin, pastor of a COGIC congregation in Paris, Texas. Not only did the Bureau believe that his actions had undermined military preparedness; it also hoped to implicate Bishop Mason. Agent DeWitt S. Winn, a former Burns Detective Agency operative, unearthed information that, if provable, could damn the entire church leadership. Kirvin was said to have referred to the Red Cross as the "blood of the Beast" described in the Book of Revelation and to have warned his flock not to contribute to that charity or wear its button. More important, Winn continued, Kirvin's congregation contributed $125 so that he could accompany Mason to Washington to gain draft deferments from Woodrow Wilson himself. Not surprisingly, the two had not seen the president but had met with a selective service official who supposedly arranged members' immunity from the draft and from Red Cross, Liberty Bond, and war thrift stamp contributions. Henceforth each member—adult and child—was assessed twenty-five cents monthly, allegedly on the authority of the president, to ensure their exemption. So ran the charges.[28]

Learning that Mason, Holt, and Kirvin were in Austin raising legal defense funds, Winn telephoned agent Claude McCaleb to urge investigation, although not a hasty arrest. McCaleb covered Mason's meeting but heard nothing incriminating.[29] Undeterred, McCaleb, Winn, and United States Attorney Clarence Merritt continued to prepare a case for prosecution. Records of Kirvin's Paris church were examined. Holt, whom McCaleb believed to be a German, had been jailed in Paris on charges of possessing a gun, which suggests that federal and state authorities were cooperating on the case. But no charges were yet leveled against Mason and Kirvin. When grilled by McCaleb, Kirvin described how, on orders from Mason, all church members had been enrolled the

27. Col. Marlborough Churchill to F. Sullens, editor, *Jackson Daily News*, 25 June 1918; Sullens to Churchill, June 29, 1918; Churchill to Bielaski, July 13, 1918 (quotation); Churchill to Intelligence Officer, Los Angeles, June 19, 1918; and Churchill to IO, St. Louis, July 13, 1918, 99-7, RG 165, MID, NA.

28. Agent DeWitt S. Winn to Bureau, July 16, 1918, OG64788, RG65, BI, NA.

29. Agent Claude McCaleb to Bureau, July 15, 1918; OG245662, RG65, BI, NA.

previous January and assessed twenty-five cents monthly for legal representation of men who might be drafted. He denied discouraging Red Cross participation and said, "I am now teaching that nations ought to chastise one another."[30]

Mason was interviewed once again. He maintained that although that part of the COGIC doctrinal statement detailing opposition to military service was first printed in 1917, after the draft law was passed, it had long been an article of faith; there had simply been no need to publish it earlier. Denying unpatriotic motives, Mason avowed that he was "just trying to teach the scriptures." Answering questions about Holt, he declared that the white man had joined the church in May 1917 as its superintendent of Spanish language missions. Concerning Holt's arrest for weapons possession, Mason explained that Holt was entitled to carry a badge and gun as a deputy sheriff in California.[31]

Henry Kirvin and Charles H. Mason were arrested on July 16, 1918. They and William B. Holt were charged with impersonating federal officers and conspiring to commit offenses against the government. The former infraction carried a maximum three-year sentence and $1,000 fine, the latter permitting a $10,000 penalty and two years' incarceration. Regarding the first charge, Mason was said to have told church members that he was an emissary of President Wilson with authority to collect twenty-five cents monthly to ensure their exemption from military service. The *Paris Morning News* cynically simplified the issue, declaring that Mason was "charged with working holy roller negroes." Holt remained in jail, unable to raise $5,000 bond, an extraordinarily high amount. The others were released on their own recognizance. Given the climate where suspicious white outsiders were assumed to be enemy agents, Holt was apparently deemed the more dangerous. A trial date was set for late October, which suited the federal prosecutors, who would have to work hard to present a credible conspiracy case.[32]

In Los Angeles, Bureau agent Killick gathered additional data on the three defendants, interviewing COGIC leader E. R. Driver—who,

30. Winn to Bureau, July 16, 18, 19, 1918, OG64788; McCaleb to Bureau, July 15, 1918, OG245662, RG65, BI, NA (quotation).

31. McCaleb to Bureau, July 15, 16, 1918, OG245662, RG65, BI, NA.

32. "Charged With Working Holy Roller Negroes," *Paris Morning News*, 17 July 1918; Winn to Bureau, July 19, 20, 1918, OG64788; McCaleb to Bureau, July 16, 18, 1918, OG245662, RG65, BI, NA. The trio was charged with violating sections 32 and 37 of the U.S. Penal Code.

incidentally, denied he was a Negro, claiming his father was an East Indian who married a black woman after the son's birth. Driver described Mason as devoted, heart and soul, to his spiritual tasks but also as sometimes misunderstood because of his lack of formal education. He claimed never to have heard Mason criticize the government or encourage evasion of military duty; rather, Mason had instructed COGIC members who were drafted to seek positions "that did not necessitate their engaging in the actual taking of human life." Killick tried to trap Driver in a logical inconsistency by arguing that noncombatant soldiers were also culpable, since they helped the actual combatants. Driver maintained that noncombatants were absolved before God of any wrongdoing. Convinced of neither the church's nor Driver's sincerity, Killick concluded that his attitude was very commanding and dictatorial, and his general personality very repugnant. "I could easily imagine that this man, if crossed and aggravated, might become wildly fanatical on any issue which might confront him. In my opinion, I do not believe that the principle of opposition to warfare was ever established as a fundamental of this church prior to the entrance of the United States into the war. . . . I believe that the members of this church were anxiously desirous of evading military service in every respect."[33]

But could conspiratorial intent be proven in a court of law? A truly impartial jury was unlikely to be convinced by the Bureau's evidence to this point.

\* \* \* \* \* \* \* \*

Meanwhile, the fear of German subversion still preoccupied army intelligence officials. Upon receipt of Winn's reports, the Military Intelligence Division requested still more surveillance to determine whether enemy aliens were promoting obstruction of the draft laws. MID operatives tapped E. R. Driver's telephone in a vain attempt to prove German associations.[34] Col. Marlborough Churchill's office waited impatiently for the trial of Mason, Holt, and Kirvin, stressing to John Lord O'Brian, the special assistant to the attorney general responsible for overseeing Espionage Act cases, that prosecution was "fairly important for our counter-propaganda work, as there are outcroppings of this negro religious agitation in

33. Killick to Bureau, July 19, 23, 25, 1918, OG64788, RG65, BI, NA.
34. Killick to Bureau, Aug. 6, 1918, OG64788, RG65, BI, NA.

other parts of the country with which we have to deal." This was a reference to the Pentecostal Assemblies of the World, Churches of the Living
God, Church of God and Saints in Christ, and black Church of Christ
congregations, all of which similarly opposed participation in the war.[35]

If the Department of Justice was to succeed in prosecuting Mason
and his associates, they would need more than hearsay evidence. Credible
testimony by church members was essential. The most promising witness appeared to be Rev. W. C. Thompson, who had left the church in
disagreement over performing military service. Interviewed by Bureau
agents in Chicago, Thompson alleged that COGIC members were discouraged from buying Liberty Bonds because Mason wanted them to
give him money for a new house. He charged further that Kirvin's anti-
war stance was simply for personal gain. To the Bureau's chagrin, however, Thompson defended Mason and Kirvin as basically patriotic, even
if mistaken. This was hardly the conclusive testimony that the Justice
Department needed in order to convict the church leaders.[36]

The government suffered another setback when the sudden death
of agent DeWitt Winn in the influenza epidemic left the Bureau without
its most informed, diligent, and professional operative on the case.[37] His
replacement, agent Lewie H. Henry, continued assisting U.S. Attorney
Merritt in preparing the case for a federal grand jury. Using the Paris
church registry, Henry took statements from thirteen members, including two lay preachers. They related how, after his trip to Washington,
Pastor Kirvin instructed the congregation to pay twenty-five cents to

35. Alfred Bettman to Lt. Van Dusen, Aug. 8,1918, OG64788, RG65, BI, NA; Carlton
J. H. Hayes, MIS, to Special Assistant to the Attorney General John Lord O'Brian, Sept.
4, 1918 (quotation); U.S. attorney Clarence Merritt to Attorney General Thomas W.
Gregory, Sept. 21,1918; case file 195341, Record Group 60, Department of Justice,
National Archives; Churchill to Bielaski, July 26, 1918, 99-7, RG165, MID, NA; Walter
J. Hollenweger, "A Black Pentecostal Concept," Concept 30 (1970) 61–63; Kornweibel,
"Apathy and Dissent," 330–31. Information on the other dissenting churches is in case
files 99-7 and 99-68, RG165, MID, NA, and case file OG27320, RG65, BI, NA.

36. Division superintendent Charles E. Breniman to division superintendent
Hinton G. Clabaugh, Aug. 31, 1918; agent R G. Habda to Bureau, Sept. 10, 1918;
agent W. Neunhoffer to Winn, Sept. 16, 1918; Neunhoffer to Merritt, Sept. 16, 1918;
OG64788, RG65, BI, NA.

37. Winn's death was mourned by his Bureau colleagues, who testified to his dedi-
cation and professionalism (tragically his daughter also succumbed to influenza on
the same day); personnel file of DeWitt S. Winn, obtained from the Federal Bureau of
Investigation through the Freedom of Information Act.

register so that the president would know who the saints of the church were. All those paying and so enrolled would not have to go to war, but those who did not would be cut off from the church and afforded no protection from military service. Women were urged to register too, so as to avoid forced Red Cross work. Members were also required to purchase, for fifteen cents, a document entitled "Doctrinal Statement and Rules for Government of the Church of God in Christ" which stated "we believe the shedding of human blood or the taking of human life to be contrary to the teachings of our Lord and Savior, and as a body we are adverse to war in all its various forms." If men were inducted, Kirvin was alleged to have said, they could use the pamphlet to plead for mercy and not be sent to the front lines. Members were admonished that they must "live the life" if they expected their church to stand behind them. Church finances were also investigated, but nothing damaging came to light. What most shocked Agent Henry was learning that Holt hugged and kissed Mason. The culturally unsophisticated Bureau agent interpreted this as a shocking display of interracial intimacy rather than as what it was: The "holy kiss," a scriptural form of Christian greeting.[38]

On October 29, 1918, even as newspaper headlines predicted the imminent collapse of Germany and its allies, a federal grand jury convened in Paris, Texas, to weigh evidence against Mason, Kirvin, and Holt. A large number of church members attended the hearing presided over by judge DuVal West of San Antonio, no stranger to cases of alleged black disloyalty. Surprisingly, despite local passions, the grand jury declined to indict on the charge of conspiring to hinder the draft, finding that the three preachers' operations "were not conducted in a way that was covered by any federal statute." It found no more merit in the charge of impersonating government officials. Disappointed but not defeated, the assistant United States attorney prosecuting the case suggested that the defendants be charged in Lamar County Court for swindling in connection with the monthly assessments. Agent Henry persuaded county attorney Grady Sturgeon to prosecute, promising access to all evidence gathered by the Bureau. So on November 1, the defendants were back in custody.[39]

---

38. Agent Lewie H. Henry to Bureau, Oct. 27, 1918, OG 64788, RG 65, BI, NARA; Capt. Moss, Los Angeles, to Department Intelligence Officer, San Francisco, Oct. 18, 1918, 99-7, RG 165, MID, NA.

39. Henry to Bureau, Nov. 2, 1918, OG64788, RG65, BI, NA; "Local News" col-

Local prosecution, where racial fears might easily be manipulated, was potentially dangerous. The press focused particularly on Holt, who was reported to have eaten and lodged with blacks and to have hugged and kissed black preachers. Kirvin and Mason made bond, but again Holt could not raise a higher sum. The *Paris Morning News*, in language common to the southern white press, reported "the white man who was arrested with the negro holy roller preachers on the charge of swindling is still in jail. None of the brethren have so far made bond for him, although the darkies have been released."[40]

This last attempt to prosecute Church of God in Christ leaders must be pieced together from only a few extant clues. The *Paris Morning News* did not mention the trio after November 5. The minutes' indexes for both the district and Lamar County courts contain no information on the disposition of the swindling case, and the county grand jury did not keep minutes in this era. It seems likely that jurors declined to support the county attorney's attempt to prosecute on evidence supplied by the Bureau of Investigation. Only William B. Holt was convicted. He pleaded guilty to vagrancy on December 6 and was fined one dollar. This was the last recorded act of harassment against the COGIC's white official.[41]

\* \* \* \* \* \* \* \*

Bishop Mason saw his legal ordeals in Mississippi and Texas as nothing less than persecution, and evidence supports his interpretation. The church's anti-war doctrines in all likelihood antedated the introduction of the draft in 1917. Clearly neither Mason nor other pastors were pro-German. Mason's sermon "The Kaiser in the Light of the Scriptures" expressed clear opposition to German policy and a willingness to support Liberty Bond drives. There was no conspiracy to obstruct either the draft or any other government operation. Nevertheless, ordinary citizens and public officials alike were disinclined to differentiate between religious objection to all wars and opposition to the present conflict. Part of the reason was that other blacks did express unmistakable political dissent.

umns, *Paris Morning News*, Oct. 30, Nov. 2, 1918 (quotation).

40. "A Complaint Against Holy Roller Negroes," *Paris Morning News,* Nov. 2; "Local News," Nov. 3, 5 (quotation), 1918.

41. Letter to author, July 23, 1982, A. M. Aiken Regional Archives, Texas State, Library, Paris, Texas; Criminal Minutes, Lamar County Court, book 12, 290.

African American socialists like A. Philip Randolph and Chandler Owen, editors of the *Messenger,* viewed the war as the inevitable product of exploitive international capitalism. Many more blacks, including ex-southerners trapped in northern urban ghettos where the Promised Land seemed as remote as ever, saw no reason to fight in a "white man's war."[42] By contrast, COGIC doctrine was apolitical. The church should have excited no more interest or disfavor than did the Quakers.

Regarding the charge that Mason impersonated a government official, the evidence was no stronger. Extant documents suggest that the twenty-five-cent assessments were to pay for the legal costs of Mason, other arrested leaders, and those seeking draft exemptions.[43] This was probably the easiest way to raise a defense fund, and the money collected seems to have gone for its stated purposes. Mason may have naively assumed from his talks with draft officials in Washington that the government approved his church's antiwar doctrines as sufficient to ensure exemption from conscription, at least for those men who were COGIC members before passage of the selective service law. Inexperienced in dealing with the wider world, Mason relied less on the nuances of law than on the strength of a sovereign God whom he knew far better.

But the mood in 1917 and 1918 was intolerant of any nonconformity. Even recognized peace churches such as the Mennonites and Quakers sustained real difficulties. Newer denominations without venerable traditions, or sects about which the government had no reliable information, were treated even less sympathetically. Given this hostile climate, and the racially biased operation of many southern draft boards, it was almost inevitable that black religious objectors and their leaders would be perceived, not as strict and devout adherents to their faith, but as pawns of the German enemy and traitors. Neither would be tolerated. In this respect white southern responses to the Church of God in Christ reflected a vocal majority of the country which had no patience for anyone, whether religious sectarian, political dissident, or slacker, who refused to demonstrate unalloyed patriotism. Wartime passions led to wartime excesses, and Bureau of Investigation agents, who were white, male, middle class, and patriotic, were not immune to intolerance. Most agents worked in areas to which they were native, so those assigned to southern Bureau

42. Kornweibel Jr., *No Crystal Stair,* ch. 1; Kornweibel, "Apathy and Dissent."

43. Neither Jones's and Cornelius's authorized histories of the denomination, nor Mason's own accounts, provide any details on the assessment.

offices were likely to hold traditional views on race relations and grave suspicions of any type of black nonconformity.

Years later, Bishop Mason recalled his tribulations during World War I. Time had blurred the accuracy of his chronology, but not the details of his ordeals:

> In 1918 1 was called to appear before the judge of the Kangaroo Court in Paris, Tex. The presiding officers [sic] looked at me and laid down his books, and said, "You all may try him; I will not have anything to do with him."
>
> In 1918, at Lexington, Miss., I took a scriptural stand against the ungodly deeds of the various races, about how many souls were being hurled into eternity without chance of seeking God for their soul's salvation, knowing that without the hand of the Almighty there could be no remedy for the same.
>
> The Holy Ghost through me was teaching men to look to God, for he is their only help. I told them not to trust in the power of the United States, England, France or Germany, but trust in God. The enemy (the devil) tried to hinder me from preaching the unadulterated word of God. He plotted against me and had the white people to arrest me and put me in jail for several days. I thank my God for the persecution. "For all that live godly must suffer persecution." 2 Tim. 3:12.
>
> Later in the same year I was called to Jackson, Miss., to answer to the charge that the devil had made against me. The presiding officers talked with me, after which they told me that I was backed up by the Scripture, and would not be hurt by them.... If God be for you, who can be against you![44]

Reasons for the federal government's inability to prosecute Mason in Jackson must be inferred from sketchy evidence. Perhaps the proceedings were simply dropped after the Armistice on November 11, 1918. But the Justice Department continued to pursue other wartime cases for many months after the end of hostilities, so it is more likely that a grand jury indeed indicted Mason—such bodies rarely failed to bring indictments in this period—but that federal attorneys, more realistically distinguishing winning from losing cases, dropped Mason's case before it came to trial. Such actions were usually not recorded, and thus the absence of information in the minutes and dockets of the district court can be understood

44. Mason quoted in Ross, *History and Formative Years*, 23–24.

as mute evidence in support of that conclusion.[45] In any case, Mason, Driver, Kirvin, and Holt were indeed fortunate.

Many federal officials during World War I believed that enemies within the gates imperiled the country. The notion that a sinister adversary was manipulating gullible blacks' loyalties was widely held, from the attorney general down to ordinary citizens. Considering the experiences of others who opposed the war on political or religious grounds, Bishop Mason and most of his associates were fortunate to find legal vindication and, with the exception of elder W. B. Holt, only brief incarceration.

The Justice Department, tasked with enforcement of selective service regulations, had a legitimate interest in the church and its leadership. The tragedy in this case is not the fact of federal scrutiny but the degree to which an over-energized Bureau of Investigation, urged on by military intelligence, compromised the possibility of objectivity by succumbing to popular fears and prejudices. Some agents, like DeWitt Winn, conducted themselves professionally, but in this and other cases his peers often imbibed the anxieties and prejudices of an overwrought white populace.

The relentless pursuit of COGIC leaders and their arrests on flimsy conspiracy and impersonation charges lend credence to Bishop Mason's claim to persecution by federal authorities, his ultimate exoneration notwithstanding. But this may be more than an example of persecution. There is likely also a hidden story of resistance. Although reliable COGIC membership figures for the World War I era are lacking, it is likely that several thousand members were drafted. An unknown number probably never appeared for induction. Some may have hidden out, while others sought the anonymity of a big city. Some undoubtedly submitted to induction even while bearing copies of the church's doctrinal statement. Given the paucity of COGIC members identified in lists of those who became absolutist war resisters—who refused to put on the uniform and who were court-martialed and imprisoned as a result—it must be assumed that COGIC objectors, once under the army's authority, were browbeaten or frightened into compliance with military orders and shouldering a rifle. Extant records, unfortunately, do not mention these individuals.[46]

45. Letter to author, Aug. 3, 1982, National Archives and Records Administration, Southeast Region, Atlanta [East Point], Georgia. I am indebted to my late colleague Richard Steele for pointing out the differing expectations of federal grand juries and federal attorneys.

46. Beaman, "*Response*: Pacifism," 88, 92 nn. 13, 14. One list of absolutist resisters is "Religious C.O.s Imprisoned at the U.S. Disciplinary Barracks, Ft. Leavenworth,

The Church of God in Christ's opposition to participating in war was both religious and political. It began with the former. The church believed that Jesus taught the substitution of brotherly love for the sin of hatred, rather than "the shedding of human blood or taking of human life." On another level, however, the COGIC stance was extremely political. The federal government never recognized the church in the sense of acknowledging the legitimacy or sincerity of its antiwar principles or granting conscientious objector status to its members. Given such hostility, it is remarkable that black men, for the most part poorly educated sharecroppers and urban laborers who had not challenged government authority in such numbers and with such persistence since the Civil War and Reconstruction, continued to cling to their convictions. Although most of them likely submitted to military discipline upon induction, their assertions of conscientious objection were politically charged challenges to white authority which could not go unheeded by those in government who had appointed themselves guarantors of white supremacy and black submission. Persecution of church members emerged from legitimate worries about draft evasion, but also from war-generated paranoia and racism. The American public, during World War I, generally condoned wholesale abridgements of constitutional rights like freedom of speech. An authority on early Pentecostal pacifism concludes that COGIC members suffered from "collusion between local intolerance and war support and the federal government's unyielding prosecution." Ironically, Bishop Charles H. Mason's reputation would be enhanced by his travails. For decades thereafter, he was perceived as a church leader who preserved faith and character intact in the face of persecution and prosecution.[47] Still, pacifism faded in the Church of God in Christ after World War I. Anecdotal evidence suggests that during World War II, at least some men whose membership antedated 1941 did not fight, but how many were successful in gaining recognition as conscientious objectors is unknown. Only twelve members worked in Civilian Public Service camps, so very likely their total number was small. As COGIC membership grew rapidly during the 1950s and 1960s, its pacifist heritage receded from view. A

Kansas," published by Mennonite minister J. D. Mininger March 10, 1919, at Kansas City. Mininger visited prisoners at Ft. Leavenworth prison and various military camps during and after the war. Professor Michael Casey, Pepperdine University, has a copy of this list.

47. Beaman, "*Response*: Pacifism," 90.

new generation of members performed combat duty in Vietnam. Today, church doctrine still states, in the exact language of World War I era documents, that "the shedding of human blood or the taking of human life is contrary to the teachings of our Lord and Saviour, Jesus Christ, and as a body, we are adverse to war in all its forms." Should members be drafted, this official statement instructs them to submit to induction as conscientious objectors, undergo only basic training while refusing instruction in "advanced weapons," and to seek non-combat roles. But few members today seem to know of, much less follow, that noncombatant doctrine. The early restorationist Church of God in Christ nurtured pacifism. But as happened in other sects that grew in membership and sought to enter the denominational mainstream, conscientious opposition to war became a forgotten tradition.[48]

# BIBLIOGRAPHY

Alexander, Paul. *Peace to War: Shifting Allegiances in the Assemblies of God*. Telford, PA: Cascadia, 2009.

Barbeau, Arthur E., and Fiorette Henri. *The Unknown Soldiers*. Cambridge, MA: Da Capo, 1996.

Beaman, Jay. "*Response*: Pacifism among the early Pentecostals: Conflicts Within and Without." In *Proclaim Peace: Christian Pacifism from Unexpected Quarters*, edited by Theron F. Schlabach and Richard T. Hughes, 82–96.

Clemmons, Ithiel C. "Mason, Charles Harrison." In *Dictionary of Pentecostal and Charismatic Movements*, edited by Stanley M. Burgess and Gary B. McGee, 585–588. Grand Rapids: Zondervan, 1988.

Cornelius, Lucille J. *The Pioneer: History of the Church of God in Christ*. Memphis: Church of God in Christ Publishing Board, 1975.

Hall, Charles E. *Negroes in the United States: 1920–1932*. Manchester, NH: Ayer, 1969.

Jones, C. E. "Church of God in Christ." In *Dictionary of Pentecostal and Charismatic Movements*, edited by Stanley M. Burgess and Gary B. McGee. Grand Rapids: Zondervan, 1988.

Jones, Lawrence Neale. "Black Pentecostals." In *The Charismatic Movement*, edited by Michael P. Hamilton. Grand Rapids: Eerdmans, 1975.

Kohn, Stephen. *Jailed for Peace: The History of American Draft Law Violators, 1658–1985*. Santa Barbara: Praeger, 1987.

48. Dr. David Daniels, McCormick Theological Seminary, Chicago, telephone conversation with the author, Oct. 15, 1992; Bishop George D. McKinney, St. Stephens Church of God in Christ, San Diego, letter to the author, Aug. 31, 1992. Regarding COGIC men in CPS camps, see Melvin Gingerich, *Service for Peace* (Akron, PA: Mennonite Central Committee, 1949).

Kornweibel, Theodore Jr. "Apathy and Dissent: Black America's Negative Responses to World War I." *South Atlantic Quarterly* 80 (1981) 322–38.

——. *No Crystal Stair: Black Life and the Messenger (1917–1928)*. Westport, CT: Greenwood, 1975.

Patterson, James Oglethorpe. *History and Formative Years of the Church of God in Christ*. Memphis: Church of God in Christ Publishing Board, 1969.

Peterson, H. C., and Gilbert C. Fite. *Opponents of War, 1917–1918*. Seattle: University of Washington Press, 1957.

Ross, German R. *History and Formative Years of the Church of God in Christ*. Memphis: Church of God in Christ, 1969.

*Second Report of the Provost Marshall General to the Secretary of War on the Operations of the Selective Service System to December 20, 1918*. Washington, DC: 1919.

Stanley, P. "Churches of God." In *Dictionary of Pentecostal and Charismatic Movements*, edited by Stanley M. Burgess and Gary B. McGee. Grand Rapids: Zondervan, 1988.

Synan, Vinson. *The Holiness-Pentecostal Movement in the United States*. Grand Rapids: Eerdmans, 1972.

Tucker, David M. *Black Pastors*. Memphis: Memphis State University Press, 1975.

U.S. Secretary of War. *Statement Concerning the Treatment of Conscientious Objectors in the Army*. Washington: Government Printing Office, 1919.

# 3

# The Foursquare Church and Pacifism

## Brian K. Pipkin

## INTRODUCTION

Aimee Semple McPherson founded the International Church of the Foursquare Gospel (commonly called The Foursquare Church) in 1923, five years after World War I ended. The movement was officially incorporated on December 30, 1927.[1] The Foursquare Church, an interdenominational evangelical Pentecostal organization, is a global movement, with 97 percent of its members and adherents residing outside of the United States.[2] The organization's "Declarations of Faith," written by McPherson,

1. Jack Hayford, "International Church of the Foursquare Gospel," in *International Dictionary of Pentecostal and Charismatic Movements*, ed. Stanley M. Burgess and Eduard M. van der Maas, 793–94 (Grand Rapids: Zondervan, 2003).

2. The denomination's theme is "Jesus Christ the same yesterday, today, and forever" (Heb 13:8). The Foursquare Church, as of 2011, represents about 1.6 percent of global Pentecostal and Charismatic Christianity (7,739,606 members), with approximately 97 percent of its members and adherents residing outside of the United States. The 1.6 percent figure is based on D. B. Barrett and T. M. Johnson's statistics identifying approximately 500 million Pentecostal and Charismatic Christians worldwide. This statistic includes members of major Pentecostal denominations equaling 65 million.

is mostly unoriginal and standard evangelical theology, with the exception of the Holy Spirit.[3]

First-generation Pentecostalism was characterized by a plain and simple reading of Scripture. Believing they were restoring the early church's beliefs and practices, many embraced speaking in tongues *and* nonviolence as authentic expressions of first-century Christianity.[4] Many early Pentecostals, both laity and clergy, had a general attraction towards Christian pacifism. For example, Jay Beaman, Pentecostal and Holiness historian, estimates that in the United States between 5 percent and 10 percent of all conscientious objectors in World War I were Pentecostal or Holiness men. "This is all the more astounding," he concludes, "since Pentecostalism as a movement was about ten years old, and was quite small."[5] Furthermore, new evidence reveals that virtually all early Pentecostal groups either officially had some form of pacifist statement against war in World War I, or in a couple of cases personal nonresistance within the movement, or in the case of exceptions, gave birth to groups that immediately had pacifist statements.[6]

The Foursquare Church, like others, was forced to deal with the widespread Pentecostal attraction toward peace. The Foursquare constituency ultimately lacked a clear consensus on militarism, as leaders wanted to be seen as loyal and patriotic citizens willing to defend their country, while also acknowledging that the New Testament prohibited

---

Charismatics, according to Barrett and Johnson, equal 175 million worldwide, with 295 million identifying themselves as Third-Wavers or Neocharismatics. In sum, they identified a total of 523 million people associated with Pentecostal-Charismatic Christianity. See D. B. Barrett and T. M. Johnson, "Global Statistics," in *International Dictionary of Pentecostal and Charismatic Movements*, ed. Stanley M. Burgess and Eduard M. van der Maas, 284–302. (Grand Rapids: Zondervan, 2003). As of 2009, women ministers currently account for 37 percent of all licensed ministers. As of 2011, the church reported 196 chaplains with 49 serving as military chaplains and 147 serving as institutional chaplains (hospitals, nursing homes, correctional facilities) and workplace chaplains (manufacturing sites, small or large businesses/industries, and places of commerce). Statistics were provided from The Foursquare Church corporate office on March 21, 2011.

3. Donna E. Ray, "Aimee Semple McPherson and Her Seriously Exciting Gospel," *Journal of Pentecostal Theology* 19 (2010) 156–57.

4. Paul Alexander, *Peace to War: Shifting Allegiances in the Assemblies of God* (Telford, PA: Cascadia, 2008) 334.

5. From Jay Beaman's Web site. See http://pentecostalpacifism.com/.

6. Jay Beaman and Brian K. Pipkin, *Holy Ghost Statements on War and Peace from the Holiness-Pentecostal Tradition* (Eugene, OR: Wipf & Stock, forthcoming).

them from bearing arms.[7] Unable to reach a decision as a movement for or against Christians bearing arms, and with no deeply rooted teaching on the subject, leaders passed a broad resolution protecting their pacifist members from combat.

The resolution, while not written to disclose the denomination's official stance on war, pledged protection and tolerance to members opposed to combatant service. The Foursquare movement, like the Assemblies of God, never prohibited their members from participating in war. Both groups encouraged noncombatant service.[8] In the spirit of self-preservation, McPherson and her movement abandoned their prior commitment to stand by their pacifists and conscientious objectors. As the movement matured, it soon began identifying more with American hegemony.[9]

While The Foursquare Church did not officially embrace the practice of peacemaking as an alternative to war, some church officials and pastors did oppose active military service and support Christian pacifism, while not necessarily using "pacifism" to describe their convictions.[10] Despite articles supporting militarism and, at times, the taking of human life in service to one's country, some ministers, including McPherson, demonstrated similar rationales for nonviolence as did early Pentecostal pacifists.

McPherson's views on politics defy easy categorization. Later Pentecostalism would be dominated by conservative politics; however, McPherson was exceptional. For example, despite being surrounded by

7. Matthew A. Sutton, *Aimee Semple McPherson and the Resurrection of Christian America* (Cambridge, MA: Harvard University Press, 2007) 254.

8. Alexander, *Peace to War*, 96. Alexander notes that the early Assemblies of God never prohibited their members from military service, although they certainly encouraged noncombatant service. Both E. N. Bell and E. S. Williams, AG General Superintendents, testify to this.

9. Matthew A. Sutton, "Clutching to 'Christian' America: Aimee Semple McPherson, the Great Depression, and the Origins of Pentecostal Political Activism," *The Journal of Political History* 17:3 (2005) 330.

10. The Selective Service defines a conscientious objector as one who is opposed to serving in the armed forces and/or bearing arms on the grounds of moral or religious principles. A combatant is someone who serves in positions of violence. A noncombatant is someone who serves in the military but in nonviolent ways such as medical personnel or military chaplains. The words *pacifist* and *passivism* are not etymologically related—they are often confused because they sound the same. The word *pacifism* comes from the Latin *pax facere*, which literally means "to make peace." A pacifist, therefore, is a peacemaker. "Blessed are the peacemakers" can be translated "Blessed are the pacifists."

a Republican-affiliated leadership team, she consistently registered as a Democrat. She also supported President Roosevelt's progressive New Deal and, unlike subsequent generations of Pentecostals, believed that Pentecostalism, liberalism, and an active state could work together.[11]

With regard to Pentecostals and war, McPherson pushed stereotypical rules. Her early ministry lamented the violence and worldliness of American culture by objecting to large-scale communal sin such as war, violence, and arms production.[12] She condemned capital punishment, supported national and international disarmament, and believed it was contrary to the Sermon on the Mount to "love your neighbor" and stick a bayonet through one's heart. In the 1930s she was attracted to pacifism but never fully embraced it. Like other antiwar advocates, she qualified her commitment to nonviolence with a statement of loyalty to the U.S. government. By World War II, McPherson had softened her peace rhetoric and abandoned her early attraction to nonviolence, choosing instead a more moderate, accommodating, and mainstream approach to war.

Although scholars have documented the acceptance and decline of Pentecostal pacifism, there has been no concerted and systematic attempt to study Foursquare pacifism in detail.[13] Research has primarily focused on the life of McPherson and her celebrity status as a religious figure. Her personal life and ministry have typically (but not always) overshadowed the retelling of the Foursquare story.

The organization's patriotic effort and wholehearted support for the United States' involvement in World War II may have led historians to assume the impossibility of any pacifistic sentiment within the movement. There was also never a "decline" of pacifism within the movement because there was never an official "acceptance" by the denomination. There were, nonetheless, nonhierarchical forms of pacifism within the early movement. With the arrival of World War II, this group likely faded.

It is rather difficult to accurately assess the probability of Foursquare objection to World War I given the fact that The Foursquare Church did not officially organize until after the war had ended. One way to locate

---

11. Sutton, "Clutching to Christian America," 330.

12. Ray, "Aimee Semple McPherson and Her Seriously Exciting Gospel," 164.

13. Matthew Sutton would be the exception. In *Aimee Semple McPherson and the Resurrection of Christian America*, Sutton dedicates the last chapter of his analysis to Foursquare Americanism, briefly describing the acceptance and deletion of the Foursquare bylaw supporting members with pacifist convictions.

Foursquare conscientious objectors to the World War I would be to obtain the military draft cards of Pentecostals who filed for conscientious objector status under a different denomination, some of whom may have later affiliated with the The Foursquare Church following the war. However, The Foursquare Church had an exceedingly low percentage of pastors migrate from other denominations since they required all pastors to graduate from L.I.F.E. Bible College, a Foursquare college founded by McPherson, in order to be a minister.[14]

Second, since there is a lower probability of pacifist belief among Pentecostal groups formed after 1917, the chance of locating pacifism within The Foursquare Church is highly decreased.[15] Nevertheless, denominational documents reveal a vocal, albeit presumably small, group of Foursquare pacifists and conscientious objectors within the movement. While some supported nonviolence and alternative forms of military service, there is no evidence that the movement, as an official organization, passed a written statement supporting the *doctrine* of pacifism. They did, nonetheless, support their members and ministers who were committed pacifists and conscientious objectors to war.

The history of Foursquare pacifism and military service is at times ambiguous and reflects what is natural to all people—inconsistencies. No one is truly arguing for war. One would be disappointed in the attempt to locate a uniform voice advocating peacemaking in the early Foursquare Church, and, for that matter, one would be disappointed in trying to locate a consistent voice promoting war. However, what Foursquare seemingly lacked in early peacemaking efforts, they made up for with a renowned organized social ministry at the Temple commissary, assisting over 1.5 million people during the Depression, regardless of color, race, or creed.[16]

14. L.I.F.E. stands for Lighthouse of International Foursquare Evangelism. The school was established by McPherson in 1923.

15. Jay Beaman, *Pentecostal Pacifism: The Origins, Development and Rejection of Pacific Belief among the Pentecostals* (Hillsboro, KS: Center for Mennonite-Brethren Studies, 1989) 30. Beaman noted that there is a lower probability of pacifist belief among Pentecostal groups formed at a later date. For instance, 62 percent of Pentecostal groups formed by 1917 gave evidence of pacifism. About 50 percent of Pentecostal groups formed between 1917 and 1934 gave evidence of pacifism. Only 20 percent of Pentecostal groups formed after 1934 gave evidence of pacifism.

16. C. M. Robeck Jr., "McPherson, Aimee Semple," in *International Dictionary of Pentecostal and Charismatic Movements*, ed. Stanley M. Burgess and Eduard M. van der Maas, 856–58 (Grand Rapids: Zondervan, 2003).

While some of the conclusions in this study are found to characterize, although not dominate, the early Foursquare movement and its relation to the topic of war and peace, the following observations do not reflect the current leadership practices or define the corporate ethos of The Foursquare Church today.

## FOURSQUARE MEMBERS REQUEST EXEMPTION FROM BEARING ARMS

During the 1934 Foursquare Northwest District Convention, with rumors, fears, and threats about the next world war looming, Foursquare ministers and leaders felt the need to investigate and draft a resolution *exempting all ministers* from bearing arms. Apparently, this group wanted to impose conscientious objection on all Foursquare members.[17] During the Foursquare annual convention, held from July 1–6, 1934,[18] a body of ministers from the Northwest District of Foursquare Gospel Churches requested that the Foursquare Committee on Resolutions submit a proposal to church officials providing religious exemption for pastors and laymen in case of war. The resolution stated: "Resolved: That all ordained ministers of the Foursquare Gospel, Incorporated, be exempt from arms in case of war. Also to file such papers with the war department at Washington, D.C., and the International Office immediately investigate for such action."[19]

## CHURCH OFFICIALS INQUIRE WITH WAR DEPARTMENT

William B. Black, Foursquare General Secretary, mailed a letter to the U.S. War Department on August 14, 1936, requesting clarification on the "exemption of ministers in the event of war." Black noted that during the Annual Foursquare Convention, questions were raised on the floor relative to "present-day legislation as to the ruling of the Government regarding the exemption of ministers." Understanding that such a request to exempt pacifists and conscientious objectors from military service could

17. R. G. Robins, *Pentecostalism in America* (Santa Barbara, CA: Praeger, 2010) 68.

18. "Convention to Be Held in Portland," *Foursquare Crusader* 8:37 (July 27, 1934) 2.

19. "Resolution from the Northwest District," 5 July 1934, corporate documents, ICFG.

easily be construed as unpatriotic and disloyal, Black inserted a loyalty clause in the second paragraph of his letter. He wrote: "We want to make it clear that the policy of this church body is loyalty and cooperation to the Government and the President of the United States and vigorously opposed to Communism or any other movement or political system that advocates the overthrow of our Government."[20]

Black's letter reveals the behind-the-scenes motivation for requesting military exemption. In his letter to the War Department, he acknowledged that church officials were concerned for their "younger ministers." He admitted that those requesting exception were "ministers or laymen" who on account of "religious convictions desire non-combatant service." These references signify that (1) the group of pacifists and conscientious objectors were mainly part of the younger generation of pastors; (2) the older generation may have been concerned over a mass exodus of their youth to war; (3) the group requesting exemption had religious convictions; and (4) the pacifist group was comfortable accepting a noncombatant role within the military.

## CHURCH OFFICIALS APPROVE PACIFIST CLAUSE

On January 9, 1937, two and a half years after the letter requesting military exemption was issued, a corporate session with 151 ministers and delegates met to discuss the proposed resolution during the fourteenth annual Foursquare Convention.[21] The main question was whether or not it would be necessary to insert a bylaw that would prohibit the movement from "engaging in war in combatant capacity." One person brought up the fact that this was a question of pacifism. Another suggested that "any action taken should be worded in such a way that we shall be recognized in Foursquaredom as a great group of American citizens."[22] William Black

20. "Minutes of Corporate Session," 9 January 1937, corporate documents, ICFG.

21. Participants in the meeting included William B. Black, Secretary of The Foursquare Church and member of the Bylaws Committee; Sidney Correll, Bylaws Committee; Frank A. Cummings, Bylaws Committee and Midwest District Supervisor; R. J. Turner, Bylaws Committee; W. B. Teaford, Dean of L.I.F.E. Bible College; Warren Koon, Foursquare pastor; Al Wildman, Foursquare pastor; Loraine Tyler Bari, Foursquare pastor; Giles N. Knight, vice president of The Foursquare Church; Melvin Neubert, Foursquare pastor in Cedar Rapids, Iowa; Myron Sackett, assistant to William B. Black and Southern California District Supervisor; Earl W. Dorrance, Foursquare board member.

22. "Minutes of Corporate Session," 9 January 1937, corporate documents, ICFG.

read the war combatant section of the Assemblies of God as a point of reference. Church officials delegated the writing of the resolution to a newly appointed subcommittee called the Committee on Military Exemption.[23]

Two days after the committee met, Foursquare pastors, delegates, and leaders unanimously approved Article XVII on Military Service and incorporated it into their official bylaws. Unable to reach an agreement on religious objection to war, the constituency approved a tolerant and broad resolution recognizing the diversity of opinions.[24] The bylaw, while not necessarily reflective of the denomination's official stance on war and peace, publicly supported ministers and laymen who were pacifists and conscientious objectors to war.

> WHEREAS our Convention Assembly has manifested by voice of opinion pro and con on the subject of Military Service in the event of war; and,
>
> WHEREAS there are Ministers and Laymen who are pacifists and have conscientious convictions not to take up arms to kill their fellow-men, according to their interpretations of the Scriptures, and in so doing feel they would endanger their souls into an eternal and everlasting Hell of fire and brimstone by incurring the wrath of God; and,
>
> WHEREAS there are those among our ministers and laymen who feel they are obligated to the government of the United States of America and would take up arms to resist invasion of our country and they interpret the Scriptures to teach entire obedience to human government and that only the rulers are responsible to God for commanding to take up arms to kill humanity; and,
>
> WHEREAS, because of this divided opinion, the General Assembly and Board of Directors are hereby appealed to;
>
> NOW THEREFORE, BE IT RESOLVED: That there be inserted in our Constitution and By-Laws a clause for the benefit and protection of conscientious objectors in this organization who, when drafted into the Military service of the United States of

---

23. Motion was made by Sidney Correll and four people were appointed to chair the committee: Dr. R. J. Turner, Watson B. Teaford, Warren Kuhn, and Al Wildman. The motion was seconded by Frank A. Cummings.

24. Sutton, *Aimee Semple McPherson and the Resurrection of Christian America*, 255.

America and its possessions, and brought before the examining Boards, may be exempt from combatant service.

RESOLVED FURTHER: That the International Church of the Foursquare Gospel, a regular accredited organization and incorporated Church Body, does hereby appeal to the President of the United States of America in such emergencies when any of its members, because of conscientious convictions, cannot take up arms, that they be delegated to noncombatant service.

RESOLVED FURTHER: That we hereby recommend that every minister and layman in this organization render service in some form to the United States Government in time of war.[25]

This bylaw sheds light on early Foursquare attitudes toward pacifism, conscientious objection, and bearing arms. First, there was a group of pacifists and conscientious objectors within the organization: "Whereas there are Ministers and Laymen who are *pacifists* and have *conscientious convictions.*" Second, the constituency was "divided" over the issue of pacifism, voicing "opinion pro and con." Third, there was a group of ministers and laymen who felt they were "obligated to the government of the United States of America and would take up arms to resist invasion of our country." Fourth, while both groups appealed to the Bible "according to their interpretations of the Scriptures" as their sole authority, they failed to agree on what the Bible actually said on the treatment of enemies. Fifth, while the bylaw secured exemption and recognition of pacifists and religious objectors, the leadership counseled their men to accept noncombatant service.

The organization was, therefore, willing to petition the U.S. government and stand behind people who refused to bear arms. Their agreement on the right of individual conscience and noncombatant service satisfied both sides of the issue and likely avoided confronting the tougher questions of a Christian response to war, patriotism, and citizenship.[26] At that time, formulating a concrete stance and picking sides on such an emotionally charged and controversial issue could have caused tension within the movement.

25. "Minutes of Corporate Session, Fourteenth Annual Convention," 11 January 1937, corporate documents, ICFG.

26. Edith Blumhofer, *Restoring the Faith: The Assemblies of God, Pentecostalism, and American Culture* (Urbana: University of Illinois Press, 1993) 148. Blumhofer applies the politics of voluntary conscientious objection rhetoric to the Assemblies of God.

## CHURCH OFFICIALS STUDY THE ASSEMBLIES OF GOD RESOLUTION ON MILITARY SERVICE

Before the official acceptance of the bylaw, church officials referenced the Assemblies of God resolution on military service. However, there is nothing in the bylaw that remotely resembled the early Assemblies of God resolution. It is a mystery how The Foursquare Church came up with supporting freedom of individual conscience only after studying the Assemblies of God resolution that unapologetically declared a commitment to Jesus' way of peace and nonviolence and to the Scriptures' prohibition against taking human life.

One hypothetical may be found in the stated versus practiced values of the early Assemblies of God movement, especially during their transition from a generally pacifist orientation to a pro-military movement shortly before World War II. In 1967 the Assemblies of God again declared that they always upheld the right of each person to choose for himself the right to fight or object.[27] As the Assemblies of God movement began to moderate their pacifism, an apparent gap between *beliefs* and *practices* began to emerge.[28]

It is possible, then, that The Foursquare Church's resolution reflected the practiced tradition of the Assemblies of God, not the stated values in their official resolution in the late 1930s. The Foursquare Church's resolution prophetically mirrored the actual practice of Assemblies of God members on the issue of war and peace—the right of individual conscience. The 1937 Foursquare bylaw was a foretaste of the 1953 and 1967 Assemblies of God updated statements on military service that omitted Scripture references while supporting the freedom of individual conscience.[29]

Additionally, when comparing both statements, it becomes clear that The Foursquare Church supported the pacifist, not pacifism. Foursquare gave denominational support to the pacifist who objected to war on biblical or conscientious grounds. Conversely, the Assemblies of God resolution, which was written in 1917, argued for pacifism by

27. Beaman, *Pentecostal Pacifism*, 117.

28. Alexander, *Peace to War*, 207. Alexander notes that in recalling the past, E. S. Williams believed the official stance of the denomination was different than what the majority of persons believed and practiced.

29. Assemblies of God General Council Minutes (1953) 80; Assemblies of God General Council Minutes (1967) 14–15.

appealing to Scripture (Luke 2:14; Heb 12:4; Exod 20:13; Matt 5:39–44) and Jesus as their sole authority.[30] The Assemblies of God statement was centered on Scripture as the "all-sufficient rule of faith and practice" and on the example of Jesus Christ, the "Prince of Peace" who commands his followers to "love your enemies."[31]

In contrast, the Foursquare resolution was not an official position or exposition disclosing the denomination's position on war and peace. Rather, it was a political-democratic move to *respect opinions* (pro and con) and to *protect* those ministers and laymen who objected to bearing arms. The Assemblies of God resolution was theologically oriented, while the Foursquare bylaw was politically oriented. The Foursquare bylaw, unlike the Assemblies of God resolution, was formulated as a political act in order to protect their pacifists from military service. Foursquare dealt with the issue politically, while the Assemblies of God dealt with it biblically and morally, taking a firm stand against killing and quoting numerous Scriptures.[32] The Foursquare bylaw, in effect for only five years, gave the conscientious objector and pacifist denominational support during war only. It did not provide them with a deeply rooted and biblically informed tradition of peace.

## THE LOGIC OF PACIFIST AND NON-PACIFIST ARGUMENTS

The Foursquare bylaw also discloses the convictions of the pacifist and non-pacifist group. The pacifist argument was not based on love for

30. *Weekly Evangel* (August 4, 1917) 6. Quoted in Beaman, *Pentecostal Pacifism*, 24.

31. Ibid.

32. Edith Blumhofer argued that the Assemblies of God resolution in 1917 did not try to engage theologically with war and peace issues but intended simply to insure exemptions from war. See Blumhofer, *The Assemblies of God: A Chapter in the Story of American Pentecostalism*, vol. 1, *To 1941* (Springfield, MO: Gospel, 1989) 347. The Foursquare Church's resolution is indeed an example of a movement dealing with the issue non-theologically, seeking only to ensure exemptions for pacifist members. When comparing both resolutions, the differences are obvious. Murray Dempster also argued that the Assemblies of God registered the denomination as a pacifist church in order to provide political protection for their conscientious objectors. Whatever the motive of the leadership of the Assemblies of God may have been in drafting the resolution, Dempster's analysis can nevertheless be applied to The Foursquare Church's passage of the military service bylaw. See Murray Dempster, "Crossing Boarders: Arguments Used by Early American Pentecostals in Support of the Global Character of Pacifism," *The Journal of the European Pentecostal Theological Association* 10:2 (1995) 75. This article has been reprinted as chapter four of this book.

neighbor or enemy, nor is there evidence they referenced Jesus' example and teaching on nonviolence. Rather, the pacifist group insisted on not killing so "they would [not] endanger their souls into an eternal and everlasting Hell or fire and brimstone by incurring the wrath of God."[33]

On the other hand, the group voicing support for fighting felt they were "obligated to the government of the United States of America and would take up arms to resist invasion." They, like the pacifists, pointed to their interpretation of Scripture. For this group, Scripture taught "entire obedience to human government," and if they were to kill a fellow human being, the government officials who commissioned them would be "responsible to God for commanding [them] to take up arms to kill humanity."[34]

Because of divided opinion, church officials were in no place to make a unanimous decision for pacifism or combatant service, nor did they favor one side over the other. The division of opinion led to the acceptance of conscience as an ethical answer to war and a middle-of-the-road resolution affirming both sides.

There is no evidence to suggest that the ethics of war and peace was discussed at a deeper level within the leadership. In the context of moral issues within The Foursquare Church, pacifism was not that important. While the Foursquare Church exhibited a general indifference toward war, writers often expressed greater concerns over the evils of smoking, dancing, gambling, and alcohol than about taking life.[35]

Ironically, Foursquare documents indicate that church officials spent more time making sure they were in compliance with the regulations of the War Department than they did investigating what Scripture and the teachings of Jesus had to say on the subject. The corporate minutes disclose that leaders wanted to be publicly viewed as a patriotic religious organization that was loyal to their government in time of war. Their motivation to be loyal to the U.S. government would eventually find home in the pro-military position, not the pacifist appeal.

33. "Minutes of Corporate Session, Fourteenth Annual Convention," 11 January 1937, corporate documents, ICFG.

34. Ibid.

35. "T. M. Arthur Spotts, Chaplain of the United States Navy, Writers of the San Diego Revival," *Bridal Call* 4:11 (1921) 18; "Birthday Greetings to Uncle Sam," *Bridal Call Foursquare* (July 1932) 26; "Prophecy Marches On," *Foursquare Crusader* (April 1943) 17; "A Rambling Report," *Bridal Call Foursquare* 19:11 (1927) 22; Aimee Semple McPherson, "Dancing on Vesuvius," *Foursquare Crusader* 13:30 (1940) 27.

## EXECUTIVE LEADERS DISCUSS DELETING
## THE MILITARY SERVICE BYLAW

The unanimously approved bylaw granting denominational support for the pacifist and conscientious objector would soon be deleted at the request of McPherson and the Executive Council; it lasted five and a half years. Even though McPherson, and the organization at large, faithfully supported military personnel, the leadership was faced with the task of returning to the issue of pacifism and conscientious objection soon after the attack on a U.S military base in Hawaii. Six months after the United States entered World War II, McPherson requested the deletion of the denomination's pacifist clause.

During an executive meeting held on June 19, 1942, Earl Dorrance, Foursquare board member, publicly stated McPherson's motive to delete the bylaw. "Sister [Aimee] feels this should be stricken from our By-Laws at this time," said Dorrance. "She feels we have unanimously taken a definite stand and attitude in this war, more than in any previous war. This is a war of Christ against the anti-Christ and [she] feels if the enemy is not overthrown eventually our churches and homes and everything precious and dear to the Christian would absolutely be destroyed and we [it] would be impossible to serve God under such a regime." McPherson believed this was a holy war.

Wesley Norgaard, superintendent of the South District of Foursquare Churches, explained that "the law grants the individual the privilege of stating his position as a conscientious objector, if he desires so to do." Giles N. Knight, vice president of The Foursquare Church, agreed with McPherson's disapproval of the bylaw. "Yes, if an individual wishes to do so he may. But as the By-Law now stands if any Minister or Layman comes to our office and asks us to fulfill this By-Law we are compelled to petition the President in their behalf, which Sister [Aimee] feels positively we should not do, and therefore, she feels this should positively be stricken from our By-Laws."[36] Officials unanimously agreed that the bylaw be presented and voted on at the convention floor with a recommendation from the Executive Council that it be stricken from the bylaws.[37] What began

36. "Minutes of the Meeting of the Executive Council," 19 June 1942, corporate documents, ICFG.

37. Participants during the Executive Council meeting included Earl W. Dorrance; Wesley Norgaard, Missionary Committee; Giles N. Knight; Harold W. Jefferies, District Supervisor and member of the Bylaws Committee; Rev. Ulphin Davis, Foursquare pas-

as a pacifist grassroots movement in 1937 to encourage conscientious objection to war was on its way to deletion by top executive leaders. While pacifist inspiration within the movement was nonhierarchical, the source of deletion was hierarchical.

## FOURSQUARE MINISTERS DELETE MILITARY SERVICE BYLAW

During the 1942 annual convention, ministers and delegates of The Foursquare Church gathered to discuss and vote on conscientious objection. There, the Executive Council recommended to the convention floor that they rescind Article XVII "on the grounds that we are in a very unfavorable light in the present world struggle for supremacy, and as a patriotic organization, we don't want it said that we have a slacker in our ranks."

Dorrance acknowledged the government's leniency on the subject *without* the bylaw. However, he explained, if anyone should "infer we have a 'yellow' in our organization, I will ask for a rescinding motion." Officials worried that if the bylaw remained, they would have to petition the U.S. president on behalf of those members wishing exemption from military service, and they did not want to be perceived as "cowards" failing to do their "whole duty." Officials confirmed that apart from the bylaw, the government will give any conscientious objector the opportunity of doing noncombatant service regardless of the organization's position.

McPherson joined the conversation. After personally checking with the government, she told her constituents that the government had given her "their solemn word" by promising that "students in [her] Bible school will be exempt" from military service. While non-pastors and non-Bible students espousing pacifism or conscientious objection were on their own, men enrolled as ministerial students in L.I.F.E. Bible College, as well as licensed ministers and evangelists, were exempt by profession. She explained that government officials had been wonderful to them, saying that they could not have "treated us more fairly if we had been Princeton or anyone else."[38]

---

tor in Woodland, California; Rev. A. A. Carpenter, Foursquare pastor in Virginia; and Rev. Ethel Singleton, Foursquare pastor in Santa Paula, California.

38. "Minutes of the Meeting of the Corporate Business Session," 26 June 1942, corporate documents, ICFG. See also *Foursquare Yearbook* (Los Angeles: International Church of the Foursquare Gospel, 1942).

When McPherson's proposal to finally delete the pacifist clause came to a vote, the session agreed to rescind the bylaw. The Foursquare constituency was informed that the church's ministers, evangelists, and Bible students were exempt from taking up arms regardless of the denomination's official stance. In fact, the *Crusader* published an article under "L.I.F.E. News" explaining that the government had promised theological students of serviceable age "exemption from war duties."[39] By the early 1940s, the college reported a total of fourteen students who were in the military, and by 1944 had a total of five chaplains.[40] L.I.F.E. Bible College repeatedly expressed gratitude to the government for upholding its promise to provide conscientious objector status for full-time ministerial students.[41]

By 1944, church officials were routinely notifying government officials regarding the status of their full-time ministers and Bible students. The message of church leaders to these ministers and students was clear: "If you expect deferment, work full-time at the ministry." It was noted, however, that ministers pioneering new churches were unable to receive deferment because some had to work outside of their ministry to supplement their income. If a minister dropped out of school or the ministry, the church was "forced to report to the draft board" the absence of that person. Cooperation with the government was strongly encouraged: "Let us comply with the draft rulings, also, for if they catch us in one case of violation, they are likely to clamp down on every minister in our organization."[42]

## MCPHERSON'S MOTIVE TO DELETE THE PACIFIST PROVISION

Was McPherson's motive to delete the bylaw that she was opposed to pacifist sentiment? Matthew Sutton writes that "McPherson refused to let the denomination support any individual who had a religious objection to military service. It was not enough that they would willingly serve in

39. "LIFE News," *Foursquare Crusader* 13:33 (1941) 19–20; "L.I.F.E. Schedule Accelerated," *Foursquare Crusader* 16:6 (1944) 11.

40. "L.I.F.E. Students Serve God and Country," *Foursquare Crusader* (December 1942) 8; "Annual Convention Report," *Foursquare Yearbook* (1944) 17.

41. Ibid.

42. "Minutes of the Meeting of the Corporate Business Session," 19 June 1944, corporate documents, ICFG.

noncombatant positions; she wanted her followers to take up arms and fight for the United States."[43] From the moment of the deletion, Sutton concludes, The Foursquare Church no longer "publicly recognized those Christians who remained committed pacifists."[44] R. G. Robins further notes that McPherson "persuaded her church to repeal its endorsement of conscientious objectors."[45]

Rather than an outright rejection of people espousing pacifism within the movement, McPherson explained that she believed her (pro-military) beliefs concerning this particular war (World War II) represented the larger Foursquare constituency. She was correct. By this time, The Foursquare Church had wholly accommodated itself to the war. Although the movement no longer recognized Christians who remained pacifists in the denomination's bylaws, McPherson's view did, in fact, represent an overwhelming majority. If any lingering pacifists remained, they would soon be forced to accommodate.

Foursquare literature reveals that The Foursquare Church as a whole took a nearly unanimous pro-military stance in the early 1940s. This is not surprising, nor is this transition unique to the The Foursquare Church. Many movements, some of which were unapologetically pacifist, transitioned (accommodated) from a strong peace position to a softened pro-military stance during World War II.[46]

Furthermore, each main organ of the church, including the *Crusader*, L.I.F.E. Bible College, Angelus Temple, and radio station KFSG (Kall Four Square Gospel), supported the United States military effort. Members of the Temple serving in combatant positions even received public recognition for their willingness to kill for the United States.[47]

43. Sutton, *Aimee Semple McPherson and the Resurrection of Christian America*, 263.

44. Ibid.

45. Robins, *Pentecostalism in America*, 68.

46. Some of the groups that wavered in their commitment to nonviolence during World War II were the Assemblies of God, the Churches of Christ, Church of God (Anderson), Baptists, Methodist, Quakers, and even some Mennonites. Many more softened their positions. See Jeffrey Gross and John D. Rempel, eds., *The Fragmentation of the Church and Its Unity in Peacemaking* (Grand Rapids: Eerdmans, 2001); D. J. Wilson, "Pacifism," in *International Dictionary of Pentecostal and Charismatic Movements*, ed. Stanley M. Burgess and Eduard M. van der Maas, 953–54. (Grand Rapids: Zondervan, 2003). Wilson notes that the decline of Pentecostal pacifism over the years corresponded to the trends in public opinion in the population at large.

47. "Temple Crusader Bombs Jap Aircraft Carriers," *Foursquare Crusader* (February 1943) 7; "Crusader Boys in the Armed Forces," *Foursquare Crusader* 15:2 (February

Articles appeared in the *Crusader* signifying a cooperative relationship with organizations that were opposed to pacifism and conscientious objection. The Temple had a consistent relationship with the American Legion, often inviting leaders to speak to the congregation on topics such as God and country.[48] The Legion, of which McPherson was made honorary colonel, frowned on noncombatants by creating a resolution endorsing combatant service only, officially condemning "the action of those responsible for protecting the men who refuse full military service."[49] Although the title "honorary colonel" was bestowed on her by the Legion, it is highly unlikely they would have done the same if she were a Christian pacifist.

In the same month in which the bylaw was deleted, KFSG gave airtime to the selling of war bonds, stamps, and announcements for the Office of War Information (OWI). "It's the policy of KFSG to cooperate with the government in helping to win the war against the Axis."[50] Elmer Davis, OWI Director, even sent McPherson a telegram thanking her for her cooperation with various "war information activities so important to America's prosecution of this war."[51]

The Bible college was also used to promote the war effort through the sale of war bonds.[52] By 1943, the majority of students were "either on the evangelistic field or engaged in war work."[53] The college even accelerated their degree programs to meet the national crisis created during war.[54]

1943) 27. Interestingly, in 1940 an evangelist spoke on the topics "Selective Service" and "Conscientious Objectors" to Temple members. It is unknown, however, what was said. See *Angelus Temple Bulletin* (October 21, 1940).

48. "Great Americanism Service," *Angelus Temple Bulletin* (October 1940) 1; "Temple, Legion Stand Shoulder to Shoulder for God and Country," *Foursquare Crusader* 6:6 (1931) 1; "I Am an American Day," *Angelus Temple Bulletin* (May 9, 1943).

49. "Sister McPherson Awarded Citation of Colonelcy," *Foursquare Crusader* 13:32 (1941) 22; *Angelus Temple Bulletin* (November 3, 1940) 1; George Seay Wheat, *The Story of the American Legion* (New York: Knickerbocker, 1919) 122.

50. Phil Kerr, "Radio KFSG," *Foursquare Crusader* 14:10 (October 1942) 12.

51. "O.W.I. Director Lauds Cooperation from Sister McPherson and Radio KFSG," *Foursquare Crusader* 15:3 (1943) 3.

52. "KFSG to Sell War Bonds," *Angelus Temple Bulletin* (September 6, 1942) 1.

53. Jack Carmain, "Radio KFSG," *Foursquare Crusader* 15:8 (1943) 11.

54. "L.I.F.E. Schedule Accelerated," *Foursquare Crusader* 16:6 (June 1944) 11.

McPherson also demonstrated her loyalty to the war effort by send-ing the *Crusader* to army camps.[55] Many front covers of the *Crusader* were dedicated to the war effort, often using American war propaganda symbols and photos. For example, the January 1943 cover advertising war bonds depicted tanks, missiles, warships, bombers, and military trucks, and an American eagle flying over the famous "I Want You" Uncle Sam photo.[56]

Furthermore, there is no record of anyone objecting to the deletion of the bylaw. Just as the acceptance of the bylaw reflected the pacifist and conscientious opinions of the movement in 1937, the deletion of the by-law reflected the non-pacifist and pro-military opinions of the movement in 1942. As a point of contrast, pastors and delegates debated at length the bylaw on divorce and remarriage. Many voiced strong opinions about divorce and what Scripture had to say on the subject.[57] However, there is no record of anyone protesting the deletion of the military service bylaw.

McPherson's notion that the movement reflected her perspective on war is also evident by the fact that leaders presented the issue as a *hypothetical scenario*: "If any minister or laymen comes to our office and asks us to fulfill the Bylaw we are compelled to petition the President in their behalf."[58] This may reveal that no one appealed their conscientious beliefs to church officials. Although two Foursquare men, Otto Charles Kapp and William Thomas DeVol, were listed as conscientious objectors *prior to the deletion of the bylaw*—both of them serving in Civilian Public Service camps—I am aware of no evidence supporting the notion that Foursquare leaders petitioned the government to exempt these men from combatant service.[59]

55. Robeck, "Aimee Semple McPherson."

56. *Foursquare Crusader* 15:1 (1943). Other front covers include *Foursquare Crusader* 14:11 (1942); *Foursquare Crusader* 15:2 (1943); *Foursquare Crusader* 15:3 (1943); *Foursquare Crusader* 15:7 (1943).

57. "Minutes of the Meeting of the Corporate Business Session," 23 June 1943, cor-porate documents, ICFG.

58. "Minutes of the Meeting of the Executive Council," 19 June 1942, corporate documents, ICFG.

59. Two men from The Foursquare Church are listed in *Selective Service in Peacetime: First Report of the Director of Selective Service 1940–41* (Washington, DC: Government Printing Office, 1942) 197. They are listed as serving in Civilian Public Service (CPS) camps during World War II in the *Directory of Civilian Public Service* (Washington, DC: National Service Board for Religious Objectors, n.d.) xviii. Otto Kapp, from Matteson, Illinois, worked as a golf course technician and enlisted in CPS

In terms of numbers, by 1942 the movement reported a total of 14,483 members in the United States and a total of 1,047 ordained pastors.[60] The Foursquare church in Portland, Oregon, reported 211 men and women in the armed forces.[61] By 1944, it was noted that there were "thousands" of young people in military service.[62] If ministers and church members were objecting to military service, why were there only two Foursquare men serving as conscientious objectors to war? In fact, by 1943, one pastor resigned from his church to join the military, receiving full support from his district: "The prayers of the entire district go with him as he enters the service of our country."[63]

Another question emerges: if ministers were exempt without the bylaw, due to their profession, why did church leaders feel the need to draft a resolution in the first place? One possibility is that during World War I, many conscientious objectors were allowed noncombatant status if they demonstrated affiliation to a religious organization opposed to bearing arms.[64] However, after the passage of the Selective Training and Service Act of 1940, the law officially clarified a provision for conscientious objectors to serve in noncombatant roles *apart* from any religious organization.[65] In other words, a person did not need to belong to a religious group professing conscientious objection to be classified as a conscientious objector. Nor was conscientious objection guaranteed by religious affiliation. If a person sought conscientious objector status, he had to exhibit before the draft board evidence of a personal commitment

---

when he was thirty-five years old. He served in CPS from 6/26/41–10/10/41 under the Brethren Service Committee. Kapp graduated from L.I.F.E. Bible College in 1944 and became a pastor in the Eastern District of Foursquare Churches. See "Hold that Line," *Foursquare Crusader* 16:10 (1944) 15; "District News," *Foursquare Magazine* 20:12 (1948) 28. William DeVol, from Glens Falls, New York, worked as a waiter. He served in CPS from 1/21/42–10/17/45 under the American Friends Service Committee.

60. Statistical information was provided by the International Church of the Foursquare Gospel archives department, 24 September 2009. The number of ordained pastors includes the United States and Canada. This number does not include non-ordained licensed ministers, of which there were 507 in Canada and the United States.

61. "Minutes of the Meeting of the Corporate Business Session," 19 June 1944, corporate documents, ICFG.

62. Ibid.

63. "New Orleans, Louisiana," *Foursquare Crusader* (January 1943) 10.

64. *Selective Service in Peacetime: First Report of the Director of Selective Service 1940–41*, 189.

65. Ibid.

to his convictions. Foursquare officials inserted the bylaw before 1940 in case members needed denominational support when drafted. After the Selective Training and Service Act was approved, granting conscientious objection status apart from any religious organization, The Foursquare Church deemed it redundant and unnecessary to maintain the bylaw and therefore deleted it, noting that "the law grants the individual the privilege of stating his position as a conscientious objector."[66]

To mitigate antiwar controversy and to reflect tolerable public opinion, some of the more patriotic leaders sought to market the organization as less radical. In essence, then, leaders used the law as an excuse to delete their pacifist clause by diverting attention away from their disapproval of pacifist sentiment. Their appeal to diversion served two functions: 1) It saved church officials the personal embarrassment of abandoning pacifist members by using the law as a pretext to delete, and 2) leaders were able to spare the organization the bad press that came with pacifist association.

One must also consider the fact that McPherson declined to ask the president of the United States to exempt a conscientious objector. She assumed appealing to the president would jeopardize the patriotic image of her organization. That she wished to maintain a strong patriotic image and alliance with the state does not, however, prove that she personally refused to support ministers holding personal convictions against war.

Since the bylaw's intention was never to disclose the movement's position on war or peace, and since the government would recognize conscientious objectors *apart* from a religious organization's position on the issue, the bylaw was deemed *irrelevant*, especially since Christian pacifism was never a concern of the denomination. Therefore, the rescinding of the bylaw was more of a deletion rather than a personal attack against pacifists. The Selective Training and Service Act made the bylaw unnecessary. Affiliation with the Foursquare name, according to church officials, guaranteed exemption from combatant service, not the bylaw. Until evidence shows otherwise, McPherson's motive to delete the pacifist clause represented the majority Foursquare constituency.

66. "Minutes of the Meeting of the Executive Council," 19 June 1942, corporate documents, ICFG.

## CHURCH OFFICIALS SEEK PATRIOTIC IMAGE

Setting aside McPherson's motive for deletion, there were two reasons church officials resisted the continuation of the pacifist provision. First, pacifism jeopardized the organization's patriotic image. There was a subtle correlation between the deletion of the bylaw and the early leadership's desire for political and national recognition. When the pacifist issue was first addressed in 1937, the leadership responded with an affirmation that they were a great group of American citizens. Because pacifist expression tended to be viewed as unpatriotic, church officials felt the need to reaffirm their commitment to their country, although never inserting a loyalty clause in their bylaw.[67] The public recognition of pacifists could have resulted in local and national criticism for supporting ministers refusing to bear arms. This could have indirectly communicated to the surrounding community that The Foursquare Church was sympathetic to the nation's political enemies by affirming acceptance of pacifist members. Some leaders believed that a pacifist was a person who failed to render his "whole duty" to government in time of war.

Second, The Foursquare Church's biggest assault on their pacifists was actually an attack on their manhood. Leaders expressed fear that by keeping the pacifist clause, people might infer they have a "yellow" and "slacker" and "coward" within the organization. Here was the direct link between war and manhood. The term *yellow* was a derogatory one used against people unwilling to fight—pacifists and conscientious objectors.[68] As will be shown, the term *sissy* was used multiple times by Phil Kerr, Temple leader, to put down pacifists. Sexism (sissy) was a rhetorical device used by Kerr to counter pacifist convictions. He portrayed them as being too weak, too feminine, and too soft on the enemy.

Therefore, the outpouring of military support during war was a concerted attempt by some church officials to demonstrate that The Foursquare Church was a patriotic organization. Pacifist sentiment and the provision protecting people unwilling to fight were, for some,

---

67. Alexander notes that the Assemblies of God limited their commitment to government by qualifying it with a commitment to nonviolence. See Alexander, *Peace to War*, 94. For examples of Pentecostal loyalty clauses during World War I, see Beaman, *Pentecostal Pacifism*, 31. Loyalty clauses (loyalty to government) were statements of compromise.

68. See Ernest L. Meyer, *"Hey Yellowbacks!" The War Diary of a Conscientious Objector* (New York: John Day, 1930).

disloyal, unpatriotic, feminine, and too radical. Refusing to bear arms in a national emergency was equated with being a "coward" and a "slacker," someone who benefited from the government but refused to fight and protect it. For some leaders, pacifists were interpreted as being passive, impractical, and disloyal to country, and it infringed on the movement's desire to be seen as a patriotic organization.

## AIMEE SEMPLE MCPHERSON ON WAR AND PEACE

Serving as the editor of the *Bridal Call*, McPherson asked for short, spirit-filled stories along the lines of salvation, healing, baptism of the Holy Spirit, and the second coming of Jesus—hence the "Foursquare Gospel."[69] She believed her readers were interested in the old story of Jesus and his love, not "politics or the disarmament of the nations."[70] Consequently, the difficulty of assessing her early position on peace and war is that the majority of her early writings were written in the heat of World War I with the enforcement of the Espionage and Seditions Acts, which criminalized antiwar speech. Many religious publications were under censorship, including many Pentecostal periodicals, because of their antiwar stance.[71]

Even the slightest incitement to resist the war could be construed as obstructing the war effort, resulting in fines, confiscation of religious periodicals, and even imprisonment. Consequently, many of McPherson's writings were apolitical. The exception, however, was an early column titled "Topics of the Day" (later it became "Editorial Comments"), in which McPherson at times sought to cautiously enlighten her readers on current issues. She discussed social issues and informed her readers about the perils of war and inconsistencies of political peace efforts. For her, any discussion of political peace efforts was superfluous because governments rejected the "Prince of Peace."[72]

69. "Writing for the Bridal Call," *Bridal Call* 4:5 (1920) 11.

70. Sister H. S. McPherson, "The Rochester Revival," *Bridal Call* (December 1921) 16. See also "Bridal Call Published Monthly," *Bridal Call* 1:8 (1918) 3.

71. Alexander, *Peace to War*, 133.

72. Aimee Semple McPherson, "The Day of Remembering," *Bridal Call Foursquare* 18:12 (1934) 2; "Coming of the Prince of Peace World's Only Hope," *Foursquare Crusader* 11:4 (1937) 1.

## McPherson's Early Usage of the Term "Pacifist"

McPherson referenced the terms *pacifist* and *pacifism* a total of four times between 1917 and 1944. Three out of the four references to pacifism appeared in a 1917 sermon in which she recognized the seriousness of war conscription and its negative effect on all Christian pacifists. In 1918 she wrote, "Today it is almost considered treason to be a pacificist."[73] Her sermon criticized the doublespeak of liberal politics that preached peace and dialogue but nonetheless, when war broke out, supported armament. Of these hypocritical liberals, she wrote: "God hates the pacificist [*sic*] who endeavors to be neutral and neither take[s] a stand for or against His cause. Neutral you cannot be."[74] She followed with a *spiritual* call to arms, reminiscent of her Salvation Army background: "The Lord is a Man of war, and He is calling not for pacifists, but for soldiers of the cross who have buckled on the whole armor of God."[75]

McPherson discussed the Hague Conventions, writing that when people cried "peace," gloom and destruction followed.[76] She referenced the first Peace Parley, acknowledging that "God's peace was broken through jealousy, which causes so much warfare today."[77] The problem with human-inspired peace, she wrote, was that it often excluded the Prince of Peace. "God's message has ever been one of peace and reconciliation but strange to say, men have not seen the need of turning to Him for peace."[78] For her, the total depravity of humanity applied to institutions and politics. She wrote, "Militarism has failed; capitalism has failed. Democracy, man's last attempt to govern the world without God, will also tragically fail, because today there is no room and no desire for Jesus Christ in its political program."[79]

---

73. Sister H. S. McPherson, "Topics of the Day: Peace Palace Parable and the Supreme Call to Arms," *Bridal Call* 1:12 (1918) 6–8. McPherson also references the concerted effort of the U.S. military to enlist new recruitments in "Modern Warfare— Over the Top," *Bridal Call* 1:10 (1918) 4.

74. Ibid.

75. Ibid.

76. Sister H. S. McPherson, "Topics of the Day," *Bridal Call* 1:1 (1917) 1.

77. Aimee Semple McPherson, "The Peace Parley," *Bridal Call Foursquare* (November 1927) 13; "When Is He Coming?" *Bridal Call* 4:7 (1920) 5–6.

78. Ibid.

79. Aimee Semple McPherson, "Behold, He Cometh!" *Bridal Call Foursquare* 15:3 (1931) 5. See also "A Christless World," *Foursquare Crusader* 7:50 (1927) 2.

McPherson's early usage of the terms *pacifism* and *pacifist* took on a negative tone. Yet this does not disqualify her early support for Christian pacifist principles. It is tempting to assume that her negative usage of the term *pacifism* automatically rules out her support for peacemaking, non-violence, or nonresistance, but this is not the case. McPherson's critique of political pacifism was a judgment against *passivism*, not peacemaking. Likewise, Samuel Booth-Clibborn, one of the major influential pacifists among Pentecostals, echoed McPherson's sentiment that it was "too late for the pacifists: for their weapons, being merely political, have failed, as everything human is bound to fail."[80]

At this point, it is important to pause and consider that the infrequent use of the term *pacifism* by early Pentecostals does not discredit their early "pacifism" or the quasi-pacifism of McPherson. One would have a difficult time arguing that simply because McPherson, and the Pentecostal movement at large, omitted the term, and in some cases used the word in a negative light (passivity), early Pentecostals were not *truly* pacifists, or that they were not as *deeply committed* to pacifism.

While many omitted the term *pacifism* when defining their convictions, they nevertheless fit the definition of pacifism. For example, early Pentecostals such as the Assemblies of God claimed to follow the Quaker tradition on peace that used similar terminology, but Pentecostals did not generally apply those terms to themselves. They fit the definition of pacifism but omitted the term. Pentecostals were not alone, however. Mennonites, Hutterites, Brethren in Christ, and even the Amish did not use the term *pacifism* to describe their peace convictions, and yet they were clearly Christian pacifists.

Professor Duane Stoltzfus of Goshen College notes that the Hutterites preferred "brothers" or simply referred to their church with the "assumption that they were believers following in the faithful way." There was no reason to say more: "Of course they were pacifists, and more, but they did not feel the need to call themselves such."[81] Amish scholar Donald Kraybill confirmed that all the traditional and old order Anabaptist communities in North America—Amish, Mennonites, Hutterites, and Brethren—used the English word for nonresistance rather

---

80. Samuel H. Booth-Clibborn, "The Christian and War: Is It Too Late?" *Weekly Evangel* (April 28, 1917) 5. Booth-Clibborn was a leader in the early British Pentecostal movement.

81. Personal e-mail conversation with Duane Stoltzfus (February 7, 2012).

than pacifism.[82] Steve M. Nolt, American Mennonite Historian, wrote that in the early twentieth century most Mennonites were "uneasy" with the word *pacifism*. This uneasiness likely stemmed from the fairly new usage of the term and its negative association with the "liberal" stream of political optimism. They did, however, feel more at home with speaking of the "nonconformed-nonresistant faith."[83] The term *pacifism* was also used "infrequently in the Brethren in Christ literature."[84] These groups opted for biblical words to describe their peace convictions.

Additionally, the term *pacifism* is recent, likely dating to the early 1900s. Since Pentecostals were starting to organize then, it is likely they were not using the term for their principled opposition to killing. So it is to be expected that they would not, and indeed could not, have used the term *pacifists* before and during World War I.

Pentecostals, like twentieth-century Mennonites, preferred the term *conscientious objector* to *pacifist* to define their ethic on war. E. S. Williams, Assemblies of God General Superintendent from 1929–1949, noted that the Assemblies of God, being the third largest church in America, "opposed war" and yet was not a "pacifist" church, but rather a church of "conscientious objectors."[85]

Ted Grimsrud, professor of theology and peace studies at Eastern Mennonite University, agrees that the term *pacifism* had "never been uniformly accepted among Mennonites as a label for their peace convictions." Therefore, in the context of Pentecostal non-usage of the term, he concludes, "I agree that one should not equate the extent of those convictions with the use of the term [pacifism]."[86] Interestingly, among present-day Mennonites (Mennonite Church USA), the term *pacifism* is becoming less popular due to its connotation of passivity, but that does not imply a diminishment of peace convictions.

Therefore, if one is tempted to "throw out" early Pentecostal pacifism due to the infrequent use of *pacifism*, then one must follow the same logic and disregard the pacifist history of the Amish, Hutterites,

---

82. Personal e-mail conversation with Donald Kraybill (February 13, 2012).

83. Personal e-mail conversation with Steve M. Nolt (February 9, 2012).

84. I am thankful to Glen Pierce, Director of the Brethren in Christ Historical Library and Archives, and his colleague Morris Sherk, who researched the term *pacifism* for me in the BIC literature between 1887 and 2004.

85. Alexander, *Peace to War*, 165.

86. Personal e-mail conversation with Ted Grimsrud (February 14, 2012).

Mennonites, and Brethren in Christ. Obviously, the widespread acceptance of Pentecostal pacifism did not endure past World War II, but then again, historic peace churches had a five-hundred-year head start, and many other groups abandoned, compromised, accommodated, or softened their early commitment to pacifism. Abandonment of pacifism was not only symptomatic of Pentecostals; it was universal and widespread among many movements.

### McPherson Supports War Bonds

During World War I, with the enforcement of the Espionage and Seditions Acts legalizing discrimination against individuals and religious groups opposing war,[87] McPherson supported the promotion of Liberty Bonds—a way for the government to finance war operations. One thing McPherson was consistent on throughout her ministry was the promotion of these bonds. Yet there is no clear evidence that she encouraged her followers to *physically* bear arms and fight. Her support for U.S. military intervention can be *implied* by such comments as, "Sacrifice and giving are absolutely essential."[88] Even so, she stopped short of calling her people to physically fight. Buying war bonds was one thing, but encouraging others to kill was another. War bond promotion was her way of demonstrating patriotism and supporting the government's use of the sword without necessarily calling on her followers to kill. While bond promotion demonstrates her support for the U.S. military, it does not reveal her attitude on Christians bearing arms. Clearly, however, by World War II, she openly supported Christians bearing arms (this will be documented later).

### McPherson's Peace Colleagues

McPherson was not unfamiliar with Christian pacifism, as evidenced by her relationships with people openly committed to peace, nonviolence, and disarmament. Her continued interest in advocating peace is evidenced by the fact that she maintained close professional relationships

87. Those who failed to promote Liberty Bonds were targeted, discredited, and humiliated. They were often portrayed as un-American and un-Christian. They were labeled "cowards" and "yellow," derogatory terms for pacifists and conscientious objectors. Mennonites, Quakers, Pentecostals, and many other groups were threatened with violence and intimidation if they did not buy Liberty Bonds. See Alexander, *Peace to War*, 17, 134.

88. McPherson, "Liberty Bonds—Over There," *Bridal Call* 1:12 (1918) 2.

with well-known peace advocates such as Howard Clinton, vice president of the World Peace Commission, whom she often invited to the Temple to speak on world peace;[89] Irving Fisher, who spoke at the Temple as a representative for peace, urging the congregation to support U.S. involvement in the League of Nations;[90] and William Jennings Bryan, who was an advocate for peace and disarmament.[91] Additionally, Bishop Mason, founder of the Church of God in Christ and a well-known Pentecostal pacifist who was arrested and jailed because of his pacifism,[92] spoke at Angelus Temple on unity and love of enemy, saying, "God has called us to be one, to love one another, to love our enemies."[93]

Mcpherson's most controversial association, however, was Gerald Burton Winrod, a polarizing personality who had a strong following among German-speaking Mennonites from Kansas. He was later indicted by the U.S. government for sedition—causing insubordination within the United States military.[94] In 1936 Winrod came to the defense of a Russian-born Pentecostal leader and conscientious objector who was imprisoned in Russia.[95]

Winrod published the *Defender*, a fundamentalist magazine founded in 1927. McPherson often republished excerpts from Winrod's *Defender*

89. "Seen Through the Lens," *Bridal Call Foursquare* 9:8 (1926) 19. He also spoke at Angelus Temple on May 31, 1925. See *Angelus Temple Bulletin* (May 24, 1925). See also "C. N. Howard Describes Wonder Woman's Work on Far East Coast," *Bridal Call* 9:4 (1925) 13. Clinton's sermon "Pearls of Paradise," given at Angelus Temple and recorded by KFSG, was discussed by a listener from the Assemblies of God. See "Young People's Meeting," *Pentecostal Evangel* (June 27, 1925) 8.

90. *Angelus Temple Bulletin* (July 13, 1924). See Sutton, *Aimee Semple McPherson and the Resurrection of Christian America*, 81.

91. William Jennings Bryan, "He Calleth Thee," *Bridal Call* 7:6 (1923) 10; William Jennings Bryan, "Is the Bible True?" *Bridal Call Foursquare* 8:6 (1924) 4. Bryan's peace stance did not deter McPherson from partnering with him in ministry, although her main interest was his antievolution position.

92. Alexander, *Peace to War*, 105.

93. "Lord, Make Us One," *Foursquare Crusader* 3:1 (1936) 2.

94. See James C. Juhnke, *A People of Two Kingdoms: The Political Acculturation of the Kansas Mennonites* (Newton, KS: Faith & Life, 1975); Leo Ribuffo, *The Old Christian Right: The Protestant Far Right from the Great Depression to the Cold War* (Philadelphia: Temple University Press, 1983) 80–127.

95. See Anton Goroshko, *The Pentecostal Movement in the Ukraine* (National Slavic District Council of the Assemblies of God, 2009). Document can be obtained at the Flower Pentecostal Heritage Center. This copy was kindly provided to me by Jay Beaman.

in the *Bridal Call* and *Crusader* under the title "Signs of the Times." She inserted excerpts that highlighted war prophecy, the horrors of battle, war brutality, and war profits.[96] McPherson worked with Winrod in the 1930s at youth rallies promoting fundamentalism, and he was invited by the Temple to speak in her absence. Following controversy over his presence, the Temple terminated his contract.[97]

McPherson's movement likely found common ground in some of Winrod's political views, especially war neutrality, as exemplified by the numerous *Defender* excerpts found in her publications. Winrod, during a radio broadcast, exclaimed, "let us mind our own business" and "war means not only the spilling of blood for America. It means dictatorship. Neutrality is therefore a necessity."[98] He said that "Christians hate war"; they believe instead in the "sanctity of human life" and the "Prince of Peace."[99] McPherson echoed his antiwar and American neutrality sentiment. "My motto," she said, is to "stay in your own back yard. Let Europe fight their own battles and let us preserve the peace of America."[100] In an editorial, McPherson wrote that despite her "protestations and neutrality, we [the Temple] may find ourselves inevitably drawn into the maulstrum [*sic*] of another World War."[101] Weeks before France and England declared war on Germany, she told her readers that the reason they could sleep peacefully at night "is because this is a nation founded upon the principles of righteousness—a nation that does not believe in war!"[102] McPherson's son, Rolf McPherson, did not go as far as to adopt pacifism, but followed his mother's perspective on staying out of war, writing that Foursquare hopes the "war will not come" and that "our nation will not be involved in foreign controversies."[103]

96. For one example, see "Signs of the Times," *Bridal Call-Crusader Foursquare* (April 10, 1935) 8.

97. Sutton, *Aimee Semple McPherson and the Resurrection of Christian America*, 251–53.

98. Gerald B. Winrod, *Radio Speeches on War and Peace* (1939, reprint Rockville, MD: Wildside, 2010) 8.

99. Ibid., 14.

100. NYNA Questionnaire from NYNA answered by ASM. Personal papers of ASM (n.d.).

101. "Editorial Comments," *Foursquare Crusader* (September 16, 1936) 2.

102. Quoted in Sutton, *Aimee Semple McPherson and the Resurrection of Christian America*, 256.

103. Rolf K. McPherson, "When They Cry, 'Peace,' There is No Peace," *Foursquare*

McPherson's early co-minister and colleague Karl Klaus, a Pentecostal evangelist and frequent writer for the *Bridal Call,* was accused by the U.S. government of preaching against enlistment and war bonds and of obstructing war operations. In 1918, prior to the arrest of Klaus by U.S. marshals and his subsequent imprisonment at a concentration camp, McPherson called Klaus in Florida to assist with a Pentecostal "colored camp meeting" to emphasize God's love for all people regardless of race.[104]

During this time, McPherson accompanied Klaus on a fishing trip in Key West, Florida, where he was later arrested. The investigating agent described Klaus not as a serious threat to national interests, but rather as someone "who does not respect our laws sufficiently." Klaus declared that he was not for or against war. He was accused of "spreading propaganda among negroes" and of issuing "disloyal utterances with respect to the draft," encouraging them to "revolt against the draft regulations and other war preparations." Mrs. Klaus explained to authorities that her husband was patriotic and that he had purchased $500 dollars worth of Liberty Bonds. Another interviewee told investigators that Klaus "was not in sympathy with any government," and that the reason he left Germany was that he "did not want to fight for Germany," nor did he want to be a soldier.[105]

Despite Klaus's trouble with the law, McPherson published many excerpts from tracts written by Klaus in the *Bridal Call.*[106] In 1918 Klaus finally addressed her constituency concerning the issue of his crimes. He attributed them to "rumors" taken to authorities by "enemies of God." He claimed that he had never said "anything for or against war since the war exists between the US and Germany." He denied claims that he had obstructed war operations and recounted that during the colored tent

---

*Crusader* (October 19, 1938) 7.

104. "Colored Camp Meeting," *Bridal Call* 1:9 (1918) 16. This article makes the point that all people are equal regardless of color. The goal of the meeting was to show the "colored people" that God loves them, and that "there is no difference between them and us in God's sight." Jay Beaman introduced me to Klaus and his relationship to McPherson.

105. The National Archives, Publication Number M1085, Series Old German Files, 1909–1921, Case Number 145148. Documents provided by Jay Beaman.

106. Karl Klaus, "Seek My Face," *Bridal Call* 1:8 (1918) 5–6; "The Lord Is My Shepherd, I Shall Not Want," *Bridal Call* 1:10 (1918) 12; "Who Are These?" *Bridal Call* 2:2 (1918) 8–9; "Tarry in Jerusalem," *Bridal Call* 1:9 (1918) 12–13.

meeting, one black preacher from the Missionary Baptist Church was upset with him because some of his members received the baptism of the Holy Spirit through a white minister.

Klaus ultimately attributed the "false" accusations to white racists in Florida who disfavored his ministry with the black community and therefore reported his peace propaganda and opposition to war with the intent of having him arrested.[107] By 1919 Klaus informed McPherson's audience that he had been released and had returned to ministry.[108] His continued contact with her publication after his arrest and detainment may demonstrate that McPherson had a pacifist subgroup within her following.[109]

### McPherson Supports Pacifist Themes

As Europe was on the brink of war, McPherson was forced to clarify her position on bearing arms. She was without a doubt attracted to the pacifist appeal in the Sermon on the Mount. Although drawn to Christian pacifism, she never fully embraced it. Pacifism at this time was widespread enough within Pentecostal circles that she was *forced* to deal with the issue, and especially with the pacifists within her own movement, and this led to the formation of a denominational pacifist clause. She haphazardly flirted with pacifism before World War II, but when the United States declared war, she abandoned her ambivalent relationship to pacifist ideals.

Although McPherson never used the term *pacifism* to describe her position, she nevertheless supported biblical themes that her contemporary pacifists would have used to advocate nonviolence and peace. For example, she contrasted trust in military weaponry and its incompatibility with God's way of victory through nonlethal means. She concluded that building bombs, tanks, and guns does not demonstrate a person's trust in God. Quite the contrary. If nations would model themselves after the Old Testament pattern, then military power would be downsized. The hallmark of God's people, wrote McPherson, was trust in God, not weaponry.

She noted the difficulty people had with taking Jesus seriously because they were taught an eye for an eye. She explained that loving enemies was proof of discipleship. She wrote that forgiveness is a Christlike

107. "Letter from Florida," *Bridal Call* 2:1 (1918) 15–16.

108. "Bro. Klaus in Field Again," *Bridal Call* 2:8 (1919) 16.

109. Karl Klaus, as late as 1936, advertised in the *Foursquare Crusader* his printing business. See *Foursquare Crusader* (December 2, 1936) 8.

quality because it surpasses the norm of reciprocity. She affirmed that "if you take the sword, you will perish by the sword."[110] Three years later, she said that Jesus prayed for his enemies, and rather than fighting, he forgave his abusers.[111] She declared that Christians should love their enemies and bless them by unexpectedly going the second mile.[112]

By 1940 McPherson began exhibiting hints of Luther's two-kingdom theology. In a sermon titled "Swords and Plowshares," she contrasted the sword of the government with the sword of the Christian, advising her followers *not to trust in the sword.* She quoted Psalm 44:6: "For I will not trust in my bow, neither shall my sword save me." In her church-state contrast, she affirmed that "God gives to the Christian a sword of life and instruction [the Bible]," *not* the "sword of destruction." She preached against the nations for manufacturing "deadly instruments of war" by "beating plowshares into swords." She pointed to many Old Testament warriors, contrasting them with Jesus' prohibition against bearing the sword, citing Matthew 26:52: "Then said Jesus unto him [Peter], put up again thy sword into his place: for all they that take the sword shall perish with the sword."[113]

### McPherson Clarifies View on Bearing Arms

McPherson not only pushed gender and social activism boundaries, but she rhetorically pushed her people toward biblical nonviolence. For years, she successfully avoided giving a clear-cut view on killing. Her position had been cloaked in spiritual, ambiguous, obscure, and vague terms. She effectively avoided giving a plain answer on the Christians relationship to war. But with war imminent, she was forced to clarify her view. When asked by a reporter, "Do you believe religion can prevent war?" McPherson responded:

110. Aimee Semple McPherson, "The Astonishing Gospel," *Bridal Call Foursquare* 8:11 (1925) 9.

111. Aimee Semple McPherson, "Love One Another," *Bridal Call Foursquare* 12:6 (1928) 7, 8, 26; "Love One Another," *Foursquare Crusader* 6:27 (1932) 2.

112. Aimee Semple McPherson, "What Shall I Do With Jesus?" *Bridal Call Crusader Foursquare* 1:4 (1934) 11; "Christ—the Spring-Tide of His Song, the Summer of His Ecstacy [sic], the Autumn of His Passion," *Bridal Call Foursquare* 14:3 (1930) 6–7.

113. Aimee Semple McPherson, "Swords and Plowshares." Personal papers of ASM, ICFG corporate documents. Sermon was given on May 30, 1940.

True religion or Christianity can prevent war because the very embodiment of Christ's teaching of the Sermon on the Mount is opposed to war. There is something appalling in the distinction which society makes between the killing of a man in the heat of anger, and the organized slaying of millions. Christ said that *hatred* was *murder*. War is not the triumph of righteousness. It is the triumph of brute force. The mere existence of the prophecy "they shall learn war no more" is a sentence of condemnation on war. Between converting a man and killing him lies a considerable distance. To love your neighbor as yourself and then to stick a bayonet through his heart is contrary to the principles of Christianity. War could be prevented if the nations would heed the command of the Prince of Peace when he said, "Love your *enemies*, bless those that curse you and pray for them that despitefully use you." So that these indescribable wars fulfill not the law of love, but the law of pride and hatred.[114]

With these words she came as close as she would ever come to Christian pacifism. This is her clearest, most explicit response to the question of bearing arms. Her use of "bayonet" is a direct reference to soldiers killing in battle. Here, on the basis of biblical grounds, she argued against taking life. For her, taking up arms to kill another person was directly contrary to the elementary principles of Christian faith—the Sermon on the Mount and the example of Jesus. She highlighted the hypocrisy of a society that would outlaw the killing of individuals but not the organized slaying of millions.

This, too, is in direct contrast to Assemblies of God leader E. N. Bell's perspective on taking life.[115] Both Bell and E. S. Williams argued that killing in war, under orders, was not murder.[116] McPherson, on the other hand, argued the exact opposite by condemning the distinction society makes between the killing of a man in the heat of anger (murder) and the organized slaying of millions (killing). The distinction Bell and Williams made between murder and killing appalled McPherson. Her

114. NYNA Questionnaire from NYNA answered by ASM. Personal papers of ASM. Emphasis in original.

115. Grant Wacker believes McPherson simply represented Bell's position on war. The story is not so simple, however. Here, I try to point out the discontinuity between McPherson and Bell. While they agreed on many points, they also differed greatly on others. See Grant Wacker, *Heaven Below* (Cambridge: Harvard University Press, 2001) 247.

116. Beaman, *Pentecostal Pacifism*, 114.

statement was also a direct criticism of politicians who legalize these "appalling distinctions."

Furthermore, McPherson, like Charles Fox Parham and Arthur Booth-Clibborn, both Pentecostal pacifists, contrasted war with missions—between converting (missions) and killing (war) "lies a considerable distance."[117] She also consistently believed in the usefulness of the Sermon on the Mount and its applicability to politics: "War could be prevented if the nations would heed the command of the Prince of Peace."

McPherson would not go so far as to push her members to refuse arms, as this would be infringing on their freedom of conscience, but she did define her opinion on killing. She later published her comments in the *Crusader*, under Charles Walkem's "Question and Answer" section, sharing with her constituency Jesus' prohibition against bearing arms. In response to another question—"What steps are the churches of the world taking to combat the tendency toward war?"—she replied, "Every true minister who occupies the pulpit is indeed a messenger of peace and is a promoter of international good-will"—not a soldier.[118]

McPherson personally believed it was contrary to the principles of Christianity to take life in war. However, she never sought to impose that belief on her movement. During the same interview in which McPherson expressed pacifist sentiment, she expressed ambiguity on the issue. When asked by the reporter if she, as a religious leader, would inaugurate a campaign against American participation in war, she replied: "In the case of *foreign* [italics mine] entanglement I would oppose any effort toward American participation. But let the enemy come to our shores and then every red-blooded American would willingly and gladly lay down his life in defense of his country and 'Old Glory.'"[119] She apparently believed it was wrong to kill unless you were defending the United States.[120]

McPherson's commitment to peace was provisional, selective, haphazard, and conditional. She was not alone. On one hand, she never qualified her commitment against capital punishment. To her it was

117. Beaman, *Pentecostal Pacifism*, 53.

118. Sutton, *Aimee Semple McPherson and the Resurrection of Christian America*, 331. I have followed Sutton here in adding the phrase "not a soldier"; Sutton likely used the phrase to contrast McPherson's proposition that to be a minister of peace and international goodwill is contrary to being a soldier, bearing arms, and killing.

119. NYNA Questionnaire from NYNA answered by ASM.

120. Sutton, *Aimee Semple McPherson and the Resurrection of Christian America*, 257.

murder. However, she qualified her antiwar conviction on the grounds of a "defensive war."[121] Although McPherson, like George Fox, opposed killing—Fox believed it was neither Christian nor something in which he himself could participate—she ultimately supported the use of force when the government was *upholding peace* and *ridding the world of evil.*[122]

McPherson, like John Wesley, never demanded total nonviolence from her followers (despite Welsey's disgust for war, he believed that *loyalty to government* sometimes justified the use of violence).[123] McPherson's perspective on peace resembled that of William Jennings Bryan, her fundamentalist ally, who, while supporting disarmament, believed government must at times use force to rid the world of evil. McPherson and Bryan were not pacifists in the sense of being opposed to the use of violence, nor did they use the word *pacifism* to describe their positions. As for war, neither opposed it under all circumstances.[124]

### McPherson Supports Disarmament

With the conclusion of World War I, McPherson moderated her tone on war and began promoting national and international disarmament. She advocated, rather publicly, for peace and disarmament in the 1920s and 1930s in conjunction with instructing Christians on biblical grounds not to use violence.[125] In the early 1930s, she officially went on record, writing an editorial for the *Los Angeles Times* in which she promoted disarmament, advocated the Sermon on the Mount, and officially disapproved of military conscription. She argued that trying to solve the world's problems by war was foolish and voiced support for the League of Nations. There is "something stupefying," she wrote, "in the spectacle of great nations whose people have not a thing in the world against each other, being taxed to the verge of starvation to build great military machines." She referenced the term "bayonet" again by sharing a story. "Don't imagine for a minute that a gentle little shoemaker from Bavaria wanted to leave

---

121. John Alexander Dowie was like McPherson on this point. For analysis on Dowie, see Beaman, *Pentecostal Pacifism*, 45.

122. Alexander, *Peace to War*, 94.

123. Ibid., 99.

124. Willard H. Smith, "The Pacifist Thought of William Jennings Bryan," *Mennonite Quarterly Review* 45 (1971) 33, 45, 152.

125. Sutton, *Aimee Semple McPherson and the Resurrection of Christian America*, 254.

his family and go out to plunge a bayonet into the heart of the father of a little family in the grape vineyards of Normandy. They had to be goaded into it."

She wrote that if nations would stop "building warships and equipping armies we would be all but overwhelmed with prosperity. Boys [soldiers] had to be poisoned with hatred," she wrote, "with tales of atrocities to make them fight." She exhibited a christocentic response to the problem of war. Jesus, the Prince of Peace, the author of the Sermon on the Mount, was the only answer to violence. The Sermon on the Mount, she wrote, "was the soundest diplomacy, the sanest business ethics, the most practical rule for success and happiness ever written or spoken in the whole history of the world." The problem with the world, she believed, is that people have succeeded in evading the simple and straightforward teaching of Jesus.

McPherson explained that people cannot get around the hard sayings of Jesus: "It can't be tinkered with; or evaded or compromised." The words of Jesus in the Sermon on the Mount are "final and inexorable." She believed that if civilization wished to be saved, people must stop participating in war, stop manufacturing weapons, stop conscripting young boys, stop big business from profiting from war, and most importantly, take Jesus seriously and follow the Prince of Peace. "The only way to disarm is to disarm," she concluded.[126]

## McPherson Challenges Capital Punishment

McPherson pushed stereotypical boundaries even further by opposing capital punishment. We may be able to narrow her understanding of the Christian's relationship to war by analyzing her attitude toward capital punishment. What makes her position exceptional is the scarcity of documents demonstrating the opposition of early Pentecostals to capital punishment. Most Pentecostals did not push that far.

McPherson argued, persuasively, that capital punishment is "medieval." She, like some Holiness pacifists, opposed the death penalty instituted by government.[127] "No, I do not believe in capital punishment" she said in response to a reporter. She turned a "deaf ear to those who argue

126. Aimee McPherson Hutton, "The Way to Disarm Is to Disarm," *Los Angeles Times*, 14 February 1932.

127. See Thomas C. Upham, *The Manual of Peace: Exhibiting the Evils and Remedies of War* (Boston: American Peace Society, 1842) 90.

society should not be taxed for support of a lifetime prisoner who has taken the life of another member of society." She believed that society, as contributors to the social order that produced the criminal, should "bear the burden of maintaining penitentiaries." She said that Jesus and the new dispensation he inaugurated overruled the Mosaic law of retribution. "It is true that the old Mosaic Law called for a life, but it also demanded an eye for an eye and a tooth for a tooth and many other retributory penalties which have no place in our present-day civilization under the dispensation of Grace."

One objection to abolishing capital punishment is that offenders, when sentenced to life imprisonment, are frequently paroled, only to return to old haunts and repeat the same violent crimes. To this objection, McPherson replied, "If the parole system is so lax that there is a constant danger of habitual and violent criminals being paroled and loosed in the midst of society, then the remedy lies in correcting the activities of the parole system—not in executing a man to prevent his parole."[128] Interestingly, in the 1930s, students at L.I.F.E. Bible College scheduled a debate on the subject: "Resolved, that Capital Punishment is Unscriptural."[129]

Regarding capital punishment, McPherson differed from E. N. Bell and E. S. Williams, who supported capital punishment. Bell believed that as long as the "sheriff who hangs the criminal as commanded by law" has no "hatred in his heart," he is not a murderer.[130] McPherson made no such distinction. E. S. Williams unapologetically supported capital punishment by citing Old Testament passages and Romans 13.[131] McPherson, on the other hand, placed Jesus and the "dispensation of grace" above the Mosaic law of an eye for an eye.

In an article addressing capital punishment, Foursquare leader Charles W. Walkem shared Martin Luther's two-kingdom theology. Walkem believed it was okay for the state to executive criminals; however, in citing Romans 13, he stated that the sword is not to be administered by Christians, but by the state. He wrote, "Christ makes it morally

128. "Campaign Aids," personal papers of Aimee Semple McPherson, ICFG.

129. "Day 'Reapers' Win in Spirited Debate," *Foursquare Crusader* (December 7, 1938) 7.

130. E. N. Bell, "Questions and Answers," *The Christian Evangel* (October 19, 1918) 5.

131. Ernest S. Williams, "Questions and Answers," *The Pentecostal Evangel* (September 21, 1935) 5; Ernest S. Williams, "Your Questions Answered," *The Pentecostal Evangel* (July 28, 1957) 19;

impossible for a Christian or disciple to be a hangman or wear a black cap."[132] While the state wields the sword, Christians, on the other hand, should not participate in the sword-wielding campaigns of the state.

Walkem's view on capital punishment is a less radical version compared to McPherson's. Both believed, however, that the Christian should not wield the sword, and both agreed that Jesus and the dispensation of grace make taking life morally wrong. McPherson took her argument further, applying it to the battlefield, believing it to be contrary to the principles of Christ to love your neighbor and then kill him. Her opinion on capital punishment was soon abandoned by subsequent leaders, and it never took root within The Foursquare Church. By 1978, the organization affirmed their position that the Bible authorizes the death penalty, but permits mercy.[133]

### McPherson Condemns War Profiteering

McPherson was likely influenced by the writings of General Smedley Butler, nicknamed "The Fighting Quaker." Butler, whose lectures on war ("War Is a Racket") from 1935 to 1937 were widely known by pacifist groups, was an outspoken critic of war profiteering.[134] Echoing Butler, the *Crusader* cited "love of money" as the cause of all wars and quoted Butler as stating that "at least 21,000 new millionaires and billionaires were made during the World War. The normal profits of a business in the U.S. are 6, 8, 10 and sometimes even 12 percent. But war-time profits— Ah! that is another mater—20, 100, 300, and even 1800 percent—the sky is the limit."[135]

McPherson developed Butler's arguments in a 1937 editorial exposing war profiteering and criticizing politicians who send their young people to battle while profiting from their sacrifice. She, like Pentecostal pacifist leaders Frank Bartleman and Charles Parham, viewed war as a commercial enterprise that produced enormous profits for the rich.[136]

132. Charles William Walkem, "Capital Punishment," *Foursquare Crusader* (January 16, 1935) 9.

133. Foursquare Position Statements (August 14, 1978), Letter from Rolf McPherson, President, to Raymond L. Cox. ICFG corporate papers.

134. Smedley Butler, *War Is a Racket* (1935, reprint Los Angeles: Feral, 2003).

135. "Signs of the Times," *Foursquare Crusader* (December 18, 1935) 8.

136. For Parham, see Beaman, *Pentecostal Pacifism*, 53. See also Murray Dempster, who notes that Frank Bartleman critiqued war because it was a machine that profited

She wrote, "The men who really make war and inflame people to a point of patriotic fervor are not the men who go to the struggle." She added, "How many Congressmen, Diplomats or Premiers bore arms or smelled the smoke of battle in the last war?" She said the "war spirit" was enthusiastically advertised by those who reaped profits by "manufacturing munitions and other war material." She continued, "As long as politicians can protect their own devoted hides and send the other fellow to the front, they clamour for war, especially when those manufacturing munitions and other war materials make it worth their while to promote the war spirit."[137]

As editor, McPherson also allowed the publication of short columns condemning violence, war profiteering, arms production, and conscription. Most are anonymous but are representative of McPherson's views. For instance, in two separate issues of the *Crusader*, she published a short piece by Charles M. Shelton titled "The Truth about War." Shelton wrote: "It is about time the truth were [sic] told about 'love of country' and 'patriotism' in times of impending war. Millions of young men have become soldiers because governments or arbitrary military powers have compelled military service."[138] Another column appeared discussing the excessive accumulation of U.S. wealth following the first war. "We raised $37,000,000,000 for war and used the money to kill and maim; why should we not raise $9,000,000,000 to keep men and women from starving?"[139]

### McPherson Says "War Is Hell"

McPherson also critiqued the carnal nature of war, saying, "Every dog of war was on the leash, every modern invention of war was put into use to destroy men, women and little children and baptize them in their

---

the rich. Dempster, "Pacifism in Pentecostalism: The Case of the Assemblies of God," in *The Fragmentation of the Church and Its Unity in Peacemaking*, ed. Jeffrey Gross and John D. Rempel (Grand Rapids: Eerdmans, 2001) 150.

137. "Editorial Comments on War," *Foursquare Crusader* 10:36 (1937) 2.

138. Charles M. Sheldon, "The Truth about War," *Bridal Call-Crusader Foursquare* 1:14 (1934) 7; Charles M. Sheldon, "The Truth about War," *Foursquare Crusader* (December 9, 1936) 6. See similar arguments in A. P. Gouthey, "World Cries and How They Have Been Met," *Foursquare Crusader* 7:14 (1932) 2; "Martin Luther Thomas, "The Crisis Hour," *Foursquare Crusader* 13:28 (1940) 6.

139. J. C. Kellogg, "The Unemployment Sign," *Foursquare Crusader* (June 1932) 7.

own blood."[140] She located the cause of war in "human greed and selfish-ness, a desire for power and for gold, [and the] human desire to rule by might."[141] She said that as "we look back over the record of wars, we find war has never brought peace . . . we see only poverty, hunger, desolation, heartbreak and sorrow . . . we have failed to learn the terrible lesson that war should have taught us."[142] She frequently used the phrase "war is hell" and affirmed that those who were killed in battle were made in the image of God. War, for her, was "mass massacre." She continued, "War is hell! [sic] and no sane person can advocate it—especially in its modern de-structive form." She continued that one cannot escape the conclusion that "Satan himself must sit in at all the councils of war today. There must be war-mad demons perched on the shoulders of every military commander and riding in the cockpit of every bombing place."[143] McPherson's disgust for war *generally* originated from the negative outcomes and motives of war—death, poverty, injustice, profit, greed—rather than Jesus' prohibi-tions against violence.[144]

One column asked, what should be the attitude of Christians toward war? The answer: "Ministers renounce war!"[145] A short column titled "Christianity and War" noted that love and peace agree with Jesus as shown in the Gospels, and that "we war not against the flesh and blood but against principalities and darkness."[146] An unknown author wrote, "War demoralizes the people. [It] makes beasts out of men if they survive

140. Aimee Semple McPherson, "The Coming Prince of Peace," *Bridal Call* 3:8 (1920) 11.

141. Aimee Semple McPherson, "The Day of Remembering," *Bridal Call Foursquare* 18:12 (1934) 2.

142. Ibid.

143. "Editorial Comments," *Foursquare Crusader* (November 3, 1937) 2.

144. Many Foursquare writers based their condemnation of war on the results (death and destruction) and on causes (sin, greed, lust of territory, power, fame, and money). See "Signs of the Times," *Foursquare Crusader* (December 18, 1935) 8; "Prophecy Marches On," *Foursquare Crusader* 11:44 (1938) 13; "Signs of the Times," *Bridal Call Crusader Foursquare* (April 24, 1935) 8; A. P. Gouthey, "Lust for Power, Fame, Money Cause of War," *Foursquare Crusader* 7:7 (1932) 1; E. McClelland, "Sin, the Cause of Nation's Turbulence, Destroyed Only by Christ's Millennial Reign," *Foursquare Crusader* 12:20 (1938) 1.

145. "Youth Faces War," *Bridal Call-Crusader Foursquare* 1:18 (1934) 11.

146. "Christianity and War," *Foursquare Crusader* 15:6 (1943) 13.

and heroes if they do not . . . It is the poor that pays with his life in time of war."[147]

## McPherson Welcomes Soldiers to Temple

McPherson's ministry attracted many soldiers, some of whom received prayer for healing.[148] Her Temple hosted dozens of patriotic services, with some including the distribution of purple hearts to soldiers.[149] Her effort to minister to the military does not signify her support for Christians bearing arms.[150] Despite the horrors of battle, which many acknowledged, war simply provided another mission field in which to evangelize soldiers and spread the Foursquare Gospel. Eventually, however, this would result in the accommodation of the Pentecostal witness to peace, as more ministers became affiliated with the U.S. armed forces in order to evangelize.

Some Temple members soon began voicing opinions in the *Crusader* that the U.S. military was ushering in "peace on earth, goodwill toward men."[151] McPherson would eventually acknowledge her approval of U.S. soldiers fighting on behalf of their country, saying, "To die in the service of one's country is a glorious and honorable end."[152] However, while she eventually succumbed to endorsing the role of the U.S. military, often interpreting it as a holy war between good and evil, she argued that fighting and dying for country is not akin to salvation. She wrote that some told their soldiers that if they were to die for Japan, the U.S., China, and the fatherland, they would be "welcomed in heaven." McPherson disagreed:

---

147. "Signs of the Times," *Bridal Call-Crusader Foursquare* (April 24, 1935) 8.

148. Some examples include "Drum of Left Ear Punctured—Healed," *Bridal Call* 3:4 (1921) 23; "Canadian Soldier Released from Steel Cast," *Bridal Call* 5:4 (1921) 5; "The Sailor Boy Whose Lung Was Healed," *Bridal Call* 1:5 (1921) 18.

149. "Order of Purple Heart Administered at A.T.," *Foursquare Crusader* 10:25 (1936) 2.

150. "Ship Ahoy!," *Bridal Call Foursquare Crusader* 10:7 (1926) 13. "Great American Service," *Angelus Temple Bulletin* (October 1940); "Free Bibles for Service Men," *Angelus Temple Bulletin* (October 1942); "Our Men in Service," *Foursquare Magazine* 17:5 (1945) 15. In 1945 ICFG launched a ministry for men in the armed forces. See also Daniel Epstein, *Sister Aimee: The Life of Aimee Semple McPherson* (San Diego: Harcourt Brace, 1994) 115, 130, 131, 426, 427.

151. "Sailors in Mid-Pacific Seek Salvation," *Foursquare Crusader* 1:20 (1927) 2.

152. Aimee Semple McPherson, "The Unknown Soldier," *Foursquare Crusader* (June 13, 1928) 3.

"No, my brother, there is only one way to get to Heaven—you must be born again."[153]

By 1943, with her rise to the status of celebrity, McPherson not only prayed for soldiers but also began distributing autographed New Testaments to soldiers, announcing that "every soldier is right at home in any Angelus Temple service."[154] It is unlikely that her messages offended them as soldiers; there is no account of soldiers protesting her peace sentiment, for example.

### McPherson Uses Military Themes and Structures

McPherson, with her Salvation Army roots, mimicked the Salvation Army's military structure, flying a Foursquare flag, using militaristic imagery, themes, music, and uniforms, and referring to her students as "soldiers of the cross."[155] She even assumed the title "Commander-in-Chief." She called her periodical the *Crusader*, and young folks of the Temple were called "crusaders." In contrast to the military draft, McPherson and her colleagues asked people to voluntarily "enlist" for service in the "army of God" under the "banner of Christ," to "battle righteousness" with "God's word" as their weapon. They called for "alternative service"— ministering in hospitals, participating in street crusades, visiting the sick, and joining the choir.[156]

McPherson was well known for sermonizing military themes. But just as her criticism of secular peace does not necessitate her disapproval of peacemaking, her usage of war imagery does not unequivocally explain her literal attitude toward bearing arms. Sermonizing on military themes cannot be cited as conclusive evidence that she supported Christian participation in warfare, although one might assume her listeners could have interpreted it that way.[157]

153. Aimee Semple McPherson, "The Zero Hour," *Foursquare Crusader* 13:15 (1939) 2.

154. "Testaments for Boys in the Service: 'Sister' Opens Campaign for 250,000 Bibles," *Foursquare Crusader* (February 1943) 3.

155. See front cover of *Foursquare Crusader* (June 20, 1934) 1; "Glimpses into Daily Vacation Bible School," *Foursquare Crusader* (July 1942) 10; Aimee McPherson, "Soldier, Salute!," *Foursquare Crusader* (June 1940) 24.

156. "God Is Calling Yet," *Bridal Call Foursquare* (December 1932) 16; Francis M. Sander, "Young People, Attention!" *Bridal Call* 6:10 (1923) 18–19; Rheba Crawford, "The White Feather: An Armistice Day Message," *Bridal Call Foursquare* 17:6 (1933) 5.

157. Sister H. S. McPherson, "Liberty Bonds—Over There," *Bridal Call* 1:2 (1918) 2;

Early Christian literature, for example, was filled with militaristic imagery and metaphors, even as Christians consistently opposed the shedding of blood. The early church was likened to an army, but a non-violent one. Thus, the use of military imagery should not be confused with endorsing war.[158] Although McPherson was extremely patriotic, her early movement was an army without weapons, without war, and without bloodshed.

### McPherson Upsets Religious Enthusiast

In the early 1930s one of McPherson's messages offended a man by the name of William W. Harris, a forty-eight-year-old visitor to the Temple, who interrupted her Fourth of July sermon. Harris, a loose cannon and frequent lawbreaker,[159] was later prosecuted in the Los Angeles Superior Court. His main criticism was the Temple's cozy relationship with militarism.

In court, McPherson testified that during the disturbance, she ordered the trumpets to "blow louder" to drown out Harris's "unseemly noise."[160] Other Temple members confirmed Harris "voiced loud protests" when the Temple gave tribute to the U.S. military. In his defense, Harris asked the judge to consider the Bible as evidence that militarism had "no place in religion,"[161] likely a stab at McPherson's patriotic leanings. The judge ordered that both the New and Old Testament be used in his defense. After ten minutes of jury deliberation, they found him guilty and sentenced him to five days in jail and a $25 dollar fine. The

---

"Modern Warfare—Over the Top," *Bridal Call* 1:10 (1918) 4.

158. Rob Arner, *Consistently Pro-Life* (Eugene, OR: Pickwick, 2010) 79–80.

159. The Los Angeles Superior Court supplied me with multiple documents showing that a William W. Harris was often in trouble for breaking the law in the 1930s, and even sentenced to jail; there is some question whether this Harris is the same man who disrupted McPherson's sermon. Some offenses are not so "pacifist," such as carrying a firearm to a union strike and initiating a fight (defending protesters with a firearm). Although the documents do not list his age, they are from the same time period and location as his disturbance at McPherson's Temple.

160. "Bible as Evidence Wins Suspension of Sentence," *Los Angeles Times*, 14 July 1931. Harris interrupted Aimee's sermon titled "Heaven's Fireworks," which was given on Saturday, July 4, 1931, at 7:30 p.m. See "At Angelus Temple This Week," *Foursquare Crusader* 5:32 (1931) 2. The sermon was later published in 1946. See "Heavens Fireworks," *Foursquare Magazine* 18:7 (1946) 8, 34.

161. Ibid.

judge later suspended his sentence.[162] Though Harris faced charges in court, including testimony by McPherson regarding his actions, he was ultimately prosecuted for his disturbance, rather than his self-proclaimed non-militaristic beliefs.

A week after Harris was prosecuted, McPherson threw a "mammoth" patriotic service, inviting 103 members of the American Legion to the Temple.[163] These meetings symbolically crafted a strong alliance between patriotism and Pentecostalism.[164] In a message titled "Christianity and Patriotism," she declared that "Christianity and patriotism go hand in hand—one must be loyal to Christ, the Saviour, and one must be loyal to this country which is a Christian republic, as the laws of our country and its jurisprudence are based upon the Scriptures."[165] McPherson was thrown a patriotic birthday party by Temple leaders with the theme "The American Flag, the Bible, and the Cross."[166] Her party opened with "The Star-Spangled Banner" and the Pledge of Allegiance.[167] She taught her followers, "We are only fulfilling the law of the Lord when we give to our own country the deep, intelligent, and unswerving devotion of our hearts—the same devotion we should give to the ruler of our lives, Jesus Christ."[168] She preached that "we have no room for any ism but Americanism."[169] She affirmed that Christianity does not destroy patriotism but develops it, and that "Christ was a patriot: His mission was first to his own nation."[170] She wrote, "You will find that patriotism is close akin to religion and that love of country and love of God go hand in hand for the success of the land and the glory of the Kingdom of the Lord."[171]

162. Ibid.

163. "American Legion Pays Tribute to Temple in Visit," *Foursquare Crusader* 5:33 (1931) 1–2.

164. Sutton, *Aimee Semple McPherson and the Resurrection of Christian America*, 248.

165. Aimee Semple McPherson, "Christianity and Patriotism," *Bridal Call Foursquare* 16:2 (1933) 7.

166. "Special Birthday Programme," *Angelus Temple Bulletin* (January 3, 1926).

167. Ibid.

168. Aimee Semple McPherson, "The Blessing of Liberty: An Independence Day Editorial," *Bridal Call Foursquare* (July 1932) 3.

169. Aimee Semple McPherson, "The Trojan Horse," *Foursquare Crusader* 13:27 (1940) 25.

170. Ibid.

171. Ibid.

Harris is an example of someone who in the early 1930s could not reconcile McPherson's double-talk on war and peace. For him, flying American flags, singing patriotic songs, and paying tribute to soldiers was contrary to the Gospel of peace. This flaunting of American militarism was probably typical of many churches in American on the Fourth of July. Despite McPherson's haphazard attempts at explaining her view on war and peace, she never succinctly explained to her congregation how she reconciled lethal defense of the nation against Jesus' prohibitions on violence. She, like her movement, remained unclear on the issue.

## ANGELUS TEMPLE, WORLD WAR II, AND THE NEW PENTECOSTALS

By World War II, McPherson abandoned her attraction to the pacifist appeal, opting for a more moderate and mainstream brand of Pentecostalism. In contrast to first-generation Pentecostals and their insistence on conscientious objection to war, she lead the way for a new generation of Pentecostals—one that was accommodated to Christian America and conservative evangelicalism. As Matthew Sutton correctly observed, McPherson, "repudiated the pacifistic tendencies of early Pentecostalism, honoring American soldiers . . . expressing her nationalism and support for American militarism."[172]

By the 1940s McPherson took a rather unambiguous stance for U.S. armament, abandoning her earlier appeals to Christian pacifism, love of enemy, and promotion of global disarmament. Despite her seeming nonviolent and antiwar sentiment, she soon took a stance that was anything but pacifistic. Her haphazard appeals to pacifist principles were habitually moderated with a commitment to defend America.

In a 1942 sermon titled "Stand by America," McPherson said that America had never carried out an "unjust war for personal aggrandizement"; rather, it had always shown great acts of "Christian benevolence to other nations." She believed America to be a Christian nation, a benevolent, innocent, and peace-loving nation. She also told her congregation that democratic government is ordained by God. Her concern, she said, was not whether God was on America's side, but whether "we are on God's side." America, she said, will protect the church.[173]

---

172. Sutton, *Aimee Semple McPherson and the Resurrection of Christian America*, 266.

173. Aimee Semple McPherson, "Stand by America!" Personal papers of ASM.

McPherson's final reference to the term *pacifism* came four months before the deletion of the military service bylaw in a 1942 article titled "Foursquaredom and Uncle Sam." Here she declared that The Foursquare Church was "one hundred percent behind our Government" and that because "our Nation is imperiled and our Churches and the Word of God are imperiled we are glad to give our very lives if need be. This is no time for pacifism."

No longer appealing to the gospel dispensation of grace, McPherson instead began looking to the divinely sanctioned killers in the Old Testament. She used their stories of divinely inspired violence to conclude that in Scripture people took up arms when their "homes and liberty were in jeopardy." She taught her followers that "freedom and the right to preach the Gospel is worth defending, worth living for, and worth dying [and killing] for." She explained the war in strict dualistic terms. "There are two worlds arrayed against one another—the antichrist and the Christian. It is the Bible against 'Mein Kampf.' It is the Cross against the Swastika. It is God against the antichrist of Japan."[174]

McPherson declared that "we must win this war," and wrote, "I say if my boy and your boy have to go, let us give them the best guns and ships."[175] She acknowledged that America was not in the market for a new flag, and encouraged her congregation to "rally as never before for God and country" because "a heathen foe is challenging us; an atheistic enemy is threatening our religious liberty."[176] She affirmed The Foursquare Church's loyalty to the U.S. war effort, declaring, "I, as a Christian, a citizen of the United States of America, want the United States to know that Angelus Temple is at their disposal for anything."[177] Adopting an ultranationalistic tone, reminiscent of the Ku Klux Klan's[178] rhetoric of

---

Sermon given on June 25, 1942.

174. Aimee Semple McPherson, "Foursquaredom and Uncle Sam," *Foursquare Crusader* 14:2 (1942) 24.

175. Aimee Semple McPherson, "This Is Worth Fighting For," *Foursquare Crusader* 14:11 (1942) 4.

176. Aimee Semple McPherson, "Happy New Year!" *Foursquare Crusader* 1:15 (1943) 3.

177. Aimee Semple McPherson, "The Four Freedoms," *Foursquare Crusader* 14:2 (1942) 5.

178. McPherson's promotion of "Americanism" was virtually identical to the nationalist rhetoric of the Ku Klux Klan, which influenced many branches of American Protestantism. The Klan, similar to the rhetoric of McPherson, sought to marry the

"the cross and the flag," she went so far as to announce that "if you don't like America, if your allegiance is to another government and system of government, get out of America!"[179] She later wrote, "The flag of America and the Church stand for the same thing . . . they stand or fall together."[180]

One of her co-ministers, Howard Rusthoi, Foursquare military chaplain and the author of the monthly column "Prophecy Marches On," exhibited the same attitude. "I believe anyone refusing to honor the American flag and that for which it stands should be run out of the country." In solidifying the marriage between Pentecostalism and Americanism, Rusthoi wrote that failing to pledge allegiance to the American flag is "definitely un-Christian!"[181]

McPherson allowed Temple members to be propagandized by the U.S. War Department, showing a number of pro-Allied war films loaned to the Temple by organizations such as the Office of War Information and the British government. Films shown included "The Doom of the Graf Spee," about the sinking of the German warship of the same name;[182] "British Commandos in Norway";[183] "Burning of the Normandie and Pearl Harbor Disaster";[184] "Washington in War Time," a war heroes colored motion picture;[185] "Know Your Enemy—The Jap!";[186] "Hitler's Children";[187] "The World At War";[188] "Target for Tonight," loaned by the British government;[189] "Norwegian Raid Film," which depicted the

---

spirit of Americanism with Protestantism by fighting against evolution, immigration, modernism, and all forces that would threaten "Christian" America. See Kelly J. Backer, *Gospel according to the Klan: The KKK's Appeal to Protestant America, 1915–1930* (Lawrence: University Press of Kansas, 2011) 94–95.

179. Aimee Semple McPherson, "Unlimited National Emergency," *Foursquare Crusader* (August 1941) 26–27.

180. Aimee Semple McPherson, "Call to the Colors," *Foursquare Magazine* 16:8 (1944) 28.

181. Howard Rusthoi, "Public Enemy No. 1," *Foursquare Crusader* (August 23, 1939) 2.

182. *Angelus Temple Bulletin* (February 4, 1940).

183. *Angelus Temple Bulletin* (February 15, 1942).

184. *Angelus Temple Bulletin* (March 22, 1942).

185. *Angelus Temple Bulletin* (August 16, 1942).

186. *Angelus Temple Bulletin* (November 8, 1942).

187. *Angelus Temple Bulletin* (March 21, 1943).

188. *Angelus Temple Bulletin* (April 16, 1943).

189. *Angelus Temple Bulletin* (September 26, 1943).

German rape of a Norwegian community;[190] and "Report to the Nation," a special restricted release by the War Department.[191]

During the 1942 Foursquare Convention, McPherson called down a plague on Adolf Hitler, Chancellor of Germany, and Emperor Hirohito of Japan. She said that "God is not only defensive; He has an offensive, too." McPherson asked, "How many of you would like to see Hitler covered with boils from head to foot?" She continued, "Well, I would." She then prayed for a bombardment of the Axis forces by fifty-six-pound hailstones, as described in the Bible.[192] During a war bond campaign, she requested all twenty thousand people in attendance to "drop to their knees" and pray for the success of the U.S. military effort.[193] One year later, she issued a telegram to local and federal officials registering a "protest" to the government "against the releasing of Japanese" from war camps.[194]

## MOTHER AND SON ON WAR AND PEACE

Rolf K. McPherson, Aimee's son and the second president of The Foursquare Church, expressed similar perspectives on war, peace, and patriotism. Years after the war, Rolf McPherson penned a postwar article that when compared to the writings of his mother in the 1940s, has contrasting themes about Americanism, peace, and violence. For instance, Rolf McPherson contrasted the nonviolent and non-retaliatory way of God's kingdom with worldly kingdoms built upon wealth, military strength, and "stock-piles of atomic and hydrogen bombs." He wrote that Christians follow a "King with no army," a "King without even a sword." He explained that God's kingdom has nothing to do with military might. He made clear that Jesus pointed to the fact that his disciples did not fight in his defense as proof that God's kingdom was uniquely different.[195]

By contrast, his mother, in a 1943 article titled "America's Mission to Millions," justified the use of force, if necessary, to spread and protect

190. *Angelus Temple Bulletin* (October 10, 1943).

191. *Angelus Temple Bulletin* (February 20, 1944).

192. "Angelus Temple Rally Launched," *Los Angeles Times*, 18 June 1942, 11.

193. "Angelus Temple News by the Roving Reporter," *Foursquare Crusader* 14:8 (1942) 3.

194. Aimee Semple McPherson to Governor Earl Warren, Congressman John B. Costello, and Congressman Norris K. Poulson, personal papers of Aimee Semple McPherson, ICFG; "Aimee Protests Return of Japs," *Los Angeles Times*, 9 June 1943.

195. Rolf K. McPherson, "The Greatest of All," *Foursquare Magazine* 27:1 (1954) 4.

America's messianic mission to the world. "I am for America and America is for Jesus Christ, for God the Father, and for the Holy Spirit. America will carry the Gospel to millions."[196] She declared that America is the "hope of the world."[197] She believed political freedom was worth dying and killing for. "If it takes every dollar we have and every drop of blood, we have this liberty and we intend to keep it."[198]

Rolf McPherson exhibited his mother's pre-World War II peace rhetoric. His attraction to nonviolence, like his mother's early perspective, advocated peace, not force, as the means to establishing God's will on earth. Rolf McPherson wrote, "God's kingdom can never be established by force"; all the armies of the world "could never establish his love." He encouraged readers to "bomb the world with the Word of God," and said that the most powerful weapon is "not the sword" but "God's spirit and word." Christians were not to wage war with carnal weapons, but with weapons of love. "The proof of our love," he wrote, "is not in slaying our enemies but in dying for our enemies."[199] His attraction to peace, like his mother's, was soon moderated with the institution of chaplaincy.

## SHOULD A CHRISTIAN TAKE UP ARMS IN TIME OF WAR?

It is difficult locating articles that publicly criticize taking up arms. That does not, however, imply that ministers were indifferent to war—some opposed active military service.[200] Rolf McPherson, editor of the *Crusader*, which often published sermons submitted by Foursquare ministers, noted that his editorial team found many things in writing that could "get us in trouble" by casting the U.S. war effort in a negative light.[201] The editorial

196. Aimee Semple McPherson, "America's Mission to the Millions," *Foursquare Crusader* 15:8 (1943) 2.

197. Ibid.

198. Aimee Semple McPherson, "Unlimited National Emergency," 26–27.

199. Rolf McPherson, "The Greatest of All," 5.

200 Nathaniel M. Van Cleave notes that many Foursquare people were opposed to America's involvement in World War II, and some even opposed active military service. That attitude, however, changed after the bombing of Pearl Harbor. See Nathaniel M. Van Cleave, *The Vine and the Branches: A History of the International Church of the Foursquare Gospel* (Los Angeles: International Church of the Foursquare Gospel, 1992) 158.

201 "Minutes of the Meeting of the Corporate Business Session," 26 June 1942, corporate documents, ICFG.

policy, Rolf McPherson affirmed, is that "everything has to be read carefully . . . that nothing will interfere with our country's government . . . and we don't want to displease the government."[202] He continued, "You would be surprised how many things are often in sermons that have to be removed."[203] Regardless of this censorship, a few articles were published shedding light on Foursquare attitudes toward military service.

After the acceptance of the military service bylaw, the debate continued over the question of whether or not a Christian should take up arms. In 1938 the *Crusader* published a front page article titled "Should a Christian Take up Arms in Time of War?"[204] The article noted that questions about pacifism continued to "pour into the office."[205] The subtitle of the article revealed a negative stance toward pacifism: "Clergy, Laity, Statesmen Attack Pacifistic Attitude."[206] Unfortunately, the unpublished responses that poured into the church office were likely discarded by the editor.[207] In the article, nine Foursquare ministers responded to the question of taking up arms, three of whom supported conscientious objection and noncombatant service.

C. W. Philleo, managing editor of the *Crusader*, noted that the question was perhaps a little late. "It already has been answered—in the Bible!"[208] He cited the Decalogue, saying, "Until the Ten Commandments are repealed the Christian has no alternative but to stay aloof from war and its consequent destruction of human life."[209] He explained that a person can love his country and resist taking up arms. "Prayer, wisdom and the proof of patriotic loyalty on our part, coupled with a willingness to serve our country in non-combatant service should turn the trick for any obedient child of God."[210]

---

202. Ibid.

203. Ibid.

204. "Should a Christian Take up Arms in Time of War?" *Foursquare Crusader* 11:40 (1938) 1–2.

205. Ibid.

206. Ibid.

207. Steve Zeleny, Manager of Heritage Archives Department, ICFG, e mail correspondence, 28 October 2009. Zeleny confirmed the likelihood that other responses mailed to the church office were discarded by the publisher.

208. "Should a Christian Take up Arms in Time of War?," 1–2.

209. Ibid., 2.

210. Ibid.

Myron Sackett, Foursquare pastor, wrote that while he thought Old Glory was great, "I could not conscientiously kill anybody, and still think that I was doing what the Lord wanted me to do, neither could I advise anybody else to do so."[211] If war broke out, he explained, he would do his part to defend the United States. However, he refused to take up arms to kill anyone. He believed a Christian should be a noncombatant. "I cannot give life and I do not feel that I have any right to take life."[212]

R. J. Turner, who was involved in the acceptance of the bylaw, supported noncombatant service. Citing Ezra 7:26, Romans 13:1, and John 18:36, Turner believed that while a Christian is part of two kingdoms, the Christian's ultimate loyalty belongs to God's kingdom first—a kingdom opposed to violence. He cited John 18:36, in which Jesus explained that if his kingdom was of this world his servants would fight. Referencing Luke 9:56, Turner believed that "in light of Scripture the Christian cannot destroy life."[213] He concluded his appeal with a call for every Foursquare Christian to "conscientiously protest combatant military service but be willing to render non-combatant service in time of war!"[214]

The American Legion responded by citing the book of Revelation, describing the present war as a war of aggression against the United States.[215] Phil Kerr, the manager of KFSG and a leader of the Temple, asked, "Do Christians have to be sissies?" He asserted that "becoming a Christian doesn't make a 'sissy' out of a man and becoming Christian doesn't absolve a man from his duties as a citizen."[216] Kerr believed that there was a difference between killing and murder: "The soldier who is forced to take part in a war which he did not start is not guilty of disobeying the command 'thou shalt not kill.'"[217] He also placed the blame for taking life on government officials, an argument reminiscent of the group opposing noncombatant service during the formation of the 1937 resolution declaring that "politicians who start the war are the ones who

211. Ibid.
212. Ibid.
213. Ibid.
214. Ibid.
215. Ibid., 1.
216. Ibid.
217. Ibid.

are guilty."[218] Kerr's views, similar to that of the Assemblies of God at this time, would ultimately dominate the movement.

T. R. Jackman, Foursquare pastor, agreed to take up arms because, according to him, the first Epistle of Timothy explained that "the man who fails to provide for his family is worse than an infidel."[219] Pastor Joe Jefferies believed that God sanctions justified violence by appealing to the Old Testament model of warfare and to Jesus' words in Luke 22:38: "He that hath no sword let him sell his garments and buy one."[220] Pastor Hardy Mitchell acknowledged the Bible's inconsistency on the topic and explained that the answer depends on the situation. In 1928 Mitchell affirmed that "loving enemies is to build your life on God's solid foundation."[221] Ten years later he stated, "Christians should be as ready to defend their country and freedom from foreign invasion, as any sane minded person would be to protect their loved ones if some bloodthirsty criminal would threaten to break down the door of your home to murder your loved ones. Who could stand indifferently by and say 'I don't believe in taking up arms'?"[222]

William Black admitted that the question was difficult to answer. He appealed to his personal responsibility and affirmed that he would fight to protect his family. He would not, however, fight for wars of aggression or wars for economic advantage. Black ultimately appealed to civil obedience and exempted soldiers from the crime of sin and murder. Black, like Kerr, believed that responsibility rested on the government in time of war: "If the Government conscripts a man and forces a man to take up arms, the responsibility rests upon the Government and not upon the individual."[223]

In a separate article, Giles N. Knight, vice president of The Foursquare Church, declared his position on military service. "Let us stand Foursquare behind our Government and our 'all out' national defense program . . . The writer himself would not hesitate one moment to take up arms and go into the field to destroy the forces of the enemy

218. Ibid.

219. Ibid., 2.

220. Ibid.

221. Hardy Mitchell, "Vehement Streams Cannot Shake Their Faith," *Foursquare Crusader* 2:35 (1928) 8.

222. "Should a Christian Take Up Arms in Time of War?," 2.

223. Ibid.

which are arrayed against the Church."[224] Knight later wrote a letter in 1943 thanking Congressman Norris Poulson for exempting his son, John G. Knight, from the army.[225]

## PHIL KERR'S CAMPAIGN TO DISCREDIT PACIFISTS

E. N. Bell's positions on taking life were not advocated by McPherson, but by her co-ministers at the Temple, most notably prowar advocate Phil Kerr. Kerr was the most outspoken critic of pacifism and conscientious objection within the Temple. He gave the most detailed theological and philosophical reasons for taking up arms. Kerr, like Stanley Frodsham, E. N. Bell, and E. S. Williams, believed that killing to defend one's country was not murder.[226] It is unclear whether McPherson officially endorsed Kerr's position on taking life. However, she provided him with the political platform to communicate his anti-pacifist message.

One of Kerr's most outspoken anti-pacifist sermons, titled "A Christian's Relationship to the Present War," was advertised in the Temple, on KFSG, and in the *Crusader*.[227] The same day the military service bylaw was deleted, Kerr held a seminar on the Christian's relationship to war for ministers and delegates—the same people who deleted the bylaw.[228] Kerr used three primary arguments to support his position on combatant service—arguments that likely became the church's (unofficial) position.

Kerr's first argument distinguished killing from murder, the former being justified if commissioned by civil authorities. In other words, as long as the act of killing was approved by government officials or legal entities, it was not murder. His killing-murder distinction represented the convictions of influential church leaders like Bell and Williams. They,

224. Giles N. Knight, "From Here on Out," *Foursquare Crusader* 14:2 (1942) 5.

225. "Honorable Norris Poulson Congressman: June 23, 1943," corporate documents, ICFG.

226. Jay Beaman notes that Stanley Frodsham, E. N. Bell, and E. S. Williams made a distinction between killing and murder. See Beaman, *Pentecostal Pacifism*, 113–14.

227. Phil Kerr, "A Christian's Relationship to the Present War," *Foursquare Crusader* 14:4 (1942) 6, 7, 42; *Angelus Temple Bulletin* (February 15, 1942); *Angelus Temple Bulletin* (February 22, 1942); *Angelus Temple Bulletin* (March 1, 1942). It is interesting to note that both Kerr and Aimee preached a sermon titled "A Call to Arms." See Phil Kerr, "A Call to Arms," *Angelus Temple Bulletin* (May 24, 1942); Aimee Semple McPherson, "A Call to Arms," *Angelus Temple Bulletin* (May 31, 1942).

228. "Foursquare Convention Program," *Foursquare Yearbook* (June 1942) 17.

like Kerr, represented Pentecostals who, by that time, were arguing that the word *kill* in the Decalogue really meant murder, thereby rendering Exodus 20:13 irrelevant to questions pertaining to war and capital punishment. For example, in 1917 the Assemblies of God constituency supported pacifism by quoting Exodus 20:13, "You shall not kill." By 1953 the Assemblies of God altered their statement on military service by removing the sixth commandment. The same Scripture once used to renounce killing was later used to justify its support.[229]

Consequently, limiting the scope of the commandment "You shall not kill" to "You shall not murder" (i.e., the illegal killing of a person) exempted Pentecostals (ethically and theologically) from systematically condemning topics such as war and capital punishment. The subtle transition evangelicals made by distinguishing killing from murder put in motion a new ethical direction for Christians that sanctioned all kinds of killings and atrocities that fall outside of the narrow definition of murder.[230]

For Kerr, as long as the act of killing was approved by civil authority, it was not murder: "An American soldier who kills an enemy soldier is not guilty of transgressing the Biblical commandment against murder."[231] Kerr noted that Christians are commanded to submit themselves to all ordinances of constituted government.[232] Kerr explained to Temple members that "some of you mothers have boys in the Armed Forces, behind machine-guns. When that boy is commanded by his superior officer to 'mow them down,' he is not a murderer. He is a representative of civil government."[233] The Levites, he noted, killed thousands of idolatrous people. However, they were not "blood-thirsty" people. They were simply "enforcing human law, by God's command."[234]

---

229. In the later half of the twentieth century, Assemblies of God leaders stated, "In light of this, how are we to understand the sixth commandment: 'You shall not murder' (Exodus 20:13)? The Hebrew word used here (raisach) in the ancient manuscripts is descriptive of an act of *willful* and *personal* vengeance. While the outcome may be similar to the killings of war, the motive and driving force are quite different." Web site of the Assemblies of God, "War and Conscientious Objectors." Online: http://ag.org.

230. Wilma A. Bailey, *"You Shall Not Kill" Or "You Shall Not Murder"? The Assault on a Biblical Text* (Collegeville, MN: Liturgical, 2005) 80.

231. "Killing to Defend Home Declared No Murder," *Los Angeles Times*, 23 February 1942.

232. Ibid.

233. Kerr, "A Christian's Relationship to the Present War," 7.

234. Ibid.

Kerr's second argument was based on two-kingdom theology. He taught that God punishes evil by delegating the right to take life to civil government, not the church.[235] While the principle of the government is to execute retributive justice, the principle of the church is love, forgiveness, and nonviolence.[236] However, how can a Christian forgive his enemies and in the next breath talk about going to war? Kerr responded, "Because he (the Christian) is in a different realm in the church and in civil government."[237] He explained that as a Christian one has no right to kill. However, as a representative of civil government, one has the right to take life if commissioned to do so by civil leaders. The man who pulls the switch and thus sends the murderer in the electric chair to his death is not a murderer: "He is simply carrying out the command of God that 'whosoever sheddeth man's blood, by man shall his blood be shed.'"[238]

His third argument was an appeal to his interpretation of Romans 13. This passage served as Kerr's primary proof-text to justify Christian military service, and ultimately convinced him that resisting government is equivalent to resisting the "ordinances of God."[239] He pledged loyalty to his country, stating that if "Uncle Sam ever called me and put the uniform on me, I would go, for if I did not, I should be disobeying God."[240]

Evidently Kerr had strong opinions regarding pacifists and conscientious objectors. "The trouble with all our pacifists and conscientious objectors," he wrote, "is [that] they try to control unregenerate humanity by the rules which Christians live by."[241] For Kerr, pacifism and the refusal to bear arms were socially irresponsible, and his understanding of pacifism was, like McPherson's, interpreted as passivity. "Everybody, according to your philosophy," wrote Kerr, "[says] throw away your guns, take the locks off your doors, get rid of your warships, everyone smile at everyone else, and everything will be just lovely."[242]

Despite government's commissioning the Christian to take life, Kerr, like E. N. Bell, encouraged his listeners not to harbor enmity in their

235. Ibid., 6.
236. Ibid.
237. Ibid.
238. Ibid.
239. Ibid., 7.
240. Ibid.
241. Ibid., 6.
242. Ibid.

hearts. He concluded his message with a call to obedience and a disapproval of the convictions of conscientious objectors. "Service to Christ does not free a man from service to government . . . and peace will not be brought about by Christians who say, 'Lay down your arms and love everybody.'"[243]

## CONCLUSION

McPherson pushed boundaries theologically, socially, and politically. She challenged the status quo with her Salvation Army–style, justice-oriented, outcast-friendly urban ministry to the most vulnerable and dispossessed in society. The portrait of her early movement challenges the present-day assumption that she simply accommodated herself and her movement to mainstream "conservative" political and religious values. By World War II, she relaxed her attraction to pacifism and repudiated the pacifistic orientation of first-generation Pentecostals, choosing instead a mainstream approach to war that has come to define contemporary Pentecostalism.

Foursquare literature shows that McPherson did not structure her movement around themes that would have sustained pacifism, nor did the majority of leaders in her movement foster a religious environment conducive to upholding people with theological or conscientious convictions against combat. While she discussed war and peace in general, she never *consistently* explained her position on the Christian's relationship to war.

By the 1930s McPherson came close to pacifism, while never fully embracing it. She supported disarmament; she condemned government conscription and war profiteering; she believed that to love your neighbor and then kill him contradicted Christian teaching; she highlighted the discrepancy between killing in the heat of anger and the organized slaying of millions; she promoted U.S. neutrality; she disapproved of the shedding of blood, based on the gospel dispensation of grace; and she openly disapproved of capital punishment. In the context of her relationship to pacifism, either (1) she was a pacifist in disguise, resorting to self-censorship in a prowar nation; (2) she played the allegiances of both sides (pacifist and pro–military) because of the people she attracted to her movement; or (3) she was personally confused regarding what she believed, defaulting to ambiguity or avoidance.

243. Ibid., 42.

E. N. Bell's ethic of taking life was not pushed by McPherson. Rather, it was pushed by some of her affiliates, such as Kerr. It is possible, however, that by this time McPherson's position on bearing arms potentially corresponded to Kerr's justifications for taking life. This is uncertain. While McPherson eventually rooted her justifications for fighting on defending a "Christian America," Kerr justified taking life as rendering "entire obedience" to civil authority. Both, however, arrived at the same conclusion—taking up arms to kill is at times justifiable.

McPherson's contradictory statements on peace and war may have arisen from the type of people she attracted to her ministry. Since pacifism was widespread in Pentecostal circles, she was pressured to clarify her position on bearing arms. Her irreconcilable statements on nonviolence and national defense may disclose that she was a non-pacifist trying to keep pacifists on board with her movement. While she likely succeeded at mollifying pacifists with some type of nonviolent sentiment, she ultimately could not bring herself to fully embrace pacifism, although she took pleasure in flirting with pacifist rhetoric.[244]

For other Foursquare pastors, the Old Testament narrative on warfare, defending the weak, the instinct to defend one's nation, and loyalty to government were cited as a justification for killing. Others, like McPherson, saw a radical difference between converting a person and then killing him. In the end, however, the teachings of Jesus received little attention in relation to the question of bearing arms. Jesus' role in the majority of articles was to explain the signs of war (Matt 24), not to give an example of how to love enemies (Matt 5).[245]

The Foursquare Church ultimately followed the trajectory of the Assemblies of God in rendering issues of killing to individual conscience. Killing in war was not seen as murder. One way the U.S. government was able to successfully override people's instinct to kill was by displacing the responsibility for killing onto authority figures, such as the government, politicians, and sending officers.[246] The Foursquare Church and the

244. Jay Beaman, e-mail correspondence, 5 November 2009. I am thankful to Beaman for helping me work through some of these scenarios.

245. "War! War! War! What Does It Mean? *Bridal Call* 1:2 (1917) 3; "Predicted the War," *Bridal Call* 3:8 (1920) 20; "When Is He Coming?" *Bridal Call* 4:6 (1920) 3, 6; "Over the Top," *Foursquare Crusader* 12:20 (1938) 3.

246. See Dave Grossman, *On Killing: The Psychological Cost of Learning to Kill in War and Society* (Boston: Back Bay, 2009). This book borrows from S. L. A. Marshall's studies from World War II in which he studied the reason many soldiers during war

Assemblies of God adopted this logic. In the end, Jesus received relatively little or no attention.

The irony and inconsistency of how early Pentecostals applied Scripture to a broad range of issues is apparent. For example, peacemaking and nonviolence are core teachings of the New Testament and early Christianity. Yet The Foursquare Church demoted nonviolence and peacemaking to a matter of personal conscience. The classical doctrine of speaking in tongues as initial evidence, for instance, has considerably less biblical support than nonviolence, but more than enough for North American Pentecostal groups to make it doctrinally mandatory for their members.[247]

Moreover, the appeal to conscience as the ultimate authority is typically only applied to issues of killing—capital punishment and war. Other issues such as adultery, abortion, gambling, tobacco, dancing halls, and drinking were never regulated to a matter of conscience.[248] While Pentecostals have recently come to apply issues such as alcohol, dancing, and theater to individual conscience, killing remains a personal choice.

Foursquare ministers were likely exempt from participation in war due to their religious profession, not necessarily because they were conscientious objectors to war, and most, when drafted, were probably comfortable serving in noncombatant roles. The passage of the military service bylaw was never intended to disclose the denomination's stance on war and peace, but to ensure exemptions to ministers and laymen holding to pacifist convictions.

Despite the movement's pro-military stance taken during World War II, it is unlikely that the primary motive to delete the bylaw was to deny support for the personal convictions of ministers seeking military exemption. Since any person could claim for himself conscientious objector status apart from a religious organization, the bylaw was considered irrelevant, and therefore removed. Today, The Foursquare Church does not have an official position on bearing arms in defense of country, but they acknowledge "we favor this."[249]

---

would not fire their weapons due to people's innate resistance to kill. Online: www.killology.com.

247. Alexander, *Peace to War*, 340.

248. Ibid., 336.

249. Foursquare Position Statements (August 14, 1978), Letter from Rolf McPherson, President, to Raymond L. Cox. ICFG corporate papers.

# 4

# "Crossing Borders"

## Arguments Used by Early American Pentecostals in Support of the Global Character of Pacifism

### Murray W. Dempster

The 1989 publication of Jay Beaman's book, *Pentecostal Pacifism: The Origins, Development and Rejection of Pacific Belief among the Pentecostals*,[1] was a cause for celebration. On the one hand, Beaman masterfully orchestrated the hints and the pieces of information found in previous studies on the subject into a single volume.[2] On the other hand, through his own

1. Jay Beaman, *Pentecostal Pacifism: The Origins, Development and Rejection of Pacific Belief among the Pentecostals* (1989; reprint, Eugene, OR: Wipf & Stock, 2009).

2. Many people still express astonishment when they first learn of the pacifist heritage within classical Pentecostalism. One of the main reasons for this information gap can be traced to the secondary interpretations of early Pentecostalism. The first histories on early Pentecostalism by academically trained historians – Carl Brumback's *Suddenly from Heaven* (Springfield, MO: Gospel, 1961) and Klaude Kendrick's *The Promise Fulfilled: A History of the Modem Pentecostal Movement* (Springfield, MO: Gospel, 1961)—were both published in 1961 by the Assemblies of God publishing house and made no mention of the pacifist stance of early Pentecostal leaders. Nils Bloch-Hoell's 1964 study, despite its title, *The Pentecostal Movement: Its Origins, Development and Distinctive Character* (New York: Humanities, 1964) was silent on pacifism. John

original research of books, magazine articles, pamphlets, correspondence and denominational minutes, Beaman uncovered a goldmine of information about Pentecostal pacifism. From these sources Beaman narrated the story of Pentecostal pacifism in a fresh and illuminating perspective, highlighting the fundamental change in pacifistic belief that has occurred among Pentecostals during their short history.

Beaman's work, though largely focusing on Pentecostalism in the United States, sought to establish the fact that the Pentecostal movement was almost entirely officially pacifistic during World War I until certain events and developments of the 1940s and 50s triggered a basic shift in Pentecostal belief about Christians bearing arms in military service. The predominant "rejection of pacific belief among the Pentecostals," according to Beaman, can be traced to the assimilation that Pentecostals experienced into the cultural and religious mainstream during World War II and beyond. The "moral" interpretation of World War II, the institutionalization of the Pentecostal chaplaincy, the leadership role of the Assemblies of God (AG) and its membership in the National Association of Evangelicals, and the social and economic mobility experienced by Pentecostals since World War II are the factors Beaman identifies in accounting for the movement's cultural accommodation and the corresponding demise of pacifism among Pentecostals.[3]

Given the "sect" type profile that characterized much of early Pentecostalism and the transition over time into a "church" type, Beaman's sociological explanation of the loss of pacifistic belief among Pentecostals makes good sense. However, as I have stated elsewhere, "something is not quite kosher in this portrayal of a majority pacifist movement shifting to a non-pacifist movement within such a short period of time, especially in light of the intensity with which the pacifists held their convictions

---

Thomas Nichol's *Pentecostalism* (New York: Harper & Row, 1966), published in 1966, did mention the pacifism of the International Pentecostal Assemblies, but portrayed its pacifist stance as an isolated aberration of the movement as a whole. The first histories to mention the pacifism of early Pentecostalism were William W. Menzies, *Anointed to Serve* (Springfield, MO: Gospel, 1971), Walter J. Hollenweger, *The Pentecostals: The Charismatic Movement in the Churches*, 2nd ed. (Minneapolis: Augsburg, 1972), and Robert Mapes Anderson, *The Vision of the Disinherited: The Making of American Pentecostalism* (New York: Oxford University Press, 1979). Roger Robins, a person with a Pentecostal background who pastors a Mennonite church, has published articles in the *Assemblies of God Heritage* and *Pneuma* which have focused on pacifism in the Assemblies of God.

3. Beaman, *Pentecostal Pacifism*, 107–21.

on this matter."[4] What Beaman's thesis presupposes is that during World War I and through the interwar years, pacifism among early Pentecostals was rooted in their anti-worldly sectarianism. With that assumption intact, the cultural assimilation theory gives an intelligible explanation for the loss of Pentecostal pacifism. Certainly the link between pacifism and the "sect" character of early Pentecostalism that Beaman assumes has a grounding in fact that can be readily demonstrated. The question is whether or not alongside the sectarian strain of pacifism other kinds of pacifism can also be found.

From my own research into North American Pentecostal pacifism, I have found that the arguments used by those Pentecostals who were absolute pacifists in advocating Christian pacifism reflected a variety of theological and ethical convictions.[5] Some of these arguments did not reflect an anti-cultural, "come-outers" mentality but related pacifism to the global character and witness of the church. Arthur S. Booth-Clibborn, his son Samuel H. Booth-Clibborn, Frank Bartleman, Stanley Frodsham, and Charles Parham were five of the major influential absolute pacifists among American early Pentecostals who advocated pacifism as part of the church's redemptive witness to the world.[6] Pacifism was the moral

4. Review of Beaman's *Pentcostal Pacifism* in *Pneuma: The Journal of the Society for Pentecostal Studies* 11 (1989) 59–64.

5. My analysis of these arguments was first developed for the 7th Annual Pentecostal Lectureship at Regent College, Vancouver, Canada, Oct 12–13, 1988, and later published in a slightly revised form under the title, "Reassessing the Moral Rhetoric of Early American Pentecostal Pacifism," *Crux* 26 (March, 1990) 23–36. The arguments are selected intact out of this larger article and presented with changes in wording only.

6. Although Arthur Booth-Clibborn was an Englishman, he is included in this analysis of North American Pentecostal pacifism because of the influence of his writings on Pentecostals in the United States. His major book *Blood Against Blood*—the second edition appearing in 1914—was promoted with great fanfare for the consumption of American believers. In 1915, for example, *Word and Witness*, under the editorship of E. N. Bell, ran repeated ads on behalf of the Gospel Publishing House for *Blood Against Blood*; in one instance, calling it "A most striking, realistic and forceful book by Arthur Sydney Booth-Clibborn, an English Pentecostal Evangelist and Elder, who has put into words the principles burning in the hearts of all the Pentecostal saints on the subject of whether a Christian should go to war or not." 12 (October 1915) 2. The *Weekly Evangel* was more explicit in identifying what the principles were which burned "in the hearts of all the Pentecostal saints" in its promotion of the book: "The Gospel Publishing House is now in possession of a powerful book entitled, *Blood Against Blood,* written by Arthur Booth-Clibborn, an English Pentecostal brother. . . . We recommend that you purchase it and become imbued with the spirit of its contents, in a complete opposition and protest against war and the shedding of blood" (19 June 1915, 1).

stance required by Pentecostals in fulfilling the missionary mandate of "crossing borders" and preaching the gospel to the uttermost parts of the globe. At least three principal arguments reoccur frequently in the popular level advocacy literature of Arthur Booth-Clibborn and his four American compatriots, and each argument is really a variation of the basic theme that pacifism provides a moral authentication of the universal truths of the gospel.

The purpose of this paper is to examine three of the principal arguments for pacifism that were circulating among North American Pentecostals during the period of World War I and shortly thereafter. The examination will focus on analyzing these arguments to identify the various roles that pacifism played in creating an authentic witness to the universal claims of the gospel. Based on my analysis, a proposal to revise Beaman's cultural assimilation thesis will be offered. One basic line of argument, which I will analyze first, claimed that pacifism was part of the restoration of the true apostolic faith.

## 1. RESTORING THE APOSTOLIC FAITH: PACIFISM AS THE MORAL SIGN OF A RESTORED NEW TESTAMENT APOSTOLIC CHURCH

The leaders of the Pentecostal movement chronicled its "restorationist" character from its inception.[7] In 1912, Charles Parham recollected his own restorationist vision: "My first position, given July 4th, 1900, was a God-given commission to deliver to this age the truths of a restored PENTECOST, during which time I was called the Projector of the

---

7. Charles F. Parham consistently weaves the restorationist theme through many of his articles in *The Apostolic Faith*. See especially, "The Apostolic Faith Movement," *The Apostolic Faith* 1 (1912–13) 1–2. For other restorationist interpretations see Frank Bartleman, "God's Onward March through the Centuries," *The Latter Rain Evangel* 2 (1910) 2–8, and his later *How Pentecost Came to Los Angeles—How It Was in the Beginning*, published in 1925 and reprinted unabridged as *Azusa Street* (Plainfield, NJ: Logos International, 1980); D. Wesley, Myland, *The Latter Rain Covenant and Pentecostal Power* (Chicago: Evangel, 1910) and B. F. Lawrence, *The Apostolic Faith Restored* (St. Louis, MO: Gospel, 1916), both reprinted in *Three Early Pentecostal Tracts* as volume 14 of the Garland Series, "*The Higher Christian Life*": *Sources for the Study of the Holiness, Pentecostal, and Keswick Movements*, edited by Donald W. Dayton (New York: Garland, 1985); Elizabeth Sisson, "Acts-Two-Four: Past and Present," *Weekly Evangel*, 1 December 1917, 2–3. For an interpretive analysis of the restorationist character of early Pentecostalism, see Grant Wacker, "Are the Golden Oldies Still Worth Playing? Reflections on History Writing Among Early Pentecostals," *Pneuma: The Journal of the Society for Pentecostal Studies* 8 (1986) 81–100.

Apostolic Faith Movement."[8] The modern day worldwide outpouring of the Holy Spirit, commonly associated with Azusa Street, Los Angeles, was proclaimed by Pentecostals as the restoration of the Baptism of the Spirit and the supernatural work of the Spirit from the New Testament times to the twentieth-century church. Azusa Street was the Day of Pentecost revisited, a latter rain of the Spirit that portended the soon return of Jesus Christ. A code phrase within early Pentecostal discourse that symbolized this restorationist interpretation of the twentieth century outpouring of the Spirit was, "Bible days are here again." "This reversion to the New Testament," B. F. Lawrence told his readers "was directly responsible for the Movement." Lawrence recognized that the church had a history only in order to highlight his claim: "The Pentecostal Movement has no such history; it leaps the intervening years, crying 'Back to Pentecost.'"[9]

In contrast with Lawrence's denigration of church history, some early Pentecostal leaders actually employed an apologetic construction of church history to support their restorationist claim. Frank Bartleman and some other leaders of the movement delineated the historical scenario of restoration as follows. The early church was a vibrant organism

---

8. "Leadership," *The Apostolic Faith* 1 (1912) 7. After establishing his formative role in instigating the Apostolic Faith Movement. Parham reports autobiographically that in 1907 "I distinctly felt the commission of God lifted and my return to the ranks as one of the brethren only. Since then I have been honored by the people as the founder of this Latter Rain Apostolic or Pentecostal Movement." Parham also sought in this article to discredit the apparent claim circulating that William Seymour and the Azusa Street Mission in Los Angeles was the birthplace of the fledgling movement: "Seymour, in his first paper, gave a true account of the origin of the work but after he was made Pope by his followers, and I refused to acknowledge the fanaticism of Azusa as the work of the Holy Ghost, he, drunken with the power and flattery, used all his papers to prove that Azusa was the original 'crib' of this movement, and a Negro the first preacher." Parham told of his confrontation with other would-be leaders of the movement—Fink, Lupton, Piper, Fisher and Durham—and warned others as "the senior preacher of the movement, that all men who seek leadership in this work and assume power that alone belongs to the Messenger of the Covenant – the Holy Ghost, will fall . . ." Parham concluded his piece on this adamant note: "The Apostolic Faith Movement has its origins in the College of Bethel, in the city of Topeka, Kansas, January 1, 1901" (7–9).

9. Lawrence, *Apostolic Faith Restored*, 12. At times this leap back from the twentieth century made Pentecostalism appear almost ahistorical in character. An analysis of the nature and the consequences of this ahistorical character of early Pentecostalism can be found in Grant Wacker, "A Profile of American Pentecostalism," a paper read at the Thirteenth Annual Meeting of the Society for Pentecostal Studies, November 3-5, 1983 and printed in *Pastoral Problems in the Pentecostal-Charismatic Movement*, Harold D. Hunter, ed. (Cleveland, TN: Society for Pentecostal Studies, 1983) esp. 24–36.

that proclaimed the Apostolic faith found within the New Testament through the first three centuries of Church history. The *Pax Romana* that eventually joined Church and State in the common cause of promoting Christian civilization culminated in the Dark Ages in which the light of the Gospel finally flickered out. The once vibrant organism had become "a backslidden" organization, baptizing with holy water the world and its ways.

God by his grace, however, intervened in the church's history in order to restore New Testament Christianity. Starting with the Reformation, God used Martin Luther in restoring to the church the reality of justification by faith. During the Great Awakening, God used John Wesley in restoring to the church the reality of sanctification through consecrated holy living. In the twentieth century, God sovereignly acted again in restoring the reality of Spirit baptism and the supernatural gifts to the church through the outpouring of the Holy Spirit. This "Latter Rain" outpouring of the Spirit was sent by God to empower Christians to gather the harvest of lost men and women into the Kingdom before the approaching return of Jesus Christ.[10]

Variations on the restorationist theme were present among Pentecostal leaders; however, all shared in the view that the full gospel of the New Testament proclaimed by Jesus and the apostles was being restored to the church through the Pentecostal movement. Moral commitment to pacifism among early Pentecostals must be appreciated against this restorationist understanding of church history. From the Pentecostal perspective, militarism entered the church's life when it backslid and forged a political alliance with the Roman State. Pacifism, in this context, represented the restoration of the Christian ethic from the Apostolic church of the New Testament to the twentieth-century church.

As a consequence of this logic, one of the apologetic features of the Pentecostal argument was to demonstrate that pacifism was the normative position on military service within the early church. "For the first three centuries," according to Samuel Booth-Clibborn, "Christians abstained totally from carnal warfare."[11] In providing evidence for such an

10. For a good analysis of Frank Bartleman's view of this "process of restoration" see the "Introduction" by Cecil M. Roebeck, Jr., *Witness to Pentecost: The Life of Frank Bartleman*, volume 5 of the Garland Series, *"The Higher Christian Life": Sources for the Study of the Holiness, Pentecostal, and Keswick Movements*, edited by Donald W. Dayton (New York: Garland, 1985) esp. xviii–xxi.

11. Samuel H. Booth-Clibborn, *Should A Christian Fight? An Appeal to Christian*

assertion, both Booth-Clibborns, for example, serially listed pacifist quotations from the church fathers. They also gave anecdotes about Roman soldiers becoming converted and immediately casting their weapons to the ground.[12] Early "Church History simply swarms," according to the younger Booth-Clibborn, with conversion accounts which transformed soldiers into pacifists.[13] In addition, Bartleman claimed that until the fifth century, Roman soldiers were denied Holy Communion because they engaged in the immoral practice of killing other human beings.[14] The moral implications of this apologetic for the normativity of pacifism in the early church in light of the restorationist interpretation of church history is clearly drawn out by Arthur Booth-Clibborn in his culminating argument in *Blood Against Blood*: ". . . wherever there is a revival of the spirit of Apostolic Christianity, there also appears a revival of the conviction and the testimony that war is anti-Christian."[15]

Pacifism, from this Pentecostal restorationist perspective, was the concrete moral practice that signaled the recovery of the eschatological character of the original Apostolic faith of the New Testament. The key phrases most typically used by Pentecostals to portray the eschatological character of Christian life which pacifism encapsulated were "the heavenly citizenship of the Christian" and of "the pilgrim role of the church." Frank Bartleman orchestrated these themes together in his forthright challenge to the Pentecostal readership of *Word and Work* shortly after the war began:

> War is damnation in the end to all concerned . . . The present nations at war declare they will fight to a finish . . . [T]he hopelessness of all such efforts for peace should cause every true Christian to separate himself from it, confessing themselves but "strangers and pilgrims" in this world . . . We are not of this world, but "our citizenship is in heaven" from whence we await our Savior. We must be separate from "nationalism". . . The early

*Young Men of All Nations* (Swengel, PA: Bible Truth Depot, n.d.) 32.

12. Arthur Sydney Booth-Clibborn, *Blood Against Blood* (New York: Charles C. Cook, n.d., reprint of preface from the Second Edition dated 1914) 106–10; S. Booth-Clibborn, *Should A Christian Fight?* 32–35.

13. S. Booth-Clibborn, *Should A Christian Fight?* 33.

14. Frank Bartleman, "Christian Preparedness," *Word and Work* (circa 1916) 114.

15. A. Booth-Clibborn, *Blood Against Blood*, 146.

church occupied a position of separation from nationalism completely separated unto God, and so must the church of the end.[16]

Charles Parham drew out the positive universal value implicit in this
eschatology more directly in *The Apostolic Faith*: "As citizens of heaven
and sojourners, strangers and pilgrims here, we have no part in the political affairs of any of the nations of this world. We preach a universal
brotherhood—a kingdom not bound by governments."[17] Based on the
believer's heavenly citizenship and pilgrim role, Stanley Frodsham in
the October 1915 issue of *Word and Witness* criticized the viewpoint of
his fellow Pentecostals who argued in *The Evangel,* "the children of God
should preserve an attitude of strict neutrality to the warring nations
in Europe." From Frodsham's view, to remain neutral on the war issue
was to support the patriotism that fired up the war spirit. Such national
pride, according to Frodsham, was an "abomination in the sight of God."
Moreover, "one of the old things that pass away when one becomes a
new creature in Christ," Frodsham reminded his fellow Pentecostals, is
"that cultural love for the nation where one happened to be born." To
be translated into the Kingdom of God's dear Son, Frodsham continued,
means that "loyalty to the new King should swallow up all other loyalties."
This new center of loyalty destroyed the possibility that a Christian could
remain neutral concerning the war. A Pentecostal who sings "this world,
this world is not my home" should not remain neutral toward "the nations who have drawn the sword to kill those of the same blood in other
nations . . . with their policy of 'War on earth and ill will toward men.'"
Because the bellicose rulers of this world denied the truth that God "hath
made of one blood the nations of men," Frodsham claimed that they have
set themselves "against the Lord and against His anointed." The options
were clear: "Is any child of God going to side with these belligerent kings?
Will he not rather side with the Prince of Peace under whose banner of
love he has chosen to serve?"[18]

Some aspects of Frodsham's argument are enigmatic and the meaning is difficult to track, but what needs to be noted is that his conception
of an eschatology that "made this world not his home" did not mean that
pacifism was a way of standing aloof from the world. To be a heavenly

16. Frank Bartleman, "War and the Christian," *Word and Work* (circa 1915) 83.

17. Charles F. Parham, "Wet or Dry?" *The Apostolic Faith* 1 (1912) 2.

18. Stanley H. Frodsham, "Our Heavenly Citizenship," *Word and Witness* 12 (1915)
3.

citizen, a pilgrim en route to the next world, did not translate into a passive withdrawal from the world. Pacifism was a proactive witness to the universal values of the gospel.

Despite their efforts to show that pacifism was a moral imperative grounded in the Apostolic faith the Holy Spirit had restored to the church, these five spokesman experienced a growing antipathy from their fellow-believers as the war progressed. The government's concerted effort to clamp down on pacifist activity coupled with the patriotic spirit that swept through the country after America entered the war caused many Pentecostal Christians to break ranks with those who were conscientiously opposed to the war. When the war was over, Frank Bartleman stated his view bluntly: during the war, "Pentecostals failed to stand by the Lord."[19] But for Bartleman there was a more far-reaching tragedy than the disappointing way in which Pentecostals had responded to the particular events of World War I. The war had robbed "the church of her sacred calling and 'pilgrim' role" and plunged it headlong "into the vortex of world politics and patriotism, with all its fallen prejudices and preferences, avarices, cruelties, hates and murders."[20] Bartleman's deep sense of sorrow that the church as a whole had betrayed its eschatological character as a pilgrim people who stood for universal values also hints at the notion that the church had a prophetic mission to unmask the sinful pretensions of the world. During the war, this second line of argument reoccurred with rhythmic frequency.

## 2. "UNMASKING THE REALITY OF SOCIAL EVIL": PACIFISM AS A MORAL CRITIQUE OF THE EXISTING SINFUL SOCIAL ORDER

The prophetic indictment of the war by Pentecostal pacifists also was based on a fundamental conviction about fallen human nature. War was both rooted in and an expression of human sinfulness. As the Apostle James declared in his fourth chapter, verse 1, war arose from "the lusts of man." Therefore, war bore all the features of human sin—cheating, greed, hatred, hypocrisy, lying, murder, pride, spying, vengeance, and so forth. Marked by such vices, war explicitly exploited the victim while it subtly

---

19. Frank Bartleman, "War and the Christian," tract (circa 1922) 4.
20. Frank Bartleman, "Christian Citizenship," tract (circa 1922) 2.

dehumanized the victor. Thus for Bartleman, "War is insanity, madness. A great insane asylum turned out of doors."[21]

War, according to Bartleman and other absolute pacifists, was more than individual human sinfulness on the loose. It was institutionalized evil that reflected the sinful power structure of the world system. "Men's laws of destruction," "organized iniquity," and "systematized sinning" are some of the phrases that Arthur Booth-Clibborn used in *Blood Against Blood* to characterize the reality of war.[22] "The Scripture shows us," he wrote, "that organized sin is much worse in the sight of God than are the sins of individuals." The church, to its shame, has been complicit at times in legitimizing "the organized slaying of millions in the wars" through an "unholy alliance" with emperors and governments.[23]

Two groups within the power structure—the ruling politicians and the rich class—were targeted by early Pentecostal pacifists because their political policies and practices revealed the structural evil that war represented and perpetuated. The ruling politicians, Bartleman believed, used the war machine in order to consolidate their power. Weaker nations were blamed for the failed domestic policies and international relations of stronger ones, and thus, were cast into the role of the enemy. Military conscription of civilians provided a mechanism to acquire the soldiers to fight the enemy, and, as a consequence, to ameliorate the unsolvable social problems of their respective countries.[24] Sounding like Old Testament prophets, the pacifist preachers would catalog the warring nations, unmask the sins they each tried to cover and pronounce the war as God's judgment on them for their "brazen hypocrisy."[25] Samuel Booth-

---

21. Bartleman, "War and the Christian," tract, 4.

22. A. Booth-Clibborn, *Blood Against Blood*, "men's laws of destruction," 39, "organized iniquity," 82, "systematized sinning," 73.

23. Ibid., 87–88.

24. These indictments are repeatedly made by Bartleman in a variety of articles: "Present Day Conditions," *Weekly Evangel*, 5 June 1915, 3; "The European War," *Weekly Evangel*, 10 July 1915, 3; What Will The Harvest Be?" *Weekly Evangel*, 7 August 1915, 1; "The War—Our Danger," *Word and Work* (November 1915) 300–301; Christian Preparedness, *Word and Work* (circa 1916) 114–15; "Not of this World," *Word and Work* (circa 1916) 296–97; "The World War," *Word and Work* (July 1916) 296–97; "The World Situation," *Word and Work* (circa 1916) 344–45; "In the Last Days," *Word and Work* (September 1916) 393–94; "The Money God," *Word and Work* (circa 1916/17) 274–75; "A Time of Trouble," *Word and Work* 39 (April 1917) 185–86.

25. S. Booth-Clibborn, *Should A Christian Fight?* 19. Frank Bartleman also used this rhetorical technique. See especially "Present Day Conditions," 3; "What Will the

Clibborn, for example, lists the social sins which generated "the present cataclysm":

> *England* is being punished for her increasing and overbearing pride, coupled with wretched hypocrisy in trying to cover such sins as her cowardly Boer War, her Chinese opium scandal, her drunkenness and oppression of the poor . . .

> *Germany* for her military pride and greed of conquest, her boastful and blasphemous philosophies which have developed unbelief in numberless young minds, and for her subtle and clever higher criticism which has been Satan's best weapon for undermining man's faith in God's Holy Word as being true and inspired.

> *France* for her blatant infidelity and unspeakably vile morals . . . trying hard to beat Sodom's record for disgusting immorality, (while) making frantic but useless efforts to cover it all up with an outward show of art, architecture and science.

> *Belgium* for her recent Congo atrocities, her widespread immorality and drunkenness . . .

> *Russia* for her continual and cruel treatment of God's chosen people, the Jews, not to speak of her over-bearing tyranny on her own subjects.

> *Italy* for her general wickedness and anarchy, which sins have been encouraged rather than reproved by the Roman Catholic Church, the "harlot" of Revelation (see Rev. 17:5,9).[26]

And the United States is also being brought under divine judgment for her blatant idolatry. The war was God's judgment on America for "her degrading and long-continued worship of the golden calf—the almighty (?) dollar."[27] War camouflaged these national sins and provided a mechanism for the rule of the stronger nations under the guise of patriotism to compete for "the spoils" of the weaker ones.[28] Drawing a clear distinction between civilian populations and government officials,

Harvest Be?" 1; "The War—Our Danger," 300.

26. S. Booth-Clibborn, *Should A Christian Fight?* 19–20.

27. Ibid., 20.

28. Bartleman, "War and the Christian," *Word and Work*, 82; "What Will the Harvest Be?" 1.

Bartleman unhesitatingly blamed the government bureaucrats for the carnage of war:

> Crimination and recrimination among politicians . . . proves to us beyond the shadow of doubt that human governments are simply rotten. Men in public office and ruling positions rule their fellow-men, produce wars or avoid them, according to their own fancies and welfare. . . . The souls of men are used up as so much fodder for their own wills and wishes.[29]

But if the politicians used the military system for the accumulation of power, economic expansion and ameliorating social problems at home, then the beneficiaries of this material production, in the pacifist's judgment, were the rich class of the world's nations—and this was especially true in the United States. This American "'money bag' despotism"—as Bartleman labeled it[30]—of the ruler and the capitalist exploited the poor and working classes in at least two ways. Economically, war resulted in the increased disparity between the rich and the poor: the rich get richer and the poor get poorer until finally "the rich man's dog gets more meat than the poor man's family."[31] The capitalist viewed the war as a commercial enterprise that provided a way to make a profit. The profits came, however, from exploiting the misfortune of others. During a war economy, the prices for munitions, wheat, and the other staples of life were driven up for profit. And who were the beneficiaries of the price hikes? Bartleman lists them: "Wall Street interests, Pork Barrel administration, Brewer's Corporation, Syndicate and Monopoly, Steel Trust and Armor Plate, Powder Trust, etc. without end."[32] And at the same time, Bartleman noted, "The poor must live on half rations. The sick must die. We cannot buy new clothes. We cannot buy good food. We cannot travel. Rent prices are criminally high." The most galling part of this hypocrisy, in Bartleman's view, was that the politicians who had enough power to "commandeer a nation" into war did nothing about this "handful of

---

29. Ibid., 83.
30. Bartleman, "The War—Our Danger," 301.
31. Bartleman, "In the Last Days," 393.
32. Bartleman, "War and the Christian," *Word and Work*, 83.

exploiters."[33] Bartleman characterized these monopolists as "Human leeches."[34]

Observing the shrewd way the rich used the government promotion of patriotism to their own benefit, Bartleman chided the rich for their ingenuity in finding schemes to rip-off the common worker in a war economy:

> Patriotism in most cases has proven to spell "Graft." "Dollar" patriotism. War bonds are reduced in price until the poor man is either forced or frightened into unloading. Then they suddenly soar above par. Stung again! They are now in the hands of the patriotic Broker.[35]

Individual greed, the capitalist free market system and the politicians who made public policy coalesced together in the institutionalization of the unequal distribution of wealth. In Bartleman's judgment, the distance between the classes in wartime constituted such an egregious criminal act that it "cries to heaven." He challenged his readership, "Think of Charlie Chaplin, the popular movie actor, getting around a half million dollars and over for one year's salary while millions are starving."[36]

Economic exploitation of the poor by the rich was only one area of the evil social functions of war. The other area that came under the pacifist's indictment was the cost in human life. Charles Parham stated categorically that "the ruling power of this old order has always been the rich, who exploited the masses for profit or drove them *en masse* to war to perpetuate their misrule."[37] From the outset of the war, the pacifists emphasized that it was the American wealthy class that profited financially from the bloody transaction of human killing. Samuel Booth-Clibborn, for example, recalled how the rich profited without regard to human suffering when the Allies looked to U.S. firms for millions of tons of munitions.

33. Bartleman, "War and the Christian," tract, 4.

34. Bartleman, "In the Last Days," 393.

35. Bartleman, "War and the Christian," tract, 4.

36. Bartleman, "Christian Preparedness," 114.

37. Charles F. Parham, *The Everlasting Gospel* (Baxter Springs, KS: Apostolic Faith Bible College, 1911) 48. Reprinted in *The Sermons of Charles F. Parham* as volume 36 of the Garland Series, *"The Higher Christian Life": Sources for the Study of the Holiness, Pentecostal, and Keswick Movements*, edited by Donald W. Dayton (New York: Garland, 1985).

Did these millionaires "stand by the president" by keeping strict-ly neutral??? No!!! Not while there was a chance of piling up dollars, even though every one of them was dripping with the blood and tears of tortured Europe.[38]

A new pool of the poor and working class helped to revitalize this "blood money" exchange of human lives for profit after America entered the war. And the ultimate irony that Bartleman saw in this exploitation was that "the innocent are sent to do the killing, and be killed" while "those responsible for the wars are generally beyond its reach."[39]

Arthur Booth-Clibborn recalled a personal incident when the systemic evil involved in this exchange of life for money became crystal clear to him. He visited a dock at Cork where a ship was en route to war. He saw first-hand the "organized inequity" which, in his own words used "human flesh as 'food for cannon'":

> . . .As I looked at a mass of . . . factory lads from Lancashire packed on the forward deck of a great transport ship . . . and talked to them from one ship to the other, there was a horrid squeezing at my heart. The scene reminded one of slavery, or the Irish cattle market preceding the shambles. Poor lads! How hollow their laughter sounded. How shy they looked when I passed them across some religious literature. A shilling a head was their price. The Queen's shilling, taken perhaps outside some corner saloon. And some widow's prodigal boys were probably among them. My heart felt like bursting.[40]

The Booth-Clibborns, Frank Bartleman and Charles Parham were absolute pacifists who shared in the belief that war was institutionalized violence under the cover of law. For them, a Christian resisted complicity in the social evil called the war through the practice of pacifism. Living by the principles of Christian pacifism was a way to critique the power structure of the world order in concrete moral action. An essential part of the Church's moral witness was to remind the world—its military, economic, and political systems—of God's judgment on human sin, both individual and corporate.

The first two principal arguments might be summarized as follows. The pilgrim church was a counter-community, an alternative society

38. S. Booth-Clibborn, *Should a Christian Fight?* 42.

39. Bartleman, "War and the Christian," tract, 4. Cf. "The War—Our Danger," 301.

40. A. Booth-Clibborn. *Blood Against Blood*, 83.

centering in the person and the teaching of Jesus Christ. Resisting cultural assimilation into the world's power structure was the only way to maintain loyalty to Jesus Christ and keep its true identity as an eschatological community. Pacifism was grounded in these theological and ethical convictions. Bartleman stated it without pulling his punch: "The war church is a harlot church"—it persecutes pacifists in order to sell its own members for blood money in exchange for the favor of the powerful and the rich.[41] A commitment to pacifism was the moral way of expressing the truth that "the 'body of Christ' is not the Body of 'a harlot.'"[42] But for some of these pacifists, the church as a counter-community did more than stand over/against the world: the church was also a counter-community because it stood proactively for the values of human life.

### 3. "AFFIRMING THE VALUE OF HUMAN LIFE": PACIFISM AS THE CERTIFICATION OF THE UNIVERSAL VALUE OF HUMANITY

Participating in the practice of war-killing or in the practice of peace-making disclosed the ultimate loyalties, values, and dispositions of Christians. To kill another human being in war was to demonstrate one's ultimate loyalty, through one's conduct, to what Arthur Booth-Clibborn called "the Earth Empire." The earth empire "selfishly cuts up humanity as a whole in the supposed interest of a part," "places kings and countries between the soul and Christ," disseminates propaganda for "the organized discouraging of any good and kind information about 'the hereditary enemy' or rival nationality," and then willfully cultivates a "blind and narrow spirit" which is "the seed of war."[43] In contrast, Christians were those who gave their ultimate loyalty to Jesus Christ and who experienced a genuine conversion to God. This life-changing transformation, in which all Christians share, lifted their minds, in Booth-Clibborn's words,

> above the fogs of prejudice or party, of politics or nationality
> . . . [and made them into] overcomers, whose spiritual stature
> makes [sic] their heads come over little partitions which separate
> nations and organizations—enabling them to examine universal

41. Bartleman, "War and the Christian," tract, 4.

42. Bartleman, "War and the Christian," Word and Work, 83.

43. A. Booth-Clibborn, Blood Against Blood, 26.

truths in a spirit of universal love, and recognize fellow men everywhere and brethren in those born again.[44]

The brand of pacifism that Arthur Booth-Clibborn promoted among early Pentecostals needs to be explicitly identified. Pacifism was not ultimately grounded in anti-militarism for him, nor in what H. Richard Niebuhr labeled the "Christ Against Culture" type. Rather, it was, in Booth-Clibborn's own words, "pro-Christian."[45] To build international harmony, therefore, without a true spiritual life only leads to the delusion of a false peace, because the real war can only be won by killing "the war spirit" within through spiritual transformation.[46] "In the trans-Calvary empire alone," Booth-Clibborn wrote, "can peace be found either for a world or for an individual soul. But those who have been born again alone dwell there. The words 'enemy' and 'foreigner' are not in their language."[47] What ultimately distinguishes between "the Earth Empire" and the "trans-Calvary Empire" is "an essential difference in *spirit* and *disposition* and *in the means employed to remedy the evils in the world.*" For the unregenerate, "it is carnal power and worldly war, expressed in hatred and ending in death; to the Christian, it is spiritual power and gospel war, expressed in love and ending in life."[48]

Christian pacifism not only reflected a pursuit of peace based on a spiritual foundation; pacifism provided concrete moral certification to the gospel that the church proclaimed to a war-ridden world. Thus, Bartleman stated flatly that when a Christian went to war against his fellow human beings he betrayed "the principles of the Christ who died for all men."[49] "God's grace and Gospel are international," he declared; "Christ died for all men."[50] Samuel Booth-Clibborn, in the same vein, expressed his disbelief at the dehumanizing effects of war. War caused people to become calloused toward the very human lives whom Jesus came to save: ". . . the rending of thousands upon thousands of precious souls *for whom Christ died* being blasted into eternity or sunk in the ocean, causes the av-

---

44. Ibid., 31.

45. Ibid., 125.

46. Ibid., 99.

47. Ibid., 95.

48. Ibid., 14 [emphasis his].

49. Bartleman, "War and the Christian," tract, 3.

50. Bartleman, "Christian Citizenship," 2.

erage person no more feeling than as if they were so many swatted flies or drowned rats."[51] In the view of these pacifists, however, those spent lives had value, a value placed on them by Jesus Christ in his redemptive death.

The value that God places on all people was not only certified by the redemptive death of Jesus Christ. Redemption only disclosed that which God had deemed of value in the Creation. "In Adam," all people were part of a common humanity, a humanity whom God loved. Killing in war, therefore, denied this central truth of natural law; killing, by definition, denied that all people are a part of a common humanity. Arthur Booth-Clibborn eloquently expressed this pacifist sentiment: "Those persons who died out yonder belonged, after all, to no empire, to no church, to no organization or sect. They belonged to God, to humanity, to each of us, as we belong to them." According to Booth-Clibborn, the truly converted person recognized that in belonging to Christ he also belonged "to humanity and not to any nation, and this will settle the question of war for him forever."[52]

When a Christian believer kills his fellow-Christian in war, according to this logic, there was a double moral evil involved. Booth-Clibborn emphasized this two-fold denial of truth as follows: "In war the worldling denies one kind of tie in killing his fellow-creature; the Christian denies two kinds—he kills his *fellow-creature* and his *fellow-Christian*."[53] Bartleman agreed with this conviction. The very idea of "converting men by the power of the Gospel, and later killing these same converts, across some imaginary boundary line," Bartleman wrote, "is unthinkable."[54]

Christians killing Christians was both a violation of natural law and a violation of Christ's law; it also violated the church's identity as the community that embodied the new humanity that exists in Christ. Samuel Booth-Clibborn emphasized this principle from Paul's teaching. Booth-Clibborn quotes the following three passages: 1 Corinthians 12:13, "For by one Spirit are we all baptized into one Body whether we be Jews or Gentiles, whether we be bond or free;" Colossians 3:11, "Where there is neither Greek nor Jew, circumcision nor uncircumcision, Barbarian, Scythian, bond nor free; but Christ is all and in all;" and Romans 12:5, "So we being many, are one Body in Christ, and every one members of

---

51. S. Booth-Clibborn, *Should A Christian Fight?* 18.

52. A. Booth-Clibborn, *Blood Against Blood*, 30.

53. Ibid., 32.

54. Bartleman, "Christian Citizenship," 1.

another." From these biblical affirmations, Booth-Clibborn adduced that the Body of Christ is composed of people of different national identities who have been united into "one mystical Body of which Christ is the Head." "As a member of that Body," Booth-Clibborn claimed that a Christian "must love its members irrespective of their nationality." In the younger Booth-Clibborn's mind, Paul's portrayal of the church was inconsistent with the practice of Christians from their respective countries fighting, hating, and killing each other. Therefore, in saying his "Yes" to Christ, the Christian, as a member of Christ's Body, must say his "No" to the wars of the world.[55]

But whether the argument against killing in war was based on the value of a common humanity created by God, the value of a humanity headed toward redemption in Christ or the value of a new humanity already existing as the Body of Christ, the ethical question, according to Arthur Booth-Clibborn, boiled down to the same basic moral value. "And so, as in all such questions of right and wrong," he reflected, "everything comes finally to a point, and that point is *life*—human life."[56] Pacifism, in this theological context, was moral because it valued all humanity created by God and for whom Christ died, and it gave visible expression to this pro-life witness in its own transnational community of regenerated believers.

The theological and ethical grounds for Christian pacifism from all three arguments can be synthesized as follows.

Christian believers constitute an eschatological community of pilgrims already living as citizens of their future heavenly home. Given this fundamental eschatological mindset, Christians need to resist being assimilated into the values and behaviors of the world and its power structure. Instead, Christians, both individually and corporately, are called to embody the values and behaviors of the new humanity "in Christ," which values include the worth of all human life created by God and for whom Christ died.

On the basis of this analysis of the arguments used by early Pentecostals to justify their pacifism, let me return to Jay Beaman's study of Pentecostal pacifism and suggest a revision to his thesis.

---

55. S. Booth-Clibborn, *Should A Christian Fight?* 14–15.
56. A. Booth-Clibborn, *Blood Against Blood*, 16.

## 4. "REVISING THE CULTURAL ASSIMILATION THESIS": A NUANCED REVISION FOR A BETTER UNDERSTANDING OF THE DEMISE OF PACIFISM

The theory of cultural assimilation advanced by Jay Beaman to account for the demise of pacifism among Pentecostals makes good sense. The thesis presupposes the veracity of the fact that pacifism was an expression of "sect" type Christian attitudes that fell by the wayside when Pentecostals later assimilated into the cultural mainstream and took on the accommodation characteristics of the "church" type. The thesis also presupposes the veracity of his claim that pacifism was the majority view in Pentecostal circles through World War I and the interwar years. On the face of it, both of Beaman's claims seem irrefutable. However, the analysis of the actual arguments found in the popular literature—when coupled with other factors that I will identify—suggests that the cultural assimilation thesis needs to be nuanced to include a basic theological and ethical factor in explaining the loss of Pentecostal pacifism.

First, the theological and ethical grounds for pacifism disclosed a variety of justifications for this normative moral position. Pacifism was tied to the restoration of a vibrant Apostolic faith, to the practice of resisting assimilation into an exploitive, war ridden world, and to the affirmation of the value of human life. Accordingly, pacifism was viewed as the moral sign of a restored New Testament faith, the moral critique of the existing sinful social order and the moral certification of the universal value of humanity: a humanity created by God, redeemed by Jesus Christ and finding visible expression in the church. The dissonance that early Pentecostals felt toward the world of human culture—including its military system—resonates from all these arguments. Early Pentecostals made it clear that this world was not their home, and a pacifistic way of life was, without question, an expression of this sojourner's mentality.

But the content of the arguments they made in support of the normativity of pacifism indicates just as clearly that early Pentecostals viewed a pacifist way of life as a positive expression of the truth of the gospel. Pacifism was understood as a way of life that both resisted accommodation to the world and expressed the universal truths of God's love for all human beings. It validated the church's proclamation that God was the creator of human life, that Jesus died to save all people and that the church was a multinational community.

Given the content of these arguments and the intensity with which the pacifists presented them, the loss of pacifism seems almost incredible within such a short timeframe if pacifism was the majority position among Pentecostals. Moreover, these arguments were marked by a definite advocacy character. Persuasion was their goal. They were written by Pentecostals to other Pentecostals. While the popular-level literature functioned in expressing and consolidating already existing sentiment, it also functioned in evangelizing others into the pacifist fold.

When the theological and ethical content and the persuasive functions of these arguments are coupled with other factors of the time, they suggest that the cultural assimilation theory needs to be nuanced in an important way in order to account for the demise of Pentecostal pacifism. What are some of these other historical factors? First, the 1917 Pacifism Statement that was sent by the Executive Presbytery of the Assemblies of God to President Woodrow Wilson officially declaring itself as a pacifist church was later justified to the Pentecostal constituency as a whole on the grounds that pacifism represented the movement's "Quaker principles," that pacifism represented "every branch of the movement, whether in the United States, Canada, Great Britain or Germany," and that some part of the movement needed to take responsibility to speak for the movement as a whole in light of the US government's Conscription Law.[57]

While the allusion to Quaker principles is enigmatic, the claim that pacifism pervaded all branches of the Pentecostal movement can be demonstrably documented. The issue of the scope of pacifism pervading all sections of the movement, however, is logically discrete from the degree to which pacifism represented a majority of Pentecostals within all branches and sections of the movement. Pacifism appeared controversial among North American Pentecostals from the time of the original discussions about it. Three years prior to the 1917 statement, from 1914 and onward, the *Christian Evangel* and its successor the *Weekly Evangel* had carried exchanges—sometimes rather pointed—on the pacifist/military service issue. Although the editorial policy of these magazines from 1915 on moved cautiously but deliberately toward a pacifist posture, the backlash of reaction gave clear indication that not all the preachers agreed with the editorial policy of the official magazine.[58]

---

57. "The Pentecostal Movement and the Conscription Law," *Weekly Evangel*, 4 August 1917, 6.

58. This pacifist-militarist exchange is analyzed by Roger Robins, "A Chronology

Additional reactions from the clergy came on the heels of the 1917 resolution. For example, the Texas District Council—a strong regional power—in its 1917 session resolved to cancel the credential of any preacher who, in their pacifistic zeal, spoke against the government. Sensing the pressure of the Texas delegation about the inappropriateness of anti-government statements made by some pacifists, the General Council in 1917 concurred by official action "that such radicals do not represent this General Council."[59]

But the last justification provided by the AG executives for registering the denomination as a pacifist church is really a disguised confession. Under both the press of deadlines imposed by the Federal Government and the conditions established by the Congress for religious denominations to qualify their members for conscientious objectors status, the AG executives registered the denomination as a pacifist church.[60] This action, therefore, was politically necessary in order to protect those Pentecostals who were pacifists—whatever their number—from military service. Accordingly, the statement itself, and the rationales developed to justify it, may not provide faithful measures to determine the degree of pacifistic sentiment that characterized the movement as a whole.

Then there were Bartleman's eyewitness accounts of how the war spirit invaded the Pentecostal churches during the war. His conclusion was unequivocal, "the Pentecostal failed to stand by the Lord" during the war."[61] In his two-part article published in the *Pentecostal Evangel* in 1930, Donald Gee concurred with Bartleman's assessment that the church as a whole imbibed the patriotic spirit during World War I and betrayed its

---

of Peace: Attitudes Toward War and Peace in the Assemblies of God: 1914–1918," *Pneuma: The Journal of the Society for Pentecostal Studies* 6 (1984) 3–25.

59. The *Minutes of the General Council of the Assemblies of God in the United States of America, Canada and Foreign Lands*, 1917, reported the following consensus reached on Thursday, September 13th, 1917, under the heading, "Loyalty to the Government": "Brother E. L. Banta spoke on the importance of our loyalty to the powers that be, since they are ordained of God; and told of some so-called Pentecostal preachers who thought they were doing honor to God by insulting the flag and of the humiliation to them that followed. Bro. A. P. Collins followed and said we were on Bible grounds in honoring the government. And said that the flag stood not only for civil freedom but also for religious liberty; and that at the Texas District Council they had purposed to cancel the credentials of any preacher who spoke against the government. This body also agreed that such radicals do not represent this General Council" (17–18).

60. "The Pentecostal Movement and the Conscription Law, *Weekly Evangel*, 6.

61. "War and the Christian," tract, 4.

pacifist principles.[62] That a majority of Pentecostals were pacifists during World War I and remained so through the interwar years may be a faulty assumption based on these factors. The "official" position adopted by the church may not have reflected the "majority" position of the movement's overall membership, but may have been an action that was necessary to take in order to permit those who were pacifists the option of claiming conscientious objectors status.

So, based on these reflections and my analysis of three moral arguments for pacifism, I submit my thesis for discussion: Given the political nature of the 1917 statement, the advocacy character of the pacifist literature, the theological and ethical content of the pacifistic arguments and the eyewitness appraisal of pacifists like Bartleman and Gee, *the change in the Pentecostal position on military service makes more sense if explained as a loss of a prophetic minority of pacifists*. These pacifists, while holding overlapping ideas and common arguments, used a variety of theological frameworks and ethical principles to justify Christian pacifism.[63] But before they had an opportunity to cultivate a pacifist *tradition* based on a shared theology and ethics, history had overtaken them and the patriotic war spirit invaded the house never to leave. Without a theologically-informed ethical tradition to sustain their numbers and to perpetuate their beliefs to subsequent generations of believers, the demise of pacifism was only a matter of time. The loss of this prophetic strain of pacifists within the movement was the theological and ethical condition that allowed the very factors of cultural accommodation that Beaman identified to occur.

---

62. Donald Gee, "War, the Bible and the Christian," *Pentecostal Evangel*, 8 November 1930, 6.

63. Even a cursory examination of representative pacifist literature suggests to the reader that no unified set of theological convictions and ethical principles were used by early Pentecostals to justify Christian pacifism. A typology of different kinds of North American Pentecostal pacifism might be characterized as follows: "sectarian" pacifism (Frodsham), "dispensationalist" pacifism (S. Booth-Clibborn), "prophetic" pacifism (Bartleman), "populist" pacifism (Parham) and "ethical humanitarian" pacifism (A. Booth-Clibborn). Other pacifists in addition to the five examined in this paper might expand the database within each one of these types or expand the variety of the kinds of Pentecostal pacifism within the typology.

# 5

# Pentecost and the End of Patriotism

## A Call for the Restoration of Pacifism Among Pentecostal Christians

### Joel Shuman[1]

## THE WAR CHURCH IS A HARLOT CHURCH[2]

This essay is intended to be prophetic in nature. By this I do not mean that it is written to foretell future events or to express its author's particular charismata, but that it is meant instead to "reinforce a vision of the place of the believing community in history, which vision locates moral

---

1. Joel Shuman (PhD, Duke University) is a professor of theology and ethics at King's College in Wilkes-Barre, Pennsylvania. This chapter first appeared as Joel Shuman, "Pentecost and the End of Patriotism: The Call for the Restoration of Pacifism among Pentecostal Christians," *Journal of Pentecostal Theology* 9 (1996) 70–96. Used by permission.

2. From Frank Bartleman's tract (circa 1922) entitled "War and the Christian," 4. Quoted in Murray Dempster, "Reassessing the Moral Rhetoric of Early American Pentecostal Pacifism." *Crux*: 26.1, March 1990, 30.

reasoning."[3] The argument presented here is hardly a complex one; simply put, I claim in what follows that the 1967 decision of the Assemblies of God officially to abandon its historical position as a pacifist church was a grievous error; that it was, as Murray Dempster has said, "a funeral service for the conception of the church associated with it."[4] In making official its transition from a pacifist church to a non-pacifist church, I shall argue, the Assemblies of God ceased to exist in a way consistent with the radical eschatological vision which energized it from its beginning.

This is perhaps an unusual, albeit not unique, claim about the demise of Pentecostal pacifism. In his 1990 article, "Reassessing the Moral Rhetoric of Early American Pentecostal Pacifism," Dempster correctly identifies an increasing militarism among contemporary American Pentecostals, a disposition that is one particularly noticeable sign that these communities have abandoned their heritage and have become highly accommodated versions of what Yale Professor Harold Bloom refers to in his book of the same title as "The American Religion." In Bloom's interesting examination of American Christianity, the Jesus who gathered a community of women and men to follow him in the way of the cross is replaced by an altogether different figure, "a very solitary and personal American Jesus, who is also the resurrected Jesus rather than the crucified Jesus or the Jesus who ascended again to the Father."[5] This different figure, it seems, is the conceptualization of Jesus which has become more common among North American Pentecostals.

---

3. John Howard Yoder, "The Hermeneutics of Peoplehood," *The Priestly Kingdom: Social Ethics as Gospel* (Notre Dame: University of Notre Dame Press, 1984) 29. Yoder remarks: "Prophecy is described as both a charisma distinctly borne by some individuals and a kind of discourse in which others may sometimes participate as well." I take my writing to be an expression of the latter understanding. This understanding of prophecy, says Yoder, "is a matter of simple trust that God himself, as Spirit, is at work to motivate and to monitor his own in, with, and under this distinctive, recognizable, and specifically disciplined human discourse." Yoder suggests that persons engaging in this discourse may be referred to, alternatively, as Agents of Direction; in either case, the intent is to suggest to the community the need for a reorientation of its moral vision.

4. Dempster, "Reassessing the Moral Rhetoric," 33. My arguments here are concerned with the Assemblies of God, simply because this is the community of which I am a member and with which I am most familiar. Insofar as the Assemblies may be regarded as a paradigm for much contemporary American Pentecostalism, however, the arguments presented here are applicable to that wider community.

5. Harold Bloom, *The American Religion* (New York: Simon & Schuster, 1992) 32. Professor Bloom's account of American Pentecostalism, although not entirely convincing, is nonetheless quite compelling.

Dempster's article, which he says "aims to analyze the moral rhetoric of early pentecostal pacifists in order to determine the way they thought theologically about the church's moral responsibilities to the larger society,"[6] will serve as a significant conversation partner here. Where Dempster delimits his purpose to exclude the providing of "a basis from which to assess the normative relevance of pacifism for today,"[7] I shall make the provision of such a basis my principal objective. In other words, I want to offer a theological rationale for my assertion that the gradual and eventually complete loss of its pacifism is among the most compelling signs that the Assemblies of God has, at least in practice, abandoned its self-understanding as a community of radical Christian witness. In this regard I agree with Stanley Hauerwas, who has said that nonviolence is "the hallmark of the Christian moral life . . . not just an option for a few, but incumbent on all Christians who seek to live faithfully in the kingdom made possible by the life, death, and resurrection of Jesus."[8]

I begin here by showing that contemporary Pentecostal self-understanding has its origins in the Christian restorationist movement of the nineteenth century. Characteristic of this movement, I argue, was a way of reading Scripture and of conceptualizing the presence of God in the Christian community that emphasized a return to the ecclesial forms and practices of the New Testament, especially to those represented in the book of Acts. It was from this particular hermeneutic that both the unique doctrines and the atypical social ethics of early Pentecostalism emerged.

Second, I shall attempt to account for the loss of pacifism in the Assemblies of God as being the consequence of that community's gradual loss of identity as an eschatologically driven church and its eventual captivity to American nationalism and the conceptual categories of democratic liberalism. This accommodation, I argue, was to a significant extent the consequence of two closely aligned factors. The first of these is the insidious presence of an incorrect understanding within American Christianity which held that the United States, based on its democratic polity, was a nation structured according to Christian principles which, therefore, enjoyed a position of particular favor with God. The second

6. Dempster, "Reassessing the Moral Rhetoric," 23.

7. Ibid.

8. Stanley Hauerwas, *The Peaceable Kingdom* (Notre Dame: University of Notre Dame Press, 1983) xvi.

factor, which is closely related to the first, is the eventual complete acceptance of Pentecostalism into the highly nationalistic American evangelical mainstream.

Finally, I shall argue that the self-understanding of early Pentecostals, which made possible their pacifism, has not totally disappeared. A space, albeit a narrow one, still exists within the beliefs and practices of the Assemblies of God from which a return to that community's pacifist heritage might be initiated. Whereas Dempster argues that a historical division between Pentecostal spirituality and social ethics has prevented Pentecostals from reembodying their once radical social ethic, I maintain that this is only partly correct, and that the division of which he speaks is a reparable one.[9] In response to his call for the formulation of a social ethic based upon the "distinctive testimony" of the Assemblies of God, I will attempt to show that this testimony is an inherently eschatological one and that the moral ramifications of the doctrine of Spirit baptism must be understood eschatologically (as they initially were) in order to undergird a restoration of Pentecostal pacifism.

In his outstanding genealogy of Christian nonviolence, *Christian Attitudes to War, Peace, and Revolution*, John Howard Yoder counts contemporary Pentecostalism as one of the many inheritors of nineteenth century restorationism. Yoder notes that many of the restorationist communities were pacifist from their beginning. He identifies a general tendency toward the avoidance of unnecessary attachments to the world and a "literal obedience to a word of scripture without rationalizing it."[10] As two significant characteristics of these movements, he notes, moreover, that among these communities:

> . . . there is the absence of a cultural commitment to social responsibility. As was somewhat the case with the camp meeting, so it will be more the case with Pentecostalism, that the absence of commitment to social responsibility correlates with being of the lower classes, who don't have the money or the leisure or the training anyway, to be social leaders in the traditional elite ways.[11]

9. Dempster, "Reassessing the Moral Rhetoric," 32.

10. John Howard Yoder, *Christian Attitudes to War, Peace, and Revolution: A Companion to Bainton* (Elkhart, IN: Co-Op Bookstore, 1983) 307–8. The "literal obedience" to which Yoder refers here is meant, I believe, as a compliment.

11. Yoder, *Christian Attitudes to War, Peace, and Revolution*, 307–8.

Yet, as Yoder makes plain in his monograph, it was not their socio-economic location per se that led the first Pentecostals to be pacifists. "The simplest reason [for their pacifism]," he says, "is that they take the whole Bible straight."[12] It was, in other words, a particular way of reading the Bible that led nascent Pentecostals to maintain that it was simply wrong for one human to take the life of another.

This unique hermeneutic clearly plays a role in determining the four characteristics of restorationism identified as having "particular significance for Pentecostalism" by historian Edith Blumhofer.[13] The first of these, she says, was the restorationist call for Christian perfection, which "tended to advocate purifying religious forms and examining practices and beliefs against the New Testament standard."[14] Second, she notes, was the restorationist tendency to view the true church as being united, to look past "the turmoil and heterodoxy that had marked Christian beginnings. An emphasis on shared origins promoted hope of renewed 'family harmony.'"[15] The third of these characteristics was the restorationist tendency to see itself as a church on the cusp of the eschaton; this aspect of restorationism, like the preceding two, arose primarily from the way these communities were trained to read the New Testament. Finally, restorationists supported a flight from denominational Christianity, which they saw as irreparably contaminated by the world.

> From this perspective, restorationist views molded the subculture in which Pentecostalism flourished; its participants had already separated from the mainstream. Their attitudes about the world were shaped by their conviction that cultural values necessarily opposed true faith; they interpreted persecution as a measure of spiritual strength. They volubly opposed much of their culture, and the sense that they offered a viable, satisfying alternative to this-worldliness attracted adherents.[16]

What is common to each of these characteristics is the tendency of those who embodied them to see themselves as being part of a tradition with very direct ties to the apostolic church represented in the first chap-

12. Ibid., 308.

13. Edith Blumhofer, *The Assemblies of God: A Chapter in the Story of American Pentecostalism*, (Springfield: Gospel, 1989) 18.

14. Ibid., 19.

15. Ibid.

16. Ibid.

ters of the New Testament book of Acts. This association became increasingly overt among Christian leaders from a wide variety of traditions at the end of the nineteenth century, all of whom expressed extraordinary dissatisfaction with the level of commitment demonstrated by Christians of that day. Leaders among both liberal and conservative Protestant groups called for a renewed holiness among their constituents: the story of the coming of the Spirit at Pentecost was frequently referred to as the source of this renewal.[17]

Dempster is correct when he asserts that the "Pentecostal moral commitment to pacifism has to be appreciated against this restorationist understanding of church history."[18] Pentecostals of the early twentieth century saw themselves as being the contemporary restoration of the New Testament church, a community that had become increasingly unfaithful in the time between the Pentecost of the first century and that of the twentieth. Central to the church's fall during that interim era was its entry into political establishmentarianism: "Militarism entered the church's life, from the Pentecostal perspective, when it backslid and forged a political alliance with the Roman State."[19] A general attitude of social and political disestablishment was consequently seen as an integral part of the Pentecostal renewal.

This disestablishment was accentuated by the initial rejection of Pentecostals by the evangelical mainstream. This rejection served to enforce their tendency to see themselves as being citizens not of any earthly nation, but of the kingdom of God.[20] Taking their inspiration from Hebrews 2, they regarded themselves as "pilgrims and strangers on earth," says Blumhofer.[21] Participation in war was regarded as incompat-

---

17. Ibid., 39–41. Blumhofer notes that Walter Rauschenbusch, the founder of the Social Gospel movement, was among those who called for such a renewal. On pages 40–41 she says: "In terms that could have been borrowed from conservatives, for example, Rauschenbusch maintained that, throughout history, the Church had repeatedly been 'rejuvenated by a new baptism in [the] Spirit.'" Rauschenbusch is quoted from "The New Evangelism," in *American Protestant Thought: The Liberal Era*, edited by William R. Hutchinson, 115–16. New York: Harper & Row, 1968.

18. Dempster, "Reassessing the Moral Rhetoric," 27.

19. Ibid. I discuss this phenomenon of "Constantinian" versus "anti-Constantinian" Christianity at some length below.

20. Blumhofer, *Assemblies of God*, 179–80; cf. Dempster, "Reassessing the Moral Rhetoric," 28.

21. Blumhofer, *Assemblies of God*, 343.

ible with such citizenship not simply because the violence inherent in war was wrong, but because the allegiances demanded by war were trivialized by comparison to the allegiance demanded by God. "Pentecostals considered themselves engaged in a conflict," Blumhofer notes, "infinitely more important than any earthly struggle."[22] Nationalism was consequently regarded by many Pentecostals as a sin of no little significance: "Pride in nation and race was an abomination."[23]

The outbreak of World War I and the development of strict United States' government policies with regard to religious objectors would force American Pentecostals to develop an official position with regard to their participation in war.[24] Although Blumhofer implies that the initial response of the General Council of the Assemblies of God was rooted as much in political pragmatism as it was in sincere theological leanings, the statement's explicitly theological language and logic speak volumes.[25] Claiming that they wrote from "the established principles or creed of all sections of the Pentecostal movement," several members of the leadership of the Assemblies of God produced an official resolution in April, 1917.[26] The resolution, which became the official policy of the fellowship, reads as follows:

> While recognizing Human Government as of Divine ordination and affirming our unswerving loyalty to the Government of the United States, nevertheless we are constrained to define our position with reference to the taking of human life.
> WHEREAS, in the Constitutional resolution adopted at the Hot Springs General Council, April 1–10, 1914, we plainly declare the Holy Inspired Scriptures to be the all-sufficient rule of faith and practice, and

22. Ibid., 345.

23. Ibid., 350–51. Blumhofer offers here an excellent account of the anti-nationalist rhetoric employed by Pentecostals at the outset of World War I. Dempster's article also gives a good deal of attention to these matters.

24. From this point forward I shall engage in the admittedly somewhat questionable practice of seeing my own fellowship, the Assemblies of God, as representative among Pentecostals. While admitting to the questionability of this move, I would also note that North American Pentecostalism comes as close as any strand of the Christian tradition to possessing the uniformity that would make such a move possible.

25. Blumhofer, *Assemblies of God*, 352.

26. From *The Weekly Evangel*, 4 August 1917, 6. Cf. Blumhofer, *Assemblies of God*, 352–53.

WHEREAS the Scriptures deal plainly with the obligations and relations of humanity, setting forth the principles of "Peace on earth, goodwill toward men," (Lk. 2.14); and

WHEREAS we as followers of the Lord Jesus Christ, the Prince of Peace, believe in implicit obedience to the Divine commands and precepts which instruct us to "Follow peace with all men," (Heb. 12.14); "Thou shalt not kill," (Exod. 20.13); "Resist not evil," (Mt. 5.39); "Love your enemies," (Mt. 5.44; etc.), and

WHEREAS these and other Scriptures have always been accepted and interpreted by our churches as prohibiting Christians from shedding blood or taking human life;

THEREFORE we, as a body of Christians, while purposing to fulfill all the obligations of loyal citizenship, are nevertheless constrained to declare we cannot conscientiously participate in war and armed resistance which involves the actual destruction of human life, since this is contrary to our view of the clear teachings of the inspired Word of God, which is the sole basis of our faith.[27]

What is especially notable about this statement, apart from its explicitly theological tenor, is the way in which it clearly explicates so much of the restorationist self-understanding of Pentecostalism noted earlier in this essay. Although there is an implicit recognition in the first paragraph of the document that impending American participation in the war was the impetus for the formulation of the resolution, there is also a strong claim in paragraphs three, four, and five that the Scriptures, according to the Pentecostal reading, "deal plainly" with the matter of Christian participation in war. Moreover, because Pentecostal Christians understood their primary citizenship to be in God's kingdom and their first obligation to be obedience to God's will, their resolution concludes it would be a matter of disobedience (and suggests it may even be a sort of treason) for a Pentecostal to take human life in the name of America or any other nation.

Whether the newly developed policy was primarily theological or pragmatic in character, it served the purpose of earning members of Assemblies of God churches exemption from United States military service during World War I. Ultimately, they were granted this exemption under the thirteenth of several 'Claims for Discharge' enumerated in a

27. Blumhofer, *Assemblies of God*, 352–53.

War Department document dated July 14, 1917. This document noted
that among those not required to participate in combat were

> . . . a member of any well-organized religious sect or organiza-
> tion organized and existent May 18, 1917, and whose then exist-
> ing creed or principles forbade its members to participate in war
> in any form and whose religious convictions are against war or
> participation therein in accordance with the creed or principles
> of said religious organization.[28]

In spite of the fact that the resolution met the War Department requirement by presenting the Assemblies of God as an unequivocally pacifist community with significant theological convictions in that direction,
there existed from the outset two closely related strands of thought which
mitigated this presentation. These ways of thinking are identifiable as the
basis for the ultimate abandonment of pacifism among Pentecostals. The
first is the presence of a certain amount of dissenting rhetoric among
some Assemblies of God constituents. Most of this dissension took the
form of concerns that the resolution was worded in such a way as to lead
Pentecostals to engage in blatant expressions of disloyalty to the United
States government. At the same 1917 General Council that produced the
statement of official pacifism, the minutes note that these concerns were
voiced:

> Bro. E. L. Banta spoke on the importance of our loyalty to the
> powers that be, since they are ordained of God; and told of some
> so-called Pentecostal preachers who thought they were do-
> ing honor to God by insulting the flag and of the humiliation
> to them that followed. Bro. A. P. Collions followed and said we
> were on Bible grounds in honoring the government, and that
> the flag stood not only for civil freedom but also for religious
> liberty; and that at the Texas District Council they had purposed
> to cancel the credentials of any preacher who spoke against the
> government. This body [the General Council] also agreed that
> such radicals do not represent this General Council.[29]

28. Ibid.

29. From the *Minutes of the 1917 meeting of the General Council of the Assemblies
of God*, 17–18. It is worth noting that the minutes of the General Council of the following year (1918) show that by that time the sentiments expressed here had become
official policy as expressed in the following resolution, found on p. 9: "Resolved, That
the General Council hereby declares its unswerving loyalty to our government and to
its Chief Executive, President Wilson, and that we hereby restate our fixed purpose to

The second strand of thought that mitigated the denomination's nonviolent witness was one whose presence was acknowledged even before the War Department's final approval of the pacifist resolution. In the May 19 issue of the Assemblies of God's official publication, *The Weekly Evangel*, an article intended to explicate the recently drafted resolution appeared. It explained that although the resolution's purpose was "to interpret as clearly as possible what the Scriptures teach on the subject," adherence to it would be voluntary, rather than obligatory. Concerning the adherence of church members to the position voiced by the resolution, the article noted that:

> It is not intended to hinder anyone from taking up arms who may feel free to do so, but we hope to secure the privilege of exemption from such military service as will necessitate the taking of life for all who are real conscientious objectors and who are associated with the General Council.[30]

What is more remarkable about each of these views is that they are a subtle representation of the very sort of establishmentarian Christianity that Pentecostalism's restorationist heritage led it to repudiate. Rather than seeing the state as being an agency of the world whose purposes were ultimately at odds with those of the kingdom of God, as did the restorationists, this more established way of thinking tended to see the state as an agent whose power could be employed in the service of the kingdom of God. What both views suggest is that the state is at the very least the necessary establisher and protector of a cluster of personal and institutional freedoms which are necessary for the good of the church.

A temptation toward accommodation has existed in even the most radically antiestablishment churches for most of the history of Christianity. This is partially the consequence of the evolution of ethics as a discrete discourse with little attachment to specific theological convictions; it has been widely held for some time that although women and men must be informed of the gospel message, they simply "know" right from wrong as a function of their being human.[31] "The realm of the social," notes John Howard Yoder, "is accordingly the one where the

---

assist in every way morally possible, consistent with our faith, in bringing the present 'World War' to a successful conclusion."

30. From *The Weekly Evangel*, 19 May 1917, 8.

31. John Howard Yoder, "The Authority of Tradition," in *Priestly Kingdom*, 72–73.

dynamics of accommodation and the tendencies to sell out are the strongest, as the church lives at the interface with the world of unbelief, its powers and pressures."[32]

Although Yoder suggests that the historical roots of this accommodation lie, among other places, in the church's gradual departure from its Jewish roots as it encountered the Hellenism of Asia Minor and southern Europe, he maintains that the most significant locus of the tendency is found in the church's legitimation of war. In this legitimation, he claims, "the view of Christians on the morality of violence in the public realm was reversed."[33] This acceptance of violence is not traceable to any theological position held by the earliest Christians, but instead represents a significant departure from the primitive Church's normative practices:

> The new stance rejects the privileged place of the enemy as the test of whether one loves one's neighbor. It rejects the norm of the cross and the life of Jesus Christ as the way of dealing with conflict. It assigns to civil government, not only to Caesar as an ecumenical savior figure but even, later, to fragmented local regimes, a role in carrying out God's will that is quite incompatible with the fruit of the progressive relativization of kingship from Samuel to Jeremiah to Jesus and Jochanan ben Zakkai.[34]

Although a number of particular sociopolitical factors could be cited as possible reasons for the church's acceptance of state violence, the most likely is almost certainly related to the fact that during the time of this acceptance the church had gradually come to enjoy a place of privilege in the Roman Empire. Yoder notes that the conversion of Constantine and the subsequent establishment of Christianity as the Roman state religion provide an appropriate symbolic representation of this transition. For when the leader of a government becomes Christian, he notes, "The assumption tends to be that in order to continue being a sovereign, he needs to continue to act the way a (non-Christian) sovereign 'naturally' acts, thereby creating some tension with what the later prophets and Jesus taught about domination, wealth, and violence."[35]

What Yoder suggests here, in other words, is that this Constantinian accommodation had its origins not in newly developed theological posi-

32. Ibid., 73.
33. Ibid., 73–74.
34. Ibid., 75.
35. Yoder, "The Kingdom as Social Ethic," in *Priestly Kingdom*, 82.

tions, but in the perceived need to create a space for the church to occupy a position of relative power and mutual affirmation with regard to the civil authorities. This abandonment of the particular ethical convictions of the Christian faith inevitably had a significant effect, however, on the ways in which the Church articulated its theology. Yoder notes a number of ways in which this is so; two of these are especially relevant to the changing attitude with regard to members of Assemblies of God congregations participating in state violence and therefore worth discussing here.

Yoder explains that the first significant theological shift in the Constantinian Church was toward a new ecclesiology and a new eschatology. In the New Testament church, prior to its being accepted as the state religion of Rome, the Christian community was an empirical entity, a visible, confessing gathering whose members were subject to active opposition by the state. With the establishment of Christianity, however, this situation was reversed. There were suddenly a variety of reasons to be a member of the church, and it became necessary to postulate the existence of an 'invisible' church, operating within the confines of the larger visible one; it was to this invisible community that those with genuine Christian faith were believed to belong.

In the pre-Constantinian church, Jesus was seen not only as risen savior but also as ascended Lord of the universe. The earthly powers, including the civil authorities, were believed to be under the control of Christ and were thus being used, in spite of their rebellious nature, to fulfill the purposes of God's kingdom. With the establishment of Christianity, however, this situation was also changed. The evidence of God's reign over history was no longer a matter of faith, but was instead plainly shown by the presence of the emperor, who was now at least nominally a Christian. According to Yoder, before Constantine

> one knew as a fact of everyday experience that there was a believing Christian community but one had to "take it on faith" that God was governing history. After Constantine, one had to believe without seeing that there was a community of believers, within the larger nominally Christian mass, but one knew for a fact that God was in control of history. Ethics had to change because one must aim one's behavior at strengthening the regime, and because the ruler himself must very soon have some appro-

bation and perhaps some guidance as he does things the earlier church would have disapproved of.[36]

The second of these theological/philosophical transitions came in the form of a changed view of history and the way changes within history were regarded. The established powers of civil government, and not the "average person or the weak person," were now seen as "the main bearer[s] of historical movement."[37] A church enjoying a position of favor with the government tends to adopt that government's "eulogistic" view of history whereby it is assumed that "the only way to read national and political history is from the perspective of the winners."[38] When the relative power of the existing regime increases, it is seen by the established church as a sign of God's blessing. Ultimate standards of right and wrong are thus changed: "A moral statement," says Yoder, "is tested first by whether a ruler can meet such standards."[39]

One might legitimately question whether any of this accurately represents the situation encountered by Pentecostal Christians in the United States of the early twentieth century. The answer to such a question, Yoder would say, is affirmative: "Perhaps the strongest proof of the great reversal," he notes, "is the fact that it survives even as the situations which brought it forth no longer obtain."[40] If anything, the form taken by Constantinian Christianity in modern democracies proves to be an even stronger corrosive force with regard to the faithfulness of the church:

> Once the separation of church and state is seen as theologically desirable, a society where this separation is achieved is not a pagan society but a society structured according to the will of God. American patriotism remains highly religious. For nearly two centuries, in fact, the language of American public discourse was not only religious, not only Christian, but specifically Protestant.

36. Yoder, "The Constantinian Sources of Western Social Ethics," in *Priestly Kingdom*, 136–37.

37. Ibid., 138.

38. Yoder, "Kingdom as Social Ethic," 95.

39. Ibid. Ostensibly, Yoder would agree to the addition of "and still maintain control" to this sentence. In *Christian Attitudes*, 259–61, he offers the example of the Quaker's peaceable rule in late seventeenth- and early eighteenth-century Pennsylvania, noting that it was faithfulness to their convictions (among which was the refusal to exert coercive force to maintain power), and *not* an unwillingness to rule that led them to hand over power to others.

40. Yoder, "Constantinian Sources," 141.

> Moral identification of church with nation remains despite in-
> stitutional separation . . . Let us call this arrangement "neo-
> neo-Constantinian." The social arrangement has been changed
> deeply and formally, but remains informally powerful.[41]

Those voices speaking from within the Assemblies of God that argued for the freedom of the individual to follow his conscience and the necessity of the state to preserve that freedom clearly represent an instance of Yoder's "neo-neo-Constantinian" disposition.[42] These voices, which were evidently present from the beginning in at least an embryonic form, eventually became a dominant force within the fellowship. This dominance may be accounted for on the basis of two interdependent factors, both of which continue to manifest their presence within contemporary American Christianity.

From the beginning, the twentieth century Pentecostal movement saw itself as uniquely carrying the burden of bringing salvation to a lost world about to experience Christ's return.[43] *The Weekly Evangel* article written to explain the adoption of the resolution on pacifism began not with a statement about the evils of war, but with the following claim about the mission of the fellowship:

> From its very inception, the Pentecostal Movement has been a
> movement characterized by evangelism, studiously avoiding any
> principles or actions which would thwart it in its great purpose.
> All the wings of the movement, which have grown out of the
> work that originated in the Southwestern States and the Pacific
> Coast are a unit in this respect.[44]

41. Ibid., 142.

42. I am grateful to my colleague Bill Cavanaugh for first pointing this out to me when I wrote a short unpublished essay on the philosophical foundations of the Assemblies' 1967 revocation of pacifism.

43. Blumhofer (vol. 1, p. 13) makes this point very well when she quotes Bennett Lawrence's *Apostolic Faith Restored* (a compilation of a series of articles written in 1916 for *The Weekly Evangel*), one of the earliest book-length accounts of contemporary Pentecostal Christianity: "This movement of God has resulted in the salvation of hundreds of thousands of sinners, both in so-called Christian lands and in those called heathen. . .hundreds have felt the missionary zeal of the first evangelists and have gone to the uttermost parts of the earth in one of the most spontaneous and widely spread missionary efforts the world has seen since the days of Pentecost."

44. *Weekly Evangel*, 4 August 1917, 6.

As in other sectors of Pentecostalism, evangelistic passion became the driving force in the Assemblies of God. Arguably, it was a concern to be as effective as possible in this regard that led the fellowship to make a series of small departures from the ethos represented by Pentecostalism's restorationist beginnings less than ten years earlier. Blumhofer notes:

> At least since 1916, the Assemblies of God had exhibited tendencies that separated it from other Pentecostal denominations . . .
>
> After they disowned Oneness advocates in 1916, Assemblies of God leaders opted for courses of action that distanced the denomination in important ways from what others regarded as the essence of Pentecostalism: The Assemblies of God became increasingly organized; it quickly developed educational institutions to train its ministers, encouraged affiliated churches to utilize various techniques for Christian education, developed an aggressive missionary program, implemented programs, and devised statistical measures of success.[45]

Evangelistic growth came, and the Assemblies of God quickly became the largest denomination in the Pentecostal movement.[46] It was the nature of this growth, suggests John Howard Yoder, which proved at least partially responsible for the ultimate abandonment of pacifism by the fellowship.

Their rapid success in numerical growth swept all kinds of additional people into the movement, many of whom had not restructured their views on anything except the gift of tongues. Their distinctiveness was located at other points that did not relate to critiquing Constantine or to the church as a distinctive community.

So Pentecostalism's original pacifism was rapidly diluted. Already in the first World War, when it was only a ten-or-fifteen year-old movement, pentecostal pacifism was softened in order to send people to evangelize among the troops. There was a beginning of a kind of awareness that we now call "church growth theory," namely, that you go where people are mobile and are worried and are away from home, not in their own cultural context, with a new message.[47]

The new members who swelled the ranks of Assemblies of God congregations (as well as those of the other parts of the Pentecostal

---

45. Blumhofer, *Assemblies of God* (vol. 2), 14–15.

46. Ibid., 15.

47. Yoder, *Christian Attitudes to War, Peace, and Revolution*, 309.

movement) during this time were women and men who had been at least somewhat conditioned by the neo-neo-Constantinian ethic of a still nominally Christian American culture. They had been trained by the highly religious rhetoric of late nineteenth-century patriotism and had come to believe that their nation was a special locus of divine activity.[48] The Social Gospel movement of the early twentieth century emerged, to some extent, as one of the progeny of this belief; its spokesperson Walter Rauschenbusch, while not going so far as to say that America was a uniquely Christian nation, did call for a repentance that could not be accomplished without the active involvement of the United States government.[49]

Rauschenbusch's claims were rooted first of all in his tendency to see Christianity as having deep philosophical affinities with democracy. He asserted that the Judaism of the early prophets, for which he expressed a tremendous admiration and of which both Jesus and John the Baptist had in his mind been faithful expressions, had been essentially democratic.[50] The United States was consequently positioned ideally before God in a way that other nations were not:

> In this absence of social caste and this fair distribution of the means of production, the early times of Israel were much like the early times in our own country. America too set out with an absence of hereditary aristocracy and with a fair distribution of the land among the farming population. Both the Jewish and the American people were thereby equipped with a kind of in-grained, constitutional taste for democracy which dies hard.[51]

48. See 140 n. 40, above.

49. I offer the following observations on Rauschenbusch based not upon any sort of perceived connection between his account of Christianity and that of the early Pentecostals, but rather on account of his rhetoric, which freely blended a call for repentance with the notion that such repentance was possible only in America. I am grateful to Dr. Gary Smith of Grove City College, who corrected my earlier assertion that Rauschenbusch was the Social Gospel movement's *founder*, rather than its spokesperson.

50. Walter Rauschenbusch, *Christianity and the Social Crisis* (Louisville: Westminster John Knox, 1991/1907), 13, 52–53. I am grateful to Dr. Stanley Hauerwas for this understanding of Rauschenbusch, and for highlighting the undeniable influence of Ernst Troeltsch on Rauschenbusch's work.

51. Rauschenbusch, *Christianity*, 15.

Democracy, Rauschenbusch maintained, was the essential notion underlying the founding of both Israel and the United States. As such, he maintained, it was also the fundamental principle of Christianity: "Approximate equality is the only enduring foundation for political democracy. The sense of equality is the only basis for Christian morality."[52] The problem, he believed, was that America, like Israel before it, had departed from the democratic ideals upon which it had been founded.[53] A return to these Jewish/Christian democratic ideals could be achieved only through the combined efforts of the church and the presumably democratic state:

> When the State supports morality by legal constraint, it cooperates with the voluntary moral power of the Church . . . When the Church implants religious impulses toward righteousness and trains the moral convictions of the people, it cooperates with the State by creating the most delicate and valuable elements of social welfare and progress . . . Church and State are alike but partial organizations of humanity for special ends. Together they serve what is greater than either: humanity. Their common aim is to transform humanity into the kingdom of God.[54]

The purpose of this digression is to display broadly the particular form taken by American neo-neo-Constantinian Christianity around the time that contemporary Pentecostalism was emerging and establishing its identity. The growth and subsequent institutionalization of the Pentecostal movement was rapid enough, as an earlier reference from Yoder indicates, that the community was unable to continue defining itself in ways consistent with its restorationist heritage. It is not unlikely that many of those entering the fellowship at least tacitly shared sentiments akin to those expressed by Rauschenbusch.

The departure of the Assemblies of God from restorationism reached a critical mass in the early 1940s, when the movement took its most significant steps toward an establishmentarian ecclesiology. In the minutes of the General Council of 1941, Article XVI of the Assemblies of God Bylaws still affirmed the Assemblies as a pacifist denomination. By this time the official position had been moderated only slightly through a combination of the initial pacifist resolution of 1917 with a

52. Ibid., 247.
53. Ibid., 15.
54. Rauschenbusch, *Christianity*, 380.

version of the loyalty resolution of 1918.[55] Yet, the movement's continued growth and prosperity made it increasingly difficult to maintain this
view; the Assemblies of God was on the verge of entering the evangelical
mainstream.

Beginning in 1940 there emerged a number of loosely related movements among fundamentalist Christians calling for the formation of an
organization that might counter the public influence of the mainstream
Protestant Federal Council of the Churches of Christ.[56] At the front of
these fundamentalists' minds was a concern that liberal Protestantism
represented a serious threat to their own freedoms; they were persuaded,
notes Blumhofer, that the Federal Council "had become . . . nothing less
than a front for those conspiring to subvert fundamentalists' civil and
religious liberties."[57] Their efforts culminated in a meeting in St Louis,
Missouri, in April, 1942, at which the Assemblies of God was represented
by a delegation of three; the organization founded there came to be
known as the National Association of Evangelicals, and the Assemblies of
God was counted among its members.[58]

The NAE of that day was characterized by what Blumhofer rightly
calls a "reverent patriotism," fueled by then-president Harold John
Ockenga's "grand vision for American culture." Ockenga's vision was for a
Christian America, and his rhetoric, which was both highly patriotic and
strongly anti-Catholic, was a product of his conservative Reformed theological heritage.[59] An excerpt from his address to the first Constitutional
Convention of the NAE is worth quoting at length:

> I believe that the United States of America has been assigned a
> destiny comparable to that of ancient Israel which was favored,
> preserved, endowed, guided, and used by God. Historically,
> God has prepared this nation with a vast and united country,
> with a population drawn from innumerable blood streams, with

55. What I here call a "slight" modification is arguably a significant one. Attached to
the original pacifist declaration is the statement, "At the same time the General Council
hereby declares its unswerving loyalty to our Government and to its Chief Executive,
and we purpose to assist the government in time of war in every way morally possible."
I take up the issue of Christian loyalty to government at some length below.

56. Blumhofer, *Assemblies of God* (vol. 2) 20–21.

57. Ibid., 21.

58. Ibid., 23–25. Blumhofer notes (211–12 n. 45) that the Assemblies of God soon
became the NAE's largest member denomination.

59. Ibid., 27, 29–30.

a wealth that is unequaled, with an ideological strength drawn from the traditions of classical and radical philosophy but with a government held accountable to law, as no government except Israel has ever been, and with an enlightenment in the minds of the average citizen which is the climax of social development.[60]

What is especially remarkable about this rhetoric is the fidelity with which it represents both Rauschenbusch's attitudes about Israel and the United States and Yoder's account of a neo-neo-Constantinian Christianity. Both Rauschenbusch and Ockenga express the tacit assumption that there is a sort of philosophical principle undergirding both Christianity and the United States Constitution and that this principle is in a sense more significant than the Gospel, which is but a historical manifestation of the principle. Given this perspective, it is fairly easy to understand how one could justify certain types of military action in order to preserve the principle. "It is hardly coincidence," notes Blumhofer, "that Assemblies of God views on war and country changed significantly at about the same time the denomination affiliated with the NAE."[61]

The most profound expression of the change Blumhofer mentions occurred at the General Councils of 1965 and 1967. By 1965 a significant number of questions had arisen concerning the official position as it stood to that time. A resolution was presented, calling for a special committee appointed by the Executive Presbytery to study the matter further.[62] At the 1967 Council the committee brought the following proposed modifications to what had become Article XXII of the denominational bylaws:

> WHEREAS, The 31st General Council in session requested the appointing of a committee to study the adequacy of our statement on Military Service as found in Article XXII of the Bylaws; and
> WHEREAS, Subsequently a duly appointed committee has carefully examined said Article XXII, together with the expressed opinions of chaplains, pastors, evangelists, and

---

60. Blumhofer, *Assemblies of God* (vol. 2) 30. Blumhofer takes this quote from p. 10 of Ben Hardin's letter in "United We Stand: NAE Constitutional Convention Report," taken from the Herbert J. Taylor papers at the Billy Graham Center Archives. Cf. Blumhofer, *Assemblies of God*, 210 n. 35, 212 n. 53.

61. Ibid., 212.

62. From the minutes of the 1967 General Council of the Assemblies of God, 14. Obtained from the Assemblies of God Archives in Springfield, Missouri.

correspondence from young men currently involved in the draft; therefore, be it

RESOLVED, That we retain Article XXII as it now appears in the Bylaws; and be it further

RESOLVED, That the following paragraph be added thereto: We hereby express our desire to continue to extend fellowship and sacramental ministries to those who do not choose non-combatant service.[63]

Given the rise of nationalistic sentiments in American evangelical-ism beginning in the 1940s, the position expressed by this amendment is surprisingly moderate. By resolving to "retain Article XXII as it now appears," a great respect is shown for the pacifist heritage of American Pentecostalism. The addition of the paragraph concerning the ecclesial status of those who did choose to take part in war was not a particularly new claim; it merely stated explicitly what had been implicit from the beginning. Clearly, however, the committee members wished to preserve as much of the denomination's traditional pacifism as they possibly could in the face of changing opinion.

This amended resolution, however, was not adopted. The minutes explain that its reading was followed by "[C]onsiderable discussion . . . concerning the Assemblies of God position on military service." During this discussion it was decided that the resolution should be re-referred to the committee and that the committee should be expanded by the addition of three members "representative of a cross section of the fellowship."[64] Three days later the expanded committee reported back to the Council, proposing a change much more significant than originally suggested:

WHEREAS the ideal world condition is that of peace, we as Christian citizens should use our influence in promoting peaceful solutions to world problems; and,

WHEREAS we live in a world in which there may arise inter-national emergencies which will lead our nation to resort to armed violence in the defense of its ideals, freedom, and na-tional existence; and

WHEREAS, our first loyalty is to God, we recognize neverthe-less that human government is ordained of God, and that

63. 1967 minutes, 14.
64. Ibid., 15.

there are obligations of citizenship that are binding upon us
as Christians; and,
WHEREAS we acknowledge the principle of individual freedom
of conscience as it relates to military service; therefore be it
RESOLVED, That Article XXII of The General Council Bylaws
be deleted and replaced with the following article:

Article XXII. Military Service
As a movement we affirm our loyalty to the government of
the United States in war or peace.
We shall continue to insist, as we have historically, on the
right of each member whether to declare his position as a combatant, a non-combatant, or a conscientious objector.[65]

What is more remarkable about this particular revision of Article
XXII (which the minutes note without remarks was passed and made
part of the official policy of the Assemblies of God[66]) is the clearly different rationality at work in contrast to the original resolution of 1917. That
particular article made an allowance for the place of civil government,
but was clearly more concerned to affirm the Christian position toward
violence described in the New Testament and interpreted by contemporary Pentecostalism. These were matters, said the original resolution, that
were presented quite plainly by the New Testament and which were to
be modeled by a faithful community. The "inspired Word of God," it had
claimed ". . . is the sole basis for our faith."[67]

No such reasoning is evidenced by the resolution of 1967. In contrast
to the original statement, which looked almost exclusively to Scripture
for its warrants, this article is void of any such references. It acknowledges
the peaceableness of an "ideal world" but insists that such a world is far
from being a present reality. It suggests that the real world is a violent one,
and in a violent world violence is sometimes necessary in the defense of
the good. That good is described variously here—as the "ideals, freedom,
and national existence" of "our nation," or "the principle of individual
freedom of conscience"—but it is always a good that exists in a realm of
principles and ideas rather than history, always a good whose preservation requires the support of the state. The clear implication is that the existence of the kingdom of God is dependent not upon God's acts toward

65. 1967 minutes, 35.

66. Ibid.

67. *Weekly Evangel*, 4 August 1917, 6.

and within a faithful Christian community, but upon a sword-bearing American state that can militarily defend the principles that make possible the existence of any Christian community at all.

Such reasoning is patently fallacious on historical and philosophical, as well as theological, grounds. The church has existed and can continue to exist as a minority community at odds, rather than in partnership, with the state. America's founding, moreover, was by no means an explicitly Christian event; as Mark Noll, Nathan Hatch, and George Marsden so succinctly put this matter in their book *The Search for Christian America*, "early America does not deserve to be considered uniquely, distinctly or even predominately Christian, if we mean by the word 'Christian' a state of society reflecting the ideals presented in Scripture. There is no lost golden age to which American Christians may return." If anything, they say, "evangelicals themselves were often partly to blame for the spread of secularism in contemporary American life."[68] The historical record suggests that the Constantinianism of the American church has operated to the detriment of the cause of the Gospel.

As the church has deepened and complicated its alliances with government, that deepening has demanded an ever-increasing reliance on principles and ideals and a corresponding abandonment of the scriptural accounts of Jesus and the church. The result, says John Howard Yoder, has, to say the least, been problematic:

> If *kenosis* is the shape of God's own self-sending, then any strategy of Lordship, like that of the kings of this world, is not only a strategic mistake likely to backfire but a denial of gospel substance, a denial which has failed even where it succeeded. What the churches accepted in the Constantinian shift is what Jesus rejected, seizing godlikeness, moving *in hoc signo* from Golgotha to the battlefield. If this diagnosis is correct, then the cure is not to update the fourth-century mistake by adding another "neo-" but to repent of the whole "where it's at" style and to begin again with *kenosis*.[69]

I stated at the beginning that the possibility for a return to pacifism still exists in American Pentecostalism based on the eschatological nature of its origins and the priority it gives the book of Acts among the New

68. Mark Noll, Nathan Hatch, and George Marsden, *The Search for Christian America* (Colorado Springs: Helmers & Howard, 1989) 17.

69. Yoder, "Constantinian Sources" 145.

Testament Scriptures. One might say that the way Pentecostals had been trained to read the Bible by their restorationist heritage gave them the sense that they were the contemporary manifestation of the 'last days' community founded in Acts. Although this imminent eschatological sense has been diminished by the passage of time and the relative institutionalization of Pentecostal communities, the privileging of Acts remains a contemporary characteristic of Pentecostalism. It is here, then, that I shall begin to develop a reconstructed theological argument for Pentecostal pacifism.

The Pentecostal arrival of the Holy Spirit in the book of Acts was clearly understood by the first Christians as an eschatological event. Jesus' promise of the imminent and powerful advent of the Holy Spirit was made in the context of his followers' questions concerning the final restoration of Israel (Acts 1:6–8), a promise sealed by the angelic assurance that he would "come in the same way as you saw him go into heaven" (Acts 1:11).[70] Peter's proclamation to those who were witnesses to the Spirit's coming, moreover, framed the Pentecost event in the context of the eschatological prophecy from the Old Testament book of Joel, by which God made the promise:

> In the last days it will be, God
> declares,
> that I will pour out my Spirit
> upon all flesh . . .
> Then everyone who calls on the
> name of the Lord shall be
> saved. (Joel 2:17, 21)

As I noted above, this eschatological aspect of the Pentecostal experience was a significant part of the way the earliest twentieth century Pentecostals understood themselves, some of which has continued to find expression up to the present day.[71] The sense that the coming of the Holy Spirit brings an empowerment by which the Christian community is made a radical community of witness to the life, death, and resurrection of Jesus still remains broadly palpable.[72] This sense, I believe, was the

70. All Scripture references, unless otherwise noted, are taken from the New Revised Standard Version.

71. Edith Blumhofer offers an account of the eschatological expectations of the restorationists in *Assemblies of God*, 1:2–26.

72. The 1993 Constitutional Declaration of the Assemblies of God, for example,

implicit basis for the Pentecostal social ethic that included a strong commitment to pacifism; it has also, however, served as the basis for a denial of the importance of social ethics in the face of an impending eschaton.[73] Dempster is thus correct in his assertion that Pentecostalism's failure to explicitly link its "distinctive testimony" to its early pacifism "has had, and continues to have, an almost lethal impact on the task of constructing a Pentecostal social ethic."[74] This link, however, continues to offer itself as a possibility through a reclamation of the moral significance of the story of Pentecost.

There are two particular reasons for making the story of Pentecost central to the recovery of a nonviolent Christian social ethic. The first of these reasons is literary. Stanley Hauerwas has argued that the Christian life has a particularly narrative character, and that this "narrative mode is neither incidental nor accidental to Christian belief. There is no more fundamental way to talk of God," he claims, "than in a story."[75] Stories are theologically fundamental because God's self-revelation is specifically narrative in its character; God has, in other words, revealed godself "in the history of Israel and in the life of Jesus."[76] Christians are "justified" and "sanctified" through our participation in this story; the use of this language requires that we remember, though, that these terms are "not meant to be descriptive of a status."

Indeed, part of the problem with those terms is that they are abstractions. When they are separated from Jesus' life and death, they distort Christian life. "Sanctification" is but a way of reminding us of the kind of journey we must undertake if we are to make the story of Jesus our story. "Justification" is but a reminder of the character of that story—namely what God has done for us by providing us with a path to follow.[77]

---

says that "the priority reason for being of the Assemblies of God is to be an agency of God for evangelizing the world . . . [it] exists expressly to give continuing emphasis to this reason-for-being in the New Testament apostolic pattern by teaching and encouraging believers to be baptized in the Holy Spirit, which enables them to evangelize in the power of the Spirit with accompanying supernatural signs . . ." From the *Minutes of the 45th Session of the General Council of the Assemblies of God*, 125.

73. Blumhofer, *Assemblies of God*, 1:24–25.

74. Dempster, "Reassessing the Moral Rhetoric," 32.

75. Stanley Hauerwas, *Peaceable Kingdom*, 25.

76. Ibid., 28.

77. Ibid., 94.

Participation in the stories of Israel and of Jesus rightly calls into question the supposition that Christians must calculate ways to protect themselves and to control their own existences; it names as a lie the notion that human existence in a world filled with violence necessarily relativizes the way of life presented in Jesus' life, death, and resurrection.[78] Such deceptive illusions are at the root of Christian participation in human violence, for they perpetuate the idea that "we are our own creators—and that only we can bestow meaning on our lives, since there is no one else to do so."[79]

Constructively, our participation in the Christian story offers an altogether different possibility for our existence, a possibility grounded in the claim that as we make the story of Jesus' life, death, and resurrection our own, we are brought into the immediacy of God's kingdom. The presence of this kingdom constitutes a substantive reality in which we are called to learn how to live.[80] We are thus able to see the world from a distinctively eschatological perspective.[81] As we are made part of a people who are learning to live according to this perspective, we are taught to understand not simply that God rules, but also "*how* God rules and the establishment of that rule through the life, death, and resurrection of Jesus."[82] It is through our participation in the world constituted in this rule that we may "learn to be creatures, to have characters appropriate to God's Lordship, to be redeemed."[83]

78. Ibid., 142.

79. Ibid., 94.

80. The work of George Lindbeck is especially helpful here. He notes in a discussion of the notion of intratextuality in his important book *The Nature of Doctrine* (Philadelphia: Westminster, 1984) that classical texts (of which the Christian Scriptures are ostensibly one example) "shape the imagination and perception of the attentive reader so that he or she forever views the world to some extent through the lenses they supply . . . These same considerations apply even more forcefully to the preeminently authoritative texts that are the canonical writings of religious communities. For those who are steeped in them, *no world is more real than the ones they create* . . . Intratextual theology redescribes reality within the scriptural framework rather than translating Scripture into extrascriptural categories. It is the text, so to speak, that absorbs the world, rather than the world the text" (116–17; 118).

81. I think here of Paul's take on this matter in 2 Cor 5:16: "From now on, therefore, we regard no one from a human point of view . . ."

82. Hauerwas, *Peaceable Kingdom*, 82–83.

83. Ibid., 69.

Among Christians, Pentecostals are uniquely well positioned to understand that peaceableness is central to lives that truthfully bear witness to the reality of this kingdom. For Pentecostals understand, by virtue of their privileging the story told in the book of Acts, that in baptizing Jesus' disciples in the Holy Spirit, God was acting definitively to create a new world and a new people capable of living in that world. Hence the remarkable change in the disciples' demeanor after Pentecost; they were a people, to borrow a phrase from Paul, who found themselves living in "a new creation" in which "everything has become new."[84]

The centrality of peaceableness to those who would live as witnesses to this new creation becomes apparent when the story of Pentecost is understood as one part of the entire story of God's life with God's people. For in Pentecost, notes Stanley Hauerwas, we see the restoration of that which was destroyed at Babel.[85] This destruction, which consisted in the scattering of humanity into "separate peoples isolated into homes, lands, and histories and no longer able to cooperate,"[86] was God's judgment on a people who believed they were capable of living without the acknowledgement of their own creatureliness, and hence without God.[87]

The consequence of the divisions created at Babel was the birth of war, "as the fear of the other became the overriding passion which motivated each group to force others into their story or to face annihilation."[88] The presence of difference became an intolerable one as each group sought to make itself the absolute standard for being human.

Humans became committed to destroying the other even if it meant their own death. Better to die than to let the other exist. To this day we thus find ourselves condemned to live in tribes, each bent on the destruction of the other tribes so that we might deny our tribal limits. Our histories become the history of war as we count our days by the battles of the past.[89]

---

84. 2 Cor 5:17. I am grateful to Dr. Richard Hays, as well as to Dr, Steve Long, both of whom have helped me see that the most satisfying translation of this passage is one that sees the phrase "new creation" as referring to the world itself, rather than to the individual believer.

85. Stanley Hauerwas, "The Church as God's New Language," in *Christian Existence Today* (Durham: Labyrinth, 1988) 48.

86. Hauerwas, "The Church," 49.

87. Ibid., 48.

88. Ibid., 49.

89. Ibid.

The story of Babel, however, is not the story of the ultimate fate of humankind. After the tragedy of Babel, the redemptive call of Abraham is issued, through whom "God creates a rainbow people so that the world might know that in spite of our sinfulness God has not abandoned us."[90] The story of Israel is thus born, and through Israel comes Jesus, whose life bears witness to the existence "of a new possibility of human, social, and therefore political relationships."[91] These are the relationships instantiated in the community called into existence by Jesus' proclamations concerning the reign of God; a community intended, as Yoder says, to be "a visible socio-political, economic restructuring of relations among the people of God, achieved by his intervention in the person of Jesus as the one Anointed and endued with the Spirit."[92]

Pentecost therefore represents a culmination of the story begun with the call of Abraham, a story of God's gracious response to the tragedy of Babel. Those Jews who had gathered in Jerusalem for the festival came from all over the world and spoke a multitude of different languages. The glossolalia engendered by the coming of the Spirit was heard by each of them in his or her own language, a sign that in Pentecost God had begun the final work of gathering together the world's scattered peoples into one new people.[93] The remarkable life of the newly created community, including the signs and wonders done by the Apostles and the free sharing of resources, was a sign that Jesus' promise of power sufficient for the faithful bearing of witness was being fulfilled.[94] The hostilities arising from the divisions established at Babel were overcome.

The glossolalia of Pentecost represents the Spirit's creation of a new language that is not restricted to the utterance of words. "It is instead a community whose memory of its Savior creates the miracle of being a people whose very differences contribute to their unity."[95] This is the community called the church,[96] the community which looks forward to the time when God will complete the work of gathering together "a great multitude that no one can count, from every nation, from all tribes and

---

90. Ibid.

91. John Howard Yoder, *The Politics of Jesus* (Grand Rapids: Eerdmans, 1972) 63.

92. Yoder, *Politics*, 39.

93. Hauerwas, "Church," 50.

94. See Acts 2:42–47.

95. Hauerwas, "Church," 53.

96. Ibid.

peoples and languages, standing before the throne and before the Lamb, robed in white, with palm branches in their hands."[97] The existence of such a people is surely a sign that "we really do have an alternative to Babel, to fear of one another, and finally then to war. Even more happily it means that insofar as we are the church, we do not just have an alternative, we are the alternative. We do not have a story to tell but in the telling we *are* the story being told."[98]

Pentecostals, of all such people, ought to be faithful embodiments of this story. For it is our "distinctive testimony" that at Pentecost God made possible the existence of a community whose willingness to live "filled with the Spirit" makes present to the world the reality of God's kingdom. A reality centered around so peaceable a vision certainly precludes any level of participation in killing. May we be transformed by the recovery of this vision.[99]

---

97. Rev 7:9.

98. Hauerwas, "Church," 54.

99. I am especially grateful to the staff of the Assemblies of God Archives in Springfield, Missouri, for their assistance in gathering a number of the materials used in the composition of this essay, and to Dr. Grant Wacker, who directed me to the work of Murray Dempster.

# 6

# Prophetic "Patriotic" Pentecostal Peacemaking

## Early Assemblies of God Pacifism and the Twentieth Century[1]

### Paul Alexander

The blending of nationalism and the body of God reminds me of one of the most violent games ever invented, and one of my favorites, an entertainment that unites emperor and clergy, military and peasantry in an attempt to defeat the enemy and perpetuate one's own kingdom. The game, of course, is chess. On the chessboard, the bishops, the representatives of the people of God, stand closest to the king and queen—they are even closer than the cavalry (the knights) or the siege towers (the rooks).

---

1. This chapter is a revised version of "Speaking in the Tongues of Nonviolence: American Pentecostals, Nationalism, and Nonviolence," *Evangelical Review of Society and Politics: An Interdisciplinary Journal for the Christian Analysis of Social and Political Issues* 1:2 (2007) 1–19. I also presented an earlier version of this chapter at the American Academy of Religion/Southwest Commission on Religious Studies on Saturday, March 4, 2006, in Dallas, Texas, three days before Southwestern Assemblies of God University in Waxahachie, Texas, informed me that my faculty contract would not be renewed. I later learned that a well-meaning student at the conference had given a copy of this paper to his Assemblies of God pastor, who passed it on to university administration.

Chess is a great pastime, but it portrays a rather unfaithful theology and practice: the church entangled with the empire, seeking first its kingdom, striking at an angle for the color of its national kin. In real life, nationalism and the body of God form a lethal combination.

We are now at the one hundredth anniversary of the Azusa Street revival in Los Angeles, California (1906–1909). Pastored by William Seymour (1870–1922), an African-American from Louisiana, this revival greatly influenced the birth of the Pentecostal Charismatic movement that now numbers almost six hundred million people around the world, representing over twenty-five percent of global Christianity.[2] What is the nature of the relationship between Pentecostalism and the nationalistic violence represented in the game of chess?

Robert Beckford has noted that "at the heart of the birth of Pentecostalism was an anti-oppressive focus expressed in *glossolalia*— speaking in tongues. . . . William Seymour linked *glossolalia* with social transformation [and his] church developed an anti-racist, anti-sexist and anti-classist ministry."[3] Though scholars dispute the extent and duration of these characteristics,[4] I would like to explore whether we may add anti-nationalist and anti-violent to the list of first generation Pentecostal impulses. Do American Pentecostals have the historical and theological resources to critique nationalism and war? Beckford claims, "Azusa street teaches us that the Spirit of God is a force for challenging social structures that discriminate in the world today," and that it was a "socio-political happening with profound effects for ecclesiology." If this statement is true, one might anticipate finding early Pentecostal voices prophetically critiquing politics and cultures. Indeed, research affirms that many first generation Pentecostals encouraged interethnic worship when doing so was dangerous to their persons and their families, they promoted women in ministry and leadership before women could even vote in the United

2. "Global Statistics" in Stanley M. Burgess, editor, *The New International Dictionary of Pentecostal and Charismatic Movements* (Grand Rapids: Zondervan, 2002) 287.

3. Robert Beckford, "Back to My Roots: Speaking in Tongues for a New *Ecclesia*" (The Bible in TransMission, Summer 2000) 2. Also see *Dread and Pentecostal: A Political Theology for the Black Church in Britain* (London: SPCK, 2000).

4. See Mel Robeck, *The Azusa Street Revival and Mission* (Nashville: Nelson, 2006); Estrelda Alexander, *The Women of Azusa Street* (Cleveland: Pilgrim, 2005); and Leslie Callahan, "Fleshly Manifestations: Charles Fox Parham's Quest for the Sanctified Body" (PhD diss., Princeton University, 2002).

States, and they opposed war vociferously though it meant they might be tarred, feathered, jailed, or shot.

Harvey Cox has observed that in U.S. Pentecostal circles speaking in tongues often functions simply as performance rather than as "protest or as prophecy."[5] The chess-set worldview often lacks Spirit-empowered prophets who, by their protest, provide an alternative to nationalistic and violent civil religion. Yet many first generation Pentecostals believed that God poured out the Spirit to create just such a community to speak truth to power. Though not always received as a gift by either the church or the world, perhaps the Pentecostal movement can yet offer something prophetic in these days of imperialism and war.

Such a contribution would have to include a critique of the power and place of nationalism (from *ethnos*, ethnicity) and patriotism (from *pater*, father) while encouraging the nonviolent faithfulness of the church. Early Pentecostals addressed these identity-challenging and character-transforming issues by carefully critiquing both patriotism and nationalism, "Christians must lose their national preferences and prejudices. . . . God's people must all get to this place, where national prejudices must die and where the glory of God only will be sought."[6] The (predominantly Anglo) Assemblies of God (AOG) and the (predominantly African-American) Church of God in Christ (COGIC), along with the majority of Pentecostal denominations, professed that Christians should not "participate in war or armed resistance which involves the actual destruction of human life since this is against the clear teachings of the inspired Word of God which is the sole basis of our faith."[7] I long to draw from the wells of Pentecostalism to discover, explore, encourage, and refine a prophetic community able to withstand the fierce gales of nationalistic pride and militarism. I hope to reveal that Pentecostals have been powerful witnesses to the conviction that the holy Christian *ethnos* transcends not only race, gender, and culture, but also political borders. I pray that doing so will inspire present day Pentecostal communities to embody, in both belief and practice, the non-nationalistic, nonviolent, peaceable

5. Harvey Cox, *Fire From Heaven* (Reading, MA: Addison-Wesley, 1995) 297.

6. J. Roswell Flower, "What Will the Harvest Be? Article in Last Week's Evangel Receiving Just Criticism," *Weekly Evangel*, 14 August 1915, 2.

7. "The Pentecostal Movement and the Conscription Law," *The Weekly Evangel*, 4 August 1917, 6.

theology of many early Christian communities and their own Pentecostal forerunners.

## EARLY ASSEMBLIES OF GOD PACIFISM AS A MAJORITY WITNESS

Grant Wacker proposed that the AOG only "permitted a variety of views in its official publication until 1917, when the United States entered the conflict" and that "after May [1917], no more articles supporting pacifism appeared in official publications."[8] However, extensive evidence shows that the AOG published pacifist articles and encouraged conscientious objection and noncombatant service during American participation in World War I[9] and continued to do so after the war ended, throughout the 1920s and 1930s, and into the early 1940s.[10] Furthermore, attempts

8. Grant Wacker, *Heaven Below* (Cambridge: Harvard University Press, 2001) 243, 245. A more thorough treatment of this issue is in Paul Alexander, *Peace to War: Shifting Allegiances in the Assemblies of God* (Telford, PA: Herald, 2009).

9. The following authors argued for pacifism and conscientious objection in 1917 and 1918, during World War I. These were all printed in *The Weekly Evangel* (which later became *The Pentecostal Evangel*). Baron D'Estournelles de Constant, "The Sinister Education of War," *The Weekly Evangel*, 20 January 1917, 2. "What is War?" *The Weekly Evangel*, 21 April 1917, 2. "The Crisis," *The Weekly Evangel*, 21 April 1917, 7. Samuel H. Booth-Clibborn, "The Christian and War. Is it too Late?," *The Weekly Evangel*, 28 April 1917, 5. "Compulsory Military Service: An English Conscientious Objector's Testimony," *The Weekly Evangel*, 28 April 1917, 7. Samuel H. Booth-Clibborn, "The Christian and War," *The Weekly Evangel*, 19 May 1917, 4. J. W. Welch, "An Explanation," *The Weekly Evangel*, 19 May 1917, 8. "The Pentecostal Movement and the Conscription Law," *The Weekly Evangel*, 4 August 1917, 6. "The Pentecostal Movement and the Conscription Law," *The Weekly Evangel*, 5 January 1918, 5. Oscar Barl, "Reports From the Field: Fort Riley, Kansas," *The Weekly Evangel*, 19 October 1918, 14. A. B. Cox, "In Prison and Out Again," *The Weekly Evangel,* 29 June 1918, 14. Arthur Sydney Booth-Clibborn, "Nigh, Even At The Doors," 7 September 1918, 2.

10. The following authors argued for pacifism and conscientious objection in the years following World War I and during World War II. Lydia Hatfield, "The Law of Christ for Believers," *The Christian Evangel*, 12 July 1919, 3. Arthur Sydney Booth-Clibborn, "European Pentecostal Notes," *The Pentecostal Evangel*, 6 March 1920, 11. D. M. Panton, "Coming War," *The Pentecostal Evangel*, 25 November 1922, 10. Stanley H. Frodsham, "From The Pentecostal Viewpoint," *The Pentecostal Evangel*, 21 June 1924, 4. Donald Gee, "War, the Bible, and the Christian," *The Pentecostal Evangel*, 8 November 1930, 6. Donald Gee, "War, the Bible, and the Christian," *The Pentecostal Evangel*, 15 November 1930, 2. "War Behind the Smoke Screen," *The Pentecostal Evangel*, 6 December 1930, 3. Ernest S. Williams, "In Case of War," *The Pentecostal Evangel*, 19 March 1938, 4. "The Christian and War," *The Pentecostal Evangel*, 29 July 1939, 2. "War and Christianity," *The Pentecostal Evangel*, 23 September 1939, 10. Edmund B. Chaffee, "The Early Church and the Sword," *The Pentecostal Evangel*, 27 January 1940, 3.

to change the pacifist article in the constitution and bylaws of the AOG failed in the late 1940s and were unsuccessful until 1967. This timeline alone shows that pacifism was a significant part of American Pentecostal tradition that did not disappear during World War I.

In the spring and summer of 1918, Americans experienced the announcement of the Selective Service Act (May 18, 1917) and the wide unveiling of the famous "I Want You" posters, amid extremely high patriotism and popular support for the war. At this time, with American flags draping buildings and avenues throughout the United States, the executive presbytery of the AOG confidently proclaimed that "the principles of the General Council were in opposition to war from its very beginning" and that "the General Council meets every requirement of the law relating to religious bodies . . . whose religious principles are opposed to participation in war."[11] This witness by the AOG, in the face of intense nationalism and support for the war, led the U.S. government to correctly recognize it as a pacifist church. The anti-combatant articles continued to significantly outnumber the pro-combatant articles in the AOG publications.

Wacker surmised, "no one requested prayers for conscientious objectors. . . . One can only assume that they were either too few to count or that editors screened out such requests, knowing how most readers would react."[12] Yet the April 28, 1917 edition carried exactly such a request, along with the testimony of a Pentecostal conscientious objector.[13] Wacker reasons that published prayer requests for soldiers demonstrated a lack of commitment to conscientious objection, yet the very issue he quotes (October 5, 1918) also contained Arthur Booth-Clibborn's article advocating nonviolence, "the true conscientious objector is the sort of Christian who is gladly willing to go unarmed among the savage heathen, far beyond the 'protecting' reach of a six inch shell. He is equally willing to dispense with all 'protection' in 'civilized lands.'"[14]

11. Ibid., 7.

12. Wacker, *Heaven Below*, 247.

13. "Compulsory Military Service: An English Conscientious Objector's Testimony," *The Weekly Evangel*, 7.

14. Arthur Sydney Booth-Clibborn, "Nigh, Even At The Doors," 5 October 1918, 6. It was possible that Booth-Clibborn purposely contradicted E. N. Bell's earlier appeal to American forces for the protection of Pentecostal missionaries. E. N. Bell, "Wars and the Missionaries," *The Christian Evangel*, 12 September 1914, 1.

E. N. Bell (1866–1923), General Superintendent of the AOG in 1914 and from 1920–1923, supported Christian participation in war more than any other leader in the early AOG. Wacker suggested that "there is no evidence that any elected official within the denomination publicly resisted Bell or his point of view."[15] However, ample evidence indicates that at least thirteen different authors wrote articles in the *Evangel* that opposed Bell's view. These included three General Superintendents, two General Secretaries who also served as editors of *The Pentecostal Evangel* for a combined thirty-six years, and a college dean.[16]

In fact, shortly after Bell's death the "darkening clouds" of war prompted an article by elected leader and editor Stanley Frodsham in which he encouraged constituents to refrain from participation should the occasion arise. He quoted a Quaker resolution passed in Philadelphia that called violence "unchristian" and renounced "all participation in war."[17] He then stated:

> When the editor [Stanley Frodsham] of the paper [*The Pentecostal Evangel*] received a copy and handed the same to the Chairman of the Council [General Superintendent], Brother Welch expressed the warmest sympathy for the sentiments of the Friends. The statement on our Council minutes concerning nonparticipation in war is somewhat stronger than the above.[18]

Frodsham confidently and rightly recognized that the AOG's own stance against war was stricter than that of the Quakers themselves, and this in 1924. While in wartime Bell cautiously supported the authority of the Christian's individual conscience to allow him to fight, those preceding him and most of those following him for the next two decades consistently presented conscientious objection as the Pentecostal path of faithfulness.

Even while Bell was General Superintendent, several articles promoting pacifism were published. In 1920 Arthur Booth-Clibborn claimed

15. Wacker, *Heaven Below*, 247.

16. John W. Welch, Earnest S. Williams, and Donald Gee (in Great Britain) were superintendents and Burt McCafferty was a college dean and founding member of the Assemblies of God. Stanley Frodsham was elected as General Secretary (1916), Missionary Treasurer (1917), and then editor of all Assemblies of God publications (1921–1949). J. Roswell Flower, also a founding member of the Assemblies of God, served as its first Secretary-Treasurer (1914) and founder and first editor of the *Evangel* (1913–1920). He continued in elected leadership until 1959.

17. Frodsham, "From The Pentecostal Viewpoint," 4.

18. Ibid. Emphasis added.

that any participation in warfare cheapened both Calvary and Pentecost and was "a disaster of untold magnitude."[19] In 1922 the *Evangel* printed an article by D. M. Panton (1870–1955) which stated:

> The Church's right attitude to war [is to] at least refuse to partici-
> pate in war herself, and so make good her profession of peace.
> In the first two centuries of our era, so swordless was the Church
> of Christ, that Celsus, the Gnostic, in the first written attack
> ever made on the Christian Faith, grounds his censure on this
> very fact, and says: The State receives no help in war from the
> Christians.[20]

Bell did not represent the majority attitude of the AOG, and the pacifists seemed not to be the minority voice. Rather, it seems that Bell was nearly a lone voice unable to silence conscientious objectors. Pacifist authors contributed articles to the primary AOG publications before, during, and after Bell's time in office.

In fact, a peace witness within the AOG persisted right up to World War II. In 1938 the General Superintendent of the AOG in the United States reprinted the pacifist position statement, wanting to reflect on war "while free from the emotional effects of such events."[21] He desired to "assist the thinking of our youth in the event that they should be called for military service," and emphasized the nonviolence to which the AOG committed itself. "Could not such a one [if drafted] serve as a cook, a helper in a hospital, a stretcher carrier, a driver of an ambulance, or of a truck? There are many services which one could fulfill without 'armed resistance which involves the actual destruction of human life.'"[22]

In 1939 the *Evangel* published articles declaring, "War does not fit in with the teaching and example of our Lord Jesus Christ. This is in accordance with the Christian teaching of the first three centuries," and "it was usual for a soldier to lay down his sword when he accepted the truth of Christ. The declaration of faith has become historic: 'I am a Christian, and therefore I cannot fight.'"[23] A powerful promotion of conscientious

19. Arthur Booth-Clibborn, "European Pentecostal Notes," 11.

20. D. M. Panton, "Coming War," 10. Although Panton was not a Pentecostal, Stanley Frodsham quoted his articles quite often from 1919–1925. Panton also founded and edited the British end-times periodical *The Dawn*.

21. Williams, "In Case of War," 4.

22. Ibid.

23. *The Pentecostal Evangel*, 29 July 1939, 2. *The Pentecostal Evangel*, 23 September

objection by Donald Gee, the leader of the AOG in Britain, appeared in May, 1940.[24] The timing of the release of this article, by the American AOG, revealed that they tried to hold to their peace witness. One month later the American General Superintendent quoted the *Pacifist Handbook* as listing the AOG, with 173,349 members, as the third largest church in America that "opposed . . . war."[25] He then said, "The AOG may well be classified among the 'conscientious objectors.' It is doubtful that it could be classified among the unqualified 'pacifists,' since it is pledged to 'assist the Government in time of war in every way morally possible.'"[26] As late as October, 1940 the *Evangel* proclaimed that the "*universal* feeling in the ranks of the AOG [is] that military service is incompatible with the gospel of Jesus Christ, and that a Christian cannot fully follow the teachings of his Lord and Master if he engages in armed conflict."[27] The author exhorted the constituency to be sure that they were true conscientious objectors and not just "hid[ing] behind the position of the church to which they belong."[28] He also recommended the *Pacifist Handbook*. The leaders of the AOG, in 1940, claimed that the "general belief" of AOG members was that combatant participation in war was wrong.[29] While the sincerity of this claim can be doubted, it is significant that AOG leadership continued to teach conscientious objection.

Due to the significant participation of AOG men in World War II, the 1947 General Council appointed a committee to evaluate the appropriateness of the article on military service. They realized that their actions as a fellowship had not exactly corresponded to their stated position. However, the committee reported that they had not found it necessary to change the position:

---

1939, 10.

24. Donald Gee, "Conscientious Objection," 4.

25. Ernest S. Williams, "The Conscientious Objector," 4. The two larger ones were the Churches of Christ (433,714) and the Brethren (192,588). The Quakers were listed as having 105,917 members.

26. Ibid.

27. "The Attitude of the General Council Toward Military Service," *The Pentecostal Evangel*, 13. Emphasis added. Based upon the context of the other articles that supported noncombatant service, this article probably referred to combatant military service.

28. Ibid.

29. Ibid.

> After considerable thought and prayer on this very vital subject, your committee feels that it will be unable to formulate an article on Military Service that will better represent the attitude of the AOG than that which is now a part of our General Council By-laws.[30]

They adopted this report *without debate*. One may question the popularity of AOG pacifism in 1947, but its ministers and elected officials unequivocally opted to maintain pacifist doctrine. Perhaps, at this point, the fellowship was hesitant to undermine its strongly worded and Jesus- focused scriptural support for nonviolence, or perhaps so much of the leadership still agreed with it that they did not want to change it. Whatever the explanation, the AOG reaffirmed its pacifist doctrine in 1947. Their statement would stand another twenty years before the Vietnam-era constituency finally deleted it.

My research into pacifism within the early AOG, and early Pentecostalism in general, supports those scholars who argue that pacifism was early Pentecostalism's majority position.[31] First generation Pentecostals wrote about and promoted conscientious objection in official publications quite often, denominational leadership continued to support the stance publicly until at least 1941, and the constituency reaffirmed it in 1947. Furthermore, the "quite a large number"[32] of conscientious objectors and noncombatants in the third largest peace church in America during World War II is best explained by the interpretation that first generation Pentecostals integrated pacifism deeply and broadly into their worldview.

Perhaps this reading of AOG history provides Pentecostals today with a "usable past" that, while certainly not flawless, can be legitimately employed to help them imagine Pentecostal practices of faithfulness that

---

30. *General Council Minutes*, 1947, 13.

31. Jay Beaman, *Pentecostal Pacifism: The Origin, Development, and Rejection of Pacific Belief Among the Pentecostals*. Foreword by John Howard Yoder (Hillsboro, KS: Center for Mennonite Brethren Studies, 1989); Roger Robins, "A Chronology of Peace: Attitudes Toward War and Peace in the Assemblies of God: 1914–1918," *Pneuma* 6 (Spring 1984) 3–25; Howard Kenyon, "An Analysis of Ethical Issues in the History of the Assemblies of God, (PhD diss., Baylor University, 1988); Dwight J. Wilson, "Pacifism," in *Dictionary of Pentecostal and Charismatic Movements*, edited by Stanley M. Burgess and Gary B. McGee (Grand Rapids: Zondervan, 1988).

32. J. Roswell Flower, "The Plight of the Christian in the Present World War," *The Pentecostal Evangel*, 12 June 1943, 6.

are less nationalistic and less violent than those of the contemporary American AOG. Harold Bender (1897–1962), a prominent Mennonite theologian, and many of his students, one of whom was John Howard Yoder (1927–1997), provided just such a "usable past" for Mennonites by carefully studying sixteenth-century Anabaptism.[33] Mark Thiessen Nation observes that this past was "usable" because "what was learned from the sixteenth century was to be used to bring critique and renewal to contemporary Mennonite life."[34] Yoder himself explained that they had

> gone beyond studying the Anabaptists and admiring their depth of conviction and reached the conclusion that on many points they were right and should be followed. The claim is not that the Anabaptist movement was infallible but that on a surprising number of points they were led to right answers which retain an exemplary value for our time.[35]

Yoder devoted his life to directing this message toward "both Mennonites and non-Mennonites."[36]

It should be clear from the work in this book that a usable past does not have to be fabricated; it emerges organically from a careful examination of the primary sources. Early Pentecostals, as fallible as they were, identified, adopted, and proclaimed a faithful theology when they took their stand as peace churches. I hope that subsequent historical revisionism, which perhaps reflects embarrassment about our early peace witness, can be corrected, making way for Pentecostal peacemaking theology to resurface. To one beginning attempt we now turn.

## PROPHETIC PATRIOTIC PENTECOSTAL PEACEMAKING, OR SPIRIT-EMPOWERED NON-NATIONALISTIC NONVIOLENCE

First generation American Pentecostals prophetically protested violence and nationalism. They combined the practices of biblical interpretation and social critique. They focused on Jesus, highlighting the biblical themes of justice, peace, mission, the Kingdom of God, and Spirit em-

33. Albert N. Keim, *Harold S. Bender, 1897–1962* (Scottdale, PA: Herald, 1998) 33.

34. Mark Thiessen Nation, *John Howard Yoder: Mennonite Patience, Evangelical Witness, Catholic Convictions* (Grand Rapids: Eerdmans, 2006) 42.

35. John Howard Yoder, "What Are Our Concerns?" *Concern* 4 (1957) 20–21, as quoted in Nation, *John Howard Yoder*, 43.

36. Ibid.

powerment. These contrasted with their analysis of the social situation of the world: one they saw marred by injustice, war, jingoism, and xenophobia. American Pentecostals have, in their heritage, the theological resources to critique contemporary nationalism and war, and should seek a post-critical re-appropriation of this counter-cultural witness. I propose prophetic "patriotic" peaceable Pentecostalism as a possible way forward.

First, the prophets of God name and expose injustices and violence among the people of God, then they do so in all the nations of the world. *Vox populi* (the voice of the people) and *realpolitik* (pragmatic politics) do not determine their actions or dictate their messages. They humbly and powerfully speak the words of God in a sinful world, and as a result often experience popularity problems: the kings tortured Jeremiah, the empire and the religious elite crucified Jesus, and an assassin's bullet felled Dr. King.

A historically important passage of Scripture for Pentecostals is Acts 2, part of which is a quotation from Joel, "in the last days I will pour out my Spirit upon all flesh. Your sons and your daughters will prophesy . . ." To prophesy, even to be eschatologically driven, is not to predict the imminent end of all things; rather it is to speak courageously in public, in the tradition of biblical prophets, about the idolatry of nationalism, about hoarding wealth at the expense of the poor, and about dependence on military strength and violence for security. This prophetic voice was one significant reason why Pentecostals were disliked by both liberal and fundamentalist Christians in the early twentieth century. Pentecostals blamed compromising Christians for slavery, massacres of Native Americans, and war. The charismatic prophet today, if influenced by these aspects of early Pentecostalism, would illuminate connections between a complicit church and the injustice and violence of the state. This places her in a dangerous tradition.

Second, American Christians of almost every political type argue about who is the most patriotic. Anti-war folk consider the most patriotic action in support of the military and the nation would have been to forego the invasion of Iraq in 2003. They would bring the troops home now (or soon). Those who support the war in Iraq say they are being patriotic by continuing the fight. Most want to be considered American patriots and cherish the label. But the prophetic, politically radical, Pentecostal Christian need not seek that title. Many early Pentecostals would have said, "You think I am not patriotic; perhaps your patriotism is a worshipping of false gods." Nevertheless, patriotism is a powerful concept that may be put to work within the Pentecostal prophetic tradition.

Pentecostals are called to be citizens and patriots in the Kingdom of God, a kingdom that, according to Christian claims, transcends and outlasts all other kingdoms, empires, and states. Pentecostalism highlights this important biblical theme as a true freedom. It enables an internationalism not captivated by or subordinated to any particular nation. Prophetic patriotic Pentecostals should be able to say again, "we speak without fear or favor, we favor no country," for Yahweh is our God and God's kingdom transcends and outlasts all other kingdoms and nations. To be eschatologically driven is to live *now* in Jesus' "kingdom that will never pass away."

I advocate neither withdrawal from society nor abdication of one's ethnicity, nationality or gender, but a thoroughly Christian relationship to each. I think Miroslav Volf achieves a reasonably healthy balance with his explanation of distance and belonging. [37] Like Abraham, we must depart our country (national loyalties), cut the ties that so profoundly define us, and become strangers. [38] Jacob Neusner demonstrates how monotheistic traditions (Christianity, Judaism, and Islam), "insist upon the triviality of culture and ethnicity, forming trans-national, or trans-ethnic transcendental communities." [39] Like Muslims or Jews who place their faith above their nationality, we Pentecostals should never be Nigerian, Mexican, Korean, British, or American first, for "at the very core of Christian identity lies an all-encompassing change of loyalty, from a given culture with its gods to the God of all cultures." [40]

But departure and distance need not end in isolation, empty identity, or disdain or contempt for one's nationality, ethnicity, or gender. We remain embodied selves of a particular hue, gender, ethnicity, and nationality. Our "bodily inscribed differences are brought together" in the Pentecostal unity of the Spirit who "does not erase bodily inscribed

---

37. Miroslav Volf, *Exclusion and Embrace: A Theological Exploration of Identity, Otherness, and Reconciliation* (Nashville: Abingdon, 1997) 35–55. Volf was reared in a Pentecostal pacifist home in Croatia.

38. Volf, *Exclusion and Embrace*, 39.

39. Jacob Neusner, "Christmas and Israel: How Secularism Turns Religion into Culture." In *Christianity and Culture in the Crossfire*, edited by Daved Hoekema et al. (Grand Rapids: Eerdmans, 1997). As quoted in Volf, *Exclusion and Embrace*, 39.

40. Volf, *Exclusion and Embrace*, 40.

differences" but grants access to all.[41] Our particularities and genealogies matter, as do our nationalities, but we resist the temptation to ascribe any religious or holy significance to them. To de-sacralize, to take the "holy" away from one's nation, especially America at this point in history, is radical and can sound treasonous, but it is necessary. Ultimately, our allegiance belongs to God and *Christ's* body is the Holy Nation (*ethnos hagion*).

How then do we live? Departure and distance are not spatial categories but "take place within the cultural space one inhabits."[42] Therein, we belong within our particular cultures, nations, and ethnic groups, and do not have to leave them, but they should never be the primary source of a Christian's identity. We must have belonging and distance. "Belonging without distance destroys," for if I'm so white that I can't love a black sister, I'm too white. If I'm so American that I can't love a Palestinian, I'm too American. As a Pentecostal preacher might say, "if I bleed red, white, and blue then I need a blood transfusion so I can bleed Jesus." "Distance without belonging isolates" and can degenerate into living a hateful and exclusive way of life that expresses unchristian vitriol toward one's own nation, ethnicity, or gender. Pentecostals should be truth tellers who speak as honestly as their perceptions allow about the good, the bad, the ugly, and the beautiful in any nation.

Third, Pentecostals have a strong history of pacifism, though they have shunned the label. They did not passively avoid conflict; they did risk their lives for the gospel. But, they ejected the belief that Christians should kill for their own safety or for the preservation of their nations. Prophetic patriotic peacemaking is non-nationalistic and nonviolent, but not as a position in response to a nation or war, per se.[43] It proceeds from a conviction that the peasant from Galilee, Jesus of Nazareth, revealed the way of God to the world *and* that the Spirit of this God empowers the followers of Jesus to prophetically challenge the idolatrous nationalism that requires the sacrifice of its enemies for its own continued existence.

John Howard Yoder noted that early Pentecostal pacifism "wrought by the synergy of enthusiasm. . .did not mature into a solid ethical

41. Ibid., 48.

42. Ibid., 49.

43. See Lisa Sowle Cahill, *Love Your Enemies: Discipleship, Pacifism, and Just War Theory* (Minneapolis: Fortress, 1996).

hermeneutic."[44] I agree and hope to rectify this, and am not the first to call for the restoration of peacemaking among Pentecostals.[45] I echo Yoder to claim that Pentecostalism calls the whole church to nonviolence in ways not readily accessible within the Historic/Living Peace Churches. Having drunk deeply at the Pentecostal and Anabaptist wells, I am convinced that the most faithful and authentic Pentecostal witness practices nonviolent and proactive peacemaking.[46] Peacemaking in Pentecostalism can be a gift to the church, particular in its inflections, and is at the core of our truest identity.

The majority of Pentecostals in the world are not citizens of the United States. Only five percent of the AOG's forty-eight million adherents are in the USA. This is significant because the majority of Anglo Pentecostals in America practices nationalism and enthusiastically supports war.[47] Yet the passionate and articulate multi-ethnic voices in Pentecostal history are resources within the "Spirit filled church" that can provide more international and less violent ways of practicing Pentecostalism.

Moving away from nationalism, which carries with it *de facto* support of war, to just war tradition would be a positive development among American Pentecostals since just war tradition begins with a strong presumption against violence. According to Martin Ceadel's categories, the AOG transformed from pacifist (Christians should never kill humans) to crusading (offensive and preemptive war to establish justice and peace) in less than a century.[48] Adopting a critical defencist position (governments

---

44. John Howard Yoder, "Foreword," in Jay Beaman, *Pentecostal Pacifism*, iii–v.

45. See Joel Shuman, "Pentecost and the End of Patriotism: The Call for the Restoration of Pacifism among Pentecostal Christians," *Journal of Pentecostal Theology* 9 (1996) 70–96. A revised version of this article is now chapter four of this book.

46. For a comparison of early Quakerism and early Pentecostalism, see Paul Alexander, "Historical and Theological Origins of Assemblies of God Pacifism," *Quaker Theology* 7.12 (2005–2006) 35–76.

47. Paul Alexander, "Spirit Empowered Peacemaking: Toward a Pentecostal Charismatic Peace Fellowship." *Journal of the European Pentecostal Theological Association* 22 (2002) 78–102. A survey of American Assemblies of God ministers conducted in April 2001 revealed that ninety-three percent agreed with the statement, "It is appropriate for a Christian to support war." Sixty-five percent of these Assemblies of God pastors agreed that "The principles of Jesus support war." An even greater number, a significant seventy-one percent, said that they "would kill in a war." These were not Pentecostal lay people who support war and would kill, these were the pastors of the Assemblies of God churches in the USA five months before September 11, 2001.

48. Martin Ceadel, *Thinking About War and Peace* (Oxford: Oxford University Press, 1987). For a detailed account and analysis of this transformation see Paul Alexander,

may take military action for self-defense as a last vresort) that takes just war tradition seriously would be a significant improvement. Hopefully, the American AOG will encourage their theologians and ethicists to provide respectful and nuanced arguments in support of Christian pacifism, just peacemaking, and just war traditions so that Pentecostals may more clearly discern Jesus' call to peacemaking.

Finally, rather than being ashamed of the term "Pentecostal," which I was for many years, I now recognize the necessity of emphasizing the enabling of the Spirit to live (and perhaps die) as prophetic nonviolent citizens in the Kingdom of God. Becoming a Christian peacemaker helped me appreciate my Pentecostalism. Pentecostals believe that God empowers followers of Jesus to witness faithfully. Acts also says, "you will receive power when the Holy Spirit comes upon you, and you will be my witnesses (*martures*, martyrs). . . ." I do not advocate "witnessing" or missions as triumphalistic colonialism, though this is undoubtedly what many early Pentecostals had in mind, but I would argue for the possibility and necessity of a postcolonial Pentecostal witness. Radical Pentecostals who transcend and critique political parties and national policies must rely on the Spirit of God for their sustenance as they participate in the immanent untidiness of peacemaking. Public prophetic witness toward justice and peace is good news for the poor and the weak, as well as for the rich and powerful, though the rich and powerful may not receive it as such. Being wisely led and enabled by the Spirit for this mission is indispensable. Pentecostalism exists primarily in previously colonized and majority world countries, the underbellies of empire, and in the biblical narratives this is exactly where the Spirit enables prophets to speak and sustains them as their words and actions challenge oppressors. Luke's Jesus-from-an-occupied-territory says, "The Spirit of the Lord is upon me and has anointed me to preach good news to the poor." Pentecostals should be able to say the same.

All Christians should embody aspects of Hispanic American Pentecostalism as described by Eldín Villafañe:

> In a real historical sense they are a pilgrim people. . . . Being a border people, no matter where we live, we must serve as a means of communication between the rich, over affluent and misdeveloped world of the North, and the poor, exploited and

---

*Peace to War: Shifting Allegiances in the Assemblies of God* (Telford, PA: Cascadia, 2009).

also misdeveloped world of the South. This . . . requires that we continue to be bilingual and bicultural.[49]

I propose that the entire Church, not just the Pentecostal family, be a humble, prophetic, transnational, nonviolent, and Spirit-empowered *ethnos* who lives and speaks God's counter-intuitive will and way while being on the chessboard, but not of the chessboard.

49. *The Liberating Spirit: Toward an Hispanic American Pentecostal Social Ethic* (Grand Rapids: Eerdmans, 1993) 89, 163, 165, 171, 198–99.

**Part II**

Pentecostal Peacemaking in the Twenty-first Century

# Rebuild Afghanistan

*A Declaration of Faithfulness / A Transforming Initiative*

September 25, 2001

## Paul Alexander

Rebuild Afghanistan! That is the call of God to the church today. It is the call of God to all people everywhere, of all faiths and nationalities. The evil of the few will not bring our wrath on the many; we will not be defined by their hatred and not be reduced to the pursuit of revenge. Christians are to be characterized by our Jesus, who did and taught more than mere lack of anger or retaliation. He called us to initiate new and better relationships by being reconciled to our enemies by seeking their good. In the face of adversity, the followers of Jesus feed and clothe, shelter and comfort. By so doing we win the true victory in true power by revealing the very way of God. We will be named "builders of streets with homes" for we have learned that mercy is better than sacrifice. We will spend ourselves on behalf of the hungry for our food loses its flavor when we eat only with those who can feed us.

Our mourning and fasting for the fallen in New York City, Washington, DC, and Pennsylvania will not end in quarreling and strife, but with the rebuilding of ancient ruins and age-old foundations. We will not be seduced into selfishness and pride, focusing only on ourselves and our cities; we will neither wallow in self-pity nor lash out as we have been lashed. We will respond with overwhelming mercy and compassion. Our desire for reconciliation will challenge the very foundations of the world. We do not attempt to buy peace, but willingly and joyfully sacrifice ourselves for our God who leads us toward each other. We will neither lie about our righteousness nor lie about our enemies; instead, we will speak truthfully about the sins of the Many, who have enjoyed prosperity and luxury at the expense of much of the rest of the world. We, the followers of Jesus, have learned well that we must continually remove logs from our own eyes, so that we will not be the blind leading the blind into the pit. No! We acknowledge our sins and, in view of God's mercy, offer ourselves as living sacrifices. As acts of worship we will devote our time, effort, work, money, and resources of all kinds to building infrastructures that help the people of Afghanistan. Effort and expense for the United States will be matched and devoted to Afghanistan. Unselfishness and concern for the hurting will outshine all else.

Criticism and rejection from those who would scoff at this path of reconciliation is expected and even understood. But these detractions do not change the fact that this is the way of God: forgiveness and redemption are better than bitterness and retribution. Loving those who do not return love, lending to those who do not repay, and doing good toward those who do no good for you leads to exclusion, insult, and rejection by many. This is why the church is hated, because we reveal the Son of Man. We then rejoice and leap for joy when we are treated as were the prophets. This is not a time to be rich, well-fed, or applauded as are false prophets. Knowing that judgment, condemnation, and forgiveness are pressed down, shaken together, and poured back into our laps with the very measure we use to dish them out, we will instead be faithful and dish out mercy until it overwhelms our enemies. For God is kind to the ungrateful and the wicked (and we recognize ourselves in that description), and we are to be merciful because God has shown us mercy.

Rebuild Afghanistan! Though the savagery of war has barely touched the United States, violence has taken its toll on that land for decades. The call of God to the church around the globe, and especially to those offended in America, is to root out the perpetrators that remain and eat with them. The church knows that vengeance is not ours, that God repays—and he has chosen to repay by having his people overcome evil with good. This is neither an abstract principal nor an unreachable ideal, it is as concrete as concrete. We do not rely on other political entities to do this, we *are* a political entity and our politics are those of Jesus. As his body on this earth, as the transformed ones who no longer regard anyone from a worldly perspective, we practice and live the service of reconciliation.

Therefore, we let the world know that people around the globe are uniting and raising funds to rebuild Afghanistan. This is happening before any American violence even takes place there, for our action is not to be reactive but proactive. But how can we do this for a nation that oppresses women the way the Taliban does? Please consider: if nations can kill these same women and call them collateral damage, then we can build them homes with running water, electricity, and toilets. If nations can kill hundreds of thousands of Arab people and still build for themselves at home, we can build for a nation that kills in proportion. All are called to account for their selfishness and violence, and all enemies of the Way are invited to dinner, even those in Afghanistan.

Paul Alexander
September 25, 2001
Waxahachie, Texas

# 7

# Jesus-Shaped and Spirit-Empowered Peace with Justice

## *Toward a Christomorphic Pneumatology¹*

### Paul Alexander

That many early pentecostals believed that participation in the destruction of human life, even in warfare for one's own nation, was not congruent with a fully pentecostal understanding of the euangellion (gospel) has been brought to light. This theological and ethical position of our ancestors has been excavated, examined, and discussed for several years

---

1. I first presented this chapter as a paper, then entitled "Toward a Pentecostal Theology of Peacemaking," at the Society for Pentecostal Studies conference in March 2002, one year before the official U.S. invasion of Iraq. I refrained from editing it for this volume, but it contains the seeds of the concept of christomorphic pneumatology that I am developing more fully in another book. I had not arrived at the term until 2008, although the motto for Pentecostals and Charismatics for Peace and Justice (PCPJ) has been "Jesus-Shaped Spirit-Empowered Peace with Justice" for several years. Christomorphic pneumatology is simply a theologically technical way of saying Jesus-shaped and Spirit-empowered. Another way I like to think of incarnational theological ethics is "Dios con carne"—God with meat.

now.[2] This historical research has been appropriate and has challenged those who would privatize their pentecostalism[3] at the expense of social concerns. However, simply echoing the passionate professions of the past, as significant and necessary as that endeavor is, will not sufficiently enable contemporary pentecostals and charismatics to fully live into Spirit-baptized discipleship in the kingdom of God at this time. For that to happen, we must reexamine the scriptures together with our heritage to see whether early claims for nonviolence and peacemaking can once again be supported as a faithful testimony to the story of Israel, Jesus, and the church. This conversation has already begun in Joel Shuman's 1996 article entitled "Pentecost and the End of Patriotism: A Call for the Restoration of Pacifism Among Pentecostal Christians."[4] This paper is meant to continue that discussion as a response to his call.

My objective is to show that a Pentecostal theology well grounded in the scriptures will prescribe peacemaking as a fundamental characteristic of Spirit-filled communities. This is quite a claim when we consider that many Pentecostals have advocated the opposite for much of the twentieth century. We have fought for many nations, for many causes, and we have shed much blood. Nevertheless, I believe that if we take the time to examine who we say we are and allow ourselves to be God's vessels, then we will conclude that peacemaking should characterize our Christian faith.

I believe God is calling the church to be obedient to the way of Christ in all things, and to therefore be a peacemaking church. This peacemaking encompasses seeking justice for the poor, promoting reconciliation between divided brothers and sisters in the faith, and reserving ultimate allegiance for God above all sectarian and Constantinian boundaries erected by nations, classes, genders, ethnicities, and geography. It addresses economic and social issues such as consumerism and globalization, it inspires our speaking truth and witnessing authentically to the

2. A detailed account of the American Assemblies of God story can be found in Paul Alexander, *Peace to War: Shifting Allegiances in the Assemblies of God* (Telford, PA: Herald, 2009).

3. From this point forward I will use the term pentecostal to refer to both Pentecostals and Charismatics as those who trust the power and gifts of the Spirit and the authority of scripture to help them follow Jesus. This is similar to the way James William McClendon, Jr. uses "baptist" to refer to those who recognize the authority of scripture and their continuity with it [*Doctrine* (Nashville: Abingdon, 1994) 45]. CA: Council of Mennonite Seminaries, 1970) 5.

4. *Journal of Pentecostal Theology* 9 (1996) 70–96.

way and life of Christ in everything. The call to make peace is not inventive; it does not impose a foreign substance on the gospel. To make peace means to unleash and take seriously the very heart of God as revealed in the incarnation. It is to accept and submit to the truth that "the wisdom that comes from heaven is first of all pure; then peace loving, considerate, submissive, full of mercy and good fruit, impartial and sincere. It is to believe that "peacemakers who sow in peace raise a harvest of righteousness (justice)."[5] This is public and social, private and individual. It encompasses everything because it is based in the faith that Jesus Christ is actually Lord.

Where does one begin in this endeavor to help the church once again realize that violence and division, retaliation and enmity are not appropriate for those empowered by the Spirit of God? The Assemblies of God began with evangelism as the basis for their pacifism during World War I: "From its very inception, the Pentecostal Movement has been a movement of evangelism, studiously avoiding any principles or actions which would thwart it in its great purpose."[6] They believed that telling the story of Jesus to someone, only later to kill that same person in combat, amounted to blatant hypocrisy. Evangelism is a fine place to examine peacemaking and war, and in chapter fourteen I examine peacemaking as the opportunity for evangelical integrity, but I here will begin where the identity of the *Christ*-ian might begin, with Jesus Christ himself.

## CHRISTOLOGY AS THE *SOURCE* OF PENTECOSTAL PEACEMAKING[7]

My father always told me to "seek Jesus." Little did he or I know that this would lead me to advocate peacemaking as an integral part of the gospel.

5. James 3:17–18 (NIV).

6. "The Pentecostal Movement and the Conscription Law," *The Weekly Evangel*, 4 August 1917, 6. This introduction was followed with "The laws of the kingdom, laid down by our elder brother Jesus Christ, in His Sermon on the Mount, have been unqualifiedly adopted, consequently the movement has found itself opposed to the spilling of the blood of any man, or of offering resistance to any aggression. Every branch of the movement, whether in the United States, Canada, Great Britain or Germany, has held to this principle."

7. I would like to thank Craig Carter for allowing me to use his analysis of Yoder's thought in *The Politics of the Cross: The Theology and Social Ethics of John Howard Yoder* (Grand Rapids: Brazos, 2001) as the basis for the titles in this paper. More development along these lines will be done with ecclesiology as the shape and perhaps eschatology as the context of pentecostal peacemaking. I highly recommend Carter's book as an excel-

This priority of place for the Messiah is certainly appropriate when addressing anything, but especially peacemaking. Jesus is the one who said, "blessed (good for you!) are the peacemakers" and "love your enemies, do good to *them*." When Jesus' life, death, and resurrection are joined with his words, it reveals a peacemaking way of life that becomes the imperative model for the children of God. Simply put, joint-heirs with Jesus will share in his sufferings as well as his glory. Pentecostals especially should be appalled at the marginalization of Jesus when it comes to discussions of ethics. We should start and end with Jesus, the author and finisher of our faithfulness, who revealed to us the way of God. It is by him that we have been redeemed and for him that we seek the redemption of the world. Oppression, exploitation, greed, nationalism, and violence are difficult to justify without moving Jesus to the side, and this should not be acceptable for pentecostals. Jesus was faced with real options and temptations in his life that were not the Way, yet he was obediently faithful to God, and we must follow his example.

Getting to know the Jesus of the Christian scriptures is a wonderful adventure, but it is also a continual challenge. Jesus himself said, "blessed is the one who does not fall away on account of me," and Peter confirmed this later by calling Jesus the stumbling block (skandalon) that makes people fall. We must be sure that we identify the correct reasons why Jesus is a stumbling block to following God, for our description of the Messiah will determine our understanding of who we are to be. So I will attempt the all-important task of interpreting the revelation of Jesus' life, murder, and resurrection and then applying it to contemporary pentecostals in a way that is faithful to the New Testament. If it challenges us to change our self-understanding, our loyalties, and our actions, then may the Holy Spirit empower us to be faithful.

In facing temptations, Jesus rejected the use of economics to avoid the cross and become king, and he rejected the authority and wealth of the kingdoms of the world because hunger for power and nationalism were not the ways that God would redeem the world.[8] Jesus rejected safety, security, control, and coercion even though they were real options. Instead,

lent introduction to the work of Yoder and his relationship to Karl Barth and Reinhold Niebuhr.

8. John Howard Yoder, *The Politics of Jesus* (Grand Rapids: Eerdmans, 1972) 26. Carter notes the point of the biblical story is that the idolatry of nationalism is on the same moral level as Satan worship, *Politics of the Cross*, 96.

Jesus allowed himself to be rejected and thus challenged economic power, nationalism, and violence. He consistently taught and demonstrated that "servanthood replaces domination."[9]

As much as we may try to avoid it, the human Christians claim was the incarnate God created a new social reality that was supposed to live like he did. Wealth, defense, and control are temptations that our generous, nonviolent, and submissive (though not always obedient to the powers) Messiah rejected. Jesus generously fed the hungry, but not for status, recognition, or power. We should do the same. Jesus accepted his own death at the hands of his enemies, and when we do the same we are taking up the cross and following Christ. God allowed God's own son, and many others, to die while forgiving and seeking reconciliation with their attackers. Jesus did not force the cross on others, but he lived his life in such a way that challenged the status quo and forced them to deal with him, thus offering them an alternative way of dealing with conflict and hostility. He issued open invitations to participate with God in redeeming the world through aggressive love, obedient to God but submissive to those who stone the prophets.

Jesus even told his hometown that he was there not only for them but also for the outsiders, the poor, prisoners, the blind, and the oppressed. He made this so clear to them that they attempted to murder him because they did not want peace with their enemies. From Jesus' life we learn that making peace creates both friends and enemies—just like switching on a light in a dark room where oppression is taking place makes some rejoice and others angry. The oppressed rejoice but the oppressors are threatened. When we do not support the establishments that others around us worship, or at least highly admire, we are at odds with those who hold the (alleged) power. Valuing immigrants because we realize that this is not our land anyway, it is God's, and it used to belong to somebody other than us, is similar to when Jesus told the people of Nazareth that Elijah and Elisha could have healed the Israelites but ministered to foreigners instead. Siding with the poor, hungry, weeping ones while also being foolish enough to say "watch out!" to the rich, well-fed, laughing ones will bring hatred and exclusion. But Jesus called into being a "community of voluntary commitment, willing for the sake of its calling to take upon itself the hostility of the given society."[10] Peacemaking admits that there is

9. Carter, *Politics of the Cross*, 97.
10. Yoder, *Politics*, 37.

hostility and confronts it, it does not lie passively by. It attempts to destroy enmity by turning enemies into friends.

When Peter confessed Jesus as the Messiah, Jesus immediately told his disciples that he would suffer, be rejected, be killed, and be raised to life. He also did not hesitate to tell them that they themselves would also die. "Taking up the cross" was a not symbolic or figurative idea as Jesus taught it. It was true that, each day, following Jesus could get you killed. His call to imitate himself, both as servant and as a murder/execution victim, was a call that the New Testament church understood very clearly. It took the resurrection and Pentecost to get them back to the Way, but even Peter went from denying Christ with the sword to exhorting the church:

> when they hurled their insults at him he did not retaliate; when he suffered he made no threats. Instead he entrusted himself to him who judges justly. . . . Do not repay evil with evil or insult with insult, but with blessing because to this you were called.[11]

Jesus renounced the Zealot option numerous times during his ministry. It is possible that several of his disciples were Zealots who desired a violent revolution that would establish God's rule and reign on earth after the pagans were driven out of the land.[12] He rejected insurrection as an option after feeding the multitudes, after cleansing the temple and, for the third time, in the Garden. Instead, he drank from the cup that the Father presented him. The temptation to take over and bring about peace and justice with force is a serious enticement; it is usually presented as the responsible or realistic way. But Jesus knew that the way of God is to bring conciliation through sacrificial love, not through force, for a coerced love is not love at all. Pentecostals today must also resist the temptation to take matters into our own hands through force. We must not think ourselves powerful enough to make things turn out right. A healthy Christology allows plenty of room for action but no room for violence, regardless of the alleged good that could come from it.

Jesus, the Christ who makes peace, must be seen as a real threat to the status quo, to establishments, and to powers. There are those with vested interests who gain position, power, and wealth through division and enmity. This is true both in religious institutions and in nations. We should avoid so overly spiritualizing the life of Jesus that we make the

---

11. 1 Peter 2:23; 3:9 (NIV).

12. Yoder, *Politics*, 47.

mistake of thinking that the Jews and Romans misinterpreted Jesus when they thought they had to kill him to keep their order.

> Both Jewish and Roman authorities were defending themselves against a *real* threat. That the threat was not one of *armed*, violent revolt, and that it nonetheless bothered them to the point of their resorting to irregular procedures to counter it, is a proof of the political relevance of nonviolent tactics, not a proof that Pilate and Caiaphas were exceptionally dull or dishonorable men. . . . Jesus' public career had been such as to make it quite thinkable that he would pose to the Roman Empire an apparent threat serious enough to justify his execution.[13]

People really hoped he would redeem Israel and they were rightly expecting a kingdom of God since that is what Jesus consistently talked about. The misunderstanding was that the life that leads to the cross, the faithfulness of the Messiah, was the inauguration of the kingdom. This is the way it happens.

> Here at the cross is the man who loves his enemies, the man whose righteousness is greater than that of the Pharisees, who being rich became poor, who gives his robe to those who took his cloak, who prays for those who despitefully use him. The cross is not a detour or a hurdle on the way to the kingdom, nor is it even the way to the kingdom; it is the kingdom come.[14]

It is to this moment that pentecostals and charismatics are called to be faithful witnesses. We should be able to look at the power structures in this world and speak the truth to them, calling out the injustice and oppression that promotes greed and holds itself above moral reproach. Nations that train their people in materialism and consumerism must be offered an alternative, a better way that is the way of God. I believe that God revealed to us in Jesus "an ethic marked by the cross, a cross identified as the punishment of a man who threatens society by creating a new kind of community leading a radically new kind of life."[15] Radical Christianity is supposed to be the hallmark of pentecostals, and it is appropriate to recognize that this involves living in communities (churches) that are threats to injustice and social/structural evil around us. Jesus'

13. Ibid., 49–50.
14. Ibid., 51.
15. Ibid., 53.

death is integrally related to his life, for he was killed because of the life he lived.

I am convinced that if we live as faithful witnesses to Jesus we very well may endanger ourselves and our families. There is always the hope that the offender will be won over by our love, but there is no guarantee. The calculating link between obedience to God and its efficacy has been broken by the cross; while we offer reconciliation we may be rejected and killed just like Jesus was. Indeed, by aggressively addressing racial and ethnic tensions, we will cause those benefiting from the conflict to demand silence, even by force. In addressing economic or gender issues, we hope that there will be confession, repentance, and restoration, but there may be retaliation instead. God has known this risk from the beginning. The faithful prophets in the Hebrew Scriptures received their punishment for speaking the truth; the faithful Son and children of God in the New Testament were prepared for it as well. This is why we are told to submit to the authorities in the context of enemy feeding and love as the fulfillment of the law (Romans 12–13).[16] If you feed the state's enemies, you may be sentenced to hang for treason. You then submit to the state when you accept this consequence. In doing so, you must never underestimate or overlook the exact way that Jesus responded to his executioners, "Father, forgive them." Stephen took this so seriously that he almost quoted his Messiah as he was being executed, and we too are to face our deaths with this compassion and forgiveness. This is not an unreachable ideal of perfection that is only futuristic—that response simply avoids the real lordship of the Messiah in our lives. This way of sacrificial and suffering love is the way things really are if we believe that the God of Abraham, Isaac, and Jacob came in the flesh in Jesus of Nazareth.

Just as Jesus' death resulted from the life he lived and the truth he spoke, so his resurrection was God's vindication that this is God's way. Jesus trusted the Father to raise him from the dead, and was thus obedient even to a shameful death on a cross. Jesus, knowing that peace is made only by unselfishness and sacrifice, poured himself out in suffering and his glory came later. We who claim to be his followers can expect no easier road; we cannot claim to bring about peace, justice, or joy through the suffering of others for our God demonstrates otherwise. In suffering

16. Christians are not to suspend moral judgment and obey the state if it commands something that is against the way of God. See John Howard Yoder, *The Original Revolution* (Eugene, OR: Wipf & Stock, 1998).

with and for others, we ultimately, and without reservation, place our hope in God and God alone because we know that only God can raise us from the dead after we are killed. If Jesus was not raised, then all the beatings, imprisonments, and testimony deaths are truly crazy and we are to be pitied for our foolishness. But, if Jesus really is the Son of God, then we can make peace with our enemies just like Christ did, even when it costs us our lives, because we believe that God himself will vindicate our faithfulness. We trust God to judge justly. Christ's death falls between his life and resurrection. This sequence should be taken seriously in order to have a healthy Christology: Christ's sacrificial death is the result of his peacemaking life, it is in itself our peace exemplified, and his resurrection is the hope that we who make peace have in God. If we share in his suffering, we do so with the faith that we will share in his glory.

Thus far, I have focused mainly on the actual life of Jesus as presented in the biblical narratives. But the epistles also identify reconciliation and peacemaking as the very essence of the good news, for it is *good* because it is a non-coercive invitation to be united in God, and it is *news* because if it were not for Jesus the way would not be fully known. I do not here have the space to present how prevalent this unforced, yet proactive peacemaking centered in Christ is throughout the New Testament, so I will discuss only a couple of passages and note how we are by no means exempt from the call.

Jesus as a maker of peace is stated explicitly in Ephesians 2:

> For he himself is our peace, who has made the two one and has destroyed the barrier, the dividing wall of hostility, by abolishing in his flesh the law with its commandments and regulations. His purpose was to create in himself one new person out of the two, thus making peace, and in this one body to reconcile both of them to God through the cross, by which he put to death their hostility. He came and preached peace to you who were far away and peace to those who were near.

Paul saw Jesus creating a unified body out of divided peoples, specifically Gentiles (the ethnicities/nations) and Jews. This peace and reconciliation came through real, material sacrifice and suffering. This is why Paul repeatedly mentions participating in Christ's suffering, which is so small compared to Christ's glory (the reconciliation of divided peoples). Christians are told to imitate God, not abstractly but in a concrete and particular way, "just as Christ loved us and gave himself up for us as a fragrant offering and sacrifice to God." Paul calls the faithful disciples "letters from Christ" who have the ministry and message of reconciliation (2 Cor 3–5) and who suffer terribly because of it (2 Corinthians 6).

Peacemaking is an essential Christian practice because it is the essence of Jesus the Christ, the precise Jesus of Nazareth presented in the scriptures who made peace between peoples and with God. This Jesus is portrayed as the fulfillment of the hope of the Hebrew Scriptures and the call to Israel to be the prophet, priest, and witness to the world. This is a new covenant that reads the old covenant through the revelation in Jesus and calls the obedient to follow in his way. But love of enemies and forgiveness for one's murderer, hospitality for strangers and speaking truth to those with the power to kill, attempting to unite factions and divided people, these things seem quite difficult and almost impossible. How can this happen? What makes this a possibility for us rather than just a foolish dream? The answer to this question has been supplied by pentecostals for years, but it is time to link our fascination with the Holy Spirit to a Christology that is faithful to Jesus and his invitation to us.

## PNEUMATOLOGY AS THE *MEANS* OF PENTECOSTAL PEACEMAKING

It has been shown that Luke's pneumatology continually empowers people to turn to God's way (seen best in Jesus) both in actions and speaking.[17] From Elizabeth, Mary, Zechariah, and John to the disciples after Pentecost, the Holy Spirit is crucial to the embodiment and declaration of what God is doing through Jesus and his followers. Jesus himself is also described as being "full of the Holy Spirit," "led by the Spirit," and "in the power of the Spirit" (Luke 4:1, 4:14). This is necessary because the path of reconciliation which involves healing demon possessed outcasts at the expense of thousands of dollars worth of livestock is dangerous (Luke 8).[18] The call to sacrifice and suffering in order to bring peace is made

17. James B. Shelton, *Mighty in Word and Deed: The Role of the Holy Spirit in Luke-Acts* (Peabody: Hendrickson, 1991). Roger Stronstad, *The Charismatic Theology of St. Luke* (Peabody: Hendrickson, 1985). By calling the Holy Spirit a means to an end is immediately to risk objectifying the Spirit rather than respecting the Spirit as a person of the Trinity. However, I view the Spirit this way based on the biblical presentation of the goal of Spirit baptism/filling as particularly described in Luke-Acts. Specifically in Acts 1:8, "you will receive power when the Holy Spirit comes on you, and you will be my witnesses (martyrs). . . ."

18. Valuing people above stock (corporations, returns, dividends, etc.) today can

possible only through God's gift of the Holy Spirit. We are not called to be super-human—we are not expected to simply will ourselves into loving our enemies with some sentimental affection. Instead, we are called to be filled with the Spirit and imitate Christ. Jesus was empowered to love and value the rejected (women, lepers, thieves, foreigners, etc.) as a Spirit-filled human. The Lukan narrative recounts Jesus introducing his first public proclamation of good news to the poor, imprisoned, blind, and oppressed with his declaration, "the Spirit of the Lord is upon me." Christology shows us how to live and die while making peace, pneumatology enables it. This is a christomorphic pneumatology.[19]

Luke makes a special point to show that Jesus relied on the Holy Spirit to help him through the temptations. James Shelton believes that "the way Jesus overcame temptation is a paradigm for the way his followers would overcome temptation" and that "the temptations of Jesus are real . . . he overcomes the evil as God expects all people to triumph—through the power of the Holy Spirit."[20] I agree and would like to move past an abstract concept of overcoming of "temptations" to discuss the exact ones with which Jesus dealt. Jesus was offered many opportunities to use force or coercion to bring about the kingdom of God, but he prayed and trusted in the empowerment of the Spirit each time to reject this realistic and truly tempting option. He rejected the use of evil means to obtain a righteous end, but instead entrusted himself to God. It is no accident that he instructed his disciples to pray that they would not fall into temptation in the Garden, and then told them to receive the power of the Spirit from on high so that they could disciple the nations. Making disciples requires an empowerment greater than can come from within oneself. Reconciling with enemies, loving outcasts, and challenging the status quo all necessitate the same empowering that the prophets of old and the Messiah himself were described as having.

Acts also portrays the relationship between the Holy Spirit and imitating Christ in reconciliation. The witness (marturioV), or martyr, was for the entire world and crossed all linguistic and ethnic boundaries.

---

have the same effects: healing for the dispossessed and anger accompanied by invitations to leave from the stockholders.

19. I am exploring christomorphic pneumatology more fully in a theological ethics book I am currently writing.

20. Shelton, *Mighty in Word and Deed*, 58–60. He lists the temptations that bothered Jesus during his life as popular views of righteousness, taking short cuts, and condoning evil to do good.

The sixteen nations represented in Acts 2 all came together and formed Christ's body of which he is the head, with even Gentiles being brought in later. However, pentecostal pneumatology has only recently been linked with the biblical witness to christocentric peacemaking, and this needs continued attention.

A pentecostal pneumatology will remind us that we have God's empowering presence to realistically live lives that imitate Christ's forgiveness of enemies and sacrifice for reconciliation.[21] To be the unified yet broken body of Christ in the world, to practice the transforming initiatives of peacemaking given by Jesus, and to truly be ministers of reconciliation is to fully depend on the empowerment of the Holy Spirit.[22] The Spirit was the enabling means for Jesus to live in tension with his enemies while inviting them to repent, and the Spirit is God's gift to empower the church to be what we claim to be: the people of God who hope to glorify God as we daily pick up our instruments of execution and follow Christ.

I have briefly tried to show that Jesus is the source for our commitment to making peace between divided people. The parameters of this peace initiative extend as far as our worst enemy and as close as the people in our own homes, recognizing that our efforts will sometimes bring a sword, instead of peace, upon ourselves. Any disagreement about the primacy of peacemaking will have to be a discussion about how seriously we are to take Jesus as the Messiah, as our Lord, and as our example.

I have also attempted to show that Christology as a source for peacemaking is not sufficient because we cannot do it on our own. Just as we need God to show us the way in Jesus Christ, we need God to enable us to walk in it and follow. Thankfully, God has done this in Pentecost when he created a Spirit-empowered people who rely on and trust that this really is the way of redemption. Baptism in the Holy Spirit is the means by which we are enabled to be faithful even when it hurts, and to remember that peace and patience go together.

21. This is a reference to Gordon Fee, *God's Empowering Presence: The Holy Spirit in the Letters of Paul* (Peabody: Hendrickson, 1994).

22. Glen Stassen, *Just Peacemaking: Transforming Initiatives for Justice and Peace* (Louisville: Westminster John Knox, 1992). 1) Acknowledge your alienation and God's grace realistically; 2) Go, talk, welcome one another, and seek to be reconciled; 3) Don't resist revengefully, but take transforming initiatives for peace; 4) Invest in delivering justice; 5) Love your enemies with actions, affirm their valid interests; 6) Pray for your enemies and bless them; persevere in prayer; 7) Don't judge, but repent and forgive; 8) Do peacemaking in a church or a group of disciples.

I am overjoyed and overwhelmed by the possibilities that Christ-centered, Spirit-empowered peacemaking presents to pentecostals and charismatics. At the beginning of this twenty-first century, we number six hundred million that God has empowered to follow Christ as peace-makers who sow in peace. It must not be efficacy that determines our witness, but faithfulness to Christ alone. We may not always transform our enemies, but we can be faithful and seek their friendship by offering forgiveness and love. May the Spirit who led Israel, Jesus, and our ancestors in the faith lead us as well.

8

# What the Church Teaches about War

## *A COGIC Conscientious Objection Principle*[1]

### Elder David A. Hall, Sr.

What does the Church of God in Christ (COGIC) teach about war? How is the church preparing the coming generation to deal with the brutality and insanity war continuously afflicts upon every generation? Off and on many nations are engaged in the timeless pursuit of making war, symbolized in the current generation by the September 11th suicidal terrorism, in which hijackers destroyed magnificent symbols of American society and claimed the lives of over three thousand people. I, as an American, as a black American, and particularly as a Pentecostal American, have come to an ethical and enigmatic dilemma. That dilemma forces me to ponder whether I should desire the death of those who attacked America. Should we send our sons and daughters to fight for the preservation of liberty? In the Church of God in Christ, saints have been taught that conscientious objection is our official position on war. Our forbearers and later generations taught peace, committing the saints to nonviolent

1. Adapted with permission from *Essays to the Next Generation: Issues Vital to Life, Salvation and Spirituality of the Church of God in Christ* (Memphis: Hall, 2004).

205

interaction—even during declared war.[2] Many present day youths do not practice this basic philosophy, lifestyle, and tenet of faith. If our commitment to conscientious objection does not regain its rightful place, more of our children will actively and aggressively go to war.

*The Church must ask our youth to understand and accept again the principles of conscientious objection* while loving America and serving America. Our greatest challenge may be to produce a faithful conscientious generation of militants for peace, those against the brutality and insanity of war—a generation committed to the same historic principles of conscientious objection as taught by Bishop C. H. Mason.

The Church of God in Christ is at a crossroads: while teaching youth to believe in and perpetuate the legacies of this country, especially as such traditions may challenge our faith, our direction must be to keep today's youth faithful to the COGIC religious heritage of holiness, pacifism, and conscientious objection. For this generation, the critical question is whether they as Americans, and especially as Pentecostals, can stand with America. Certainly our youth should know that throughout our Church's history our committed proclamation has been resoundingly, "We stand with America as always!" That stand of support has heretofore been as conscientious objectors. There was a time when that stance was not ambiguous but clarion, and with peaceful intent we served America, even on the front lines of battle. The Church of God in Christ historically taught Bishop C. H. Mason's principles of conscientious objection, and our members did their patriotic duty during the wars of the twentieth century. Bishop Mason taught tenets of patriotic conscientious objection at the same time that W. E. B. Du Bois explained the harsh reality of the double-consciousness blacks were forced to endure in America in *The Souls of Black Folk*. Then, as now, loving America was often incongruous and contradictory in the conflicted souls of black folk.

War is as old as civilization. Nations will rise up against nations because of politics, race, economics, terrorism, or even less essential issues. Bishop C. H. Mason dared to resist war as a pacifist and was imprisoned due to his belief. His radically different approach to war is recorded in the book, *The Formative Years*.[3] What white America failed to understand

---

2. See Theodore Kornweibel's chapter in this book for a detailed account of early Church of God in Christ pacifism.

3. J. O. Patterson, German Ross, and Julia Mason Atkins, editors, *The History and Formative Years of the Church of God in Christ* (Memphis: Church of God in Christ, 1969).

was why Mason practiced pacifism and encouraged his ardent members to be conscientious objectors. The day of Jim Crow usually meant black folks did what they were told without complaint. In the South, blacks were considered unworthy to wear the uniform of America. Often handed the menial and dirty jobs, blacks served the country's military while suffering mockery and humiliation. How confusing it must have been to be black and encouraged to participate in war but then to be met with racial scorn and ridicule for wanting to demonstrate loyalty. Mason's speech and practice incited the wrath of the Ku Klux Klan and criticism from the government itself. The black struggle was the classic "catch-22." Blacks were cursed if they did not fight and cursed if they did.

Conscientious objection runs deep in my family. My father, Elder Cleophas Hall, Sr., was drafted into the army in 1942 and went to the Pacific Theater, where he faced battle on the frontlines without a gun. Recently, I looked through the medals the U. S. government presented to him for courage in battle. He was honored with a Good Conduct Medal, an American Campaign Medal, two Asiatic-Pacific Campaign Medals, a WWII Victory Medal, a Philippine Liberation Ribbon, an Honorable Service Lapel Button WWII, and the Purple Heart. Bishop Mason taught that saints did not take life, and my dad went through World War II without a gun. In a segregated medical unit, he braved intense battles and sustained nearly fatal wounds on the front lines. God spared his life, and after the war he became nationally known as a great evangelist, referred to as the "Church Doctor" and "Mr. Bible." My brother, Elder Cleophas Hall, Jr., was drafted into the army during the war in Vietnam, and he too never carried a weapon. My brother was in the medical corps as well. I was an anti-war protestor and another type of patriot. Each of us registered as conscientious objectors and followed the teachings of Bishop Mason. COGIC youth of the World War II and Vietnam Eras were Americans, but COGIC Americans were conscientious objectors. My two sons have been trained to register as conscientious objectors, and each of them was frankly surprised that many of their COGIC friends did not register as conscientious objectors.

I discussed conscientious objection with former Presiding Bishop G. E. Patterson, and it was clear our experiences were analogous. He revealed that as a youth he declared his conscientious objector status and was called before his draft board. There, he defended the tenets of the faith and teachings of C. H. Mason. He made clear his willingness to serve his country, but only as our faith would allow. After his encounter and their understanding of the nature of his commitment to God and country, he was reclassified. It takes courage to serve in the military, and it takes another type of courage to stand on the principles of peace. I too made my choice and selected a course of open defiance to the war in Vietnam, and yet I feel no less patriotic than my brother who did serve as a non-combatant conscientious objector. Today's youth are simply not being taught the principles of conscientious objection.[4] This is wrong!

What should the world expect from the saints of The Church of God in Christ? What should the saints expect from the world? The saints in America are praying that our nation will come through this difficulty and have the resolve to end terrorism. This effort will cost lives on both sides. Our leader, President Barack Obama, and his advisors have their hands full. Our prayers and support should give them confidence and the heart and resolve to press forward. Certainly, the decisions of this nation's leaders affect us in the balance of history. The Church of God in Christ has always been loyal to America, but that loyalty is not like the Hebrew *herem* (total destruction of an enemy), which is an absolute that could lead to radicalism, bearing arms, and merciless killing. The bishops of our Church have always encouraged prayers for leaders, and so, we shall give Mr. Obama that prayerful support. For us, however, God and country are not analogous, and shedding blood for the country is not a possibility. Neither does God ask us to support the killing of others by our nation's military.

COGIC believers should be realistic; we have accepted that nations feel justified for committing to so-called just wars although many of them do not satisfy traditional just war criteria. What most often happens is that many claim that God is on our side, and, consequently, America feels it has a "moral high ground" upon which to act. But then historical

4. I feel it necessary to add a personal twist on conscientious objection and pacifism. COGIC persons are not defenseless because we will not pursue and kill our enemies. This does not mean I would not or could not kill another individual. Every person has the right to self-defense, and should someone kill as a result of an act of self-defense, that person has not broken faith and commitment to conscientious objection. Does this sound contradictory? For example, if someone attacks my wife, I will not allow that to happen unchallenged. That individual will have to cease or with all my power and God given strength, I will stop him! My intent would be to stop him but not to kill him. Should he die in the struggle to make him stop, God will judge my intent; and my wife and I will be safe. This is an ethical determination I have made, knowing how easy it is to have troubling situations overtake one.

realities often modify perspectives and tend to marginalize the decisions that precipitate so-called just wars. All nations address the issue of defense and tend to declare a moral high ground that is used to retaliate against those who commit murderous attacks. *In the Church of God in Christ, our youth should believe the moral high ground is a commitment to conscientious objection, which makes killing an enemy unacceptable.*

However, our sons and daughters are currently choosing to fight and possibly take human life for this country. What has happened to our basic belief? Unlike some religious combatants who kill for their God because they understand God to be an ultra-nationalistic being totally committed to their side, COGIC youth should not be trained that way. Our youth clearly view the military as a career option. They have been seduced by the system and powers of the state, and they have forgotten about the God who calls us to peace. The commitment to military service as a volunteer makes one a combatant, for there is no room for conscientious objection in the voluntary armed services. The Church of God in Christ has not changed the conscientious objection taught by Mason, thus it should sound strange to hear that so many COGIC youth serve in the military! Look among your own congregation and see how many have voluntarily joined the military service. We have youth serving and killing Iraqi and Afghani soldiers, and willful killing should not be an option for saints. Serving is an honorable choice, but it is hardly consistent with our Pentecostal heritage and Mason's pacifism. Our tradition was one of military service only if one was conscripted, but now our youth volunteer! In all candor, this country has too often forgotten about the needs of blacks and minority youth with respect to education and occupational success in the job market, and high rates of unemployment and underemployment directly contribute to the high rate of blacks volunteering for military service. *In reality, our youth are killing for money and political reasons, not for self-defense.* I say this because I question the legitimacy of the current wars.

*Historically speaking, the Church of God in Christ is anti-war, and I hope we will remain so in the future.* Bishop C. H. Mason was a practical pacifist, and he believed that war was the result of pride. He opposed the Great War in Europe, even though it was fought as "the war to end all wars." Mason saw no moral value in the fighting, and he knew the complexities of international relations would spark continued difficulty. He was guided by the scriptures and based his belief in conscientious objector status on God and the sacredness of human life. Jesus was the primary model, and he taught that Luke 9:56 demonstrated the Son of Man did not come to destroy lives but to save, and by his possible death may come peace. For preaching an anti-war message, Bishop Mason was imprisoned, his life was threatened, and he was eventually banished from Lexington, Mississippi. Bishop Mason was called a "Kaiser Lover" by the "good" white people of Lexington, Mississippi and put in jail. Black soldiers were often beaten and stripped of their uniforms because we were not considered worthy to wear the uniform. This was a difficult time for the saints, and we were damned on both sides, but being popular and in tune with the larger society was not our call. *The Formative Years*, edited in part by Bishop German Ross in 1969, showed that Bishop Mason was not anti-government or anti-national, only anti-war. On killing, Mason preached:

> The son of Man is not come to destroy men's lives, but to save them. Future events showed, before he would kill he offered up himself, and by his death came peace, and if the Kaiser had been willing to die rather than shed the blood of his fellow men, we would now have peace.

How did Mason support the U.S. government? Mason said, "I cannot understand, after preaching the gospel for twenty years and exhorting to peace and righteousness, how I could be accused of fellowshipping with the anti-Christ of the Kaiser." He then encouraged the saints to do as he and buy government bonds, of which Bishop Mason bought $3,000 worth. "Brethren, we are living by every word of God-Matthew 4:4. Our government is asking us for a loan, and we are in no violation of God's word in granting it, and not only to loan, but loan, hoping for nothing to gain-Luke 6:35."

Mason preached to people of color who were close to the ground. American secular society impacted black folks differently—though poorly educated and economically desperate, we held on to our American ideals. Bishop Mason's message was liberating and challenging for the emerging black population. Our men came home from France and were beaten and lynched for wearing a military uniform. We believed America would change and recognize her African sons and daughters whose blood spilled in Cuba, the Philippines, and France. Again, historically, in contrast to whites, black Americans believed in general the reports that our country held the moral high ground in life and death commitments. Bishop Mason was not deceived and knew that blacks died disproportionately in war. The poor, the underprivileged, and masses of innocents died first and most often. In relation to this country, we are still forced to grasp false hopes with big smiles, knowing the results of institutionalized bigotry and Jim Crow Laws controlled our destiny. We loved America in spite of our American experience. In *The Soul of Black Folks*, W. E. B. Du Bois wrote that we black people live two lives. This reality we could hardly deny; our democratic guarantees were often marginalized by racism, lack of privilege, double standards, and permanent second-class feelings. "Racial situations" in America have been nothing more than a social science and cold economic statistics since days of slavery. It is a historic fact that America has measured and exacted harm and punishment upon the victims of its systematic racism. America has elevated prejudice to an art while singing the traditional jargon of patriotism to the melody of the "Star Spangled Banner." Though the brutal reality is a history of broken promises, we black Americans run life's gauntlet of oppression while the promises of America are presented to others without contest.

It is time for the clerics of Islam, the rabbis of Judaism, and the clergy of Christianity to speak not in the language of politics, culture, or military retaliation, but rather the speech of God, a speech of conscientiousness. My faith and sense of purpose challenge me to believe in love, peace, and preservation of life, and I believe these qualities are found in the simple truths of these religions and that spreading these ideals can make a positive difference. Whether Islamic, Jewish, or Christian, the belief in a higher being should help reasonable humans not want to see the world reduced to trash. Like our conscientious father, Bishop C. H. Mason, religionists the world over need to aggressively pursue peace. Following the examples of Dr. Ralph Bunche and Dr. Martin Luther King, Jr., boldness and commitment to principle must be primary in the pursuit of life.

Lastly, what is the future generation to do? What should our bishops and pastors teach as dogma to make this clear? There is a moral imperative for the Church to be an advocate for peace even during times of war. *The Church that Bishop Mason founded should proclaim peace even when war is considered "just" because war is the last act in willful pride. To be COGIC should mean being a militant for peace, and this should be basic to the character of coming generations. Our bishops and pastors should revisit the doctrine of conscientious objection and discourage our children from joining the military.* Bishop Mason believed we should serve when conscripted, but today there is no draft, and we should not have youth in the military. Certainly, we do have fine young people in the military today, and I personally pray for their safety, but I also pray that none of them has to take a human life in the service of this country.

The Church of God in Christ should be progressively challenging people around the world to promote anti-war activities. The world should be upset with our continuous resolve for peace. The General Board of Bishops should join the international peace community and educate the world about our COGIC position. *The bishops should work to restate our conscientious objection tradition within the organization and then approach the world with numbers of ardent supporters.* The General Assembly should commission an office headquartered in Memphis dedicated to dialoguing and promoting world peace. It is time for religionists to speak not the language of politics, culture, race, or military retaliation, but rather the speech of God. The COGIC tradition should challenge the coming generation to believe that the principles of love and preservation of life are found in the simple truths of faith, especially as expressed by Bishop C. H. Mason. The General Board should take immediate and committed action by consecrating an auxiliary bishop to promote peace with others, whether Islamic, Jewish, or Christian.

The Church of God in Christ should make formal contact with all relevant governmental agencies and ancillary groups involved with international relations and announce the formation of an Institute for Peace. This institute should be composed of religious groups who have rejected the use of violence and are avowed conscientious objectors. Funding for the institute should be through participant dues, making it independent of any secular government or agency. This will preserve the institute's freedom and pragmatic approach to resolving problems. What real relevance or transforming power would a group have if it were inextricably tied to or controlled by an outside force? The institute, just like the Church, must have its independence because any outside control would take away its real relevance and transforming power. Philanthropic organizations and persons of means would be welcomed contributors, provided they would allow the institute its autonomy and God-centered principles. The institute should be totally committed to pacifism. Association with the world court shall be a tenet of establishment because there is not peace without justice. An elected president should have emissary credentials and be granted observer status at the Untied Nations. In return, the Institute of Peace would grant observer status to a representative of the United Nations.

Killing is too easy, and the numbers killed daily throughout the world suggest the world's technology for killing is unparalleled. The institute could sponsor ecumenical peace conferences. Religionists should come together and ask whether or not the great religions can reach agreements regarding essential theological truth, supporting meaningful pursuits that express and affirm peace among humanity. There should be an awakening to the consanguine reality that all creation is indeed of one family and of one destiny. The whole of humanity should rediscover that we share a common progenitor: the God of Peace. Our common heritage and kinship suggest there is common ground upon which God's children can walk. The consultation for peace could allow people of faith to confer together about the content of our varied scriptures and find inspiration to live together. Perhaps our scriptural insights could transcend diverse theological apologetics and affirm God's presence.

This conference should ask how to help all people desire righteousness and equality. We should value all civilizations on the face of the earth! Representing God only, the purveyors of peace and faith must speak boldly to geopolitical structures and prepare a place at the table of essential ideas for the coming generation. Our greatest idea is that our world can have peace while futility and inhumanity can cease to exist. Our practical imaginations labor under such an ideal circumstance. The next generation must understand that there may be times when some claim that violence is considered necessary to save life and that such a time will be under pressure of moral and ethical scrutiny. Conscientious objection can rise to relevancy and immediacy, making it clear that stopping the killing is God's will. In fact, the order of the day will affirm that saving one's enemy from annihilation is the first step in preserving one's own humanity.

The next generation must signal a rebirth of Bishop Mason's commitment to conscientious objection, and our church must be recognized for its passionate militancy for peace. To maintain COGIC integrity, the saints must take every opportunity and speak against cultural bias, economic exploitations, nationalistic boundaries, and racial issues, thereby promoting the sanctification for which we are known. This current generation should lay the groundwork to forge a practical theology for public scrutiny and publish the realities of individual sanctification in the form of a collective treatise. This treatise should be used as a vital bridge between warring groups whose chief individual concerns have too long negated human respect and mutual dignity of all life. All people must be dedicated to separation from sin, separation unto God, and being conformed to the image of Christ. As a group of conscientious objectors, the Church of God in Christ could correlate these various theological principles for the world while reinforcing our founder's teachings. Our practical application of Bishop Mason's desire for peacemaking could emerge as genuine and provide a response to the existential and community questions that are often divisive and self-interested. The desperate need for survival everywhere shows that the time is now. The zeal to kill or die for a cause has now surpassed the wholesome desire to strive for a workable peace. A religious organization committed to peace can help sanctify a humanity in need of theological answers and forge collaboration among non-combatants, professional arbitrators, and belligerent, fatally-engaged parties. The Church of God in Christ, the children of Mason, has an opportunity to participate in public process, and we can help the world recognize the mutual interdependence that all peoples have.

Finally, this collaboration will mean the mobilization of a new and public faith-based initiative to work toward worldwide peace. What a time to dream, to reclaim the dignity and Godly quality the Creator bestowed upon His creation! What a time to sanctify the blood and memory of so many lost and wasted lives and to birth countless souls into new perceptions of living! The simple ability to converse using peaceful constructs is the first step toward purification and redemption for all people and an end to philosophies that justify war.

*Come behold the works of the Lord,*
*Who has made desolations in the earth.*
*He makes wars cease to the end of the earth;*
*He breaks the bow and cuts the spear in two;*
*He burns the chariot in the fire.*
*Be still, and know that I am God;*
*I will be exalted among the nations.*
*I will be exalted in the earth!*
Psalm 46:8–10

# 9

## Send Judah First

*A Pentecostal Perspective on Peace*

### Marlon Millner

I have the privilege of running a listserv dedicated to pastors, scholars, and laypeople who want to talk about Pentecostalism throughout the African diaspora, including Oneness Pentecostalism. We have discussed and debated various issues since the listserv was started, especially the need for Pentecostals to engage in more collective action.

During the one-year anniversary of September 11, I noticed that white Evangelicals were endorsing President Bush's plan for a preemptive war with Iraq via open letters and opinion articles. They couched their endorsements in Christian language, giving the impression that to not support war was not just un-American, but non-Christian. I knew many good Pentecostals (white, black, other) who felt otherwise, but had not voiced their opinions; so I initially crafted "Send Judah First: A Pentecostal Perspective on Peace." I went through three or four revisions, gaining input from various persons, and learning more about Pentecostals' history of pacifism.

Finally, the letter was completed in early October, 2002 and we started an all-out blitz to get signatures. I contacted over thirty bishops and leaders of Pentecostal and Apostolic organizations, especially Apostolics—Pentecostal Assemblies of the World (PAW), Church of Our Lord Jesus Christ, Bibleway—because this is my tradition. I was sorely disappointed by the bishops' general lack of response. We deliberately reached across many denominational barriers, but most of the signers are Pentecostal, including several academics in the Assemblies of God, and one Hispanic Oneness group. The most important Apostolic ecclesiastical leaders to sign the letter are Bishop Charles Ellis, Bishop of the International Young People's Union of the PAW and pastor of Greater Grace Temple in Detroit, and Bishop James Clark, presiding Apostle of the Church of Our Lord Jesus Christ of the Apostolic Faith and pastor of Christ Temple in New York.

The letter was delivered to the White House by an official lobbying firm in November 2002, but we received no official response. I think this lack of response is, in large part, because they know Pentecostals tend to follow Evangelicals politically so they have nothing to lose. If Bush could basically brush aside the protests of millions in early February 2003, a letter with 40 names would not have been of much significance.

One of the key themes of the letter is that if Pentecostals are so different from Evangelicals because we are actually "baptized" in the Holy Ghost, we ought to have a different opinion about war. Our history indicates that historically, we have, but we have lost that zeal as we have become comfortable with the world.

We have pressed on, and now many of us are a part of an effort to form Pentecostals & Charismatics for Peace & Justice—not a new denomination, but an alliance of Pentecostals and Spirit-filled Christians who are concerned that our witness includes a manifest commitment to peace, reconciliation, and justice. If being baptized in Jesus' name and baptized in the Holy Ghost, with the initial sign of speaking in tongues, *truly* makes any difference while here on the Earth, this is one of the times it should.

I encourage Oneness Pentecostals to be more informed. We need Pentecostals and Apostolics by the millions to pray, praise, and protest. We need to harness our Holy Ghost resources to combat this evil if we believe we have the power to "bind and loose."

Jesus knew His power lay not in dispatching angels to eradicate the "Evil Ones" but in suffering to redeem those controlled by the powers of darkness. He offered the primary biblical example (more than Exodus, more than I Chronicles, more than Jeremiah, more than Galatians, more than any other source in the Bible): the Gospel of God provides the resources not for living in fear but for staying in the middle of God's will, even in the face of death.

Being that we believe this is the "end time," why would we support a war to "preserve our safety" and the current order of this world, which is sinful? We should pray "Come, Lord Jesus" and stand against violence in the confidence that God himself will radically manifest Himself when we declare the name of Jesus and refuse to take human life, and even suffer death, rather than inflict it.

## AN OPEN LETTER TO PRESIDENT GEORGE W. BUSH

November 12, 2002

The Honorable George W. Bush
President of the United States of America
The White House
1600 Pennsylvania Avenue NW
Washington, DC 20502

To President Bush:

In a national dialogue over the prospect of war with Iraq, the voices of secular ideology have dominated. The undersigned of this letter believe now is the time for a Spirit-filled and prophetic Christian voice for peace. Mr. President, you have determined that the only way to bring peace is through war. The notion of waging war—even acting preemptively—to bring peace is not new, nor is it a proven remedy to eradicate those manifest forces of evil that plague our world. Christians have debated the right or wrong of the U.S. striking Iraq and opening the door to what surely will escalate into a much larger battle against forces. We humbly ask you to consider our ideological view—entitled, *"Send Judah First: a Pentecostal Perspective on Peace."*

We speak first and foremost as Christians, not experts in military strategy, political theory, or international diplomacy. However, we are not naive about the functions of those areas of secular society, but we claim that even the secular society operates within sacred space—God's good creation of the whole inhabited Earth.

Moreover, we say this is a "Pentecostal Perspective," to indicate that we place primacy on the present activity of God in the Earth through God's Spirit. The Spirit of God is what enlivens our faith, transforms our mentalities, enables, empowers, and equips us to live our lives out of a new set of realities. Indeed, we no longer give into fear, rather, we are enabled to love unconditionally, empowered to be agents of change, and equipped to exercise self-restraint, particularly in the use of force or violence of any means to bring about the peace and justice the world seeks.

We humbly propose that American Christians, the President included, radically rethink the rules and tools of engagement with powers of darkness, whether they are individual, societal, or military weapons of mass destruction. In essence, we challenge them to be filled with the Spirit of God.

"Send Judah First" is an expression used in Spirit-filled churches to suggest that by praising God we can defeat evil as manifested in Saddam Hussein. There are many biblical examples that could be appealed to, but here is just one that is popular in Pentecostal and Charismatic churches:

> They rose early in the morning, and went out into the wilderness of Tekoa; and as they went out, Jehoshaphat stood and said, "Listen to me, O Judah and inhabitants of Jerusalem! Believe in the LORD your God and you will be established; believe in his prophets." When he had taken counsel with the people, he appointed those who were to sing to the LORD and praise him in holy splendor, as they went before the army, saying, "Give thanks to the LORD, for his steadfast love endures forever." As they began to sing and praise, the LORD set an ambush against the Ammonites, Moab, and Mount Seir, who had come against Judah, so that they were routed. (2 Chronicles 20:20–22, NRSV)

In this popular story of the Old Testament, the portion of the former ancient nation of Israel in the South, known as Judah, faced enemies on all sides. Overwhelmed and afraid, the leader of the nation, King Jehoshaphat sought God and asked for His help. In the end, God Himself promises to fight for the nation, and they praise God (speak well, compliment, exalt God) and sing. They go out, but they send their praisers and singers first. Judah can be translated as 'praise.'

In the war debate between liberal and conservative Christians, Evangelicals have dominated the ideological battlefield, and they are, in fact, the people to whom Bush actively caters. A September 28th *Washington Post* article quoted Richard Cizik as saying, "In this instance, the president has articulated a faith much like our own." Cizik is vice president for governmental affairs at the National Association of Evangelicals. The article goes on to say, "That faith includes a stated belief in Jesus Christ and the existence of 'evil' in the form of people like Hussein, Cizik said." The article also quoted Richard Land, a leader on public policy issues for the Southern Baptist Convention, as calling religious leaders who oppose Bush "well-intentioned and naive." Land was quoted further as saying, "My educated surmisal is that the president and intelligence community believe Saddam is much closer than we know he is to getting these weapons. Time is on Saddam's side, not ours. I'd rather be safe than sorry," Land said.

Noticeably absent from the article are comments from Pentecostal and Charismatic church leaders, for it is in fact our branch of Christianity that is the fastest growing, both in the U.S. and around the world. And it is on this issue of war that we believe clear distinctions and tensions between progressive Pentecostals and socially and theologically conservative Evangelicals should be contrasted for the purpose of articulating a prophetic and Spirit-filled voice for peace.

Mr. President, we are sure Land would consider our warfare theology of praise naive and probably not even well intentioned. Land, Cizik, and other Evangelicals often do not believe in the felt, tactile presence of God—known in the person of the Holy Spirit—and typically do not believe that modern phenomena such as "speaking-in-tongues" or prophecy or faith-healing are legitimate expressions of miraculous gifts described in New Testament scriptures. Such a wooden, non-experiential, and fundamentalist faith often supports the status quo politically.

But consider that many leading historians of antiquity believe that it was the spread of Christianity (often fueled by religious experience) that ultimately led to the downfall of the Roman Empire. While Western civilization is often the celebrated rediscovery of Greco-Roman antiquity, it can hardly be considered paradoxical that much of what is rationalist-Enlightenment thought, rooted in ancient philosophical foundations, was defeated by the phenomenological and experiential forces of a living God mediated through a new community of believers in Jesus Christ.

These were believers that often emphasized the immediate presence and activity of God through the Holy Spirit, even as one after another was killed, murdered, slaughtered, and martyred for their faith.

In modern times, many African-American Christians actually waged war against slavery, then de facto segregation, lynching, and state-supported oppression through praise. Leaders, such as Martin Luther King, Jr. and many other preachers, led marches against the enemy with prayer and singing. Thousands went to jail on their knees, not in defeat but in prayer. Thousands faced dogs, water cannons, and bullets through praising God. In a wonderful book, *Protest and Praise: Sacred Music of Black Religion*, Dr. Jon Michael Spencer portrays an experiential faith in action, in which people are empowered to engage their enemies without fear, but they do not fight on the terms of evil.

> I ask that when I am present I need not show boldness by daring to oppose those who think we are acting according to human standards. Indeed, we live as human beings, but we do not wage war according to human standards; for the weapons of our warfare are not merely human, but they have a divine power to destroy strongholds. We destroy arguments and every proud obstacle raised up against the knowledge of God, and we take every thought captive to obey Christ. We are ready to punish every disobedience when your obedience is complete. (2 Cor 10:2–6, NRSV)

It is no surprise that some church leaders would be ready to make educated surmisals of being safe rather than sorry when one is not being prompted by the Spirit but by spy intelligence and military war doctrine—not the doctrines of God. It is also clear, and unfortunate, that those who would question American political leadership would be called un-Patriotic, and even un-Christian, as if Jesus is the patron savior of the U.S. alone. A prophetic voice challenges a nation and goes against conventional thinking when it is rooted in the ways of the secular institutional superstructures.

And yet, should Christians provide unwavering support of war with Iraq, especially if those with training and experience in war doubt the mission will be effective?

In a Reuters article from October 10th, retired Marine Corps General Anthony Zinni said that military conflict rarely accomplishes the goals politicians intended. Zinni is quoted saying, "If we look at this (attacking

Iraq) as the beginning of a chain of events that means that we intend to do this through violent action, we're on the wrong course." What's more, Zinni, who has served both President Clinton and President Bush, listed several priorities ahead of war with Iraq: putting Middle East peace talks back on track, ensuring that Iran continues to move toward reform, helping Afghanistan and other central Asian states, patching up relations with Arab states, and reopening dialogue with the people of the region.

One wonders if those other goals may be achieved if Christians are complicit with a "might means right" doctrine, while our own scriptures suggest that God has chosen the weak things of this world to confound the mighty?

We agree with the priorities of construction and creation, rather than destruction through war. We also believe the humanizing power of God's love leads us to engage even our enemies, with our hopes not in men but in God's ability to transform persons and institutions. Only through dialogue, mutual investment, and self-sacrifice can we demonstrate our Christian love, binding us together only as we work for peace. This is the true effect of praise, for the writer of the letter to the Hebrews reminds us not only to "continually offer a sacrifice of praise to God, that is the fruit of lips that confess his name," but he adds, "Do not neglect to do good and to share what you have, for such sacrifices are pleasing to God."

Self-righteous engagement based on narrow interests will only create new regimes that may no longer simply threaten the United States, but are often the worst enemy of the nation's own people. Regime change must begin in us. A regime or religion of words from our lips but not works from our hands tells others to believe Jesus for who we say He is but not for the miraculous works of our hands done through God's empowering Spirit. American Christians must demonstrate our commitment to a region, while American interests have often resulted in abandoning nations to the point that we no longer identify their struggle as our own.

Christians who believe in the primacy of the Holy Spirit have long been convinced that by mediating metaphysical reality through prayer and praise, Christians can in fact affect the material world and provide jobs, health, good relationships, mortgages, and cars. The power of the Spirit engages us to help shape our own personal world into a place of God's destiny. The supporters of this letter challenge each American Christian and the whole church to now extend the privatization of the praise ethic to the world of foreign affairs and social conflict in both word and deed.

In the early years of Pentecostalism, many American leaders were opposed to World War I as pacifists. The conviction that the outpouring of the Spirit should be viewed as the agent of ushering in a new reality through Jesus Christ made Pentecostals unwilling to be complicit with the politics and warmongering of their day, no matter how justifiable. But alas, waiting for manifestations of that eschatological social re-organization made Pentecostals doubt their experience would soon bode major social change, and they retrenched in denominations based largely on race, class, and dogma. By the second World War, many were trying to preserve their own existence, rather than trusting in the ways of the Holy Spirit to eradicate evil, which is no less present in the world now than then. If it is true that God does not give us a Spirit of fear but of power, of love, and of self-control, then we, the undersigned, challenge all Christians, including you Mr. President, to re-orient their thinking to trust that "Sending Judah First" may in fact be the only way for Christians to truly say they trust God to deliver them in the face of imminent attacks of a grave nature and to work for peace even in the face of grotesque evil.

In the Spirit of truth,

Marlon Millner
Student, Harvard Divinity School
Minister, Apostle Church of Christ in God
Washington, DC/Winston-Salem, NC

Ruth Lewis Bentley, PhD
Director of Administration/Treasurer
National Black Evangelical Association
Member of Church Board
Progressive Beulah Pentecostal Church
Chicago, IL

Dr. Robert Franklin
Former president, Interdenominational Theological Center
Elder, Church of God in Christ
Atlanta, GA

Rev. James Brooks, PhD
Chairman, Department of Religion & Philosophy
Bethune-Cookman College
Dr. James Brooks Ministries Inc.
Port Orange, FL

Garland J. Owensby
Assistant Professor
Southwestern Assemblies of God University
Waxahachie, TX

Paul Alexander, PhD
Associate Professor, Bible & Theology
Southwestern Assemblies of God University
Waxahachie, TX

Antipas Harris
Student, Boston University School of Theology
Minister, A House of the Living God, Church of Jesus Christ
Manchester, GA

Superintendent Herbert R. Davis, MDiv
Instructor, North Carolina Bible College
Pastor, Nehemiah Christian Center Church of God in Christ
Durham, NC

Rev. Craig Scandrett-Leatherman
Urban Studies Consultant, Greenville College
Pastor, Lighthouse Free Methodist Church
St. Louis, MO

Rev. Don diXon Williams
Bread for the World
Field Representative, United Way of the Cross Churches International
Danville, VA

Dr. Lynda Jordan
Student, Harvard Divinity School
Evangelist, United Holy Church of America Inc.
Greensboro, NC

Rev. Herbert Daughtry
Presiding Bishop, The House of the Lord Pentecostal Church
Brooklyn, NY

Rev. C. Christopher Smith
Coordinator, Kingdom NOW
Home church Pastor, Common Ground Christian Church
Indianapolis, IN

Bishop James I. Clark, Jr.
Pastor, Christ Temple Church of Our Lord Jesus Christ, Inc.
New York, NY

Rev. Dr. Roswith Gerloff
Evangelical Church of Berlin-Brandenburg
African Christian Diaspora in Europe: Council of Christian Communities
of an African Approach in Europe
Leeds, UK

Dr. Albert G. Miller
Professor, Oberlin College
Pastor, The House of the Lord Pentecostal Church
Oberlin, OH

Superintendent Cornelius E. Anderson, Jr.
Pastor, Temple of Deliverance Church of God in Christ
Durham, NC

Dr. Karen Kossie-Cherrnyshev
Assistant Professor of History
Texas Southern University
Minister of Music, Latter Day Revival Center
Houston, TX

Rev. Estrelda Alexander
Associate Dean for Community Life
Wesley Theological Seminary
Washington, DC

Michael McBride
Student, Duke Divinity School
Youth Pastor, Bible Way Christian Center
San Jose, CA

Rev. Oscar Dace
Pastor, Bible Way Christian Center
San Jose, CA

Dawn L. Henson
Student, Harvard Divinity School
Member, National Baptist Convention
Chicago, IL

William Paul Franks
Student, Talbot School of Theology
Member, Assemblies of God
La Mirada, CA

Daniel Ramirez
Student, Duke University
Guest Scholar, Center for Comparative Immigration Studies
University of California, San Diego
Member, Apostolic Assembly of the Faith in Christ Jesus
San Diego, CA

David Michel, S.T.M.
Student, Chicago Theological Seminary
Minister, Church of God (Cleveland, TN)
Chicago, IL

Mark Jennings
Student, Harvard Divinity School
Minister, Church of the Olive Branch
Washington, DC

Rev. Mark Johnson
Pastor, Church of the Olive Branch
Washington, DC

Dr. David Daniels
Associate Professor of Church History
McCormick Theological Seminary
Elder, Church of God in Christ
Chicago, IL

Elizabeth Dermody Leonard, PhD
Department of Anthropology/Sociology
Vanguard University
Costa Mesa, CA

John R. M. Wilson
Professor of History
Vanguard University
Costa Mesa, CA

Katy Attanasi
Student, Harvard Divinity School
Associate member, Fairfax Assembly of God
Fairfax, VA

Luc Caltrider
Student, Harvard Divinity School
Ministerial Student, The Wesleyan Church
Boston, MA

Rev. James Richardson, Jr., MDiv
Pastor, Mt. Sinai Apostle Church
Presiding Bishop, The Apostle Church of Christ in God
Martinsville, VA
Rev. Delman Coates, PhD Candidate
Columbia University, Department of Religion
Youth Pastor, Metropolitan Baptist Church
Newark, NJ

Tonia Dermody Collinske, MA
Asst. to Executive Director, University Relations
Vanguard University
Costa Mesa, CA

Josef Sorett
Student, Harvard University
Graduate School of Arts and Sciences
Itinerant Elder, African Methodist Episcopal Church
Boston, MA

Rev. Robert Benson III
Elder, Church of God in Christ
Washington, DC

Bryan Dahms
Associate Pastor
Olathe Covenant Church
Olathe, KS

Bishop Charles H. Ellis III
Senior Pastor, Greater Grace Temple
Detroit, MI

Richard G. Foss
Pastoral elder
Plow Creek Mennonite Church
Tiskilwa, IL

Randall Jones, Jr.
M.T.S. Student
Boston University School of Theology
Boston, MA

Dr. Anthea Butler
Professor
Loyola Marymount University
Los Angeles, CA

Rev. Jason Clark
Pastor
New Friendship Baptist Church
Baltimore, MD

# 10

## Toward a Pentecostal Contribution to the Just War Tradition

### Michael Beals

In the spring of 1915, my paternal grandmother, Violet Anderson Beals, graduated from nursing school in Kansas City, Missouri. In the years that followed, she developed her skills as a surgical nurse and, by the latter half of 1918, was working with mustard gas victims returning from the Great War. This experience left a life-long impression on her. By her own admission, working with the carnage of wartime atrocities extinguished an optimism about the future that she had previously shared with others of her generation in the early years of the twentieth century. My grandmother died in 1985 at the age of 89; her life spanned the terms of 17 presidents, and while she demonstrated resilience and courage through the seismic social, economic and technological shifts of the twentieth century, the optimism of those early years was never fully restored.

In 1919, while the gruesome effects of trench warfare were eroding my grandmother's optimism, Aimee Semple McPherson wrote a hymn which captured the essence of the contemporary Pentecostal expectation of the imminent return of Christ.

*THE FORMER AND LATTER RAIN*

*Now the great and final harvest day is drawing nigh,*
  *And our Lord is pouring from on high,*
*Pentecostal show'rs to ripen up the golden grain:*
  *Have you received this latter rain?*

*Lift up thine eyes and behold the latter rain,*
*Calling to-day to ripen up the grain;*
*For our Lord is coming soon, and with Him we shall reign,*
*Jesus is coming soon, again.*[1]

In these lines, as elsewhere in her ministry, Sister Aimee brought into focus the sustaining hope shared among believers of the approaching eschaton. For many persons such as my grandmother, who did not embrace a biblical perspective, 1919 was a year of disorientation and anxiety over the shape of the post-war world. Pentecostals, conversely, were comforted and sustained by the belief that a time was coming when those who "loved his appearing" (2 Timothy 4:8) would be delivered and vindicated for their other-worldly orientation. For now, the Lord had poured out his Spirit in these last days to "ripen up the grain."

Even among Spirit-baptized believers awaiting Christ's return there was a significant divergence of views and opinions as to how his faithful ones should conduct themselves in this interim. To be sure, evangelism and missions were cornerstones of Pentecostal engagement with the world, yet Pentecostal individuals and groups were forced to deal with the proximate reality of armed conflict. Some had few qualms about supporting the effort of the Allied Powers to repulse the aggression of the "criminal Hun."[2] For others, such support at best represented the misguided zeal of patriotism, which itself gave evidence of a lingering loyalty to the things in this world (1 John 2:15). Others more critically viewed Pentecostal support of the war effort as the church's abandonment of Christ himself. This struggle was publicly enacted in the Assemblies of God. Constituencies collided over the involvement of Christians in war in a manner that reflected the foundational commitments of the newly formed Pentecostal movement and shaped the scope of its engagement and effectiveness in the society in which it sprang to life.

---

1. Aimee Semple McPherson, "The Former and the Latter Rain" (Course syllabus, *History of Pentecostalism*, Cecil M. Robeck, Jr., Fuller Theological Seminary, Fall, 1999) 198.

2. E. N. Bell, "Questions and Answers," *The Christian Evangel* 19 (1918) 5.

In April of 1917, twenty-two days after the United States declared war on Germany, the Assemblies of God articulated its official position regarding military service to the U.S. Government in the form of a "Resolution Concerning the Attitude of the General Council of the Assemblies of God Toward any Military Service which Involves the Actual Participation in the Destruction of Human Life."[3] The resolution recognized "Human Government as of Divine ordination" and affirmed their "unswerving loyalty to the Government of the United States" while concluding that they, as a body of Christians, "while purposing to fulfill all the obligations of loyal citizenship, [were] nevertheless constrained to declare that they could not conscientiously participate in war and armed resistance which involves the actual destruction of human life, since this was contrary to [their] view of the clear teachings of the inspired Word of God, which was the sole basis of [their] faith."

Cracks in that resolve began to show immediately. They took the form of a moral migration away from the pacifism plainly visible in early official documents toward a *laissez-faire* position on Christians and military service. And although this direction was set by the end of the Great War, the journey lasted almost fifty years. During this period, the many minor emendations made to the Assemblies of God position on military service served only to reinforce a moral course set during World War I. In his essay, "Pacifism in Pentecostalism," Murray Dempster observes that in "each biennium from 1927 to 1965 a slightly modified version appeared in published, official minutes of the denomination's General Council."[4] As a final emendation, the era of Assemblies of God Pentecostal pacifism officially concluded at the 1967 General Council with the resolution to delete the long-standing "Article XXII. Military Service" from the Bylaws. The new article succinctly stated:

> Article XXII. Military Service
> As a movement we affirm our loyalty to the government of the United States in war or peace.

3. General Council of the Assemblies of God, "Resolution Concerning the Attitude of the General Council of the Assemblies of God Toward any Military Service which Involves the Actual Participation in the Destruction of Human Life," in *Combined Minutes of the General Council of the Assemblies of God in the United States of America, Canada and Foreign Lands* (Springfield: Gospel, 1917) 11–12.

4. Murray W. Dempster, "Pacifism in Pentecostalism: The Case of the Assemblies of God," in *Proclaim Peace: Christian Pacifism from Unexpected Quarters*, edited by Theron F. Schlabach and Richard T. Hughes (Urbana: University of Illinois Press, 1997) 52 n. 1.

> We shall continue to insist, as we have historically, on the
> right of each member whether to declare his position as a com-
> batant, a non-combatant, or a conscientious objector.[5]

Among the explanations of what precipitated this fundamental
change in denominational identity, three interpretive frameworks are
recognized as the most plausible explanatory systems.

## JAY BEAMAN: *CULTURAL ASSIMILATION*

In the final chapter of his book, *Pentecostal Pacifism*, Jay Beaman argues
that cultural assimilation provides the best explanation for the loss of
pacifism in the Assemblies of God.[6] Along with the establishment of the
chaplaincy, in Beaman's view, this cultural assimilation is evident in two
additional areas. The first concerned the sheer numbers of Pentecostal
men who were enlisting in the military in World War II.[7] Tens of thousands volunteered for active duty as an expression of national loyalty. This
forced a reckoning between the formally stated position of the denomination and the actions and needs of a large portion of its constituency.
The second avenue of cultural assimilation was Pentecostal "upward mobility" through membership in the National Association of Evangelicals
(NAE) in 1942.[8] According to Cecil Robeck, the NAE is "an association
of evangelical, Holiness, and Pentecostal individuals, local churches, and
denominations formed in 1942 to provide visibility and advocacy for
the concerns of conservative Christians in the U.S."[9] In Beaman's view,
moderating the stance on military service was necessary in the quest for
mainstream recognition and so pacifism was left behind.

---

5. Joel Shuman, "Pentecost and the end of Patriotism: A Call for the Restoration of
Pacifism Among Pentecostal Christians," *Journal of the European Pentecostal Theological
Association* 9 (1996) 88–89.

6. Jay Beaman, *Pentecostal Pacifism: The Origin, Development, and Rejection of
Pacific Belief among the Pentecostals* (Hillsboro, KS: Center for Mennonite Brethren
Studies, 1989) 107–18.

7. Ibid., 109.

8. Ibid., 111–12.

9. Cecil M. Robeck, Jr., "National Association of Evangelicals," in *Dictionary of
Pentecostal and Charismatic Movements*, edited by Stanley M. Burgess and Gary B.
McGee (Grand Rapids: Zondervan, 1988) 634.

## Murray Dempster: Theological Insufficiency

While Dempster does not refute Beaman's assimilation thesis, he believes it does not completely explain why the denomination lost pacifism as rapidly as it did. He points out the failure of early Pentecostals to integrate pacifism into the "distinctive testimony" of the Pentecostal outpouring of the Spirit.[10] In other words, pacifism was not recognized as a restorationist theme. If modern Pentecostals were unable to locate pacifism in the teaching of the Apostles or in the practices of the early church, it would not be considered a core element of the contemporary outpouring. Further, Dempster refers to the loss of a *prophetic pacifist minority*.

In Dempster's religious framing, the Assemblies of God suffered the loss of a prophetic pacifist minority. These minority pacifists, while holding some overlapping ideas and common arguments, used a variety of theological frameworks and ethical principles to advance Christian pacifism. Before they had an opportunity to cultivate a pacifist *tradition*, however, history had overtaken them: the nation's patriotic war spirit invaded the house, never to leave. Without a theologically informed ethical tradition to sustain pacifists' numbers and to perpetuate their beliefs to new generations, the demise of Pentecostal pacifism within the Assemblies of God was only a matter of time.[11]

## EDITH BLUMHOFER: DUAL ALLEGIANCE

Blumhofer explains that the complex attitude of the Assemblies of God toward war can be understood not merely in terms of an accommodation to culture along an upwardly mobile path, but as a "dilemma of dual allegiance."[12] Pentecostals held in tension the apostolic exhortation of "subjection to governing authorities" (Rom 13:1–2) and reminder that "our citizenship is in heaven" (Phil 3:20–21). Both were expressions of loyalty, but Pentecostals had to prioritize their allegiances and contextualize their understanding of a greater loyalty. Blumhofer explains, "Pacifists declared their identity as pilgrims; others, while concurring, claimed an obligation in that pilgrimage to counter evil; this readily adapted to

10. Murray W. Dempster, "Reassessing the Moral Rhetoric of Early American Pentecostal Pacifism," *Crux* 26 (1990) 34.

11. Dempster, "Pacifism in Pentecostalism," 51.

12. Edith L. Blumhofer, *The Assemblies Of God: A Chapter in the Story of American Pentecostalism*, vol. 1, *To 1941* (Springfield: Gospel, 1989) 347.

identifying morality with the Allied cause—or other causes they could conceive of in moral terms."[13] At its heart, the difficulty is in reconciling the responsibilities of both pilgrim and citizen.

During a century replete with examples of international aggression justified as the protection of national interest, the proliferation of increasingly sophisticated and destructive weapons, and the horrors of human suffering broadcast into every household, this Pentecostal denomination lapsed into a silence tantamount to uncritical patriotism. In view of the exalted roles of glossolalia and prophecy among Pentecostals in general and in the Assemblies of God in particular, it is ironic that a movement so focused on biblically-based utterances should be mute on the biblically-grounded issues of justice and peace.

It is unlikely that the Assemblies of God will make any significant return to its pacifist roots, yet it is imperative that the denomination embrace a moral vehicle for cultural engagement on the issue of war. The just war tradition could be such a vehicle. And to the extent that other Pentecostal movements and groups have experienced similar migrations away from pacifism, the engagement of Pentecostal distinctives with the just war tradition could signal the restoration of a prophetic voice concerning the nature and legitimacy of war and make constructive contributions to a long-standing moral tradition with a rich heritage. By regaining a moral voice on the justice of war, Pentecostals will be able to speak to twenty-first century realities of violence and armed conflict in the characteristic tone of eschatological hope.

## THE JUST WAR TRADITION

From its earliest roots in Greek philosophy and Christian reflection to its contemporary influences both within and outside the Catholic church, common themes of the various contributions have congealed into the just war tradition. While there is no single, authoritative statement of the components of the tradition, criteria emerged that are generally accepted as falling under two categories: *jus ad bellum* (justice in the resort to war) and *jus in bello* (just conduct in war).

---

13. Ibid.

## jus ad bellum

The first *jus ad bellum* criterion is *legitimate authority*. By this standard, only those who bear prior responsibility for the common good of a sovereign political entity can resort to war. As a consequence, there are no legitimate private wars. Only the declaration of war by a legitimate authority overrides the *prima facie* duty of non-maleficence, the duty to not injure or kill others, and justifies the participation (if not all the actions) of those who do the actual fighting. Legitimate authority also implies competence for war: the ability to maintain control of military resources in the conduct of war and to cease hostilities as necessary.

Even if the authority to declare war is legitimate, there must also be a *just cause*: precipitating circumstances that are serious enough to warrant the intentional killing of human persons. Among recognized just causes are the defense of the national sovereignty or territorial integrity of a state, the protection of non-combatants from indiscriminate killing, and the defense of human rights.

Motives for war are considered in the criterion of *right intention*. Starting with Plato and Aristotle and moving forward, the intentions most clearly deemed "right" are the vindication of justice and the restoration of peace. National vengeance, hatred of the enemy, the selfish promotion of economic interests or the pursuit of geopolitical dominance provide no justification for war.

The prudential assessment of whether the ends sought are likely to be achieved is the basis for a *reasonable hope of success*. This criterion is frequently invoked by those who oppose the annihilationist commitment to the use of nuclear weapons as a deterrent, and by others who call into question the use of concrete military operations in order to pursue war on the abstract principle of terror.

The final *jus ad bellum* criterion is *last resort*. Before resorting to war, peaceful alternatives to resolving the conflict must be explored, if not exhausted. If justice can be vindicated and peace restored by negotiation or non-military pressure, then war cannot be justified.

## jus in bello

The just war tradition also includes two criteria that are guidelines for justice *in* war: *jus in bello*. The first is *discrimination* or *noncombatant immunity*. This criterion points to the immorality of intentionally killing innocent persons. Michael Walzer writes, "Just wars are limited wars; their conduct is governed by a set of rules designed to bar, so far as possible, the use of violence and coercion against noncombatant populations."[14] Two issues have been especially problematic with respect to discrimination. The first is the standard by which we judge a person to be a noncombatant. Should every member of a hostile nation be considered either an actual or potential combatant regardless of their age or capacity? By way of example, during World War II the Allied command apparently answered this question in the affirmative as a justification for the indiscriminate incendiary bombings of Dresden and the nuclear detonations over Hiroshima and Nagasaki. The second issue pertains to the idea of collateral damage, the unintended killing of civilians in a military operation. If civilian populations are granted immunity from direct harm, the justification for their unintended deaths is a function of the measures taken to protect them.

The second *jus in bello* criterion is *proportionality*. According to this criterion, the harmful consequences of the war must not be greater than the evil to be fought. This serves to limit the means used in the prosecution of war so that both parties may pursue peace and productivity in the post-war period. Proportionality, then, concerns more than the loss of human life. The degradation of health and welfare services, the destruction of political and economic infrastructure, and even irreparable damage to the environment are consequences to be considered.

## ESSENTIAL PRACTICES OF DISCERNMENT

Examining the models of Pentecostal spirituality and decision-making in the works of Stephen Parker and Steven Land, five essential practices associated with discernment become clear. These practices enable Pentecostals to evaluate the source and significance of their experiences. The following are suggested headings for these practices: *prayer, reflection, dialogue, orientation,* and *decision.* Taken together, these practices provide the basis by which Pentecostals may constructively engage the just war tradition.

14. Michael Walzer, *Just and Unjust Wars: A Moral Argument with Historical Illustrations* (San Francisco: Basic, 1977) xvii.

## Prayer

Regarding prayer, Steven Land observes that it "is the primary theological activity of Pentecostals. All worthwhile knowledge must be gained and retained prayerfully because only the Spirit can lead into all truth."[15] For this reason, prayer is central to the practice of discernment. Prayer is a recognition that our lives are a gift and a reminder of the contingency of our existence. Prayers of praise and thanksgiving are offered in recognition of our dependence on God and as expressions of gratitude for life, for salvation, and for the ongoing, gracious attention that God gives to our needs, faults, and dreams.

Intercessory prayer is a means for believers, Pentecostal or otherwise, to reach out beyond the situation of the self to touch others with the transforming power of God. It is human compassion in partnership with the purpose of God to see his will accomplished in the life of another. As Land points out, it is also an expression of the longing of Pentecostals for the conversion of the lost and the consummation of the ages.

In intercessory prayers, Pentecostals weep over the lost and afflicted and long for the coming of the Lord. Intercessory prayer may become deep sighing, as is sometimes evoked by the Spirit who groans and sighs with all creation as we await the full and final manifestation of the sons and daughters of God (Rom 8:26).[16] It is often in the context of praying for another that God makes himself and his purpose for the intercessor most clearly known.

Glossolalia is a third form of prayer, and the one with which Pentecostals, by definition, are most closely identified. Land describes speaking/praying in tongues as "a form of prayer which is especially edifying to the individual; it gives assurance, confidence and courage. This eschatological speech indicates that the power of the end is breaking in now."[17] There is a distinction between the public gift of tongues, with an accompanying interpretation, for the exhortation or edification of the gathered community, and the personal endowment of tongues as a prayer language for the edification of the individual believer. Land clarifies:

---

15. Steven J. Land, *Pentecostal Spirituality: A Passion for the Kingdom* (Sheffield, UK: Sheffield Academic, 1993) 166.

16. Ibid., 172.

17. Ibid.

Tongues, when interpreted, are, like prophecy, good for the whole body (1 Cor 14). All will not exercise this gift in tongues in the body; but for Pentecostals, all may speak in tongues in self-edification which will, in the unity of the body, ultimately, if indirectly, edify the whole.[18]

Glossolalia is the most intuitive form of prayer, but the mind is not (and cannot be) detached from the experience. As noted above, the edification that one receives through this type of prayer may take the form of assurance, confidence, or courage. At times, these insights may amount to little more than a general sense of well-being, but when glossolalia is exercised in conjunction with reflections on persons or circumstances, the resulting assurance, confidence, or courage have special significance. Praying in tongues while reflecting on the nature of a spiritual experience, then, becomes an important element in the process of discerning the validity of that experience.

It is important that prayer, in all forms, attends each of the other practices of discernment. Prayer is the superintending practice in that it provides for ongoing interaction with God throughout the process. The four other practices below presume an ongoing prayer posture.

### Reflection

Stephen Parker suggests that discernment requires "a time for attending to the intuitive, affective dimensions of discernment and decision-making."[19] This is the practice of reflection. It involves setting aside time and space to consider, within oneself, the content, nature, and implications of the experience in question in view of the impressions and feelings it evokes. Parker explains, "'Feelings' connected to issues under consideration are understood, not as 'things that get in the way' of decision-making, but as important and necessary to good decision-making."[20] The ability to articulate these impressions and feelings is important, but not essential, to the process. This is an intuitive practice, and there is time (and need) for clearer articulation later. It is more important at this juncture to organize

---

18. Ibid.

19. Stephen Eugene Parker, *Led by the Spirit: Toward a Practical Theology of Pentecostal Discernment and Decision-Making* (Sheffield, UK: Sheffield Academic, 1996) 190.

20. Ibid.

and identify the types of impressions: positive, negative, fearful, empow-ering, disorienting, hopeful, etc.

The practice of reflection is also intended to clarify the situation of the self in relationship to the experience. That is, to identify motivations, vulnerabilities, dispositions, or resistances within the self that may con-tribute artificially to the patent, uncritical rejection or reception of the validity of the experience.

## Dialogue

Several years ago, I listened to a recording of Chuck Colson giving an ad-dress on ethics to the Harvard Business School. In the address, he spoke of his involvement in the Watergate scandal that brought down the Nixon presidency. Colson explained that at the heart of the encroaching cor-ruption that finally landed him in prison was an "infinite capacity for rationalization," and he believes that this infinite capacity is common to all persons.

The dialogical dimension of discernment moves the consideration of the validity of an experience from an inward reflection to an outward discussion. I agree with Colson that we all have an infinite capacity for rationalization. Because of this, subjective, interior impressions and de-terminations should be tested in the light of day, and dialogue is a means of doing so. James described godly wisdom in the following way:

> But the wisdom from above is first pure, then peaceable, gentle, reasonable, full of mercy and good fruits, unwavering, without hypocrisy. (James 3:17, NASB)

The Greek word translated as "reasonable" is εὐπειθής/eupeithēs. According to Louw and Nida, this word carries "the implication of be-ing open to reason or willing to listen."[21] Wisdom, in James' view, was discussable. Such willingness and openness to dialogue is critical to the process of discernment. Stubborn entrenchment or resistance to dialogue ought to raise immediate suspicions as to whether God is the source of the experience being protected.

Stephen Parker recommends "a time for attending to and de-scribing claims to experiences of Spirit leading. This element basically

---

21. Johannes P. Louw and Eugene A. Nida, *Greek-English Lexicon of the New Testament: Based on Semantic Domains*, vol. 1, *Introduction and Domains*, 2nd ed. (New York: United Bible Societies, 1996) 33, 305.

involves the sharing of experiences, moving discernment and decision-making from an individual experience to a communal endeavor."[22] When the practice of dialogue takes place within the community, it permits reflection on the experience in light of both the normative biblical narratives and of the interpretations of the narratives within that community. If it cannot pass this simple test of defeasibility, it should be rejected without further consideration.

## Orientation

The third practice of discernment seeks to establish a broader horizon for consideration of the experience. Once dialogue has taken place within the community, it is important to attempt to gain an external perspective to avoid insularity. Parker describes this process as "enriching the description of Spirit leading experiences from multiple perspectives.[23] These perspectives may be sought from both within and outside the Pentecostal tradition.

From within the Pentecostal tradition, the experiences and affirmations of other groups of Pentecostals are helpful to orient the experience in a broader range of manifestations and expressions. A connection to the heritage of Pentecostalism is an important goal, though convoluted relationships should be recognized as species of rationalization. The context of the experiences in other circumstances must also be closely considered. Perspectives outside the Pentecostal tradition are important as well. In Parker's view, this is the process of mutually, critically correlating traditions.[24]

Pentecostals have not always been quick or willing to acknowledge the role of the larger Christian tradition (or even the role of their own tradition), believing the immediacy of the Holy Spirit to be sufficient for their decision. Yet, as this study has shown, their own traditions and the wider Christian tradition are both important to their practices and a chief source of norms for judging these practices.

A century of rejection of Pentecostal manifestations by many in the broader Christian community makes this aspect of orientation very difficult for Pentecostals. But the focus here is not on the legitimacy of

22. Parker, *Led By the Spirit*, 191.

23. Ibid., 192.

24. Ibid., 195.

Pentecostal experience, *per se*. It is, rather, the attempt to recognize in a particular experience some broader theme or practice that transcends denominational boundaries. Reconciliation, mercy, wholeness, and sacrificial service would be examples of these reiterated themes and practices.

### Decision

The final practice of discernment requires a decision. As Parker observes:

> at some point judgments are made as to whether a given experience was the Spirit's leading. Discernment and decision-making is not an endless exercise in enriching description: at some point judgments are made, sometimes tentatively, sometimes with finality.[25]

In essence, the decision constitutes a response to the experience which has passed the referendum of discernment. The basic decision, then, is whether the experience is to be rejected or received. Rejection of the experience is typically based on a denial of God as the source. This supports the repudiation of the content or the consequences. With regard to affirming validity, Pentecostals tend to use the word "receive" rather than "accept." To "receive" a prophetic word from God, or any other experience, has several implications. It invokes gift-oriented language as an acknowledgement that God is the source. It also implies inclusion of the word or experience into the accepted themes or practices of the community. Ultimately, it is an affirmative statement regarding the validity of the experience, the veracity of the pronouncement, and/or the reliability of the directive.

## TOWARD A PENTECOSTAL CONTRIBUTION TO THE JUST WAR TRADITION

In *Theological Roots of Pentecostalism*, Donald W. Dayton identifies a Pentecostal "four-fold pattern" as the basis for Pentecostal theological and historical analysis.[26] The elements of this pattern are the theological

---

25. Ibid., 197.

26. Donald W. Dayton, *Theological Roots of Pentecostalism* (Peabody, MA: Hendrickson, 1987) 21–22.

distillations of the Pentecostal revival, and together these themes provide a *gestalt* of Pentecostal theology.[27] In this pattern:

1. Jesus saves us according to John 3:16,

2. He baptizes us with the Holy Spirit according to Acts 2:4,

3. He heals our bodies according to James 5:14–15, and

4. Jesus is coming again to receive us unto Himself according to 1 Thessalonians 4:16–17.

This four-fold pattern is clearly evident in the theological positions of both the Assemblies of God and the International Church of the Foursquare Gospel.

To the extent that the four-fold pattern reflects deep truths of Pentecostalism affirmed by the Assemblies of God, they provide a relevant and useful framework by which to propose a constructive Pentecostal perspective of the just war tradition. On the basis of each element, I suggest a point of engagement with the just war tradition which integrates the practices of discernment in a concrete process.

## REDEMPTIVE ENGAGEMENT WITH THE WORLD: DISCERNING BARRIERS AND BRIDGES

### 1. Jesus Saves Us According to John 3:16

Jay Beaman's thesis of cultural assimilation offers important insight into the loss of Pentecostal pacifism in the Assemblies of God as a search for acceptance that went beyond mainstream Christian movements to include the broader American society as well. This is seen as early as the start of World War I, when recognition by the government of the legitimacy of the denomination secured exemption from military service. This search for acceptance, however, is anomalous to the degree of suspicion and aloofness that generally characterizes Pentecostal engagement with the world. John the Evangelist's injunction, taken seriously, "Do not love the world, nor the things in the world. If anyone loves the world, the love of the Father is not in him" (1 John 2:15, NASB) served to distance Pentecostal subculture from mainstream American culture. H. Richard Niebuhr described this relationship to the world as a "Christ against culture" position:

---

27. Ibid., 16.

> That world appears as a realm under the power of evil; it is the
> region of darkness, into which the citizens of the kingdom of
> light must not enter; it is characterized by the prevalence in it of
> lies, hatred and murder.
>
> It is a culture that is concerned with temporal and passing
> values, whereas Christ has words of eternal life; it is a dying as
> well as a murderous order.[28]

It is a sad irony that Pentecostal biblical justifications for the
"Christ against culture" position can undermine the first element of the
Pentecostal four-fold pattern. God's motivating love for the world, "that
He gave His only begotten Son, that whoever believes in Him should not
perish, but have eternal life" (John 3:16, NASB), makes a uniform detach-
ment or resistance to the world antithetical to Pentecostal convictions.

At the heart of the plan of salvation is a profound love for the world.
While this love is not for the world system abjured in John's letter, this
focus on human persons is the context of the use of κόσμον in John's gospel.[29] Persons organize themselves in various kinds of social institutions
and, in certain circumstances, protecting the institution is the means of
protecting the people which constitute it. Thousands of Assemblies of
God Pentecostals gave their lives in the wars of the twentieth century to
protect American social institutions and, officially, this was not viewed
as compromise. Formal military resistance and aggression were seen as
justifiable. Working for peace and justice concerns, then, may be recon-
sidered as a redemptive engagement that further aids and protects that
for which one has already demonstrated a willingness to die.

Pentecostal contribution to a redemptive engagement with culture
takes the form of discerning barriers and bridges to peace in an impending or existing conflict. Seeking wisdom and direction through prayer
is essential. Glossolalia in particular, as the focal prayer modality of the
Pentecostal, is the source of the assurance, confidence, and courage necessary to take proactive steps to promote peace and justice.

28. H. Richard Niebuhr, *Christ and Culture* (New York: Harper Torchbooks, 1951)
48.

29. William Arndt, *A Greek-English Lexicon of the New Testament and Other Early
Christian Literature: A Translation and Adaptation of the Fourth Revised and Augmented
Edition of Walter Bauer's Griechisch-Deutsches Worterbuch Zu Den Schrift En Des Neuen
Testaments Und Der Ubrigen Urchristlichen Literatur* (Chicago: University of Chicago
Press, 1996) 446, §5b.

The first biblical dimension of the four-fold pattern addresses God's actions to redeem humanity. These actions were divine initiatives taken despite the helplessness and hostility of human persons to himself. Paul describes this in three different ways in the fifth chapter of Romans (NASB):

v. 6 For while we were still helpless, at the right time Christ died for the ungodly.

v. 8 But God demonstrates His own love toward us, in that while we were yet sinners, Christ died for us.

v.10 For if while we were enemies, we were reconciled to God through the death of His Son, much more, having been reconciled, we shall be saved by His life.

Discerning barriers and bridges to peace is a means of identifying and promoting redemptive initiatives which take into consideration more occluded perspectives and motivations of the enemy. It asks, despite the rhetoric of official postures, what are the substantive issues that stand between the parties? In the cultural ethos of the enemy, what question does this military action answer that is indiscernible through the demonizing and dehumanizing propaganda waged against them?

Pentecostals have been known to retreat into the insularity of an eschatological worldview; an absence of redemptive initiatives signifies a retreat into one's monolithic perspective and interpretation of events. An appeal to "last resort" may be made before all issues and avenues have in fact been exhausted. In contrast, a redemptive initiative employs the practice of reflection to discern at various levels our true motivations and goals. This is an intuitive process, but it can produce very tangible results.

Very often the chief barrier to peace is the perceived recalcitrance of both opponents. As a result, negotiations more clearly resemble contemporaneous monologues than constructive dialogue. In this case, even the justice of the cause can become a barrier to peace. The process of reflection in Pentecostal spirituality creates space for consideration. It situates the self in relation to events or experiences. Applied to the evaluation of the justice of a cause, it makes room to clarify contributing factors on both sides of a conflict that narrow negotiations may not permit.

As a part of the broader just war tradition, reflection as a means of discerning barriers and bridges can be a tool for determining the "comparative justice" proposed by the National Conference of Catholic

Bishops.[30] The concern for comparative justice shifts the focus away from absolute claims to the justice of a cause. Instead, it raises the question of whether either side is sufficiently justified in the resort to war. The intuitive practices of prayer and reflection in the discernment of barriers and bridges, then, provide an integration of Pentecostal theological/ethical praxis and the just war criteria of just cause and last resort.

## PEACEMAKING AS A WORK OF GRACE: DISCERNING THE WAY OF PEACE

### 2. He Baptizes Us with the Holy Spirit according to Acts 2:4

Early Pentecostals were divided over the number of works of grace. Salvation and Spirit baptism were two they agreed upon, but division arose over the issue of sanctification. Notwithstanding the number, at issue here is a Pentecostal understanding of works of grace and of grace at work. From a Pentecostal perspective, the in-breaking of the Kingdom of God in history and the reconciling work of peacemaking become progressive, Spirit-empowered processes to limit violence and establish peace and justice. I propose that this Spirit-empowered process particularly concerns the just war criterion of right intention and involves the integration of all beneficial forms of dialogue.

Beginning with Plato and Aristotle, war-oriented intentions have been justified only as they are linked to the vindication of justice and to the restoration of peace. In summary, peace is the goal of justified war. Aside from unilateral disarmament or unconditional surrender, the journey toward peace begins, before or after bullets are exchanged, by talking about peace. This may be a formal negotiation, but it may also take the form of a discussion. Dialogue, as a practice of discerning the intentions of the other and the way of peace, takes place both among and between the parties to the conflict. By means of dialogue, the goal of peace can stay plainly in view.

This demonstration of grace in the practice of dialogue presents a contrast between the worldviews of the parties in conflict. Just as the contrast between the Christian and the world is not to be a preemptory judgment in advance of the eschaton, so too communications about and between parties should be seasoned with language designed to promote peace. In an active, grace-infused dialogue that accounts for the very real

30. Ibid., §92–96.

issues of controversy, avenues to peace which would otherwise be un-
available or overlooked can present themselves.

## EXTENDING THE HORIZON FOR HEALING: DISCERNING THE ENEMY AS NEIGHBOR

### 3. He Heals Our Bodies according to James 5:14–15

Divine healing is a signature doctrine for Pentecostals, but as Frank
Macchia has observed, the limitation of the scope of healing to sickness
and the human body in typical Pentecostal teaching and practice is an
example of the individualism and isolationism of much Pentecostal theology and practice. He explains that since the earliest days of the movement, healing of the body "provides a potential corrective to a one-sided
emphasis on the inwardness and other-worldliness of Pentecostalism."[31]
This corrective, however, does not go far enough to connect the practice
to the broader scope of healing that God intends.

The problem with much of the popular teaching of Pentecostal
evangelists on healing is its implicit isolation of sickness from the broader
plight of human injustice and suffering. Also involved in this emphasis
is the isolation of healing from the work of the Spirit of God in all of
creation to bring redemption and liberation.[32] The horizon for healing,
then, extends beyond human illness to encompass *human injustice and
suffering*.

Spirit-empowerment for healing enables Pentecostals to respond to
the social plight of human persons and not just to the condition of their
bodies. For this to take place, Pentecostals must embrace the work of the
Spirit in the *renewal of creation*.[33] Macchia urges Pentecostals to achieve
"deeper solidarity with the oppressed and the suffering creation as well
as with the Spirit of redemption at work in healing."[34] For Pentecostals
to do so, however, requires the "revisioning of Pentecostal eschatology."[35]

---

31. Frank D. Macchia, "The Struggle for Global Witness: Shifting Paradigms
in Pentecostal Theology," in *The Globalization of Pentecostalism: A Religion Made to
Travel*, edited by Murray W. Dempster, Byron D. Klaus, and Douglas Petersen (Oxford:
Regnum, 1999) 20.

32. Ibid., 21.

33. Ibid., 22.

34. Ibid.

35. Ibid., 23.

Apocalyptic fervor marginalizes human suffering and the exploitation of creation as necessary precursors to the eschaton. For this reason, these conditions lose their significance against the backdrop of a pre-apocalyptic landscape. Extending the horizon for healing, then, also requires Pentecostals to shift focus from the prophetic horizon to the present and its concrete needs.

In this regard, there is much to learn from the pathos of Catholic concern for the suffering of human persons around the world. This suffering is not limited to the consequences of war only. The National Council of Catholic Bishops believes, "When we accept violence, war itself can be taken for granted." [36] The bishops, and the broader Catholic moral tradition, call us to look into the many faces of violence. In *The Challenge of Peace*, they describe some of these faces as: "oppression of the poor, deprivation of basic human rights, economic exploitation, sexual exploitation and pornography, neglect or abuse of the aged and the helpless, and innumerable other acts of inhumanity." [37] True peace calls for reverence of life, and "all of the values in the letter rest ultimately in the disarmament of the human heart and the conversion of the human spirit to God who alone can give authentic peace."

If Pentecostals will not accept violence at face value, but see the face of Christ in all those who suffer, even the enemy, then the active promotion of peace and justice for the common good will extend the horizon for healing beyond a personal experience to bring healing to the nations. Within the just war tradition, a particular contribution that Pentecostals can make is to extend the horizon for healing toward the discernment of the enemy as neighbor.

In the overture to the parable of the Good Samaritan in Luke's gospel, the narrative indicates that the lawyer's question, "And who is my neighbor," was intended to justify his narrow definition of the objects of neighbor-love in the commandment.[38] But, no doubt to the surprise of many who were listening, Jesus' parabolic response brought even the despised within the sphere of neighbor. Jesus told the story in such a way that it reoriented the relationship of two groups who persisted in deeply held animosities. By way of application, the horizon for healing

---

36. *The Challenge of Peace: God's Promise and Our Response* (Washington, DC: United States Catholic Conference, 1983) §285.

37. Ibid.

38. Luke 10:29, NASB.

can be extended to bring the opposing parties in armed conflict within the neighbor-sphere as well.

This can shape convictions about the personhood of enemies and restrain the dehumanization of opposing parties in conflict. The just war tradition acknowledges the acceptability of killing in war under prescribed circumstances, but extending the horizon for healing re-humanizes the opposing side and thus enhances the consideration of both proportionality and discrimination in the employment of force and in the protection of noncombatants.

## RESPONSIBLE PREMILLENNIALISM: DISCERNING THE URGENCY OF RECONCILIATION

### 4. Jesus is Coming Again to Receive Us Unto Himself According to 1 Thessalonians 4:16–17

Generally speaking, the Pentecostal worldview is processed through a premillennial eschatological filter that produces a detachment from the "cares of this world." In the context of engaging peace and justice concerns and the just war tradition, it is necessary for Pentecostals to adopt a responsible premillennialism. The responsible premillennialist lives in hope of the imminent return of Christ, but that hope is neither a distraction nor an excuse. It is not a distraction because it moves the eschatological focal point more toward the realm of peripheral vision (though it is still in view) so that the focus on the faces of violence is not obscured by apocalyptic fervor. On the other hand, neither is millennial hope an excuse for languishing in deafness and blindness to the concrete needs that surround the believer while s/he waits for history to conclude.

Along with the right to resort to war, the responsibility of legitimate authority is to pursue reconciliation as well. The Pentecostal perspective of the lateness of the hour infuses a sense of urgency into the process of reconciliation and maintains the distinction between ultimate and finite concerns, and these are important contributions from the Pentecostal practice of discernment. The moral voice of urgency toward reconciliation does not suggest backing away from the legitimate resistance of evil. It does seek, however, to avoid unnecessarily protracted conflict which employs either excessive force or needlessly sacrifices lives toward an outcome that is ultimately unattainable. The Pentecostal perspective of the lateness of the hour is also a factor in discerning the distinction between ultimate and finite concerns. Appeals to national interest and national security as a basis for military action, for example, can respectfully be evaluated for the degree to which they are a façade for avarice or aggression. In summary, the practices associated with discerning the urgency of reconciliation may help to determine guidelines for proportionality and whether there is a reasonable hope for success.

In the face of unbridled aggression, the exercise of courage to resist evil is the responsibility of legitimate authority. Discerning the urgency of reconciliation requires courage as well. It is this disposition of courage that speaks out against injustice on both sides of military conflicts and initiates intermediate conditions for peace in view of the time approaching, when peace will reign.

## RE-ENERGIZING THE MORAL VOICE OF THE ASSEMBLIES OF GOD

The preceding application of the Pentecostal four-fold pattern with the practice of discernment is a preliminary example of the contributions of Pentecostal epistemological, theological, and ethical distinctives to the just war tradition. Certainly, further study and development are necessary, but reengaging these distinctives can energize the moral voice of our movement and provide redirection that corrects our moral migration from our roots in Pentecostal pacifism.

It is likely that the official silence on the justice of war belies strong opinions among the rank and file. There is no indication that any significant vestige of pacifism remains in the movement, yet neither are there signs of unreflective loyalty to the government. The problem is that there is no common language of peace to speak. A move toward the just war tradition could provide that language and eventually produce the kind of critical mass necessary to identify the Assemblies of God as a denomination concerned about justice in war once again. Having been silent for so long, our voice will sound strange at first, and initial contributions will be as tentative as those offered above. Once the denomination engages the dialogue on the justice of war, however, it is imperative that we keep speaking until we become comfortable with the sound of our voice.

# 11

## Pastoring a Peace Church

### Jonathan Martin

I will never forget the Saturday afternoon last fall when I heard horrible screaming coming from our front yard. I walked out to see Dennis and Elizabeth Donahue, a couple in leadership at our church, in a tense confrontation with another man and woman in our driveway. A founding partner of a Charlotte, NC, real estate business, Dennis is known for his jovial demeanor and disarming wit, so he was one of the last persons I would have expected to find engaged in a heated showdown outside my front door. He might even be the very last person I would expect, except for Elizabeth, who spent years as the public relations director at Sea World—the picture of cordiality and restraint. On a grassroots level, Dennis and Elizabeth have spearheaded the effort for several years to help a friend in our church community named Diane. A neighbor of the Donahues, Diane lived in poverty and an abusive relationship with her boyfriend for much of her life. Now well into her fifties, Diane had been kicked out by her landlord (who was really more of a slumlord), and Dennis and Elizabeth felt God calling them to help get her into an apartment across the street from my house. (To this day, there is a group within our church that works together to make sure all of her physical needs are provided for.) While they helped get her out of the abusive relationship, the Donahues met the wrath of her ex-boyfriend, who had a violent temper and a host of addictions. That day, this man and his mother had followed Dennis and Elizabeth from Diane's apartment until they got them to pull over in front of our house. As I stepped out on the porch, I heard the man, Randy, hurling filthy epithets at Dennis and Elizabeth. I watched Dennis (who, like me, is about 6'5") flush, about to lose his cool, as Randy directed crude, sexually explicit insults at Elizabeth. In a moment of fury, he actually threw down his glasses and started to walk past me, saying "I don't care if you are here Pastor . . ." I simply put my hand on his chest and said, "We aren't going to do that, Dennis." Though every impulse in him was screaming to fight for his wife, he didn't resort to violence. After some calming words from us (and some even raunchier attacks), Randy finally sped off, all the while shouting, "I know where you live Donahue, and I'll be back!"

The Donahues were shaken by the experience. They had been brave enough to bring peace to a woman in need, and both human and demonic principalities and powers had been threatened by their presence. The powers came back roaring—and they were resisted, but not with violence or force. Instead, the powers came eyeball to eyeball with a Christian couple who were willing to stand between the oppressor and the oppressed without fear and who would not stand idly by while their sister in Christ was abused. Such is the toughness that is demanded by those courageous enough to endure the gaze of violence in Jesus' name.

Ironically, those who embrace the call to Christian peacemaking are often stigmatized as being "passive" or unwilling to confront unjust principalities and powers as they are revealed, but our congregation has learned this is far from the truth. This is especially strange given the reality that those most committed to Christ's peace are often more likely, not less, to face down the powers of darkness.

The Donahues' story is just one example in our community of a people attempting to bring the peace of Christ in Charlotte, NC. As a product and now a preacher of "the Christ-haunted"[1] American South,

---

1. A phrase from Flannery O'Connor, who claimed, "It is safe to say that while the South is hardly Christ-centered, it is most certainly Christ-haunted. The Southerner who isn't convinced of it, is very much afraid that he may have been formed in the image and likeness of God." From O'Connor's 1960 lecture "Some Aspects of the Grotesque in Southern Fiction," originally presented at the Wesleyan College for Women, Macon, GA. The entire lecture maybe accessed at http://www.en.utexas.edu/amlit/amlitprivate/scans/grotesque.html.

I am learning along with my congregation something of how challenging it is to witness for the peaceable kingdom. In the south, we have always been good at naming our enemies. It somehow seems irresponsible, and unrealistic, to talk about making peace when the world seems to be full of enemies of the cross. At its worst, talk of peacemaking may degenerate into bland accounts of tolerance and acceptance. Christian peacemakers seem to be in denial, unwilling or unable to take seriously either the reality or the challenge of hostile times. We may be viewed as wishful-thinking hippies who lack the courage to acknowledge the violent milieu in which we live. Given the near giddiness within our church culture towards apocalyptic signs, even worse we are sometimes seen as impediments to fulfilling prophecy, those who would try to turn back the clock on events that must occur in order for Christ to return. Indeed, in the face of cataclysmic events to come and in light of our own inner violence, is there any real reason to be hopeful towards kingdom peace in apocalyptic times?

If Christian peacemaking efforts were simply a matter of playing down differences and focusing on the sunny side of life, then our critics would not be wrong. But I am neither particularly inclined to be optimistic about human progress in matters of war and peace, nor am I inclined to suggest that the church does not have real enemies in the world. As the saying goes, it is not paranoia when they really are out to get you. Thankfully, a Pentecostal vision for peacemaking is by no means contingent upon naïve optimism, and it does not pretend that there are no enemies of the cross. On the contrary, we are given the resources and the language with which to recognize our enemies. Yet the only reason we have for naming our enemies is to identify who it is that Jesus has called us to bless. We are not optimistic about human nature, the economy, or the future of American politics; we do not buy into the myth of progress, and there is nothing remotely sentimental about looking deeply into the eyes of those who would do us harm and, as Jesus did with Judas, speak the word "friend."

Even so, to speak with pastoral boldness a word of kingdom peace in a violent world is to invite suspicion and even pity from sincere people of God who assume that we have just not adequately understood the charts and graphs supplied by popular end-times enthusiasts. Dispensational theology assumes very particular outcomes and gives us the comfort of knowing what is ahead (however dark or inevitable that "future" might be). Given such inevitabilities, why fight the future—especially if it is God's future? A steady diet of such teaching has not only bred passivity among Pentecostal Christians towards issues of peace, but even hostility towards those who would harbor hope for a different ending. In the face of such prophetic certainty, to take anything less than a defensive posture towards our enemies seems not only irresponsible, but even treasonous.

## MY STORY

Yet, I am by no means unsympathetic to those in my pastoral care who are fraught with tension and ambiguities toward the Christian vocation of peacemaking. I am very aware of how much I, as a fifth generation Pentecostal, embody those same tensions myself. Shaped as I have been by a high appraisal of testimony within our tradition, I know of no better way to share my pastoral strategy for peacemaking apart from my story.

Growing up Pentecostal in the South, I was entirely unaware of the roots of the movement as a peace church. The Church of God, Cleveland, TN, was birthed in the mountains of North Carolina and Tennessee by tough people in tough times. It struck me as almost comic while reading Charles Conn's *Like a Mighty Army* to come across nicknames like "old rough and ready J. F. Buckalew" amidst a fairly straightforward account of the early history of the Church of God. It is difficult to imagine a Presbyterian pastor named "old rough and ready," but to say that they were tough is not to imply that they were violent. The toughest Pentecostal pioneers I was privileged enough to be around in their later years were the most profoundly gentle men and women I have ever known. Years of hard living were etched into the lines on their faces, which made the tenderness of their eyes more haunting and lovely.

I was raised on the Bible stories they told and the Bible stories they lived. There was something roguish about these men who had known what it was to fight and scrap, but had been more shaped by the terror of God. They were products of violence to be certain, but it was the violence of the terror and lightning of Sinai that had, somehow conversely, baptized them in tenderness. They were not people who were looking for a fight, but that is not to say they were always people who would have run from one either. When one of the best-loved pioneers in my region was famously shot at, while living in his parsonage, he loaded up his shotgun . . . and fired right back.

My maternal grandfather was a local church clerk for most of his adult life. One night he and another brother in the church were counting money after the service. The other man had had a series of escalating confrontations with their pastor that finally erupted that night. When the pastor walked in the room, the man told him he was a "yellow-bellied coward." The pastor left the little office, went to his parsonage next door, and returned brandishing a pistol by his side. He asked, "Would you like to come outside and call me that again?" The man did not take the pastor up on his offer, so thankfully his resolve was not tested. These tales, which would be wonderful raw material for the kind of gothic Southern short stories that Flannery O'Connor created, are an important part of the cultural legacy that Pentecostals inherit.

Conversely, my other grandfather, a hard, tough police officer, experienced a dramatic conversion at the nearby 15th Street Church of God and became a conscientious objector during World War II. He surrendered his police badge when he accepted the call to preach, and he never took up arms again. He died when I was only three, and I did not hear this part of his story until I was thirty.

Now, as a Pentecostal pastor, I am aware that my life is a product of all the ambiguities and tensions that characterize the movement in general and this region in particular. While the overwhelming legacy of the men and women who have come before me is that of peace, I am also aware of the ways I embody conflicting narratives at times. I suspect my struggle to appropriate my roots is not an uncommon one. Like many other Pentecostals in the South, I still find myself trying to sort out my heritage from intertwined strands of Southern fundamentalism embedded in my story.

One way to illustrate both the plight and the prescription is to apply the framework of the narrative of Joseph, Rachel, and Leah.[2] In the Genesis story, Jacob falls in love with Laban's youngest daughter Rachel while in Haran. He strikes a deal with Laban to work for seven years in order to marry Rachel. At the end of the time, Laban prepares a feast to give his daughter to Jacob. Laban instead tricked Jacob and gave him Leah. That night, Jacob has relations with Leah, only to discover in the morning that it was not Rachel, and that Laban had dealt treacherously with him. Ultimately, he had to complete seven more years of service to Laban before he was able to marry Rachel. For Pentecostals, the romance

2. Genesis 29.

with Wesleyan spirituality, with its characteristic concerns for mercy and justice in explicitly Christological terms, is natural and comes first. By an accident of circumstance and social location, those of us in the North American tradition found ourselves in the tent with Leah. It has taken us more than seven years to discover that we have the wrong partner, but there is still hope that we can be surprised (and a little frustrated) by the strangeness of the arrangement and rejoin our rightful partner. For me, discovering the roots of Pentecostalism as a peace church has been a journey I like to call "finding Rachel."

Sometimes I feel like I'm still working to find her. Loving my tradition and yet unsure of how to appropriate it, I read Steven J. Land's classic *Pentecostal Spirituality: A Passion for the Kingdom* in my early twenties and it was as if I had found some exotic new continent. I recognized much of what I saw in his constructive revision but some of it was entirely new to me. I remember being particularly struck by his claim that

> Pentecostal liberation brings great joy because peace, not violent coercive manipulation, is the means and the goal of the fruit and gift of the Spirit, respectively. The early Pentecostal pacifism, in a nuclear age of extensive poverty, is the best strategy for the church today.[3]

Reading John Howard Yoder's *The Politics of Jesus* was equally devastating, especially since by that time I was able to recognize that Yoder's Anabaptist roots were more directly parallel to the concerns of early Pentecostals than those of the magisterial reformation. Further, my roots made me distrustful of any philosophical arguments that were not fully grounded in Scripture, but no one was as capable of painting an explicitly text-shaped portrait of the peaceable kingdom as Yoder.

## ALONG CAME MARGARET GAINES

However, what ultimately shapes my life most determinatively with regard to these issues is neither a better historical understanding of the early history of the Pentecostal movement nor the powerful Christological vision of peace of Yoder: it is the life of my spiritual grandmother, Margaret Gaines. Now in her late seventies, Margaret was raised in the Church of

---

3. Steven J. Land, *Pentecostal Spirituality: A Passion for the Kingdom* (Sheffield: Sheffield Academic, 1993) 207.

God in Pell City, AL and was steeped both in the stories of the American South and the Pentecostal movement. When she was a nineteen-year-old student at then Lee College in Cleveland, TN, she accepted the call to become a full-time Christian missionary in a chapel service. Margaret would never marry, giving her life entirely over toward her call. As she has often remarked to us, "How can I give my life to a man when I had already given it completely to Jesus? It wouldn't be fair to the poor man or to Jesus." Without support of Church of God World Missions, who felt it was too dangerous for a young, single woman to travel the world, Margaret moved to Tunisia for 9 years. But it was her next assignment that would determine the rest of her adult life and ministry, when she agreed to go to a small Palestinian village called Aboud on the occupied west bank of Israel.

Aboud is called the "city of flowers" because of its charming land-scape; the mountainous village is also known for its olive trees. One of the most beautiful of the Palestinian villages, Aboud is a peaceful place where it is easy to forget the years of poverty and outright oppression its people have suffered since the Ottoman empire.[4] Margaret's life was greatly shaped by the hospitality and generosity of the Arab people, who received her as a gift to their community. She established a church and a Christian elementary school that continues to this day, though in recent years serious heart ailments force Margaret to remain in Pell City.

Currently, five Muslim villages surrounding Aboud send their children to the school. With few resources, Margaret developed the curriculum and created almost all of the visual aids when she founded the school in 1970. The many Muslims who send their children to Margaret's school know they will be taught about Jesus as part of their educational program. A leading Muslim cleric in Aboud comments, "Sister Margaret shaped and changed the entire character of this village." A delegation of Muslim leaders told her on her last visit that they wanted to build a library in Aboud in her honor, as a monument to the love she brought there.

Margaret tells a wonderful story about a time when she was accosted by a man in the middle of the crowded village market. Taking out his apparent frustration with western interference, the man began cursing her. He cursed the grave of her father, the grave of her mother, the grave of her grandparents, her God, and the God of her parents—everything he could think of. She felt the eyes of the entire village watching. As he

4. Margaret Gaines, *Small Enough to Stop the Violence* (Unpublished) 4.

hurled abuse on her, she quickly prayed for wisdom. When he was finally done, Margaret responded "I am so sorry I hurt you. I never had any intention of hurting you. God loves you and I love you. He loves this village and he wants to bless you. When you get over being angry, will you remember I'm still your friend?" Perplexed, he turned and walked away. In words that have forever marked me, Margaret told me that "Satan doesn't know how to respond to the gentleness of God's Spirit." Discouraged, she went back to her room to pray. "Oh God what was the meaning of this? Everybody in the village that could walk was out on the streets. What was this all about?" She heard God say, "That was your pulpit. Those people will never come to the church. But you preached my gospel by demonstrating my Spirit."

Margaret recalls that there were many such situations that "were unpleasant to the human heart. . . . But if we can be God's person of peace in any given situation and a witness—a living witness—to the unseen Lord . . . live out His word and live out his teaching in everyday life as he expects, then over time it makes a total difference." Margaret broke down in tears before our congregation as she said, "Oh, if every village had a living breathing Spirit of Christ walking in their midst, they would have a lot more peace. You are not going to Palestine perhaps. But you have this one little corner of the world." She taught us that when we run into human cruelty and rage, "the sweetness of the Spirit will eventually dissolve the acidity of the spirit that is coming against you—and He will bring peace."

## SMALL ENOUGH TO STOP THE VIOLENCE

For most of her adult life, Margaret watched her poor but peaceful village live through the tremors of violence around them. Having lived in Jerusalem during the six-day war of 1967, Margaret and her fellow missionary Arlene Miller were in Aboud as the only Church of God missionaries in the Occupied West Bank when the Gulf War broke out in 1991. She tells of the inaccessibility of basic resources for Arabs during the war such as gas masks, food, and water. While a strict curfew was imposed, Margaret was nearly unable to get a new mother suffering with complications from giving birth to twins through a military post to get to medical care, despite her then thirty years as a missionary in the Bel Zeit district. Margaret's life among the Palestinians gave her a unique perspective on the cycle of violence there:

> The world knows that Arabs defy tanks, machine guns and rifle fire with the act of throwing stones. Television cameras have caught this irrational act in Jerusalem, Bethlehem, Hebron, Ramallah, Nablus and everywhere in between. What the media would not film are the retaliatory raids the Jewish settlers would make. They would come to Aboud about 10 at night and stay until 2 in the morning. There would be an organized party of many cars, including an ambulance just in case anyone of them was seriously hurt. They would bring chain saws to cut down the olive trees. They would line up their cars and turn on their lights and dance the *hora* in the street, they sang loudly and shouted, "Come out, you dogs. Face us, you cowards." Then they would hurl stones and break out windows of every house lining the street. Also, the bus and exposed cars would get stoned. My car window was smashed in two separate raids. To finish their party, they would cut down many olive trees.

Haunted by these scenes, Margaret has seen the western church continue to neglect the plight of the Arabs. She became increasingly incredulous at the lack of basic necessities in Aboud—at times with little access even to clean water. "Perhaps for the price of all the Scuds and Patriots, every suffering village in the West Bank could have their basic needs met, their hope restored, and opportunities to work," she mused.[5] For a village like Aboud, the resources to build a maternity clinic or nursing home would make a tremendous difference.

In 1991, Margaret sent copies of a video and written report of such "confidence building projects" that could be undertaken to bring relief. She pondered,

> Did those who received copies think or do anything at all? I do not know. I do know that children who attended our school grew up with a vision. They are still young and do not have lots of capital, but they and others are making a difference. With little or no help from outside, they have set up their own businesses. They are working, and their goods and services encourage their people and keep many working. Maybe that is why Arab violence has been practically unknown in Aboud.[6]

5. Ibid., 48.
6. Ibid., 51.

From the leaven of Sister Margaret's life, the kingdom of God has come to the Arabs. During Margaret's time in Aboud, the villagers eventually stopped keeping rocks on the roofs of their houses, the old way of settling differences when conflicts arose.

While Sister Margaret faithfully served her people, she became convinced that the "incredible, meddlesome zealotry of the church unwittingly and constantly adds to the cause of violence in the land."[7] Despite the fact that she became a testimony to the powerful vocation of Christian peacemaking simply by sharing her life in this Arab village, Margaret watched the western church become more and more preoccupied with seeing a certain apocalyptic timetable be played out in Israel. The plight of her people garnered little response from many North American Pentecostals, preoccupied as we were with more pressing matters in the Middle East—like the rebuilding of the temple in Jerusalem as a prophetic marker of Christ's return. Although Margaret anticipates the return of Christ with characteristic Pentecostal passion, she fears that:

> The church, instead of fulfilling the Lord's last will and testament (which is to go tell every nation, tongue and people the Good News that God loves them and wants to restore them) is misappropriating their God-given health, knowledge, and wealth to try and force the end before the time. Jesus indicated that when the church finishes this missionary assignment the end will come. Maybe the church should get on with the assignment and leave the matters of the Temple to the Messiah of Israel, the singular son of Abraham and son of David (Matt.1.1), who is the rightful heir to the promises, even our own Lord Jesus Christ. For do we even realize what effect the end-time zealotry of the church is having on current events, even on the level of violence?[8]

Hoping for the end of the world, Christians in the west became less concerned with peace and more consumed with being on the right side of Armageddon, where we will have ringside seats. Never a political activist, Margaret nonetheless became increasingly incredulous as she saw the one-sided nature of Western media coverage of her people. Observing the reactions of American news to the outbreak of violence precipitated by Ariel Sharon's intrusion on the Temple Mount, she wrote:

7. Ibid., 32.
8. Ibid., 33.

The numerous scenes of violence in Israel and the West Bank . . . shocked every American. Any kind of war insults this nation's comfortable peace. All anyone knows how to say is "Stop the violence." The people who say they just want the violence to stop just want the disturbance to go away. The stone throwers are seen as inhuman, ruthless, out-of-control thugs who need to settle down so peace talks can resume . . . No one seems to care that the revolt is nothing less than the death struggle of a despairing people. The whole convulsing calamity has brought me to respond with the question, "Is there anyone small enough to stop the violence?" Many of the "big," most powerful men of recent decades have tried to find a way to stop it. Actual peace negotiations have been going on longer than most thoughtful men believed would be necessary. What caused the stalemate? Who is responsible for the gridlock? . . . All I hear are commands and questions. Nothing is new. No one reaches down to the core of the issues. Who can descend into the realities, and what can be done once they reach the bottom? Certainly the big political, religious and cultural giants are too bloated by their knowledge, achievement and position to fit into the narrow shaft of descent into the depths. It would take someone small enough to go through the "needle's eye," someone who has nothing to lose, someone who is not afraid to be counted as nothing, taking the risk and assuming the responsibilities of collective errors and admitting them, if not apologizing. Is there such a one?

Margaret's phrase, "small enough to stop the violence," arrested me. For Margaret, the task of Christian peacemaking is bound up in the embrace of seemingly miniscule acts of faithfulness. In her own words, "God says my kingdom won't come about with a lot of noise. . .it comes gently like the leaven."

In 2006, I had the life-altering opportunity to see Aboud for myself—with Margaret. As we walked through the streets of the village and talked and played with the children at the Aboud school, I was struck by the love and mutual respect between this Church of God lady from Alabama and her Muslim neighbors. Margaret's own life is a testimony of one "small enough to stop the violence," of the possibilities of Christian peacemaking in a region of the world thought to be hopelessly volatile.

Taking Responsibility for God
(the Problem with "Don't look at me, look at Jesus")

Perhaps the greatest challenge in teaching congregations the Christian vocation of peacemaking is our unwillingness to become "small enough." It is not that our congregations do not believe Jesus when he says he blesses the peacemakers, so much as it is difficult to imagine that kingdom leaven could possibly make a difference in the world.

That is why it becomes necessary as pastors to bring before our congregations lives that exemplify the "smallness" necessary to bear witness to the peace of the cross. In the Pentecostal tradition, we do not formally name "saints," but we certainly name them informally—not as objects of prayer or worship, but as exemplars whose practices we emulate. Repeatedly emphasizing her own weaknesses in her autobiography, *Of Like Passions*, Margaret fears, "In my experience, I have found too much made of the 'instruments' and too little made of the Master."[9] We have certainly recognized that the source of Margaret's unique presence is not of herself but rather the sweetness of Christ. Yet, given my understanding of saints as faithful exemplars of a Spirit-led life, Margaret has certainly been such a "saint" for our church community, Renovatus. My congregation knows that my most primal theological education came neither from the Church of God Theological Seminary nor Duke University, but from the University of Margaret Gaines. It was she who taught me that the teachings of Jesus are not glassy-eyed idealism (and certainly not instructions for the distant millennial reign, as many dispensationalists have asserted), but are intended to be lived—and in fact can be lived—in real-life. She is the person who taught me that peacemakers are still blessed, that there is still a real vocation of ambassadors of reconciliation in the world.

While she lives far from us, our entire church has adopted her as a grandmother in the Lord. She was the first guest speaker we ever hosted, only 4 months into our existence. During her last visit a few months ago, I interviewed her on stage as part of a series we did on "The Politics of Jesus" (not based directly on Yoder's book, but a broad survey of the political implications of following Jesus where we live). I have understood much of my own pastoral vocation to be simply drawing attention to the

9. Margaret Gaines, *Of Like Passions* (Cleveland, TN: Pathway, 2000) 13.

lives that have formed me, especially Margaret's. So I share her stories and bring her to our people so that they can experience her directly.

It is crucial to embed these stories into our community well, as discipleship requires imitation—which we are so often prone to forget in a culture obsessed with originality. The idea of imitation is scandalous to us because of our narcissistic focus on individuality. Yet if we are reflective about the shape of our lives, we know that we are always imitating others. Societies are ordered around imitation; there is no other way to account for how we dress, what we drive, and how we act. We learn to desire the same objects as our neighbors and thus imitate them in acquiring the same objects. It is not a question of whether we will imitate another, but whom we will imitate.

Discipleship is not about originality, it is all about imitation. There is no short cut around the ancient task of disciple-making, whereby one life is shaped and formed by a master who is skilled in the practices of Christian faith. Thus, church becomes a stage for us to display the lives of saints who can make intelligible for us the witness of the apostle Paul, who brazenly challenges the Philippians to "join in imitating me." Or as he puts it to the Corinthians, "follow me as I follow Christ." These are not the words of an egomaniac, nor should they be unique to the apostolic witness of Paul. All in the body of Christ must learn the craft of mimicking saints—men and women whose authentic walk with God is worthy of our imitation. We need to observe their practices and learn to imitate their habits. Once we have learned to faithfully imitate the lives of faithful men and women, we come to a place wherein we are free to improvise.[10] While none of us are original, we are able to find our unique expression within the body of Christ once we have become habituated.

Margaret has lived the kind of life that has, like Etty Hillesum (a young Jewish woman eventually killed in the gas chambers of Auschwitz), dared to "take responsibility for God." Commenting on the power of lives like Etty's to shape our own, Rowan Williams says that belief in God

> starts from a sense that we "believe in," we trust some kinds of people. We have confidence in the way they live, the way they live is the way I want to live, perhaps can imagine myself living in my better or more mature moments. The world they inhabit is one I'd like to live in. Faith has a lot to do with the simple fact

---

10. A central idea in Sam Wells's account of ethics. See Samuel Wells, *Improvisation: The Drama of Christian Ethics* (Grand Rapids: Brazos, 2004).

that there are trustworthy lives to be seen, that we can see in some believing people a world we'd like to live in.[11]

What a wonderfully fitting description of Margaret's influence on our community, seeing in her story "a world we'd like to live in." As Paul's example taught the early churches, Margaret's example has taught our church that it is impossible to abdicate our responsibility by glibly telling our neighbors, "Don't look at me, just look at Jesus." We have used many variations of that phrase before. It sounds humble, even pious—certainly when said with the utmost sincerity. But Margaret's life reveals to us the futility of such notions. How exactly do we get someone to "not look at us, and just look at Jesus?" Do we draw them a picture to carry in their wallets? Do we give them a statue? Or a little song that says, "I don't care if it rains or freezes/long as I've got my plastic Jesus/sitting on the dashboard of my car?" What may start out sounding good to us can have the affect of absolving us from any real expectation of living a Christ-like life. Against such sentimentality, Margaret's life bears witness to our church that most important Pentecostal message: the Spirit of God that anointed Jesus of Nazareth as He went about doing good and healing all who were oppressed by the devil still wants to make Himself known through real bodies.

## ON THE ROAD TO BECOMING SMALL ENOUGH

Inspired by the narrative of Sister Margaret Gaines, our young church has begun to accumulate our own communal stories of peacemaking, stories of sons and daughters willing to be "small enough." This year, our church took the leap to adopt one of Charlotte's more fragile, violent neighborhoods: Reid Park. As part of a prayer and service initiative called the Justice Project, our community life groups have each adopted two families in the neighborhood. They serve their adopted families in whatever areas they have need—everything from painting to fixing roofs and leaking faucets to simply going over and spending a Friday night or a meal together. Additionally, we have larger scale projects (painting days, mini-extreme home makeovers, free yard sales) in which we call on the entire body to participate. In our participation in acts of service, we hope to play our part in God's larger project to bring peace to an entire

11. Rowan Williams, *Tokens of Trust: An Introduction to Christian Belief* (London: Westminster Knox, 2007) 21–22.

neighborhood known for its violence. So we devoted an entire week of 24/7 prayer, during which we had a different individual in our church pray every hour of the week at our local prayer center with the focus of "praying down the stats." None of the projects in Reid Park have been especially large—we simply do not have the resources for that. Rather, it has been a series of small acts from "small enough" people who believe that in these acts the peace of God is announced and established.

Yet, as it is for all Christian peacemakers, compassionate service is sometimes met with resistance. This brings me back to the scene in my driveway with Dennis and Elizabeth, a couple who was "small enough" to stop the violence in the life of their friend at their own peril. Like Margaret's village, in which she bore gentle witness to the Spirit of Christ in the face of violent opposition, such neighborhood conflict afford crucial opportunity for the gospel to be preached. Her story gives us the discernment necessary to understand our own confrontations with forces of terror and violence, a narrative resource from which to appropriate her disciplined tenderness. Because of Sister Margaret's faithful witness, we are able to see these conflicts as opportunities to, in the words God spoke after her confrontation in the village, "preach my gospel by demonstrating my Spirit."

From Margaret's vision of Pentecostal peacemaking, so resonant for our Christian community, I am watching the stories of saints within our own fellowship begin to take shape. Their lives, like Margaret's, hold the promise of "taking responsibility for God" in our own city. I have seen in this congregation people learning to lives worthy of imitation, whose example demands that we "follow them as they follow Christ." As it was for Margaret, our anticipation of Jesus' return gives both clarity and passion to our call as peacemakers. Rejecting the Gnostic distortion of apocalyptic expectation into a perverse, other-worldly escapism, we are rediscovering Pentecostal urgency as a mandate to bring the peace of Christ to our community. Instead of using "the blessed hope" of His appearing as an excuse for laziness, apathy, and indifference toward a violent world, North American Pentecostals are awakening to unique opportunities to bear witness to God's shalom.

I am very much aware that there are great differences of opinion in our community over the morality of war, with some strongly committed to absolute nonviolence and others who would defend some variation of just war. Yet, despite these differences, we have attempted to make the conversation less about exceptions and more about norms, challenging each other to work for God's shalom in our community. Margaret has taught us well that the stakes of being a peaceable witness to the kingdom of God in our own village are indeed high.

# 12

## My Almost-Abortion

### A Romance in Late Capitalism

**Erica Bryand Ramirez**

The practice of making peace is something very often performed on the personal level, though one often does so with the hope that many micro-actions will yield macro-effect. I hope that my making my community a friendlier place will in fact somehow make the world a better place, and even smaller: I believe that peace in my family renders my neighborhood that much more peaceful. Making peace for me is praxis, but it is first an ethos: I seek first to live into God's always-available peace, then to extend this peace to others. My experiences in peacemaking have often been most fruitful, have even totally depended upon, my ability to first make peace with myself, to make peace with my world as I know it, before I invite others into the world as I/we make it: Peaceful.

In choosing to cover such a personal topic, abortion, I mean to locate a way in which the peace of God has played a most affecting role in my life. In working out the details of what it has meant for me to be a young girl, then a young woman, tied in specific ways to the cycles of life and death that we accept because we must, but barely survive when we actually endure them, I have witnessed God's surpassing peace-ability.

## THIS IS MY LITTLE PART TO SAY

I had not been in Boston long when it occurred to me that I was late. I was walking the streets between Jamaica Plain and Roxbury, sun lost behind grey curtains, and life was looking dim. I did not take to Boston readily: my husband's historical and cultural appreciations for it only sharpened my sense of being profoundly adrift. I am *from* Texas, from eight months a year of non-stop summer, Fiesta, and The Alamo. Paul Revere, his revolution, the deep-down chill, all played backdrop for the most affecting difference—the people of Boston, I could not pretend for a minute that I was one of them. Walking toward my new apartment, I couldn't shake the feeling of being foreign.

I burned candles at night and I played certain CDs. I cooked, cleaned, talked on the phone to friends, and waited to hear whether I would get the job I really wanted. Henry Louis Gates Jr. got arrested on his own property and I forcibly suspended my judgment. I shopped all the little grocery stores and tried not to think about the splendors of H-E-B.[1] As night closed in, I took refuge in what familiarity the TV could afford me: Mad Men and The Office were still on. Maybe life would go on as it had before.

Some things can be depended on, and the moon and my biological cadences are two of them. My being *late* has only happened once in my adulthood and that one time, I was pregnant with Judah. I took to Jamaica Plain's tree-lined streets to count the days, and then to recount: fourteen days, had it been twenty-eight days? Which was day ten, day twelve? Outside, pacing the streets, I had the sense that God could better observe my situation as it grew into a predicament. Late. Anyway I counted or recounted, no manipulating of the numbers would quell my rising alarm. I was late, and, *oh God*, this was *all I needed*. My sense of dislocation, the loss of days, the sudden unreliability of both internal and external reference markers, realized together, the counting, gave rise to a particular bewilderment: how would I have a baby in Boston?

What methods I had been employing to soothe myself, I had no illusions that they would sustain me in the soothing of a newborn. I had no

---

1. H-E-B is a chain grocery store in Texas.

calm words to whisper into ears just removed from their amniotic buffer. I had recently been doubting that I had enough sunlight in my apartment to sustain a plant. I was unemployed, and if I found a job in Boston, it would hardly cover all my living expenses and the expenses associated with daily care for a small person. Further, I could not stomach the idea of leaving a newborn in a Boston daycare, even if I could afford it. I would have an abortion.

*I will have an abortion*, I thought once, jarring myself, and then thought it louder. I was realizing it and telling God so at the same time. I would have an abortion, most especially if I did not get that job. Whatever my prior notions ever were, no matter which community or which person did not approve, I would abort a life I could not soothe, could not feed, could not agree, in good faith, to make thrive when at that moment everything I might have previously thought true now echoed back at me the void of displacement and disenfranchisement. This was an assessing of my resources and a coming up short. Motherhood, I knew what it took and knew I did not now have *it*. Abortion, it was realistic; it felt responsible to admit what I could not do. I had matured past thinking I could do anything and everything. *I can't have a baby right now.*

This is how it happens, by the way. I did not opt for an abortion *because* it was legal. I certainly had enough experience in the Pentecostal and evangelical worlds to know what Christians think about abortion. But on my rather solitary walk, I did not think about what my parents, my pastors, or prominent ethicists would think. My being pregnant was a most immediate and consuming reality, deeper down and closer to me than either my community or our ethics. Rather, in my experience, matters like the carrying and birth of a child turn on an interior logic that defies argument. I was as surprised as anyone else would have been to hear what I was thinking, and I had to reckon with what it meant about me as well as with the possibility of the pregnancy itself. A sense of regret came over me: I would have to say goodbye to the version of myself pre-abortion (I would lose something important, I knew) or live with the kind of mother I became in lieu of one. Lights out, either way: a darkening sadness gathered itself around me.

I decided I would wait to find out whether I was actually pregnant until I heard back about that job that I really wanted. This was self-protective: I didn't want to endure even a day officially expecting a baby while in job limbo in Boston. I would find out about the job first, then about my lateness. The two matters were, for better or worse, joined.

The woman who would be my boss, if I got the job, had hoped to get back to me at the end of the first week, but that had not happened. I thought this meant that I would hear from her soon after I decided to make my most important decisions contingent upon her decision. If I got the job we would have enough money, maybe, to barely squeak by with a new baby. I both did and did not think I would get the job. When I thought I would get the job, I started imagining a tight, stressful couple of years, short on time, money, and energy. Still, I thought I might mother on those terms. On the nights I thought I would not get work, I felt a creeping sense of guilt and powerlessness. I had taken measures to make sure I wasn't in this predicament and, while these are only measures, if they had failed I felt chiefly responsible. I was still essentially a student, planning to submit applications for the PhD. It was from my first-choice university that I was waiting to hear about the job. Getting that job seemed tantamount to *everything* working out. Under these circumstances, I could imagine an unexpected baby would naturally find her place in our lives and, accordingly, the world. Bad news meant otherwise, actually the opposite: an ongoing lack of resources; no ready-made work community; no obvious way to move forward with PhD plans; the burden of sustaining a job search in a recession economy; disappointed hopes in a foreign, cold, dark environment; a crying new, small, sleep-depriving Someone. I could not think what to do with a baby in that world. I closed myself into my apartment, by my fireplace, to wait my Yes or No, to mourn the possibilities I feared, and lit a candle in my soul: a vigil.

## EPOCH ONE

Ann Patchett had called to me, from the shelves of bookstores and libraries, like the name of a friend of a dear friend. Before I ever opened one of her books, I felt piqued by her book covers. I knew we were meant to be. My first Ann was her only non-fiction at the time, *Truth and Beauty*. At the close of *Bel Canto*, I wept, grieved to arrive at the end of that private, glittery universe with no hope of being able to relive it again for the first time. Ann was someone who could sit shiva with me: I was beginning her most recent book, *Run*. Upon realizing that *Run* took place on the streets of Boston, I wondered whether my relatedness to the author was always coming to these moments of confinement with only her book for real company. In waiting my news, I had withdrawn completely from the streets I couldn't navigate. *Run* only returned me to them, Patchett's voice acting as one I could trust.

Her portrait of Boston took into account what I augured of it: her protagonist, Tennessee, is a woman who watches from a distance the children she gave up because she could not sustain them. She is only able to keep one child; one we think is hers but is revealed to be the daughter of her dead best friend, a child named Kenya. Tennessee and Kenya spend their days secretly looking after Tennessee's given-up boys, whose adopted mother, Bernadette, has passed away from throat cancer. Against Tennessee's best plans, her children have grown up motherless. All their lives collide when Tennessee steps into oncoming traffic to shield her oldest son, who until that moment never knew her. In the aftermath of her injuries, under sedation, Tennessee meets her namesake, her deceased best friend in what may be a dream sequence or may be a near-death encounter. The two women commiserate over their situations and that of their children, in which I heard echoes of my own fears. But in their conversation I heard some new idea I did not recognize: while they lamented their fate and their struggles, they did so together, in a bonded and bonding way. In reading their solidarity and in witnessing their sorority, I comprehended anew my own sense of disenfranchisement. By the time I put the book down, still no phone call and no news, I was less composed than before.

In general, on these days, I felt stretched thin. Now, I also felt disrupted. The book had done it. It had suggested something, something intrusive. It had stirred something up. I had imagined that the book had been meant for me, was at just the right time and from God for me. This was comforting. It implied God knew exactly where I was in a physical and emotional sense. My map of Boston, it was an unnavigable wilderness. Ann's book was a hollering back from a parent: God could still hear me and saw exactly where I was, even could see how I saw it.

But the book seemed more than a mere response: it seemed to be saying something I did not want to hear. I could feel myself resisting some of it, detaching rather quickly from it. I could avow Patchett's enunciation of motherhood as it is a predicament. I loved the weaving of her stories: the dead best friend and the dead adoptive mother, the living birth mother, the only daughter. It was a story organized by the lives of the women in it and I could get into that. Still, I didn't want to commit to it. A few days after I finished it, I changed my mind about it. *That book wasn't for me after all:* disenchantment and the price of still being lost were the prices I'd pay to be able to get a little space between me and the indigestible story. *It's just fiction anyway,* I thought, *this has all been a fictive coincidence.*

## EPOCH TWO

Still no word from my would-be boss, still no biological news, and the days were getting shorter. The sun was never really on during this time, but now, the hours closed in on me earlier and earlier. Book taken into heart, book evicted, I was now on my guard.

I was on Facebook one night, looking at pictures and reading comments, dropping in on other people's lives undetected. I came across a little conversation between friends. The comment that struck me was from Isabel, a friend of my mother's, to a childhood friend of mine, Candyce. Candyce had written something referencing her grandmother's cooking. Her grandmother, Aseneth, has been dead for more than fifteen years, but I remember her well.

I was overcome with the desire to remember Aseneth to Candyce; I say overcome because there were little reasons I might not write to Candyce. While Isabel had commented on Aseneth's godliness, I wanted to say something about her graceful beauty. I left the comment feeling lucky to have had the opportunity to make it.

I got a response in my inbox. Candyce wrote that she had only a couple of nights before dreamt about me, that she was certain that this dream was from God, but that she felt hesitant about contacting me. She needed a sign that she should make contact with me. My comment, it was the sign and the way.

*I had a dream about you,* she began, and continued to describe what she saw as my situation: I was living on the same street as she was, in my grandmother's house, and I was deeply frustrated with my being there. I was crying. She offered that we should pray about it and we did. There was a revelation from God: I was inheriting something from my grandmother, something far more important than money. She ended there, commenting, *I don't even know if your grandmother is dead.*

My grandmother Olga is dead. My mother's mother passed away when I was six, when I was exactly the age that Judah is when I am writing this. Judah is my mother's only grandchild right now, and they are thick as thieves: each has stolen the other's heart and is fine with what they have gotten in return. I once asked Judah if his Momo had ever been wrong about anything or had ever done anything wrong. A highly scientific and incredulous child, his devotion to his grandmother might be his real religion: *No*, he blankly stared back at me, *Momo has never been or done any wrong in her life.*

I am Olga Sanchez Lopez's first-born grandchild from her only daughter (also her first child), and I was born on her birthday. But she has been dead for twenty-four long years. While my memories of her are fond, they are also limited and hazy. Still, as it is our dead that bond Candyce and me, I knew her dream meant something for me. I stopped resisting. Something was being said to me, I would listen. There is no keeping Candyce at arm's length. Candyce used to be Candy. Apparently, when we were girl-babies, aged two and diapered, our mothers put us in roller-skating lessons. We were both giant girls, weighing nearly nine pounds each at birth. By age four, our parents have engineered a tiny preschool for us, in which we study basics with our own private teacher. Candy's grandpa is a patriarchal figure with added force, he heads their family and he pastors the church we go to, in which both of his sons work. With her grandpa and her uncle's families, Candy's family lives on a hill overlooking San Antonio. The three neighboring houses make up a family compound, luxurious in its setting. Much, in fact, about Candy smacked of luxury. Her house is nice enough, but her wardrobe is also awesome. Candy is an only girl, and her mother decks her out in curls and velvet. She is allowed to be a very silly girl, and given to laughing fits. Her caramel eyes widen to tell stories, tall and often hilarious. Later, when we're older, her eyes will go wild with boy-craziness. Most of all, it's her hair: thick, honeyed, and flaxen, that bespeaks Candy's natural advantages. When I miss Candy, I think about her hair.

At ten years old, Candy is somehow in possession of a book about menstruation, sex, and pregnancy. She is actually forthcoming about where she got this book; her mother gave it to her. Still, I say "somehow" because I could not add up, at the time, how her mother, whom I loved and respected and knew so well, would give a book to Candy that my own mother would never think to give to me. Her mother seemed to want to give Candy information my mother only gave me later and because she had to, for my own sake. Candy and her mother, Becky, bonded over this sharing of information and over Candy's own impending transformation into a woman. Candy got shapely looking junior department skirts: one in particular was blue mock-velvet with a lace up waist. She was ten. At ten years old I was still being dressed in clothes that matched my six-year-old sister's outfits.

Candy took her new skirts and her book of knowledge and went stark-raving-mad boy-crazy. This girl child had a horrible, unrelenting, heated crush on our youth pastor, probably then twenty. She thought about him all the time, and since she had the book, she thought about sex with him. She tried to share her secrets with me in a way I could handle: *men and women*, she looked into my eyes with solemnity, *according to God's design, they fit together, physically, like a puzzle.*

No one stopped Candy's tween-aged depravity. At least, this is how I saw it. She was allowed to run hormonally amok. I was not allowed any amount of latitude on the subject of boys. When my dad found out about my own age-appropriate crush, at eleven years old, he was hurt and mad. Mad, because it was happening, and hurt because I had not told him about my feelings for James. I was completely at a loss about his hurt feelings; even I knew that girls didn't tell their dads about their crushes. Still, what I took away from it was my need to be pretty underground about my interests. I had very little wiggle room.

For reasons I couldn't know or understand at the time, Candy's father had to serve time. This was quite the shock for everybody, as we believed him wealthy and knew him as our associate pastor, as we knew his wife to be the personification of loveliness and grace, we could not anticipate and did not know what to make of his being found guilty of fraud. In the *federal, legal* sense. The collective mind reeled.

The family endeavored to keep it all secret in the beginning, which meant Candy was taken away from me. They thought she might spill secrets on accident. Since she was withheld from me, I moved on to other friends. I also started to pick up on things adults were growing careless about mentioning, and later, in their grief and anger, allowed themselves to diatribe about.

I gathered that Candy's mother had cancer and that it was serious. I imagine that I knew something of the situation before, but I did not appreciate it at ten the way I did when I was eleven. Things came into stronger relief at eleven for me. I think now I was getting older but also that things were getting more serious and the adults in my life were venturing to be more candid at times and had less composure at others.

All the same, my attention was drawn completely into my own life around the time Candy's father went away. I couldn't have been there for her if I had known everything. In my eleventh year, my youngest sister, Traci, then almost four, died. I was eight when she was born, early in the morning, the day after I fractured my collarbone while playing an overly fierce game of Red Rover with another Girl Scout, who significantly outweighed me. April 16, my mother in labor, I couldn't even get my shirt over my head. While I was fit for a special harness that I wailed about because I thought it meant I was crippled, like, *forever*, my baby sister was born.

Who knows why, but I and my sister Lina, we got to name her. This was fitting in a special sense since it was Lina who started asking for a baby sister before my parents were thinking about a third. The third Baby Bryand girl was a little unlike the ones before her: she didn't really look as Mexican as we do. She had really light brown hair and pale skin. We named her Traci Lynn, though the name did nothing for my mother. As she was all hopped up on the drugs they gave her for her c-section, she had little say in the matter. By the time she was recovered and coherent, baby was Traci.

When Traci was one year old, we discovered she had a terminal illness. I was then nine. At nine the idea of something or someone being terminal has nothing to which to root in the mind. It was probably something incomprehensible to me, at my age, but I cannot say for sure because I did not attempt to realize it.

I am a third generation Pentecostal. My grandfather, Francisco Lopez, husband to Olga, he was a Pentecostal minister of the Holiness persuasion. In between the years when Candy and I were in preschool and the time of that scandalous book, I had been in their little Spanish-speaking Mexican church. We had left Candy's grandpa's church, and her mother Becky, the only woman I have ever heard my mother name her Best Friend, so that we could be with my grandma Olga when she was ill. After she died, when I was six, we stayed at Iglesia Bethania as much out of respect for her memory as to keep my widowed grandpa company. Aged five, six, seven, eight, and nine years, I would spend hours in a little dusty Spanish filled church every week. Church was a way of life. Pentecostalism is the way of life I learned first in their church. My grandmother Olga Lydia, she preferred Lydia (her German doctor had named her Olga as a newborn and she didn't take to it perfectly), had stomach cancer. Of course, being quite little, I knew nothing of this. We buried our grandmother, fifty-six years old, after she died on Easter morning in 1985. By the time we leave her church to return to Candy's grandpa's church, Traci is gravely ill, but nobody yet knows it.

When we learn it, we have a large congregation of tongues-speaking, devil-rebuking, prophesying Pentecostals to support us. I spent no time trying to realize the meaning of terminal, and all my time trying to "realize" her life as ongoing. I had God on a technicality, I was pretty sure, because both my sister and I were constantly having faith for Traci's healing and, as actual children, we were innately capable of the child-like faith that is supposedly most effective. For two and a half years, I made sure to do and be exactly what I needed to so that God would see that, without equivocation, I was sure that He could heal my sister. I tripped over making that Could into Would: I wasn't sure how my faith would make God do something, but I did my part all the same. As I got older, and as Traci got sicker, I got more and more serious about the time I spent in my room, next to my bed, whispering into darkness at night. In the day, we did everything, every last thing a Pentecostal community knows to do when the prognosis is terminal. The chorus of voices did what you would do, in their shoes, if you're really Pentecostal. Of course, the devil himself was rebuked. He was chased, he was forbidden; he was unwelcome, he was a liar. Traci was frequently brought to the altar, all our most holy and most esteemed came forward to pronounce Life over her, to *insist* on her life, to put their hands over her tiny rib cage and conduct the healing. I was then part of the wider circle, the ones whose job it is to Agree in Faith, which means to say the opposite of what you see, to deny science and sight, and so will her to health. I could not afford to really wrap my head around "terminal," we all had to do our part all the time for Traci's healing. This kind of faith is really expensive and risky; it takes everything.

Our congregation, large enough, was still working overtime. Traci was sick, and in a community any child being so gravely ill occupies a lot of the collective mental space. But Becky was sick as well. Her cancer grew worse and worse. She became a kind of Lady Diana Spencer to us: she was alone, strangely now withdrawn and looking more than a little ragged, so our love for her only intensified.

If Candy had been silly, had been boy-crazy, if she had been her mother's pride and joy, she was now understandably crest-fallen. No more giggle fits and crushes, Candy's whole world was now much too serious for her to stay Candy.

By February of 1991, Traci had been ill for three years. She looked it. We continued to do what we knew to do as Pentecostals who believe in divine healing, but it went this way: she took her medicine, she lost weight, she went into the hospital, she bruised all over, she went for testing, she got bad results, she was too fragile for a heart transplant. She took more medicine, she went back into the hospital, she had a stroke, she could not breathe, she labored to breathe; she grew jaundiced, she weighed nothing, she took a sickly green hue, she closed her eyes. She could still hear me, so say *goodbye*. February 20, 1991, Traci died.

Traci died in my parents' room, in the house I moved into when I was one year old, and there were a limited number of people in the house and fewer allowed into the room and Becky was one. She was the one I buried my face into to scream my powerlessness, my muffled fury-loss and grief.

I am twelve years old when I put the only thing I knew to want more than life itself into the ground, when I learned the bitterness of His Will Not Mine. I lied, I told God Himself I understood, and then concocted my own anesthetic: I would never want anything again. You can't lose anything so precious, if you won't hold anything in your heart. I reasoned that Traci's loss was horrible, but it was surely the worst thing I could ever endure, and that I would never risk that kind of loss again. For me, the worst already here, was also a relief in that it would never come again.

I spoke at her funeral. I can still remember what I said; it would be too embarrassing to write it all here. I know for sure I didn't say the things I needed to say to someone, but would not say for a decade: that I have no worse memories than those that define the minutes of her passing, that I will never forget the exact sequence of expressions that trampled across my father's face as he struggled to process that Traci had finally passed. I wish I could have said something true, something other than what I said, which was contrived and forced, which was my best effort at defending the hearts of my family and church community from the death of someone too small. I said something about how Traci's death had brought us together, that we had prayed more and known God more during her struggle, and that might have been true. Only now, if I am honest, though we struggled for Traci's life with all the hope, faith, and prayer we could, and while that had in fact brought us together, the material of that solidarity certainly went into Traci's coffin with her and into the ground. It took all our shared resources to bury Traci, not yet four, heart failed inside her pretty little chest.

Becky, bless her, was the leader of a brigade of people who loved us and endeavored to keep us all walking in our lives, when we would surely rather faint. By her presence and by her insistence on the goodness of the Lord, by giving us little white Precious Moments bibles for Traci's funeral, by her example in the hardest time, I could see that whatever had happened, a dead baby sister did not mean that we would stop being people of God. We kept going to church.

In doing so, I had a front row seat to the hardest part of Candyce's life. At some point the following year, when we were twelve, Candyce's dad came back and shortly thereafter, Becky was pregnant with her fourth child. This was a predicament, indeed, because Becky was barely recovered from cancer: perhaps it may have been that her blood count numbers were only recently good, she was in remission, that kind of contingent health. Becky's doctor did not want her pregnant. Her doctor wanted Becky to terminate the pregnancy.

This Becky refused to consider. She would see the pregnancy through, she would honor God with her faith that he would preserve her life. When she bore her fourth child, she named her baby Benjamin Raphael, we were told it meant *God is my healer.*

My family was called to the hospital, to Becky's deathbed. Before she died, leaving Candyce behind to, at twelve years old, both mourn her and look after a brand new baby and two other brothers, she told my mother she would give her love to Traci. At the point of her death, she declared that heaven, *it was so beautiful.* She closed her eyes, aged thirty-six years, leaving an entire church bereft in her wake. We buried her about ten feet from where we buried my sister the year before, who is about ten feet from where we left grandmother Olga. To hear from Candyce, it is to be brought to that ground, sacred and terrible, where we share our dead.

\* \* \* \* \* \* \* \* \* \* \* \* \* \* \* \* \* \* \* \* \* \* \* \* \* \* \* \* \* \* \* \* \* \* \* \*

My mind had done what it would and what I did not want it to do, at times, right before the end of Traci's life; I would dare to focus on her hair, her skin, the curve of her shoulder blade and I would try my damnedest to make a lasting impression of her in my mind. I can still remember the bits and pieces of her sun-kissed highlights, or her tan little frame, but when I do, I always cry.

Making those impressions was rather costly, amounted to stolen moments, since they were tacit acknowledgments that she would not last. Then they proved costly just to hold them. Even now, to call up her memory makes me eleven again.

But these impressions were most costly right after Traci died. While we were busy marching on, while we were going to church and singing the same songs and saying the same informal Pentecostal liturgy about God's all the time goodness and God's ardent love for me, while I was still daytime "together," I spent months' worth of harrowing nights alone. I was not alone because my parents didn't check on me: they certainly did the very best that they could. I spent certain moments alone because I could not articulate their thoughts safely to anyone, so certainly devastating were they, and so certain was I that for them there really were no answers.

I became preoccupied with Traci's actual body and its condition, changing, in the ground.[2] I was concerned for her hair and for her skin; I was concerned for her face. I wasn't sure the coffin could really keep her safe from the ground's intruders and, even if it did, I mourned the disintegration of her cells, her unstoppable decomposition. I became transfixed by certain words: *putrefaction* in particular was a word I could not rescue myself from, could not speak at the time. I suppose one could argue that I had no restraint, and that my imagination was the culprit, but I hardly think it fair: we keep locks of hair and baby teeth. These, these were in the ground, falling apart.

The loss of Traci, her soul, to heaven could be reckoned with one way, but a hotness flooded my face to think of her body fallen; a pounding in my head and one in my chest stopped up my ears. In my bed, I muffled the cries that threatened to become a non-stop crescendo and I made an oath to myself and to Traci: I would not mourn her because I would not be getting over her. I would not cry because then there might be an end

---

2. It is common and predictable for an eleven–twelve year old to be preoccupied with the bodily harm associated with death. Please see http://www.hospicesupportcare.org/development.pdf, for the stages subscribed to by hospice care professionals. See also: Theresa Huntley, *Helping Children Grieve* (Minneapolis: Fortress, 1991) 17.

of my crying, and this would be a betrayal. I would not heal. Other people would go on with their lives, but I would not be doing so.

Everybody was walking around in my head after my phone call with Candyce. Their memories resurrected, intermingled, and confronted each other.

When my grandmother was a young woman, with three sons and an eldest daughter, she had a near-death experience. Her youngest was going to be hit by a car, and she put herself in the way, just like Patchett's heroine in *Name of Book*. She was, as a result of her injuries, according to our family folklore, lifted from her body and well on her way to dead when she pleaded with God: she could not leave her children. She asked God for the time to raise her children.

When my grandmother's overtime was up and she died on Easter morning, she visited each of her grandchildren in their sleep; we were all found sitting up, talking to an unseen someone in the middle of the night. Grandma had come to each of us to take her leave. I had remembered Aseneth Flores to Candyce, and she had remembered Olga Lopez to me, and we had in the process meandered over to visit Becky and Traci. In Candyce's dream, we lived on the same street and I lived in my grandmother's house. The sum total of her dream, my book, and our conversation, all of it created a sense of sorority for me.

Remarking on the time following her mother's death, Candyce says, "I could touch the grave, I was so close to death."

## EPOCH THREE

When did I read *Beloved*? After my dead had been conjured.

Everybody was, in a sense, still with me, as I poured over Toni Morrison's book, as I witnessed her Sethe bearing a baby in the grass, defenseless, on her way to Boston, and very close to death.

I saw Sethe kill her baby and I had no questions and I bore no judgment. On the contrary, Morrison's work fixed me in the center of my own hurricane, where I could in fact see myself from within while inhabiting a relatively calm space.

This is what I saw: Boston may or may not have been the wilderness I perceived it to be, but certainly there are times and there are places in the world that are not good enough to bear a child in good faith. Morrison's Sethe cuts her child's throat because she will not let her child live her entire life in rank slavery. Her maternal instinct determined the world unfit for her *best thing*, it was love that drove her choice. But in spilling baby blood, she breaks her family line and her Beloved is left with a strong desire for life, for what should have been hers to look forward to in it, and she comes back to try to reclaim a life too soon ended.

I had been keeping my Beloved company, in her death, I had stayed very near her. I had kept a promise I made to her very long ago, without even thinking about it. I had made a pact, my sorority was with *her,* with Traci whose life was ended too soon, and for whom I was bitter. The ravages of disease were not, for me, innocent for their non-personification. I was offended at the breaking of the cycles of life by the premature interruptions of death, claiming first our baby and then their mother, too early, with no respect for the order of things. I witnessed at a very influential moment in my own development the fragility and vulnerability involved in being a mother, in being a child.

It was my decision, at one moment, to refuse to live out that predicament again. I saw.

## EPILOGUE

Apparently, his bones were not broken and his body did not suffer the humiliation of corruption.[3] The Son of God, he did not contend with all the horrors of death. Did not disintegrate, did not liquefy. The text, it has the same problems I do, and for these problems it provides a resurrection of the body.[4]

I have only dreamt Traci came back to life a handful of times. Each time, I have woken up agonized and in tears. One time, she died again. Another time, she could only be around for a week, and I fretted for my parents. I can barely afford to dream my sister. Each time I wake to face a reality I had never made peace with. I have not been one to put my hope in resurrection. I did not opt for grief because it might produce healing. I did not think toward healing, because I felt this would betray my sister, and I did not think toward a resurrection because the sting of death was so convincing.

3. Psalm 16:10, Acts 13:35, John 19:36.

4. For a fascinating discussion on this matter, see Caroline Walker Bynum's *Resurrection of the Body in Western Christianity, 200–1336.* New York: Columbia University Press, 1995.

While this opting out served its purposes for my twelve-year-old self, it does not serve the woman I have become, the woman I need to be, as I am already a mother and already participating in life, and it is my testimony that the Spirit, She knew this. While I have shared the details, what I cannot impart is the abiding sense of my lost loved ones that gathered around me during this time. I believe that Spirit and my ancestors, the female ones, conspired to talk this out with me, to help move me forward, when a large part of me felt beholden to their bodies in the ground. They got together, to call me forward toward them and with them.[5]

All of this was outside of my conception of reality, outside my theology, and therefore much to my surprise. The effect of their intervention, it is cumulative and it is deeper down and closer to me than any words could be, than any system of ethics could reach. But, because I am endeavoring to testify to the peaceability of God's Spirit, I will attempt to articulate how I have benefited from this peace, as it has been a revelation and a phenomenon, in hope that it may, on some level, benefit another.

Five years before I was lost in Boston, I was driving along slushy grey streets in Wheaton, Illinois, in graduate school, when I glanced into my rearview mirror and saw a phantom baby-seat. I peered into the possibility, a mirage, and introspected for its effect on me: *Yes*, I thought, *that would be okay*. A year later, Chris and I welcomed Judah into our family. I don't fully know why my answer was *yes* before and *no* later. I only know it is important for me to be able to say both. I only know I cannot really say *yes*, if I am not allowed to say, "no." It is with this reflection that I bear witness with Becky, who named her son Benjamin, in an echoing of the naming of the son of Rachel, for whom she died in childbirth. I recognize that she knew he would be her passing and honor that she chose to give her life for his. It is with this reflection that I consider Sethe, and the woman she is modeled after,[6] whose love for her child certainly rivaled that of Becky, though her choice may look opposite. I know what it is to believe the world not good enough. I call to memory the fact that mothers and children remain among the most vulnerable inhabitants in our

---

5. For an introduction to the concept of ancestor involvement in creative transformation, see Monica Coleman's chapter "Invoking Oya: Practicing a Polydox Soteriology," in *Polydoxy: Theology of Multiplicity and Relation*, edited by Catherine Keller and Laurel C. Schneider, 186–201. New York: Routledge, 2011.

6. Margaret Garner was the basis for Toni Morrison's Sethe, and the protagonist of her opera, titled "Margaret Garner," which is reviewed by NPR at http://www.npr.org/templates/story/story.php?storyId=10986783

world, and ask that every "no" be considered thoughtfully in light of the fact that globally speaking, mothers and children occupy a precarious social position.[7] Every ninety seconds, a mother dies in childbirth. Last year more than 358,000 women died giving birth. While international cooperation on the Millennium Development Goals has seen some improvement in other areas of human suffering, it is the case that the maternal mortality rate has seen very slow and too little improvement.

It is with this reflection that I remember my own mother, who had to bury her little child, and for this reason will welcome death in a way I believe to be uncommon, when it comes. I promise to let you go in peace, as you have taught me to do for those on the point of death.

It is with this reflection that I reach toward my grandmother Olga Lydia, who somehow wrestled more time from God to mother.

And with this reflection that I love Candyce, who muscled her way through a motherless adolescence to raise her brothers, who looks like her mother, and who has since become an amazing mother to five children.

With this reflection, I stand in awe of the account of Mary's assent to becoming mother to Jesus, the Christ.[8] Mary's moment of comprehension we cannot fathom, but her response I can, for I too once said *yes*. I deeply recognize "let it be with me according to your word." It is in Mary's Magnificat that I find some anchoring for what I have grown into as Mother's hope, a hope essentially for justice. I find in her song a hope that the world be fit so that women may become mothers in good faith.

And, finally, it is with this reflection that I honor Traci: what I have mostly wanted was a world in which you were well.

I honor my circle of women: I honor that we have each met Life and Death, that we have each answered their difficult calls. All of us have found ourselves stranded on one side of the divide between living and the dead, reaching hard toward the other side. It is enough to know we are reaching toward each other, still.

---

7. Please see http://www.amnesty.org/en/campaigns/demand-dignity/issues/maternal-mortality/millennium-development-goals and http://www.unicef.org/mdg/maternal.html for a look at the state maternal health in 2010.

8. An interesting article on the agency of Mary, entitled "Hail Mary," written by James Martin can be accessed at: http://www.slate.com/id/2238981/.

# 13

## Preaching Christ Crucified

*Sharing [in] the Spirit of God's Nonviolent Future*

### Jarrod Saul McKenna

"The Cross is not a detour or a hurdle on the way to the kingdom, nor is it even the way to the kingdom; it is the kingdom come."[1]

—John H. Yoder

" . . . You will receive power when the Holy Spirit comes upon you and you will be my witnesses . . . "

—The Crucified and Risen Lord, Acts 1:8

"I don't judge you. I leave that to a wrathful, angry God to do."

—Ned Flanders to his neighbour Homer Simpson[2]

---

1. Yoder, *Politics of Jesus*, 51.
2. Tidbal, Hilborn and Thacker, eds., *Atonement*, 34.

283

The father of "Black Theology" James Cone has said, "No black preacher would dare to 'tell the story' without reference to Jesus, because he *is* the gospel story."[3] In this chapter I want to explore how many considerations of eschatology and atonement have been strangely abstracted away from "the Gospel Story." As my friend Scot McKnight has argued brilliantly in his book, *The King Jesus Gospel,* it is the story of Jesus as the world's true Lord—and this story located as the climactic fulfilment of the story of Israel—that is the Gospel. Sadly, the beauty of the Gospel narrative has been substituted with an anemic, inferior imitation, what Dallas Willard has dubbed "sin management." Sadder still for the context of this book, Pentecostals and Charismatics are often not an exception to, but rather another expression of, this cultural phenomenon; seen by a consumer culture as sin management with an experiential upgrade. I really do believe Pentecostals and Charismatics have more to offer the twenty first century than a form of "evangelicalism+," or put more crassly, sin management with the allure of better spiritual one-night stands.

I offer these questions regarding eschatology and atonement in the hope that Pentecostals and Charismatics will recover from the movement's roots its genesis with the poor, its culture of challenging racial diversity, and its eschatological pacifism. The image that came to me in prayer regarding these questions was of the tree described in the first Psalm, "planted by streams of water." It is not only the roots we must recover, they must grow deep in the rich soil of orthodox Christianity's revolutionary recovery of the centrality of the transformative nonviolence of Christ. This not only means going back to a young woman named Agnes Ozman in Topeka, and a black Holiness preacher named William J. Seymour at Azusa Street as we seek the 'Streams of Water', it means going deep into the organic matter of Eastern Orthodoxy, Anabaptism and other surprising places that will ground the experience of the Spirit "on earth" and in our discipleship. This I believe will yield fruit in season of a generation who know intimately that the genuine gift of the Holy Spirit leads to subversively Christ-like lives, not supernatural charlatans supporting systems that are costing us the earth at the expense of the global poor.

In this chapter I will seek to "tell the story" of Jesus *as* the story, in particular, the peculiarities of the scandalous Calvary-shaped nonviolence of our Lord Jesus, in which any faithful contemplation of "atonement" and "eschatology" will find its meaning. I will do this by describing

3. Erskine, *King Among Theologians.*

what I see as the problem in many discussions of the subjects of atonement and eschatology, and sketching what I hope to be a helpful (albeit
humble and incomplete) questions for Charismatics and Pentecostals. I
undertake this not as an academic but as a preacher who is no stranger to
the pulpits of Australia's largest Pentecostal and Charismatic churches, a
peace and [eco]justice activist, nonviolence trainer, and co-founder of an
intentional Christian commune, working, praying, and gardening alongside those who are marginalised in one the roughest parts of my city. I
also do this work not as a "pure bred Pentecostal" but as a uniquely Gen
Y charismatic cocktail; I'm the love child of John Wimber, Dorothy Day,
Kallistos Ware, and J. H. Yoder. Out of this context arise some 'queries'
as paleo-Pentecostals of the 17th century Quakers would say, and I will
identify them for prayerful consideration as we proclaim the Gospel to a
world groaning in eager expectation for liberation from all personal, social, ecological and cosmological violence, evil, and oppression: a world
that waits to be filled with the glory poured out at Pentecost.[4]

## SHARING "THE END OF THE WORLD AS WE KNOW IT" WITH FOUR VERY DIFFERENT PEOPLE

As I write this chapter, there are four people I have spent time with who
are on my heart. I'll call them Hannah, Tyler, Jon, and Samuel.[5] Hannah
is a remarkable young woman, taking time away from her honours
project in Law and Anthropology to take part in the MAKE POVERTY
HISTORY road trip. I had the privilege to mentor Hannah as a part of
this movement. Tyler is an equally impressive young man. He is on the
development squad for a major football team, completing his first year of
studying Social Work at the university level, and is proud of his Aboriginal
heritage and deeply committed to the healing of his own people and the
struggle for justice everywhere.

John has been a close friend since high school. Despite being the
front man for a hardcore band, Jon has always had a heart sensitive to the
pain of the world. He has overcome a drug addiction that claimed the life
of our mutual friend. Now he struggles to beat the alcoholism that has

4. Num 14:21, Ps 72:19, Isa 6:3, 11:9, Hab 2:14, 1 Cor 15:28.

5. I have changed the names of the people I mention (maybe consider it a "not yet
witnesses protection program").

repeatedly landed him in court so he can be the father to his son that he longs to be.

And finally Samuel, the Australian Minister for Foreign Affairs[6] with whom I recently discussed the global poor and Australia's foreign aid budget in an amiable yet bristly conversation in Canberra.

Reading for this chapter while at the same time keeping in mind the lives and challenges of these people, I was struck by how many of the books I was reading did not address the concerns from my context that arise when reading Scripture. Most did not link atonement and eschatology directly; nor did they consider these subjects with reference to "the Story" of which Jesus is the fulfilment and rarely with a mention of the Trinity. Perhaps unsurprisingly they also did not address the pressing concerns and challenges of Hannah, Tyler, Jon, and Samuel.

## WHERE'S THE GOOD NEWS IN ATONEMENT AND ESCHATOLOGY?

"We read to know we are not alone," wrote C. S. Lewis. This is increasingly my experience. In his succinct book *A Community Called Atonement*, Scot McKnight assures me I'm not alone when he writes, "you might be surprised to find a number of books on atonement that simply do not interact with (or even mention) Jesus' vision of the kingdom."[7]

If our Lord Jesus is right (and that's what I'm banking on), then the Gospel that he embodies is "the kingdom is at hand."[8] I don't think it's too much to suggest then, that atonement theories and eschatologies that are divorced from the Kingdom of God, "God's dream for creation,"[9] are not good news.[10] UK Baptist Evangelist and United Nations Special Advisor on Community Action against Human Trafficking, Steve Chalke asks,

---

6. Ok, I realize I might have given away the anonymity here.

7. McKnight, *Community Called Atonement*, 9.

8. Mark 1:15; Matt 4:17.

9. Desmond Tutu often says, "God has a dream" to talk of the kingdom. Brian McLaren picks up on this in (what I think is his most helpful book he has written) *The Secret Message of Jesus* when he speaks of "The Dream of God". He also suggests "the revolution of God", "the mission of God", "the party of God", "the network of God" and "the Dance of God". McLaren, *Secret Message of Jesus*, 138–48. But these semantic games are only useful in how they help us access what John H. Yoder would call "the original revolution".

10. And the Apostle Paul with no regard for political correctness would insist, "Which is really no gospel at all" (Gal 1:7).

Does the atonement speak to our government's foreign policy, the future of the Middle East, the war on terrorism, the challenge to the market economy of ethical trading, people trafficking, and climate change? Does it address the hopes, ambitions and fears of our generation? Undoubtedly, a weakness of some modern theologies of atonement has been that they have simply failed to speak to, engage with, or challenge our culture in any significant way.[11]

I am convinced that the Gospel does. Not just because it is what Hannah, Tyler, Jon, and Samuel (and so many others) need to hear, but because it is radically faithful to the Biblical witness of the early church.

Biblical scholar and historian N. T. Wright is convinced much of what passes for 'the Gospel' is "sub-biblical."[12] In a sharp and cutting critique of the book *Pierced for Our Transgressions* he wrote, "despite the ringing endorsements of famous men, it is deeply, profoundly, and disturbingly unbiblical."[13] The strength of these words is not aimed at a liberal theological agenda, but at what is the default theology that Charismatics and Pentecostals often appropriate, namely, American Evangelicalism. He goes on to explain,

> What then do I mean by saying that *Pierced for Our Transgressions* is deeply unbiblical? Just this: it abstracts certain elements from what the Bible actually says, elements which are undoubtedly there and which undoubtedly matter, but then places them within a different framework, which admittedly has a lot in common with the biblical one, but which, when treated as though it *were* the biblical one, becomes systematically misleading.[14]

According to N. T. Wright this systematically misleading distortion can lead to the Gospel sounding like "stories with an angry God and a loving Jesus, with a God who demands blood and doesn't much mind whose it is as long as it's innocent."[15] With everything Hannah, Tyler, Jon, and Samuel are struggling with, news that "God's really angry and had to take it out on someone so God took it out on Jesus instead of taking it out

---

11. Chalke, "Redemption of the Cross," 36–37.

12. Wright, "Cross and the Caricatures."

13. Ibid.

14. Ibid.

15. Ibid.

on you eternally," isn't "good" news. It's horrific. Are we Charismatics and Pentecostals often guilty of adding the dynamism of the Holy Spirit onto this "sub-biblical" distortion of the Gospel? At the risk of broad brush strokes, Lee Camp paints with prophetic clarity how both Evangelical and Liberal church cultures can empty the cross of its power,[16]

> [For evangelicals] a "personal Lord and Saviour" provides, to put it crassly, "fire insurance." The "grace of God" provides the necessary insurance that I would not go to hell. Though emphasizing "grace," in this model God remains a legalist after all, who must hand out punishment to *someone* for any infraction of his holy law—Jesus provides his blood, so we don't have to. This grace is "personal," having nothing to do with a new social order, a new kingdom order among humankind. Concerned almost exclusively with "forgiveness," "grace" is equated merely with "getting saved." "Good works" merit us nothing—though they may be constructive sampling we do out of gratitude for grace we have received. The primary task for the Christian, in this model, is to "believe" and express sorrow for one's sins.

> [For liberals] faith in Christ may be less about concern with heaven and hell, and more about inner peace with one's life. One might be called to experience inner "peace" in spite of the contradictions of one's life. When the emphasis upon an afterlife heaven and hell is removed, the same existentialist emphasis is found in the likes of Protestant Liberals like Rudolf Bultmann: one is called to respond, as an individual, to the call of Jesus in a way that gives meaning and authenticity to one's life. In this way, too, there can result disjunction between ethics and faith.[17]

So are these the options I have to offer Hannah, Tyler, Jon, and Samuel? A choice between an atonement that is a punitive deity appeasing its blood lust, or, an abandonment of a cosmic "at-one-ment" for an anaemic personal "one-ness," a rehashing of some market-spirituality in Christian-drag[18] where we can find an escapist 'inner peace,' 'happiness,' and 'fulfilment' to accompany our lives so comfortable in a society that

16. 1 Cor 1:17.

17. Camp, *Mere Discipleship*, 104.

18. And if you're in the market for a "spirituality," why not upgrade from Christianity that has such bad "branding" in the West (Christianity is so last century) to Buddhism that has better public relations? My point is that when truth claims are reduced to a Neo-liberal economic "choice" the Market becomes the only "truth claim."

survives on the silent suffering of others?[19] A choice between a variety of eschatologies that see God's *telos* (or purpose) for creation as the rescue of your disembodied 'soul' before destroying all of creation[20] or eschatological hopes projected onto modernist metanarrative projects where ideology, the Nation State or science can 'save us' from ourselves?[21] The following are some humble but I pray helpful *queries* I have for a way forward.

## HOW DID PETER PREACH PNEUMATOLOGY, ESCHATOLOGY, AND ATONEMENT AT PENTECOST?

At Pentecost we do not see Peter running electives on Pneumatology with breakout working groups on its implications for atonement and eschatology. Peter does not explain the four spiritual laws, invite people forward to say the sinners prayer and follow it up with a second altar call for those who are "yet to get the Ghost."

Scot McKnight sums up Peter's Sermon at Pentecost (Acts 2:14–39) in six revealing movements that I will comment on in light of our questions and explore in more depth later,

19. The authors of *A Peaceable Psychology* note, "Each view of atonement was a response to a particular social and historical context, and will follow this same hermeneutic." They go on to say it is significant that the dominant understanding of atonement for the early Church emerged "in response to Empires" not in accommodation to Empire. Dueck and Reimer, *Peaceable Psychology*, 28.

20. Harvey Cox writes, "One of the worst features of dispensational fundamentalism is the foreshortened time it assigns to the years before the end comes, which makes any concerns for the health of the planet's oceans and air and forests superfluous. Another is the belief that Christ will not come until a titanic battle is fought in Palestine between Christ and the Antichrist. This fatalistic conviction undercut efforts to arrive at a peaceful solution to the conflict between Israelis and Palestinians." Cox, *Future of Faith*, 147.

21. Yoder suggested that Constantinian eschatologies saw the Emperor as a parousia (Yoder, *Christian Attitudes to War, Peace and Revolution*, 63.) This contrasts sharply with the beauty of the eschatology of Martin Luther King Jr. Yoder, reflecting on how King made sense of his people's sufferings, and God's presence with them in the struggle against the Powers in relation to God's Sovereignty, wrote: "It made sense to King because his people's piety was full of the memories of the first Joshua at Jericho and the second Joshua at Golgotha. *The hope of the Christian apocalypse is not utopia, not compensation for suffering, not trust in a Darwinian or a humanistic law of progress, but reasonably founded extrapolation from the cross, the resurrection, and Pentecost.*" Stassen, Nation, and Hamsher, eds., *War of the Lamb*, 63.

*v.16–21 Peter moves immediately to the Old Testament story to explain what is happening with Jesus and his followers.*[22]

Peter starts with what is happening in the church, a sign of what the world will be, by framing that the outpouring of the Spirit is what was promised by Joel when God was going to act decidedly to set the world right side up. It's very clear for Peter, the outpouring of the Spirit is a sign that God's dream for creation is becoming their waking reality. For Peter this is eschatology underway.

*v.22–24 Peter tells the Story about Jesus: life, death, resurrection, exaltation.*[23]

For Peter the Story of what God has done in Jesus *is* the Gospel. This horrific event is God's plan, not an accident, our response to God is to kill God but death doesn't win. (Christus Victor)

*v.25–31 Jesus, the Davidic messianic nonviolent King, is foretold in Israel's Story.*[24]

The king you expect came not with a crown, not violent overthrow, but with resurrection.

*v.32–33 Dead, raised and exalted as King*[25]

What you see now is the start of the end.

*v.34–35 Israel's story once again*[26]

Enemies have become a footstool not via crusade but a cross.

*v.36 The point of the Gospel!*[27]

Our Story in Jesus is subverted with a Lord and Messiah we didn't expect.

*v.37–38a How to respond to the apostolic gospel of Peter*[28]

AFTER realizing our culpability in systems that have made a victim of the Messiah yet God has vindicated him "cut to the heart," repent (change) be baptized, immersed in the story transformed in the name of Jesus.

*v.38b–39 Saving benefits for responders*[29]

22. McKnight, *King Jesus Gospel*, 167.
23. Ibid.
24. Ibid.
25. Ibid.
26. Ibid., 168.
27. Ibid.
28. Ibid.
29. Ibid.

Forgiveness of sins was what was to happen at the end when
the world was to be set straight, receive the gift of the Spirit of
God's future to animate our lives now.

## CAN CHRIST'S TABLE HELP US RECOVER THE LITURGICAL BEAUTY OF *THE STORY'S ESCHATOLOGICAL* ATONEMENT?

James Alison insists that atonement is first not a theory but a liturgy.[30]
Alison suggests that treating atonement as "theory" means that it is "an
idea to be grasped—and once *grasped*, you have 'got it'—whereas a liturgy
is something that *happens to and at you*."[31] Atonement is not something
we merely seek to understand but something we undergo, and in undergoing it, stand-under-it in transfiguring awe. As N. T. Wright puts it,
"When Jesus himself wanted to explain to his disciples what his forthcoming death was all about, he didn't give them a theory, he gave them
a meal."[32] In the First World where increasingly people eat takeout while
watching "Master Chef" on TV, it is important to remember meals are to
be shared in, to be eaten, not merely talked about.[33] There is a very real
difference between "take and eat" and "theorize and argue." This "taking,"
"eating," "undergoing," and "receiving" in a very real sense is entering into
Mystery in *receiving participation*. This mode of *receiving participation*
intuitively and experientially fits for many Charismatics and Pentecostals
given the empowerment for mission that flows from the experience of the
Spirit's power.

Kallistos Ware notes that Mystery is "something that is revealed for
our understanding, but which we never understand exhaustively because
it leads into the depth or the darkness of God."[34] Ware writes that this

---

30. I would like to discuss the significance of Alison's work and the Jewish depths
of what he means by liturgy in contrast to what he calls our "impoverished notion of
liturgy" but space will not allow.

31. Alison, "God's Self-Substitution and Sacrificial Inversion," 167.

32. Wright, "Cross and the Caricatures."

33. N. T. Wright: "Of course, the earliest exponent of that meal (Paul, in 1
Corinthians) insists that it matters quite a lot that you understand what you are about as
you come to share in it; but still it is the meal, not the understanding, that is the primary
vehicle of meaning" (Wright, "Cross and the Caricatures").

34. Ware, *Orthodox Way*, 15.

"thick darkness" we enter into like Moses turns out to be "a luminous or dazzling darkness."[35]

The ungraspable yet practical[36] meanings of this Mystery of liturgy—where we[37] share in Christ's Feast of the Age to Come—induce awe, worship,[38] thanksgiving, praise and radical humility.[39] We undergo, remember (anamnesis) *Jesus as the Story*'s past fulfilled, and proclaim as a prophetic sign *Jesus as the Story*'s future made present.[40] The "metaphors," as Hans Boersma calls them, or "meanings" of the Meal "give direction to the future, for the ethical Christian life cannot do without metaphors. They help us envision a future in which the justice of God's hospitality holds sway. Final function of metaphors is that they are a divinely given means to avoid idolatrous claims of knowledge. Metaphors . . . are an acknowledgement that we need to access the world around us in an indirect fashion, and that the idea of direct and complete access is an arrogant illusion that violates the multifaceted integrity of the created world."[41]

N. T. Wright writes, "That meal . . . contains in itself not only all the various meanings of 'atonement' that are worth considering, but also the means by which theories can be turned into real life: personal, practical, political life; Kingdom-of-God-on-earth-as-in-heaven life. And that, after all, is what 'atonement' ought to be about."[42] Another world is [not just] possible by grace; it is present [!] through Jesus. "What 'atonement' ought to be about" may be far more accessible to Hannah, Tyler, Jon, and Samuel amongst a real people whose lives are starting to be received from

35. Ibid.

36. "[Atonement is] something we are invited to perform with God in this world. Atonement is praxis." McKnight, *King Jesus Gospel*, 114.

37. "Any theory of atonement that is not an ecclesial theory of atonement is inadequate." McKnight, *Community Called Atonement*, 9.

38. Stanley Hauerwas: "The Christian alternative to war is worship."

39. "When we speak of the Cross of Christ, we are on holy ground. We stand in a place that requires humility. We ought not to violate the very love that Christ demonstrates by firing cannon balls over Golgotha at one another. We do well to present our proposals with genuine meekness, with generosity for our rival theorists, renouncing contempt wherever it lurks. Let us not tread, though lack of charity, upon the very Cross we proclaim." Jersak, "Nonviolent Identification and the Victory of Christ," 25.

40. 1 Cor. 11:24, 26.

41. Boersma, *Violence, Hospitality, and the Cross*, 104.

42. Wright, "Cross and the Caricatures."

the nail scarred hands of God's gracious Table Host.[43] The Table Host wipes our tears and welcomes us to take our place at the table to eat of *The Final Party's Entrée* with other diverse sinners like ourselves who have been forgiven to participate in this redistribution of God's-given-future in bread.

## CAN WE RECOVER THE STORY'S FIRST-CENTURY ATONING-ESCHATOLOGICAL BEAUTY FOR THE TWENTY-FIRST?

This real meal with messy people (who are at least as problematic as we are), is not a neat commemoration of timeless truths, high ideals or even the highest example of what it is to be fully human.[44] This meal is nothing less than the celebration of "God's definitive eschatological justice-initiative [that] takes place in the death and resurrection of Christ."[45] Christian eschatology is Jewish eschatology underway, in the most unlikely of ways! God's new world has not come through the expected military Messiah but through a nonviolent crucified Messiah, who is God's fullness in the flesh.[46]

Alison writes that there is "only one reason that a Christian eschatology exists at all, and that is the resurrection." [47] Resurrection in the Jewish imagination was the "climax or grand finale" at the end of his-

---

43. Camp, *Mere Discipleship*, 174.

44. "Jesus was not just a moralist whose teachings had some political implications; he was not primarily a teacher of spirituality whose public ministry was unfortunately seen in a political light; he was not just a sacrificial lamb preparing for his immolation, or a God-Man whose divine status calls us to disregard his humanity. Jesus was, in his divinely mandated (i.e., promised, anointed, messianic) prophethood, priesthood, and kingship, the bearer of a new possibility of human, social and therefore political relationships. His baptism is the inauguration and his cross is the culmination of that new regime in which his disciples are called to share. Hearers and readers may choose to consider that kingdom as not real, or not relevant, or not possible, or not inviting; but no longer can we come to this choice in the name of systematic theology or honest hermeneutics. At this one point there is no difference between the Jesus of History and the Christ of Geschichte, or between Christ as God and Jesus as Man, or between the religion of Jesus and the religion about Jesus (or between the Jesus of the canon and the Jesus of history). No such slicing can avoid his call to an ethic marked by the cross, a cross identified as the punishment of a man who threatens society by creating a new kind of community leading a radically new kind of life" Yoder, *The Politics of Jesus*, 51.

45. Marshall, *Beyond Retribution*, 57.

46. Col 1:15–20.

47. Alison, *Living At the End Times*, 28.

tory when God would have finally put the world the way it was intended to be without injustice, death, oppression and sin reigning.[48] The early Christians believed that the Hebraic hope was not just imminent but had already begun because what was to take place at the end of history (the resurrection) had started in the middle through 'The Human One'[49] who was the first fruits (1 Cor. 15:20) of the world restored to its intended beauty.[50]

What was this Hebraic hope? Crossan writes that Jewish Eschatology was not "the evacuation of earth for God's heaven but . . . the divine trans-figuration of God's earth. It is not about the destruction but the transfor-mation of God's world."[51] Is Christian hope something less than this? I have heard it preached that those who rejected Jesus misunderstood that the Messiah was not to bring a real, political and cosmic liberation but instead a "spiritual" salvation. As my friend and mentor Lee Camp insists, we misunderstand what those who rejected Jesus misunderstood!

> Oppressed by Rome . . . Jesus corrected [the disciples] not for expecting a kingdom; he corrected them for their false construal of the kind of king who would rule the kingdom, and their false nationalistic and militaristic hopes. The Disciples indeed mis-understood; but we have too often misunderstood their misun-derstanding. That is, they were not wrong expecting a "political" kingdom as opposed to a "spiritual" one; they were not wrong for expecting a "this-worldly" kingdom as opposed to an "oth-erworldly" one. Instead, Jesus announced a kingdom that was political—in that "politics," in the classic sense, is concerned with the manner in which real communities arrange their af-fairs. Jesus announced a kingdom that was "this-worldly"—in that the rule of God was not far off in the heavens, but even then, invading human history.[52]

If this then is the shape of Jesus' Messianic role—not as a militaristic messiah who bears the sword but a Suffering Servant who bears the cross—then "how does this vocation, and its acting out in Jesus' death and resurrection, relate to the challenge he was presenting in the Sermon

---

48. Crossan, "Appendix: Bodily-Resurrection Faith," 175.

49. Walter Wink's translation of "The Son of Man."

50. Crossan, "Appendix: Bodily-Resurrection Faith," 176.

51. Ibid., 174.

52. Camp, *Mere Discipleship*, 92.

on the Mount and elsewhere, the challenge of the coming kingdom, the challenge to live in the present in light of God's in breaking future?"[53] Scot McKnight contends that any "Christian theory of atonement must begin with how Jesus understands the kingdom."[54]

For the early Christians to talk of Jesus as Messiah was to talk of God's subversion of Israel's militaristic kingdom hopes through the foolish nonviolent power[55] seen on the cross in the One who was true Israel and true Adam.[56] To quote the Apostle Paul in 2 Corinthians 5:16, "we once regarded the Messiah in this [violent] way, [because of the death of Jesus] we do so no longer."[57] In light of the resurrection, Yoder can write, "The Cross is not a detour or a hurdle on the way to the kingdom, nor is it even the way to the kingdom; it is the kingdom come."[58]

To talk of the cross is to talk of atonement. But as N.T. Wright would quickly insist "There is no clear demarcation between Jesus' kingdom announcement and his approaching death. The two belong closely together."[59] To talk of the Kingdom is to talk of eschatology, the Jewish hope that God will one day un-screw the world. But no one would talk of Jesus' cross and his inseparable kingdom message if it was not for the resurrection,[60] which is again talk of eschatology; as is talk of the outpouring of God's Spirit on all flesh.

Jesus' life, signs, wonders, teachings, death, resurrection and ascension are all one inseparable initiative of God to start the *end* of all injustice, death and oppression; God's cosmic clean-up plan for all of creation. It is all this that makes possible the outpouring of the Spirit at Pentecost that we might witness to this nonviolent King and his kingdom. Gregory Boyd succinctly answers N.T. Wright's question by stating, "what it means to experience 'salvation' is that we participate in the cosmic liberation Christ won through his incarnation, life, ministry, death and

53. Wright, *After You Believe*, 110.

54. McKnight, *A Community Called Atonement*, 14.

55. Wright, *After You Believe*, 408.

56. Wright, *Following Jesus: Biblical Reflections on Discipleship*, 46–47.

57. I have found N. T. Wright's brilliant reflections on 2 Cor 5:16 very helpful.

58. Yoder, *Christian Attitudes to War, Peace and Revolution*, 51.

59. Wright, *After You Believe*, 110.

60. Wright and Crossan, "Resurrection: A Dialogue," 175.

resurrection. Hence, to have faith in what Christ did is to walk faithful to what Christ is doing."[61]

It is God's nonviolence revealed fully in Jesus that means that grace *is* eschatology.[62] The outpouring of the Spirit is the start of our gracious participation in God's beautiful *eschaton* ('end' or 'purpose'). Why is this so hard for people to comprehend? Richard Hays suggests "One reason that the world finds the New Testament's message of peacemaking and love of enemies incredible is that the church is so massively faithless. On the question of violence, the church is deeply compromised and committed to nationalism, violence, and idolatry. (By comparison, our problems with sexual sin are trivial.)"[63] "Hence the message of the kingdom and the vocation of the cross are deeply integrated, and hence the deep-level resistance within Western culture to such integration at any level. We have preferred our kingdoms to be of a different sort, and preferred to see the shameful death of Jesus as bringing about purely heavenly "salvation."[64]

## CONCLUSION: THE SPIRIT'S INVITATION TO TAKE PART IN THE START OF THE BEAUTIFUL END

I have sought to "tell the story" and proclaim Jesus *as* the story. The scandalous Calvary-shaped messianic particularities of the Resurrected Jesus are the story in which any faithful contemplation of atonement and eschatology will find its meaning. I have held in prayer the names and lives of Hannah, Tyler, Jon, and Samuel as I have sought to *tell the story*.

Yet I have found that I cannot simply 'tell them' as if the gospel was something I had *grasped*. As if it could simply be communicated in an essay. As if 'the Story' was 'mine' instead of someone I have only started to become now that I am God's. Maybe this is what Scot McKnight means when he says, "A missional life is participation in atonement. As others are brought into contact with the kingdom of God, relations with God, self, others, and the world are restored."[65]

61. Boyd, "Christus Victor View," 47.

62. "The resurrection of Jesus is an advanced sample of the reign of God that will become visible in its fullness when Jesus returns. Discern the life and teachings of Jesus is to see how things are under the rule of God." Weaver, *Nonviolent Atonement*, 40.

63. Hays, *Moral Vision of the New Testament*, 343.

64. Wright, *After You Believe*, 110.

65. McKnight, *Community Called Atonement*, 141.

Instead I find myself wanting to invite others to be part of a community where our brokenness need not be hidden because of the Spirit of Healing Forgiveness moving towards us with the invitation to *undergo*, communities where we need not pretend that the fault lines of the world's pain are simply 'out there'. Rather we can acknowledge they run though our own hearts and lives. Our past need not be concealed because God's future (and, by gratuitous grace, our part in God's future) is being revealed as our eyes become adjusted to see that the darkness dazzles with the very Presence of God. We need communities that dare to allow themselves to *undergo* the kind of grace that pardons and empowers us to take part in the healing of creation.

With tears in my eyes for my world and myself, I want Hannah, Tyler, Jon, and Samuel to know—in ways that they undergo the reality—that the Love revealed in Jesus that went to the cross to exhaust the powers of evil, washes away our sins so we can now get our hands dirty in the soil of God's New Creation. I want them to know that the Triune God now longs to fill their lives with the nonviolent power that raised Jesus from the grave, so that our lives, despite all the hurt and pain and loss, can be a sign of the Love that will one day flood all of creation like the waters cover the seas. I want them to "taste and see" that the Gospel really is good news to our world's most pressing personal, social, ecological, and political needs.

I long for all of us to see the *dazzling Beauty* that Dostoevsky was so convinced would save the world. Kallistos Ware thinks Dostoevsky came close to expressing this beauty as "the true meaning of Christ's victory" when he wrote,

> At some thoughts a woman stands perplexed, above all at the sight of human sin, and she wonders whether to combat it by force or by humble love. Always decide: "I will combat it by humble love." If you resolve on that once for all, you can conquer the whole world. Loving humility is a terrible force: it is the strongest of all things, and there is nothing else like it.[66]

Because of the forgiveness of sins, we are now all invited to "tell the story," to undergo the story, to be immersed in the story, to eat the story, to participate in the story with our very lives, in waiting witness to the final

---

66. Ware, *Orthodox Way*, 81 (I changed the gender of the quote.).

chapter of the story. The day when the beauty of humble Love's victory, won on Calvary, will conquer the whole world.

Not by might, not by power, but by the Spirit of God.

# BIBLIOGRAPHY

Alison, James. "God's Self-Substitution and Sacrificial Inversion." In *Stricken by God?*, edited by Brad Jersak and Michael Hardin, 166–79. Grand Rapids: Eerdmans, 2007.

———. *Living At the End Times: The Last Things Re-Imagined*. London: SPCK, 1997.

Boersma, Hans. *Violence, Hospitality, and the Cross: Reappropriating the Atonement Tradition*. Grand Rapids: Baker, 2004.

Boyd, Greg. "Christus Victor View." In *The Nature of the Atonement*, edited by James K. Beilby and Paul R. Eddy, 23–49. Downers Grove: InterVarsity, 2006.

Camp, Lee C. *Mere Discipleship: Radical Christianity in a Rebellious World*. Grand Rapids: Brazos, 2003.

Chalke, Steve. "The Redemption of the Cross." In *The Atonement Debate: Papers from the London Symposium on the Theology of Atonement*, edited by Derek Tidbal, David Hilborn, and Justin Thacker, 34–49. Grand Rapids: Zondervan, 2008.

Cox, Harvey. *The Future of Faith*. New York: HarperOne, 2009.

Crossan, John Dominic. "Appendix: Bodily-Resurrection Faith." In *The Resurrection of Jesus: John Dominic Crossan and N.T. Wright in Dialogue*, edited by R. B. Stewart, 171–86. Minneapolis: Fortress, 2006.

Dueck, Alvin, and Kevin Rimer. *A Peaceable Psychology: Christian Therapy in a World of Many Cultures*. Grand Rapids: Brazos, 2009.

Erskine, Noel Leo. *King Among Theologians*. Cleveland: Pilgrim, 1994.

Hays, Richard B. *The Moral Vision of the New Testament*. San Francisco: Harper, 1996.

Jersak, Brad. "Nonviolent Identification and the Victory of Christ." In *Stricken by God?*, edited by Brad Jersak and Michael Hardin, 18–53. Grand Rapids: Eerdmans, 2007.

Marshall, Christopher D. *Beyond Retribution: A New Testament Vision for Justice, Crime, and Punishment*. Grand Rapids: Eerdmans, 2001.

McKnight, Scot. *A Community Called Atonement*. Nashville: Abingdon, 2007.

———. *The King Jesus Gospel*. Grand Rapids: Zondervan, 2011.

McLaren, Brian D. *The Secret Message of Jesus*. Nashville: Thomas Nelson, 2006.

Stassen, Glen H., Mark Thiessan Nation, and Matt Hamsher, editors. *The War of the Lamb: The Ethics of Nonviolence and Peacemaking by John Howard Yoder*. Grand Rapids: Brazos, 2009.

Tidbal, Derek, David Hilborn, and Justin Thacker, editors. *The Atonement Debate: Papers from the London Symposium on the Theology of Atonement*. Grand Rapids: Zondervan, 2008.

Ware, Kallistos. *The Orthodox Way*. New York: St. Vladimir's Seminary Press, 1995.

Weaver, J. Denny. *The Nonviolent Atonement*. Grand Rapids: Eerdmans, 2001.

Wright, N. T. *After You Believe: Why Christian Character Matters*. New York: HarperOne, 2010.

————. "The Cross and the Caricatures: A Response to Robert Jenson, Jeffrey John, and a New Volume Entitled *Pierced for Our Transgressions.*" Fulcrum Web Site. Online: http://www.fulcrum-anglican.org.uk/news/2007/20070423wright.cfm?doc=205.

————. *Following Jesus: Biblical Reflections on Discipleship.* Grand Rapids: Eerdmans, 1994.

————. *The New Testament and The People of God.* Minneapolis: Fortress, 1992.

Wright, N. T., and John Dominic Crossan. "The Resurrection: Historical Event or Theological Explanation? A Dialogue." In *The Resurrection of Jesus: John Dominic Crossan and N. T. Wright in Dialogue,* edited by R. B. Stewart, 16–47. Minneapolis: Fortress, 2006.

Yoder, John Howard. *Christian Attitudes to War, Peace, and Revolution.* Grand Rapids: Brazos, 2009.

————. *The Politics of Jesus: Vicit Agnus Noster.* 2nd ed. Grand Rapids: Eerdmans, 1994.

## Part III

Emerging Anabaptist/Pentecostal Conversations

# Letter to the Editor

*Waxahachie Daily Light*
January 2006

## Paul Alexander

January 5, 2006
Editor
Waxahachie Daily Light
Waxahachie, Texas 75165

Dear Editor,

Martin Luther King, Jr. Day of Service is worthy of more attention and respect within the community of Waxahachie, especially among the Christians. Rev. Dr. King was a follower of Jesus and a minister of the Gospel, he is our brother in Christ and the only minister to have a day in his honor.

This is not a day for African Americans only, although unfortunately I often encounter those who hold this misperception. This is a day for all people, including white people, to hope, celebrate, and work together for justice, respect, and reconciliation.

Rev. Dr. King helped reveal and heal sin in the life of America, and he did so with Christian love rather than violence. He helped America live up to its ideals of freedom and democracy in ways that it previously had not.

But Dr. King would not want the day to be about him, he would want it to be about who we are and what we are doing together to make this world a better place.

I hope that all the pastors of all the churches in the area, whether Latino, African-American, Asian, Anglo, or multi-ethnic, encourage their people to participate in the events on Monday, January 16th. I wish that more places that don't close would dismiss for the day so that their employees could better serve the community and honor the legacy of this true American hero.

I and my family will be celebrating the day and participating in the events in hope that we can do our small part to build Dr. King's beloved community, and I encourage all the citizens of Waxahachie to do the same.

Cordially,

Rev. Paul Alexander, PhD
Professor of Bible and Theology
Southwestern Assemblies of God University
Waxahachie, Texas 75165

14

# Spirit-Empowered Peacemaking as Evangelical, Ecumenical, and Pentecostal Opportunity[1]

## Paul Alexander

Pentecostals and Charismatics should honestly examine "the conviction that the renunciation of the sword to which Jesus called His disciples is one of the keys to the rest of the problem of Christian faithfulness and to the recovery of the evangelical and ecumenical integrity of the church."[2] John Howard Yoder's challenge to the church is also an opportunity, for making peace is the opposite of using coercion to get one's way. Making peace is the opportunity to overcome the unfaithfulness of consumerism, oppression (gender, economic, ethnic, religious, etc.), nationalism, and militarism. Peacemaking is indeed the opportunity to be consistent in

1. I presented this paper in March 2002 in the ecumenism interest group at the Society for Pentecostal Studies conference in Lakeland, Florida. I sent in the proposal before 9/11 but wrote this paper afterward. On September 25, 2001, I wrote "Rebuild Afghanistan" (see the introduction to Part Two) which reveals where my thinking was at the time. I have left this article mostly as it was in 2002—when I was trying to discern and practice Christian peacemaking in the months after 9/11 while teaching at an Assemblies of God university in Texas that would eventually not renew my contract because of these issues.

2. John Howard Yoder, *The Original Revolution* (Eugene, OR: Wipf & Stock, 1998) 8.

our witness to unbelievers (evangelism), in our unity with our brothers and sisters in Christ (ecumenism), and in our faithfulness to our Spirit baptism (Pentecostalism).[3]

I realize that I could have opened this chapter with a less challenging statement. However, making peace between hostiles is the essence of what Christ did through his life, cross, and resurrection,[4] and peacemaking is the heart of his call to us as his ambassadors.[5] Pentecost and the charismata—the power, reconciliation, fruit, and gifts of the Holy Spirit—are crucial to fulfilling this commission. God is leading his church in peacemaking and, just as the early Pentecostals anticipated, we can even now participate in the way of the cross.

Many of our ancestors in the faith had significant concerns regarding the appropriateness of the participation of Christians in the killing of other humans, regardless of whether or not the killing was sanctioned by a government. I believe that we should rejoice and thank God for their convictions, rather than distance ourselves from or be ashamed of them. The majority of Pentecostal denominations issued statements in the early twentieth century declaring that they could not "conscientiously participate in war and armed resistance which involves the actual destruction of human life, since this is contrary to our view of the *clear* teachings of the inspired Word of God, which is the sole basis of our faith."[6] Patriotism

---

3. I use the term ecumenism to designate the unity, not uniformity, which should be sought among all Christians.

4. "For he himself is our peace, who has made the two one and has destroyed the barrier, the dividing wall of hostility, by abolishing in his flesh the law with its commandments and regulations. His purpose was to create in himself one new man out of the two, thus making peace, and in this one body to reconcile both of them to God through the cross, by which he put to death their hostility. He came and preached peace to you who were far away and peace to those who were near." Eph 2:14–18 (NIV)

5. "So from now on we regard no one from a worldly point of view. Though we once regarded Christ in this way, we do so no longer. . . . All this is from God, who reconciled us to himself through Christ and gave us the ministry of reconciliation: that God was reconciling the world to himself in Christ, not counting men's sins against them. And he has committed to us the message of reconciliation. We are therefore Christ's ambassadors, as though God were making his appeal through us." 2 Cor 5:16–20 (NIV).

6. "The Pentecostal Movement and the Conscription Law," *The Weekly Evangel*, 4 August 1917, 6. Sixty-two percent of Pentecostal denominations formed by 1917 were pacifistic at some point in their history. However, this refers only to those denominations formed in the United States; European Pentecostals also evidenced pacifism in the early twentieth century. Jay Beaman, *Pentecostal Pacifism* (Hillsboro, KS: Center for Mennonite Brethren Studies, 1989) 30, 32–33.

and nationalism were condemned as idolatrous by some, and the kingdom of God was sought above all else because an international, dare I say "global," perspective was maintained. Many Pentecostals boldly declared that killing was incompatible with discipleship into the Way.[7] This fact needs to be actively and corporately remembered.[8]

I believe this could and should lead to the questioning of Christian participation in violence and injustice by Pentecostals, and our participation in concrete peacemaking efforts should be encouraged and supported. Opportunity should be created in Pentecostal denominations (and there are fourteen thousand of them[9]) for dialogue about these issues, and a Pentecostal theology for peacemaking should be high on the agenda.[10]

This is all the more appropriate in an ecumenical context because we are at the beginning of the Decade to Overcome Violence: Churches Seeking Reconciliation and Peace.[11] Konrad Raiser reminds us that the confession of Jesus Christ as God and Savior is the source of our reconciliation and peacemaking.

> If churches do not combine their witness for peace and reconciliation with the search for unity among themselves, they fail

---

7. In this recollection I am not seeking or claiming to have found a perfect first generation of Pentecostals that can lead us to the Promised Land. As Everett Wilson astutely observed, "is not the desire to find an ideal first generation more an idolatry than it is a frank recognition that the Pentecostal movement is essentially God's working with finite, defective, men and women whom he uses to demonstrate his purposes not because of some special merits but despite the absence of them?" Rather, the recognition that it was one time an important part of Pentecostalism can open the door to accepting its relevance now. "They Crossed the Red Sea, Didn't They?" in *The Globalization of Pentecostalism: A Religion Made to Travel*, edited by Murray W. Dempster, Byron D. Klaus, and Douglas Petersen, 99–100 (Oxford, UK: Regnum, 1999). Furthermore, other early Pentecostals were very nationalistic and supported military action. All aspects of the variety need to be recognized and the theological support for each should be analyzed and critiqued as well.

8. For a detailed telling of this story in the Assemblies of God, see Paul Alexander, *Peace to War: Shifting Allegiances in the Assemblies of God* (Telford, PA: Cascadia, 2009).

9. Burgess and McGee, *Dictionary of Pentecostal and Charismatic Movements*, 811.

10. I attempted this with "A Theology for Pentecostal Peacemaking" presented at the Society for Pentecostal Studies annual meeting, March 2002. This paper now appears as chapter six of this book.

11. I must admit my ignorance regarding this declaration, I started working toward a Pentecostal peace fellowship before I found out that this call had been issued by churches from around the world.

in their mission to the world. . .responding ecumenically to the challenge, proving that non-violence is an active approach to conflict resolution and offering in all humility what Jesus taught his disciples to do, the churches have a unique message to bring to the conflict-ridden world.[12]

Peacemaking is a multifaceted opportunity. It is first of all the opportunity to be truly evangelical: to be an active missionary presence within society, a source of healing and creativity because we live the pattern of Christ's own suffering servanthood.[13] Second, peacemaking is also the opportunity to be truly ecumenical, for ecumenism is essentially making peace between divided families. The transforming initiatives of the biblical witness open doors for reconciliation between all divisions, whether personal, denominational, or international.[14] Peacemaking is finally the opportunity to be truly Pentecostal and trust that the way of the cross is God's way of redeeming and reconciling the world. Taking the scriptures seriously allows us to be led, empowered, and gifted by the Spirit to go beyond talk to actually giving our lives as faithful disciples of the Messiah. We Pentecostals claim that we need the signs and wonders, charismata, and empowerment to be the witnesses we should be, and peacemaking is the realistic and tangible opportunity to stay true to the "whole gospel, for the whole person, for the whole world."[15]

Thus, I propose the development of a Pentecostal peace fellowship[16] that is international and ecumenical in scope that will promote dialogue, writing, cooperation, and action on these issues. Clearly, my agenda is the promotion of Pentecostal peacemaking (and I blame this on Jesus), and I invite the numerous global perspectives from among our variegated tradition into the conversation. The biblical concern for peace and

12. Konrad Raiser, "Reconciliation: A Challenge for the Churches." *Theology, News and Notes* (Spring 2001) 10.

13. John Howard Yoder, *The Royal Priesthood: Essays Ecclesiological and Ecumenical* (Scottdale, PA: Herald, 1998).

14. Glen Stassen, *Just Peacemaking: Transforming Initiatives for Justice and Peace* (Louisville: Westminster John Knox, 1992).

15. This was the language of P. C. Nelson, founder of Southwestern Assemblies of God University. An interesting side note is that the main auditorium at Southwestern was named after the Assemblies of God pacifist from Texas, William Burton McCafferty (however, it is now the second largest auditorium).

16. Such a fellowship now exists: Pentecostals & Charismatics for Peace & Justice (www.pcpj.org).

justice would best be promoted by allowing all into the discussion, for the domination of one single nation, hemisphere, gender, ethnicity, or denomination would surely lead us astray. The purpose of the fellowship could be to promote and foster a concern for and participation in active peacemaking that is supported by a solid Pentecostal theology. The work of the late John Howard Yoder, Christian Peacemaker Teams, Stanley Hauerwas, Glen Stassen, and others who promote taking the life of Jesus and the gift of the Holy Spirit seriously will assist us in being the faithful and Spirit-filled Christians that we hope to be. However, our Pentecostal contributions will assist our non-Pentecostal sisters and brothers in their endeavors to be Christian peacemakers as well. We have much to offer in this area, we have perhaps been silent for too long, and the Spirit is leading us to speak.

## PEACEMAKING AS THE OPPORTUNITY FOR EVANGELICAL INTEGRITY

John Howard Yoder's epistemology of evangel illuminates the nature of the good news and its relationship to peacemaking. It is the "noncoercive concept of the way in which God presents himself to his creatures, revealing his grace and yet doing so in such a way as to leave the creature with the option to accept that grace freely or to reject it."[17] We are supposed to proclaim that good news in the same way, not imposing truth on anyone since God does not need to be vindicated by us, but we instead bear witness to Jesus Christ by offering peace without coercion. This offer of peace to both the oppressed and the oppressors is an invitation into a community of believers that is being led by the Spirit to be the body of Christ on this earth. The scope of this mission is not limited or negated by the status or animosity of the people who would either reject or accept God's offer of friendship through us. The good news is that peace has been made between enemies because of Christ's victory through suffering, and we will live and proclaim this to everyone because it is the truth that cannot be overcome even by our deaths. It is not a naïve utopian hope that everybody will just get along because of Jesus, there is real tension between the present reality of the partially realized kingdom and the yet-to-be fully realized kingdom of God, nevertheless, we are called to be patient heralds of the lamb that was slain. This involves creativity, danger,

17. Craig A. Carter, *The Politics of the Cross: The Theology and Social Ethics of John Howard Yoder* (Grand Rapids: Brazos, 2001) 230.

action, and adventure. Evangelical peacemaking, when our lives are at stake as real powers are confronted, is a risky mission.

The good news is revolutionary. It does not support the status quo of domination and oppression, indeed it challenges it as debts are forgiven, slaves are released, and the outcasts are accepted. The fact that evangelicalism in the United States is highly nationalistic is a sign that it is dangerously out of touch with the nonconformity inherent in the good news revealed in Jesus Christ. Nationalism is sectarian in that it demands the sect of the nation-state to be defended at the expense of another sect nation-state, it demands allegiance to its own self-preservation because its existence has been deemed to be the will of God.[18] On the contrary, the evangelism of the New Testament is universal in scope and transcends sectarianism that thinks it must kill its enemies to exist. The good news, according to the scriptures, is for everybody in every geographical location and of every ethnicity, i.e. their accident of birth or even their choice of allegiance to another god does not preclude them from reconciliation with the one true God.

Pentecostals have been evangel-focused from the beginning, explaining many of our actions within the context of the priority of the mission given to us by Christ. The 1917 rejection of war by the Assemblies of God was first explained by an appeal to evangelical integrity:

> From its very inception, the Pentecostal Movement has been a movement of evangelism, studiously avoiding any principles or actions which would thwart it in its great purpose. . . . The laws of the kingdom, laid down by our elder brother Jesus Christ, in His Sermon on the Mount, have been unqualifiedly adopted, consequently the movement has found itself opposed to the spilling of the blood of any man, or of offering resistance to any aggression. Every branch of the movement, whether in the United States, Canada, Great Britain or Germany, has held to this principle.[19]

Pentecostals actually thought that the use of violence—making war—was hypocrisy for someone concerned about the conversion of

18. This is Yoder's counter to the charge of sectarianism that is leveled at those who would not fight the wars of the state. Nonconformity to the establishment is seen to be sectarian by the powers when in actuality Christian nonconformity to any one particular nation and concern for all (even the enemies that need to be killed) as subjects worthy of evangelism reveals the sectarian and divisive nature of the nation-state.

19. "The Pentecostal Movement and the Conscription Law," *The Weekly Evangel*, 4 August 1917, 6.

their neighbor, the enemy. The Pentecostal commitment to evangelism was in effect saying that they would not devote themselves to any value other than the neighbor and Jesus, for any other value would cause them to sacrifice their neighbor, thus making an idol out of their nation, social philosophy, or cause. They would not sacrifice their fellow human beings for whom Christ gave his life. This is evangelical nonconformity to the divisions of the world and evangelical transformation into the likeness of the lamb that was slain.[20]

Peacemaking should be seen as something that Christians are to be engaged in continually, not as something that is done as a duty but as a definition of who we are: we are to *be* peacemakers. To explore this from a traditional missionary perspective would be to realize that the Pentecostal claim that everybody is either a missionary or a mission field has practical implications for peacemaking. All Christians are commissioned to make disciples, and this means being ready with the "gospel of peace." Peacemaking missionaries seek to be reconciled to their unbelieving neighbors and enemies, as well as seeking for all to be reconciled to God.

## PEACEMAKING AS OPPORTUNITY FOR ECUMENICAL INTEGRITY

The theme of this conference is ecumenical opportunities and challenges for Pentecostalism. Peacemaking is both, and though it is a continually difficult challenge, it is also a rewarding and God glorifying opportunity. It is a theological imperative that the body of Christ be unified, but how can this happen realistically? I would like to propose that there are biblical initiatives that are transforming and Spirit-led that can help us in our quest for Christian unity. They are also relevant to making peace with non-Christians and, if followed, the gospel will truly be proclaimed, but these four initiatives will give us concrete actions to take in order to be restored to our separated sisters and brothers in Christ.[21]

20. Yoder, *Royal Priesthood*, 217–18.

21. Much of this section relies on the work done by Glen Stassen in *Just Peacemaking: Transforming Initiatives for Justice and Peace* and John Howard Yoder's insight regarding ecumenism from a christocentric perspective in *Royal Priesthood: Essays Ecclesiological and Ecumenical, Priestly Kingdom: Social Ethics as Gospel* (Notre Dame: University of Notre Dame Press, 1984), and *For the Nations: Essays Public and Evangelical* (Grand Rapids: Eerdmans, 1997). I am concerned that emphasizing these in relation to ecumenism might appear as if I think that they do not apply to other situations, but it

First, we Pentecostals should realistically recognize our existing alienation from one another while also seeing our need for, and the availability of, God's grace.[22] We have contributed to divisions in the global body of Christ. We have been extremely nationalistic. We have benefited from sweatshop labor, violence, and consumerism at the expense of some our very own Pentecostal family, as well as at the expense of our larger family in Christ (and of course at the expense of those of other and no faiths). We Pentecostals have stocks and mutual funds that pad our retirement accounts with profits made from life destroying addictions and policies that starve children.[23] Acknowledging our sinfulness is painful and few people enjoy a prophet pointing out hidden sins, but this is where we start: we confess our own sins and hope that a friend honors us (timaw, timao ) with a rebuke (epitimaw, epitimao) when we need one. I am an ill-suited and unqualified peacemaker, so I have to start with and continue in confession of my own sins, my university's sins, and my denomination's sins.

Second, Pentecostals as individuals, churches, and denominations should "go, talk, welcome one another, and seek to be reconciled."[24] This is a proactive rather than a reactive instruction. It is to be initiated by us, not by the other. This counteracts alienation and the dehumanizing effects that it has, it helps prevent stereotyping and the building up of resentment. Talking and eating together is almost too simple of a way to make peace, but it is so actually possible that it should remind us that we can actively follow Jesus as long as we admit conflict and seek to overcome it through reconciliation rather than avoid it. Individual Pentecostals should befriend non-Pentecostal Christians. Corporately,

should be made clear that I believe these initiatives are imperative for Christians in all situations and in all relationships. An ethic that encourages the occasional avoidance of the cross of Christ is, to say it graciously, less than faithful.

22. Stassen, *Just Peacemaking*, 59–60.

23. Only in 2001 did the Minister's Benefit Association of the Assemblies of God offer a mutual fund that screened out certain stocks (five categories) that might be morally objectionable, it "excludes companies predominantly known for or who derive a significant portion of their income from abortion, alcohol, gambling, pornography, or tobacco." Several observations could be made regarding the particular vices that are and are not avoided and the fact that they are not totally avoided, only if significant or predominant. It seeks to strike a nice balance between returns and morality. Teaching theologically responsible investing is also a service that a peace fellowship could provide.

24. Stassen, *Just Peacemaking*, 61.

we Pentecostals can unite to explore ways to practice peace in our local and global situations, and we can seek to learn how to do so from churches and denominations with a longer, more pronounced commitment to peacemaking. I propose the formation of a Pentecostal peace fellowship that would seek to be in ongoing relationship with other peace fellowships and with Christians in general. A peacemaking fellowship would promote this as well as dialogue on the difficult topics, not just information sharing but racial, nationalistic, economic, and theological offenses. Each of us within our institutions (universities, churches, denominations, etc.) should seek out people from whom we are alienated and invite them into our lives. This will be painful and messy, but it is the real way toward friendship.

The third way for Pentecostals to maintain ecumenical integrity is to pray for our enemies, both real and perceived, and to persevere in prayer.[25] Pentecostal and charismatic churches need to be taught to pray for each other and for Baptists, Catholics, Methodists, Episcopalians, etc. rather than mock them or discount them. Our selfish praying does not promote peacemaking or ecumenical integrity; instead we should turn our prayers toward our separated brethren and toward our enemies outside the body of Christ. "If the cruel torture of crucifixion could not silence our Lord's prayer for his enemies, what pain, pride, prejudice or sloth could justify the silencing of ours?"[26] Praying also actually allows us

---

25. Ibid., 81. Stassen identifies three other transforming initiatives that I will not elaborate on for sake of space, but they deserve to be listed. 1) Do not resist vengefully, take transforming initiatives. The creative ways that Jesus instructs us to deal with our adversaries can help us participate in and promote ecumenical reconciliation rather than being vengeful or bitter. It may seem odd to apply this to the church but Pentecostals have lashed out from positions of apparent weakness and have abused power when they achieved it. We can turn our cheeks of dignity when slapped in insult, thus challenging those who would belittle us to treat us as equals. We can give our coats to those who would sue for our underwear, thus confronting injustice while appearing to be without power. 2) Invest in delivering justice. Pentecostals should participate in economic, community-restoring justice. This is true righteousness that is organized in real life with actual economic interests and practices to feed and clothe. Ecumenism must involve this. 3) Love your enemies, affirm their valid interests. Love is not a feeling or sentiment, but actions, deeds, and initiatives. Others have valid concerns that need to be heard and this "de-enemizing love" can reunite a divided family and turn enemies into friends.

26. John R. Stott, *The Message of the Sermon on the Mount: Christian Counter-Culture* (Downers Grove, IL: InterVarsity, 1978) 119.

to hear God's voice as God leads us toward reconciliation, and it offers us the opportunity to ask forgiveness and to forgive.

The fourth way for Pentecostals to maintain ecumenical integrity is to refrain from condemnation, opting instead to repent and forgive.[27] This has happened to some extent among Pentecostals.[28] We should encourage one another to locate our mistakes and failures and admit them. Each denomination and group of Pentecostals should search both their history and their present to find sins for which they can repent. This is not intended as a mere gesture or meant to incite a guilt complex, but should be an honest effort to locate offended people (institutions, denominations, ethnic groups) and actually converse with them. This uncovering and confession is scary in that it can cost us credentials and positions, but "there can be no reconciliation at the expense of truth."[29] When we practice reconciliation, we will surely also be called on to forgive others for sins against us as well. Forgiveness is a gift we both give and receive.

Finally, effective ecumenism, just like effective peacemaking, is not a top down, coerced, or power-driven endeavor. Therefore, peacemaking as ecumenical opportunity should be done in churches and small groups of disciples.[30] We are all surrounded by division and hostility, and we all have opportunities to be peacemakers seeking reconciliation in our own settings. Getting our schools and churches to put into practice the concrete steps of peacemaking will assist in the lifetime process of uniting divided people. This cannot be done alone for we need each other, we need information that other groups can provide, and we need support. Pentecostals need to remember that we do not need what the world considers to be power in order to be effective or to share the gospel. Small groups of faithful Pentecostals who are compassionate and patient can work in their cities and even travel around the world promoting unity in Christ if we adopt the biblical commission to repent and forgive in humility while actively seeking reconciliation.

---

27. Stassen, *Just Peacemaking*, 84.

28. The dissolution of the white Pentecostal Fellowship of North America and formation of the interracial Pentecostal Charismatic Churches of North America (along with the so called "Memphis miracle"), and the formation of one Apostolic Faith Mission from four racially divided groups in South Africa are examples.

29. Raiser, "Reconciliation," 8.

30. Ibid., 86.

Peacemaking should be central to a Pentecostal understanding of ecumenical involvement. It should fully extend to involve economic issues as we learn to critique our own greed in light of the message of justice from scripture and of the conditions of millions of our brothers and sisters in Christ around the world. Excessive participation in a consumer society must be questioned if we are to be authentically ecumenical—where we are concerned for all Christians, and take care not to use or abuse any. The use of military and political force must be discussed if ecumenical integrity is to be maintained, for a part of the church that profits from the suffering surely compromises the integrity of the body of Christ and cannot claim to be acting in love. Trying to find unity in the kingdom of God will necessarily involve recognizing how we must differentiate from the transitory nation-states, and Christ-centered peacemaking is the way of truth that allows for authentic evangelism, ecumenism, and Pentecostalism.

## PEACEMAKING AS OPPORTUNITY FOR PENTECOSTAL INTEGRITY

Pentecostals have greatly assisted the church theologically and experientially, and we have even more to offer, but we also have much to learn. Peacemaking is a gift from God to Pentecostals and the church in particular and to the world in general. In my estimation, Pentecostal integrity would consist, at least in part, in maintaining the importance of Spirit-empowerment, signs and wonders, the gifts and fruit of the Spirit, and prayer. But these alone are insufficient to do justice to the gospel and the purpose for each of the above. Authentic Pentecostal spirituality must allow the community of believers to be divinely empowered to live the good news publicly and socially, as makers of peace, even at the possible expense of ourselves because we truly trust in signs and wonders and answers to prayer. Spirituality without peacemaking can be self-centered and superficial, while peacemaking without reliance upon the empowerment, leading, and gifting of the Spirit can be legalistic and arrogant. The combination of Christ's peace and reconciliation through suffering, sacrificial love with the empowerment of the Holy Spirit for service and discipleship, can produce an authentic witness that makes Pentecostal integrity possible.

Pentecostals can learn to be better Pentecostals while helping other Christians be more faithful as well. An example of this can be seen in the work of John Howard Yoder. Yoder has presented theological, biblical, ethical, and ecumenical studies that rightly show the cross of Christ as God's way and the call for God's people.[31] He provides a believer's church ecclesiology and a very orthodox Christology that would be a great help to Pentecostals. In fact, Yoder stands as one of the most respected and persuasive proponents of peacemaking as inherent to Christianity. However, as Craig Carter observes, though Yoder has a strong implicit emphasis on the Holy Spirit in his ecclesiology, he did not develop it enough.[32] Pentecostals can work with and contribute to the theology of scholars such as Yoder, Stassen, and Hauerwas,[33] and assist the church in finding a biblical witness to Christ that is faithful to the truthfulness articulated in Pentecostalism. We cannot be as Spirit-filled as we claim to be without emphasizing and living the importance of peacemaking, and our sisters and brothers in other parts of the body need our reliance on the Spirit to empower them as well.

Peacemaking is absolutely necessary for Pentecostal integrity. One example of why peace is crucial is the denominationally justified torture of a Pentecostal minister by another Pentecostal in South Africa. Frank Chikane, a pastor in the Apostolic Faith Mission, was beaten and tortured almost to death under the direct supervision of a white deacon of the same Pentecostal church during Apartheid in South Africa. After being told by the deacon that Chikane would die a slow painful death, Chikane kept his sanity

> by thinking about the pain Jesus endured on the cross, about the imprisonment of the apostles, and especially about the role that Christians have in completing the sufferings of Christ as Paul understood it. I told my torturers, in the words of Paul, that "for me to die is gain but to live is Christ." In some very significant ways, my Pentecostal spirituality gave me the strength to survive.[34]

31. John Howard Yoder, *The Politics of Jesus* (Grand Rapids: Eerdmans, 1972); *Original Revolution*; and *What Would You Do?* (Scottdale, PA: Herald, 1992).

32. Carter, *Politics of the Cross*, 237.

33. Stanley Hauerwas, *The Peaceable Kingdom* (Notre Dame: University of Notre Dame Press, 1983); *Resident Aliens* (Nashville: Abingdon, 1989); *A Better Hope* (Grand Rapids: Brazos, 2000); *With the Grain of the Universe: The Church's Witness and Natural Theology* (Grand Rapids: Brazos, 2001).

34. "Rebuilding a Broken Society: An Interview with Frank Chikane," *Theology, News and Notes* (Spring 2001) 20–27. Chikane is the director-general of South Africa

The torturing, oppression, or persecution of another human for any ideology or cause by a Pentecostal is a profound betrayal of Christian faithfulness as empowered by the Spirit. This hypocrisy should be obvious, but it has not been and is not even now. Thus, the opportunities afforded by faithful Christian peacemaking can and should be actualized through a fellowship devoted to such a witness.

## A PEACEMAKING FELLOWSHIP AS OPPORTUNITY FOR SPIRIT-EMPOWERED FAITHFULNESS

There are six hundred million Pentecostals in the world, in fourteen thousand Pentecostal denominations, living in almost all the nations of the world and speaking hundreds of different languages, all in one body. We are part of a body whose head is Jesus Christ, the author and perfector of our faithfulness. He revealed to us the way to be faithful to God, and he has enabled us to be so by the gift of the Holy Spirit. Pentecostals need a fellowship that encourages, enables, and sustains peacemaking as an authentic and integral part of Pentecostalism.

Our fellowship would need to be multinational and multidenominational in its leadership, membership, and ministries. I have found interest in a Pentecostal peace fellowship from Indians, Africans, Asians, Europeans, and South and North Americans as well as from several denominations. A fellowship devoted to Christocentric peacemaking between genders, races, denominations, ethnicities, and nations could not be dominated by one color or kind of Pentecostal. Furthermore, as the scope of involvement increases so does the ability of the fellowship to affect significant change.

A peacemaking fellowship could assist in providing resources to help local churches and denominations in their quest for faithfulness. We could serve as a source for education about conflict transformation, biblical and theological support for concerns about justice and peace, pamphlets and other works with practical guidelines regarding racial and gender issues, as well as perspectives on economics and immigration. Having a quality selection of tangible examples of Christian peacemaking in the form of books, films, biographies, journals, and online resources would strengthen and enable a Pentecostal witness to the peace of Christ.

and ordained with the Apostolic Faith Mission of South Africa. His autobiography is *No Life of My Own* (New York: Orbis, 1989).

A peacemaking fellowship would also be an effective way of promoting actual peacemaking around the world through Pentecostals who are called by God to participate in the concrete steps of peacemaking. Christian Peacemaker Teams (CPT) has proven that people who live and intervene in places of conflict such as Israel or Northern Ireland while serving as nonviolent international observers can help local situations.[35] Cooperation with CPT and groups such as the multinational Baptist Peace Fellowships (bpfna.org) and the Ekklesia Project (ekklesiaproject. org), along with the development of a unity among Pentecostals around the world who are concerned for peace and justice will allow Pentecostals (regardless of status) to address injustice and violence in prophetic ways. Speaking truth to power, even when it goes against the status quo, is necessary to Christian authenticity. A peacemaking fellowship will facilitate such inspired speech and actions.

Our Pentecostal denominations need to address the difficult and often avoided areas where Christian faithfulness and "politics" clash. Support for legislation like the "Peace Tax Fund," which allows conscientious objectors to direct their income taxes toward nonmilitary expenditures, should be considered by Pentecostals for numerous reasons, at the least because of our heritage and tradition of supporting this position in our communities.[36] Many Christian denominations are willing to discuss globalization, consumer capitalism, warmaking, and peacemaking. They even consider these extremely significant issues with other groups (ecumenically), but there is little focus on such theological/ethical issues (other than the ones easily dealt with by evangelicals in general) in American Pentecostalism. A peace fellowship could promote these discussions by informing Pentecostals and denominations of situations of injustice and by sponsoring periodic opportunities for discussion. Simply notifying denominations of issues and providing a Pentecostal analysis could raise awareness through official publications.

Finally, a peace and justice fellowship will witness to the conviction that Jesus Christ is relevant to all tensions, crises, and brokenness in the world. Spending ourselves on behalf of and with the hurting (Isaiah 58)

35. Arthur G. Gish, *Hebron Journal: Stories of Nonviolent Peacemaking* (Scottdale, PA: Herald, 2001). This is an excellent frontline portrayal of the theology of the cross in action in a Muslim-Jewish conflict area. It is an almost daily account of six years of work between 1995–2001 in Hebron, Israel. For more information about CPT visit www.cpt.org.

36. Just such a resolution was defeated in 1981 in the Assemblies of God.

and addressing injustice as Jesus did is theologically sound, biblically commanded, and realistically possible. As we are living letters from Jesus who share in his sufferings, we can be authentically evangelical by actively remembering that we are witnesses all the time to all; we may be authentically ecumenical by always seeking unity with our sisters and brothers in Christ; and we may live authentically Pentecostal lives when we allow the Holy Spirit to gift and empower us to be faithful to our Messiah.

# 15

## Scandalous Partners in Protest

### *A Continuing Dialogue*

## Andrew S. Hamilton and Kenneth J. Archer

## INTRODUCTION

This essay is a continuation of an ecumenical conversation that was written and presented at the Society of Pentecostal Studies conference in 2007 at Lee University. In this conversation we[1] focused upon the intersections of our narrative traditions, emphasizing the commonalities we share for the purpose of proposing an ecumenical partnership in protest, which witnesses to the full gospel of Jesus Christ. This dialogue has been an ecumenical conversation between the Pentecostal and Anabaptist/Pietist traditions. What emerged out of this conversion was that the Christian worship practice of feetwashing could provide a means to share Christian love and fellowship in a way that is inclusive of all Christian traditions. The conversation addressed important points of theological intersec-

---

1. Ashland Theological Seminary, Ashland, OH, USA and Pentecostal Theological Seminary, Cleveland, TN, USA.

tions between these two narrative traditions, specifically soteriology as a "Christian synergism" and ecclesiology as an "alternative society." A concluding conviction of the initial stage of this conversation was that these traditions must engage in ecumenical dialogue for mutual theological support in forming and sustaining these "alternative Christian communities" as protesting witness while maintaining a participatory role in ecumenical dialogue with other traditions.[2] As a continuation of this dialogue, this essay will summarize our theological narratives and the significant intersections therein that correspond to establishing and sustaining contrast communities. We presuppose that the existence of these communities will serve as a protesting witness to the violent brokenness of the world.

## INTERSECTIONS REVISITED: IDENTIFYING NARRATIVES

Pentecostalism is a revivalistic movement that emerged at the turn of the twentieth century. Pentecostals understand themselves to be a restitution of primitive Christianity, which is shaped by the "Latter Rain" motif.[3] The Early and Latter Rain motif is a promise-fulfillment pattern in which Pentecostals retrieve the Lukan promise of God's Spirit being poured out upon the confessing community in the last days. The Early Rain refers to the original outpouring of the Holy Spirit as narrated in Acts 2. Pentecostals consider themselves the embodiment of the later outpouring of the Holy Spirit that was referenced at the first outpouring. The Spirit's baptizing is a particular highlight in Pentecostal narrative, which centers around God's redemptive involvement through the fivefold gospel. The fivefold gospel is a formative doxological confession that is testimonial in nature: Jesus is the savior, sanctifier, healer, Spirit baptizer, and coming King. In their own relatedness to these aspects of Christ's identity, believers identify themselves as participants in the redemptive purpose of God. The heart of Pentecostal spirituality is the doxological confession pertaining to Jesus Christ and the Holy Spirit, which forms them as a Christo-pneumatic community. The marks of this community are most notably identified by the zealous desire for

2. See "Anabaptist-Pietism and Pentecostalism: Scandalous Partners in Protest," in the *Scottish Journal of Theology* 63.2 (2010) 185–202.

3. See Kenneth J. Archer, "Pentecostal Story: The Hermeneutical Filter for the Making of Meaning," *Pneuma* 26 (2004) 36–59.

world evangelism, holy living according to the New Testament, and concern for the "least of these." Historically they have been a movement on the margins of society. This Pentecostal spirituality "seeks to extend its self understanding as a community of the Spirit *in* the world and *for* the world, but not *of* the world."[4]

Anabaptist/Pietism is a narrative tradition uniquely formed from Pietistic narratives and shaped theologically by Anabaptism. It finds its roots in the radical reformation and revivalism. Anabaptists/Pietists are shaped by these theological convictions and values: conversion, baptism, the Lord's Supper, the importance of obedience to the New Testament precepts (especially those of Jesus), and that faith is to be lived out in community, among others.[5] Specifically, their perspective is formed from their interpretation of the New Testament, with the Gospels receiving priority and the Sermon on the Mount at the center. Historically, Anabaptists/Pietists have sought to recapture pre-Constantinian primitive (New Testament & Early Church Fathers) Christianity.[6] Anabaptists/Pietists emphasize the role of the Holy Spirit's formational and leading presence in the life of the community. This narrative tradition is highly Christocentric with the *imitatio Christi* serving as an ethical guideline for the fellowship's life. Moreover, it holds to a strong theology of suffering. This community takes seriously Jesus' teachings of nonresistance and peace, which has often led to their being persecuted. This persecution, usually at the hands of the government and/or institutional church, has so informed their perspective that the experience of persecution has become, for them, the quintessential legitimizing factor of faith.

4. Eldin Villafañe, *The Liberating Spirit: Toward an Hispanic American Pentecostal Social Ethic* (Grand Rapids: Eerdmans, 1993) 193.

5. This is not a comprehensive list. Brethren, for example, have arrived at what has been referred to as seven core convictions: noncreedalism, nonresistance, nonconformity, obedience, freedom of conscience, no force in religion, and Christian unity. See, Andrew S. Hamilton, "Counting the Cost: Brethren as a Hermeneutical Community," MPhil thesis, University of St. Andrews, 2003.

6. It is necessary to qualify this statement in order to avoid any generalization. Therefore, speaking specifically from within the Church of the Brethren (one of the several Anabaptist/Pietist traditions) perspective, the writings of the early fathers in addition to the *Didache* significantly contributed to the seminal formation of the Brethren community.

## INTERSECTIONS REVISITED: PASSIONATE POSSIBILITIES OF A SOTERIOLOGICAL ECCLESIOLOGY

From these stories we have culled a synergistic understanding of soteriological ecclesiology in which a believer's salvation is lived out in community. For Pentecostals, salvation is a personal and communal journey of following Jesus in the Spirit. For the Anabaptists/Pietists, salvation is understood as reconciliation with God through Jesus expressed in the *imitatio Christi*. These understandings, taken together, articulate that faith is expressed when the believer obediently follows Jesus in community. Living out one's faith in community necessitates the continual nurturing of relationships to wholeness through confession, forgiveness, and reconciliation.

A shared understanding of soteriological ecclesiology is a synergistic response to the initiating grace of God. It does not arise from human nature, but finds its origin and end in the holy love of God. God's grace initiates and sustains one as s/he lives in whole relationship with God and others. Implied in this soteriology is an expectation of the community to be a visible embodiment of Christ and thus the physical manifestation of Christ's presence in the world, a community that is dependent upon the Spirit's gifting for the functional ministry. The concern for holistic salvation leads these traditions to be concerned about meeting the basic needs of the poor, marginalized, and oppressed.

In addition, this ongoing conversation has brought to light three primary points warranting further discussion that could lead to excitingly new possibilities. First is the necessity for these believing communities to be contrast communities protesting the structures, systems, and institutions that tolerate, ignore, and cause brokenness and division in the world. Second, as protesting communities, Pentecostals and Anabaptists/Pietists could strengthen their witness by entering into a partnership for peacemaking as an expression of Christ's love in the world. Third, the central focus of this ministry should be establishing and nurturing whole relationships, as attested to in scripture, and thus peacemaking should be incorporated as part of the missionary witness to the world. It is our conviction that an essential portion of this process is found in the shared symbol of feetwashing. This dramatic symbol not only emphasizes relationships modeled after Jesus'—in which confession, forgiveness, and reconciliation play a primary role—but crosses traditional lines within the Christian faith. It is our proposition that feetwashing can be shared among the various Christian traditions, uniting them in the ministry of our Lord Jesus.

Traditionally our communities have existed on the margins of society, bearing a distinct witness to both the world and the rest of the church. As our communities have sought legitimization, compromises have occurred by means of adopting modern ideology. Yet, it is necessary that our communities retain their distinct identity narratives as they enter into the greater conversation."[7]

## MOVING FORWARD: FEETWASHING AS FORMATIVE PRACTICE FOR A THEOLOGY OF RECONCILIATION

While in our dialogue we are extrapolating biblical concepts that are significant to both traditions, we seek to avoid diluting our traditions by reducing them to their least common denominators. We are lifting up feetwashing as a formative practice in relationship to these concepts because feetwashing is an important practice to both traditions.[8] From our hermeneutical perspective, we are developing these concepts in a manner that is faithful to our traditions and is simultaneously expanding our horizon of understanding.[9]

Our understanding of praxis is informed by liberation theology. As such, practice is understood as action-reflection. From this perspective, practice is praxis. Praxis, as a theological and methodological procedure, embraces the notion that our actions formatively affect our beliefs, and our beliefs shape and inform our activities. A praxis approach accepts the

7. See above, "Anabaptist-Pietism and Pentecostalism: Scandalous Partners in Protest."

8. Pentecostals do practice feetwashing, however not all Pentecostal traditions affirm the practice as part of the ordinances/sacraments. Archer's tradition, the Church of God, Cleveland, TN, does affirm feetwashing as one of three (sacramental) ordinances; the other two are the Lord's Supper and (believer's) water baptism.

9. This idea of the expansion of our hermeneutical perspectives through conversation is informed by Hans-Georg Gadamer's argument that interpretation is a conversation resulting in a fusion of horizons. See *Truth and Method* (New York: Crossroad, 1985) 325ff. For a description of Gadamer's argument, see Wolfhart Pannenberg, "Hermeneutics and Universal History," *History and Hermeneutic: Journal for Theology and the Church* (New York: Harper & Row, 1963) 122–62. For an important criticism of Gadamer's argument, see E. D. Hirsch, Jr., *Validity in Interpretation* (New Haven: Yale University Press, 1967) 245–64. For Hamilton's expansion of this for a Brethren hermeneutic, see "Brethren and the Bible: Finding a Perspective," forthcoming dissertation, University of South Africa.

notion that theory and practice are really inseparably united and "mutu-ally informing."[10] We believe the practice of feetwashing is both person-ally and communally formational, and that the very activity of washing feet provides a prophetic witness of the glorious human fellowship that is to come at the consummation of history. God's eschatological reign has already been consummated in the future by his promise and his future rule is drawing the present manifestation of his rule (feetwashing) to its full consummation in the eschaton.

There are key theological presuppositions underlying this proposi-tion. An essential starting point is the *imago Dei*. This concept is a fun-damental Trinitarian understanding of God in terms of the shared, even defining, perichoretic relationship among the persons of the Trinity. It is in this Trinitarian model that humans find their true identity in coexis-tence with other humans and the rest of creation. We are created as social, relational beings for coexistence as men and women in loving commu-nity. The appropriate order of relationship between man and woman in light of the whole Gospel is not hierarchical subordinationism but mutual love, service, and submission.

Following a Johannine description of the nature of God as repre-sented in the relational manifestation of the Father, Son, and Spirit, the *imago Dei* translates to the "abiding *in*" relationships of the persons of the Trinity.[11] The image of God (*imago Dei*) describes human life in relation-ship with God and with other creatures. Being created in the image of God means human beings can be addressed by God and respond freely to God.[12]

> The perichoretic relationship of the living God is the necessary "space" for the participatory activity of each person of the Social Trinity. Because God is loving relationality, the persons of God open up to creation. This is a hospitable activity of God's rela-tional love which is shared with volitional creatures.[13]

10. Kenneth J. Archer, "A Pentecostal Way of Doing Theology: Method and Manner," *IJST* 9.3 (2007) 301–8.

11. For an extensive discussion of this description, see Jürgen Moltmann, *Trinity and the Kingdom of God* (Minneapolis: Fortress, 1981); and Clark Pinnock, *Flame of Love: A Theology of the Holy Spirit* (Downers Grove, IL: InterVarsity, 1996).

12. See Daniel Migliore, *Faith Seeking Understanding* (Grand Rapids: Eerdmans, 1991) 124.

13. Kenneth J. Archer, *The Gospel Revisited: Toward a Pentecostal Theology of Worship and Witness* (Eugene, OR: Pickwick, 2011) 55.

Therefore, the starting point is not only an understanding of the Trinity existing as "abiding relationship" but a realization that Jesus invites his followers to participate in this divine relationship: "As you, Father, are in me and I am in you, may they also be in us" (John 17:20-21 NRSV). "We have been privileged to be invited as frail human beings to join the social Trinity in the mysterious dance of authentic life, which heals the past and creates positive possibilities for the future."[14] Therefore, even as the Father, Son, and Spirit live in whole, united, and interpenetrating (abiding in) relationship, so also are believers invited to participate by abiding *in* God (Father, Son, and Spirit). However, it is not enough to end here.

It is also necessary to understand that while we "abide *in*" God, we do so together—we "abide *with*" each other. This is a further extension of the abiding relationship to which Jesus calls his disciples. It is the relationship that is dramatically acted out in John 13. Moreover, it is representative of the *via salutis* (way of salvation). The way of salvation is a living out of one's salvation according to the leading of the Spirit. Addressing the Galatians, Paul exhorts them to live by the Spirit, being guided by the Spirit. This essentially contrasts with living according to the flesh, which leads to division and broken relationships. Thus, an understanding of the *via salutis* can be articulated as living according to the Spirit of God, which is ultimately expressed through the "abiding *with*" relationships in community.

Life in the Spirit is life with each other dependent upon the gifting and leading of the Spirit to guide us in unity. Yet, how do believers live out their salvation in community? Is it enough to simply rely upon the Spirit's gifting and leading? Are there ethical guidelines that illustrate this *via salutis* bringing the community from ideals to praxis? Again dealing with divisive issues in the congregation, Paul calls the believers at Corinth to be imitators of him as he is of Christ (1 Cor 11:1). The *imitatio Christi* provides the ethical guidelines for living out one's salvation in community. Therefore, a praxis-oriented soteriological ecclesiology must emphasize the imitation of Jesus, the Christ—who provides a model lifestyle.

The grammar of Christ's life is politicized beginning in the Sermon on the Mount and finds its climax and fulfillment in the passion and

---

14. Kenneth J. Archer, "A Theology Of The Word . . . And That's The Point!" *Passover, Pentecost and Parousia: Studies in Celebration of the Life and Ministry of R. Hollis Gause*, edited by S. J. Land, R. D. Moore, J. C. Thomas, JPTS (Blandford Forum: Deo, 2010).

resurrection. It is a life marked by deference, Spirit-empowered service, desire and provisions for whole relationships, self-sacrificing love, and universal mission. This is the foundation of the Christological ethic, and it finds expression in the believing community as it works toward living out the eschatological hope, the *missio Dei*. Simply put, the *missio Dei* (mission of God) is the ultimate hope of God reconciling all things to the Father, through Christ and by the Spirit. The believing community lives this out as it stands in protest against structures, systems, and institutions that tolerate, ignore, and cause brokenness and division in the world.

As we previously state, it is our conviction that an essential portion of this process is found in the shared symbol of feetwashing. Through this symbol one discovers an emphasis on relationships modeled after those of Jesus, in which confession, forgiveness, and reconciliation play a primary role. In this symbol (within a Eucharistic context), we find a Trinitarian expression of a soteriological ecclesiology that possesses eschatological implications for not only the believing community, but the entire created world.

We will relate the following biblical concepts to the practice of feetwashing. Feetwashing creates a formative moment in which the Spirit works redemptively in the community by redirecting the attention of the participants to Jesus' historic mission of reconciliation of all things (*imitatio Christi*) and reorienting their vision to the eschatological mission of God (*missio Dei*). The very activity models reconciliation of God's people, for the participants offer confession and forgiveness through humble service. Reconciliation is the primary means for the restoration of the image of God (*imago Dei*). The practices of reconciliation are sanctifying graces for Christians on their journey in the world (*via salutis*). The practices are themselves also gifts for the world, and provide a meaningful witness to the world, but their practice also creates a discrete socio-political community not of the world.[15] We jointly see all these meaningful possibilities in the reconciliatory and constructive practice of feetwashing.

---

15. In his text, *The Politics of the Cross*, (Grand Rapids: Brazos Press, 2001) 82–83, Craig Carter extrapolates upon the theology and social ethics of John Howard Yoder. He states that "Yoder's entire concept of social ethics is built upon the premise that Jesus called the Christian community into being in order that it might be a continuing witness to him on earth and that, in order for that witness to be clear, it had to be a *community*."

## MOVING FORWARD: A MODEST PROPOSAL FOR COOPERATIVE ACTION

In this section we will sketch out a proposal for cooperative efforts in working for peace and justice. We recognize that our theological traditions are embodied in local communities, and the goal is not to create a new tradition but to foster a partnership in protest as the faithful followers come together for worship. The proposal has three primary stages: cooperative worship services, cooperative missional task teams, and friendlier long-term relationships among the members of our communities and congregations. These will provide various points of relational intersections for the building and sustaining of shalom communities.

Our conviction is that the very act of corporate worship is an act of witness, and witness is always an act of worship. In this sense, we agree with the move to understand theology as orthodoxy, orthopraxy, and orthopathy.[16] These services are not to be understood as a pragmatic activity but rather an ontological reality of the future hope. Therefore, worship is a formative, relational activity among believers that moves them efficaciously to holistic missional witness (and service).

### Cooperative Worship Services

Cooperative worship services should be planned by the leadership of both communities, both of whom should endeavor to jointly follow the guidance of the Holy Spirit in putting together a time of worship.[17] This will require gracious freedom among sisters and brothers at these worship gatherings, and it will be necessary to provide adequate opportunity for our communities to express said worship according to their narrative traditions.[18] At minimum, there would need to be a gathering

16. For a Pentecostal creative development of these concepts, see Archer, "Pentecostal Way of Doing Theology: Manner and Method."

17. For a clear presentation of Pentecostal-Charismatic worship, see Mark J. Cartledge, *Encountering the Spirit: The Charismatic Tradition* (Maryknoll, NY: Orbis, 2006) chapter 3, "Praise and Worship," 51–70. For a contemporary explanation of Anabaptist/Pietist worship (within the context of the Church of the Brethren), see Richard B. Gardner and Kenneth M. Shaffer, *Let Our Joys Be Known* (Elgin: Brethren, 1998) chapter 3, "Called to Worship God," 25–36.

18. A Pentecostal worship service is marked by expressive worship and involves the whole person. Lifting of hands, tears of joy and sorrow, running, shouting, clapping, ecstatic tongues speech (glossolalia), tongues and interpretation, participatory prayer at altar calls and singing in the spirit are possible manifestations of Pentecostal wor-

of two communities, though more would be welcome. We recommend the following elements be included in these services, and in particular, a fellowship meal that would be preceded by feetwashing. An example of this service is as follows:

- Welcome & Group Recognition

  Here the ministers and congregations are recognized and a time of greeting and introduction will take place.

- Gathering song(s)

  Leadership should be sure that the music is familiar to both congregations or can be easily learned. Songs should direct the attention of the congregants to worship God and also to the ministry of God's peace and justice.

- Responsive Scripture Reading

  o Example: 1 John 1 & 3, NRSV

  | | |
  |---|---|
  | One: | This is the message we have heard from him and proclaim to you, that God is light and in him there is no darkness. |
  | All: | If we say we have fellowship with him while we are walking in darkness, we lie and do not do what is true. |
  | One: | For this is the message you have heard from the beginning, that you should love one another. |
  | All: | We must not be like Cain who was from the evil one and murdered his brother. |
  | One: | Whoever does not love abides in death. All who hate a brother or sister are murderers, and you know that murderers do not have eternal life abiding in them. |

---

ship. Tongues speech should not be viewed as divisive but as a proleptic sign of the unity of the people groups who will be gathered together before the throne of God. We suggest an insert be added to the bulletin explaining the various Pentecostal expressions of worship. It may be necessary to provide time for conversation and briefing for the Anabaptist/Pietist participants so as to assure openness for worship with their Pentecostal sisters and brothers. Admittedly, this may take significant preparation. It would be helpful for the communities to spend some time in fellowship prior to the worship so as to begin building bonds of friendship.

All:     We know love by this, that he laid down his
         life for us—and we ought to lay down our lives
         for one another.

  ○ Other responsive readings can be developed from
    various Scripture passages. Some examples are as
    follows: Exodus 6:4; 21:21; 23:9, Leviticus 19:33–34,
    Deuteronomy 10:14–22, Psalm 133, Matthew 5:38–48,
    Luke 6:26–36, Ephesians 4:1–13, and Romans
    12:9–21.

- Pastoral Prayer
- Selection of Songs
- Sermon (Scripture can be drawn from the above list)
- Feetwashing

  ○ Feetwashing may be just among the leadership, and
    then later joint services could include the participa-
    tion of the congregations. Feetwashing must be a
    noncoercive practice, but one in which all are invited
    to participate. An alternative to feetwashing can be
    handwashing, which would be necessary in particular
    situations where washing feet is impossible (e.g., am-
    putees and other people with disabilities).

  ○ It will be necessary to instruct the participants that
    feetwashing is representative of confession, forgive-
    ness, and reconciliation as sisters and brothers open
    themselves to the cleansing work of Christ through
    service to one another. It may be appropriate to
    provide a time of quiet examination prior to the feet-
    washing service.

- Song of Response
- Closing Prayer
  This prayer should not only close this portion of the service
  but also seek God's leading for ways in which participants can
  respond in service.

- Fellowship Meal
  Here is a way the sisters and brothers can celebrate the rich
  ethnic diversity of the body of Christ. Therefore, it is suggested that food be representative of the ethnic cultures repre-

sented among the participants. An underlying understanding of this gathering is that this meal represents the great diversity created by God sharing in the necessities of life, which offers a foretaste of the marriage supper of the lamb. It is also suggested that it be done simply so as to remind everyone of the many sisters and brothers who will go hungry that day. If there is food left over we suggest it be donated to a local soup kitchen or to a ministry that works with the poor. It may be helpful to have information booths available for participants to sign up for the formation of missional task teams to take part in these ministries.

Once again, we encourage the leadership to prayerfully put together the worship services jointly. We do believe that this suggested structure will be beneficial. Feetwashing should be highlighted because it is a significant ordinance to these communities and it represents a symbol that can be shared among the many Christian traditions. We also want to lift up themes of reconciliation, peaceful witness, and development of authentic fellowship.

## Cooperative Missional Task Teams

As an outgrowth of the cooperative worship services, missional task teams should be formed according to the leading of the Spirit. These teams will extend the cooperative worship into praxis-oriented service, which addresses the issues of injustice, poverty, and peace. We recommend that these task teams meet together for a time of worship consisting of prayer, singing, and feetwashing prior to their service project. Further preparation and training may be necessary depending upon the service project. The goal of missional teams will be to cooperatively participate in tasks that will effectively express the gospel holistically. These projects are a proleptic witness to the coming eschaton. Some examples of these ministry opportunities are as follows: short-term mission projects (work camps), sponsoring the construction of a home through Habitat for Humanity, volunteer work at a local homeless shelter, sending protest letters to local congress members, participating in peacemaking teams in the hostile parts of the world, etc.

Friendlier Long-Term Relationships

As these communities work together cooperatively addressing the issues that lie at the heart of God's concern (Luke 4:18–19), the narratives as representative of the participants will become more greatly interconnected. The result would most likely be the development of significant relationships with people outside of their communities of origin. In this way, the perichoretic relationship of the Father, Son, and Holy Spirit is modeled by individuals and families as they hospitably create space for the other. These longer-term relationships give opportunity for individuals to express testimonially the work of God's grace in their lives as they interconnect with others. It also provides opportunities for communities and individuals to listen attentively to the testimony of others. Of course, we recognize the role of discernment in the relationships, however, the friendships fostered become important points of intersection for the Spirit of God to work redemptively in the Christian community and prophetically in the world.

## CONCLUDING THOUGHTS

We believe that there are more important points of intersection among the Anabaptist/Pietist and Pentecostal communities than are often recognized, and we have attempted to briefly lift up important themes of these traditions. We do believe in feetwashing as an essential tool for the work of reconciliation and a significant formative practice that can be shared among all Christian traditions. It is our conviction that the modest proposal presented here will provide various relational intersections for the building and sustaining of shalom communities— which in and of themselves are an alternative socio-political community engaging the world for peace and justice. Narratively speaking, these intersections join our narratives together as we become part of each other's story, further strengthening our communal bond and Christian witness for the gospel of peace.

# 16

## My Life as a Menno-costal

### A Personal and Theological Narrative[1]

#### Martin William Mittelstadt

My life as a follower of Jesus Christ reflects the primary source of my ecclesial journey: my childhood on a Pentecostal pew, in a Pentecostal home, in a Pentecostal pastorate, and now in a Pentecostal university. At the same time, I am more and more aware of the impact of other Christian traditions upon my faith. In fact, in recent years I began intentional exploration of this multi-faceted dynamic, and I know that I am not alone in this. A journey of diverse encounters seems inevitable in our highly connected and complex world. I am also convinced that exploration is in fact a good thing. I strive to learn and live the Christian faith not only as a member of my particular tradition but of the church universal filled with many ethnicities and traditions from around the world. In this essay, I desire to facilitate such an encounter. I wish to initiate intentional discussion of the inter-Christian theology, values, praxis,

1. I first presented this paper as part of the Schrag Lecture Series at Messiah College in April, 2008. The article is published in *Theodidaktos: Journal for Eastern Mennonite Conference Theology and Education* 3.2 (September 2008) 10–17.

and witness of two traditions within Christianity, specifically, the convergence of Mennonites and Pentecostals.[2] First, in classic Pentecostal and Mennonite form, I begin not with propositional data but with my own personal narrative.[3] As I reflect upon my Pentecostal journey, I recount the profound impact of the Mennonite tradition in the shaping of my faith. In doing so, I demonstrate that my narrative need not be a surprise. Second, and on the heels of my personal narrative, I share an unforeseen theological discovery that launches intentional pursuit of such convergence. Finally, I establish specific commonalities ranging from ethos to hermeneutics, from Christology to the nature of the Christian life. I trust such openness may lead to further dialogue, community, and cooperation between our shared traditions.[4]

## PERSONAL NARRATIVE

I begin with select examples of my encounter with Mennonites. I grew up in a blended-extended family with aunts, uncles, and cousins from Mennonite, Baptist, and Pentecostal churches. I not only enjoyed listening to adult discussion of tongues, baptism/membership, and peace but also debated with my cousins about the superiority of our own traditions.

Beyond my family connections, I cherish childhood adventures at the annual Vacation Bible School at the neighborhood Mennonite church.[5] As a typical Pentecostal teenager, I attended my quota of Pentecostal youth camps and conventions. At a summer camp before my senior year in high school, I met a special young lady named Evelyn Doerksen, a fourth generation Pentecostal from Niverville, Manitoba in the heart of the Mennonite belt.[6] While dating Evelyn, I became more

2. To facilitate such discussion, I recommend Richard Foster's *Streams of Living Water: Celebrating the Great Traditions of Christian Faith* (San Francisco: Harper, 1998).

3. Early in my academic career, exegetical and theological inquiry trumped all personal experience. Today, Pentecostals and Mennonites certainly benefit from emerging methodological approaches that include theology as autobiography.

4. Historically Pentecostals have frowned upon ecumenism. While criticisms against Pentecostals include arrogance and elitism, Pentecostal insiders tend to be worried about compromise. This seems to be true of Mennonites as well. However, note the new dialogue between Church of God (Cleveland, TN) and Mennonite Church USA.

5. I now understand that Crestview Fellowship belongs to the Evangelical Mennonite Conference Church.

6. Niverville is approximately 30 miles south of Winnipeg. Some 7,000 Mennonites migrated to southern Manitoba in the 1870s. According to a 1991 census, 66,000

familiar with the region and grew increasingly curious about Mennonite faith and culture.

After completion of my undergraduate degree at a Pentecostal college, I enrolled at Winnipeg Theological Seminary (now Providence Seminary), affectionately described by students as a non-denominational seminary in the Mennonite tradition. Years later, following my doctoral residency at Marquette University in Milwaukee, I returned to southern Manitoba to pastor a Pentecostal church in Morden/Winkler. Along the way, I built many friendships with Mennonite students, pastors, and locals. While ministering in Morden, a door opened to teach a number of courses at the now defunct Winkler Bible Institute (no connection). Because of the increasing collegiality among various ministers and churches, I also taught a number of distance education courses for Canadian Mennonite University.

Finally, I share of my first trip to Messiah College. I attended a conference on the integration of faith and Christian scholarship hosted by and based upon the work of Rhonda and Douglas Jacobsen.[7] As I sat through sessions with sizable Anabaptist majorities, I remember being flooded with memories of my roots in southern Manitoba. The conference fostered further desire to wrestle with my Pentecostal identity in light of Mennonite theology and encounter.

Evelyn and I have now been married for twenty-two years. We continue to enjoy fellowship with Mennonite relatives and friends. With family and friends named Doerksen, Toews, Wiebe, Sawatsky, Friesen, Neufeld, Loeppky, Klassen, and Peters, it was only a matter of time until I would intentionally embrace the journey. I remain a passionate Pentecostal, but I also find that my faith resonates more and more with the Mennonites. Whereas twenty years ago I might have tried to convert a Mennonite to Pentecostalism, today I reflect the blending of the two. If I could coin a word for this blending, it might be Menno-costal. While not in the dictionary, I assure you it is a word—I am one.

---

Manitobans identify themselves as Mennonite (John J. Friesen, "Mennonites" in *The Encyclopedia of Manitoba* [Great Plains Publications: Winnipeg, 2007] 446). As numbers continue to increase across this belt, I offer a conservative estimate that Mennonite churches in this belt outnumber all other churches three to one.

7. Douglas Jacobsen and Rhonda Hustedt Jacobsen, eds., *Scholarship & Christian Faith: Enlarging the Conversation* (Oxford: Oxford University Press, 2004).

## THEOLOGICAL NARRATIVE

During my seminary years, professors introduced me to the writings of an author who would later change my life. Years after reading *The Politics of Jesus* by John Howard Yoder, I rediscovered this volume and felt compelled to read Yoder more extensively.[8] Following Yoder's death in 1997, I started to follow the various attempts to locate his theological impact upon contemporary Christianity. While reading one such theological biography, I stumbled upon an obscure quote from Yoder:

> Within or beside apostate churches, He raises up in every age new movements of protest, witness, and fellowship. These "free churches" are marked by the duress which gave them birth: socially unbalanced, theologically unbalanced, poor, strangely structured, given to false starts and exaggeration—and of such is the Kingdom of Heaven.

He continues:

> Pentecostalism is in our century the closest parallel to what Anabaptism was in the sixteenth: expanding so vigorously that it bursts the bonds of its own thinking about church order, living from the multiple gifts of the spirit in the total church while holding leaders in great respect, unembarrassed by the language of the layman and the aesthetic tastes of the poor, mobile, zealously single-minded. We can easily note the flaws in Pentecostal theology, organization, or even ethics—very similar, by the way, to the faults of the early Quakers and Anabaptists, or of the apostolic churches—but meanwhile they are out being the Church.[9]

This statement proved to be eye-opening and led to my intentional pursuit of the convergence between the Pentecostal and Mennonite traditions.

I searched the scholarly literature but found few comparative analyses.[10] On the contrary, from the Mennonite standpoint, note the sub-

8. Originally published in 1972, see the revised edition entitled *The Politics of Jesus: Vicit Agnus Noster.* 2nd ed. (Grand Rapids: Eerdmans, 1994).

9. John Howard Yoder, "Marginalia," *Concern for Christian Renewal* 15 (1967) 78, quoted by Mark Thiessen Nation, *John Howard Yoder: Mennonite Patience, Evangelical Witness, Catholic Convictions* (Grand Rapids: Eerdmans, 2006) 45–46.

10. See Mathew S. Clark, "Pentecostalism's Anabaptist Roots: Hermeneutical Implications" in *The Spirit and Spirituality: Essays in Honor of Russell P. Spittler*, edited by Wonsuk Ma and Robert P. Menzies, JPTS 24 (London: T. & T. Clark, 2004) 194–211. Clark traces Pentecostal origins to the nineteenth century Holiness movement,

title of Mark Thiessen Nation's theological biography of Yoder published forty years after the statement above: "Mennonite Patience, Evangelical Witness, Catholic Convictions"—no mention of Pentecostals. Similarly, William Klassen echoes Nation: "Yoder opened up the world of the Anabaptists . . . to the ecumenical world."[11] But there remains little or no interaction with Pentecostals; Pentecostals remain on the sidelines. While I am excited about Anabaptist, Evangelical, and Catholic exchange, the time is right for intentional conversation between Mennonites and Pentecostals.

In light of the Yoder citation above, German sociologist Max Weber provides a helpful point of departure. Weber argues that movements tend to begin with a spontaneous charismatic impulse until in the second generation the charismatic elements become routinized, generally falling short of the first generation's freedom and spontaneity. Movements inevitably journey toward institutionalization in an attempt to establish doctrinal and pastoral boundaries only to suffer further routinization of the charisma.[12] Both Pentecostals and Mennonites struggle with this tension. On the Mennonite front, Nation again summarizes Yoder's lament concerning the current status of the Mennonite tradition: "By and large the Mennonite Church is often more concerned to defend its ethnic identity and retain its own children than it is to be a 'believer's church' or to embrace the Anabaptist agenda of mission and social change."[13] The late Rodney Sawatsky echoes this Weberian tension:

> Our challenge is not to decry institutionalizing as inherently less Anabaptist or less Christian; rather, it is to keep our institutions and our leaders faithful to their ever-evolving mission in the second or twenty-second generation. The Holy Spirit surely is not limited to the first generation. The charisma ever leads us into new truth. Today we need a theology for the second generation, with much less said about restituting the first, which is impossible anyway.[14]

launched by John Wesley. Clark links Wesley's inspiration to the Anabaptists thereby providing a bridge to Pentecostalism (195).

11. William Klassen, "John Howard Yoder and the Ecumenical Church," *The Conrad Grebel Review* 16 (1998) 77–81.

12. This Weberian sense also occurs in Rodney Sawatsky, "Leadership, Authority and Power," *Mennonite Quarterly* 71 (1997) 441.

13. Nation, *Yoder*, 50.

14. Sawatsky, "Leadership," 442.

Such statements surely ring true for contemporary Pentecostals. Now entering only the second century of existence, Pentecostals also crave the fervor and passion of the first generation: "Give me that old time religion," "every generation needs their own Pentecost," and "we are only one generation away from extinction." Swiss Pentecostal theologian Walter Hollenweger captures this tension as Pentecostals long for charismatic freedom in the midst of increasing institutionalization. The answer is

> not the book, but the parable,
> not the thesis, but the testimony,
> not the dissertation, but the dance,
> not concepts, but banquets,
> not a system of thinking, but stories and songs,
> not definitions, but descriptions,
> not arguments, but transformed lives.[15]

For Mennonites and Pentecostals, this kind of tension encourages serious reflection. I believe we can learn from each other. But before going any further, a brief synopsis of the core theology and praxis of these traditions is in order.

## PENTECOSTAL AND MENNONITE CONVERGENCE

Historically, Mennonites trace their roots beyond the Reformation that began under the leadership of Martin Luther and John Calvin for the trumpet calls of the Reformers that "the Just Shall Live by Faith" would not suffice. According to Anabaptists, the direct ancestors of the Mennonites, the Reformers fall short in their Reformation. First, unlike the magisterial Reformers (and Roman Catholics), Anabaptists argue that the church be comprised only of believers entering by believer's baptism. This *believer's* baptismal position establishes the church as a discrete community separate from national citizenship and reflects the Anabaptist priority to the Scriptures above the authority of civil government whenever the two come into conflict. The Scriptures provide the community with answers to questions of faith and life under the guidance of the Holy Spirit. Finally, whereas the Reformers did not emphasize the teachings of Jesus as paradigmatic, Anabaptist theology privileges Jesus' call to love both neighbor

---

15. Walter Hollenweger, "Pentecostalism: Article, Research Centers, Bibliographies and Selected Literature," <http://www.epcra.ch/articles_pdf/Pentecostalisms.PDF> (page 7).

and enemy with ultimate authority. This commanding love example provides the nonviolent distinction to Jesus' radical call to discipleship.

Like the Anabaptists, Pentecostals might be summarized as a "radical, Jesus-centered, martyr movement."[16] Pentecostals emerged as a reactionary movement at the beginning of the twentieth century. While scholars continue to debate the origin of the movement, sociologist Michael Wilkinson provides a compelling argument for the "Azusa Street Revival" in Los Angeles led by African-American preacher William Seymour. Wilkinson coins the notion of Pentecostal "Azusa-ization," a process whereby Pentecostals look for their identity in relation to this event.[17] In other words, regardless of the multiple possible points of origin for the movement, Pentecostals consistently find a model by way of Azusa. Pentecostals embrace Azusa's post-conversion encounter with the Holy Spirit (specifically Spirit baptism and the gifts of the Spirit). Jesus, the consummate man of the Spirit, serves not only as an example, but also pours out this same Spirit upon the church. New and fresh life of the Spirit coupled with strong restoration impulses serve as the foundation for radical Christianity driven by a passion for evangelism at any cost.[18] While the historical journeys of these respective movements evolve separately, I turn now to their similar impulses.

## Counter-cultural Movements

Mennonite historians and theologians offer innumerable illustrations of the counter-cultural nature of their tradition. Menno Simons wrote: "The

16. See Clark, "Pentecostalism's Anabaptist Roots," 204. Unlike Anabaptist history, Clark refers to a Pentecostal martyr motif as "sacrificial, urgent witnessing, missionary." This resonates with my findings in *The Spirit and Suffering in Luke-Acts: Implications for a Pentecostal Pneumatology*, JPTS 26 (London: T. & T. Clark, 2004) and "Spirit and Suffering in Contemporary Pentecostalism: The Lukan Epic Continues" in *Defining Issues in Pentecostalism: Classical and Emergent*, edited by Steven Studebaker (Eugene, OR: Pickwick, 2007).

17. Michael Wilkinson, "Religion and Global Flows" in *Religion, Globalization and Culture*, edited by Peter Beyer and Lori Beaman, 375–89 (Boston: Brill Academic, 2007). This view certainly reflects the emergence of North American Pentecostalism.

18. Since both traditions are far from homogenous, I am aware of the danger of such narrow definitions. I proceed with the premise that our traditional identities may benefit mutually through analysis of our similarities. Again, I want to highlight the shared loss felt by Pentecostals and Mennonites due to an uneasy relationship with Evangelicals. Pentecostals are hardly Evangelicals plus the Spirit and Mennonites are certainly more than pacifist Evangelicals.

entire evangelical Scriptures teach us that the church of Christ was and is, in doctrine, life, and worship, a people separated from the world."[19] So also Johann Loserth: "More radically than any other party for church reformation the Anabaptist strove to follow the footsteps of the church of the first century and to renew unadulterated original Christianity."[20] Similarly, the early Pentecostals took pride in their counter-cultural mission. Their mandate, based upon strong links to the Holiness movement and an intense eschatological urgency, produces an unwavering passion for the lost. As people of the Spirit, early Pentecostals were often labeled "holy rollers" and "chandelier swingers" and certainly found themselves on the fringes of the established church and society—a people "in the world but not of the world."

These counter-cultural visions contrast with the Evangelical propensity toward assimilation. Unlike Pentecostals and Mennonites, Evangelicals desire to be the dominant culture. I noticed this particularly as I moved stateside. Evangelical proclamation often fuses the good news of Jesus with an American Dream, thereby producing a political Christianity fueled by overzealous nationalism. Christianity often looks more like a commercial for a *gospel Americana* than a radical community of Jesus' followers. Yoder laments this ever-increasing seduction. In contrast to Christianity, Yoder traces Christendom to the alliance of church and state under the reign of the Roman Emperor Constantine, thereby creating the official (or unofficial) religion of the West.[21] The tumultuous history of Christianity reflects the ongoing attraction of Constantinianism. Following in the steps of the sixteenth century Reformers, contemporary Evangelicals find the lure of Constantinian power tempting.[22] While there

19. Menno Simons, *The Complete Writings of Menno Simons* (Scottdale: Herald, 1956) 679.

20. Harold S. Bender, "The Anabaptist Vision (Text, 1944)." *Global Anabaptist Mennonite Encyclopedia Online*. Accessed: March 13, 2008. <http://www.gameo.org/encyclopedia/contents/A534.html>.

21. See Yoder, *Politics*, 17, 234. For excellent resources and analysis of the complex notion of Constantinianism and Christendom, see Craig A. Carter's *The Politics of the Cross: The Theology and Social Ethics of John Howard Yoder* (Grand Rapids: Brazos, 2001). I recommend chapter 6 entitled "The Heresy of Constantinianism." I should also point out that Clark ("Pentecostalism's Anabaptist Roots") suggests a primitivistic motif in Wesley based upon a desire to return to a pre-Constantinian church (196).

22. I recommend Gregory A. Boyd, *The Myth of a Christian Nation: How the Quest for Political Power is Destroying the Church* (Grand Rapids: Zondervan, 2005) and Stephen Prothero, *American Jesus: How the Son of God Became a National Icon* (New

remains much to appreciate within Evangelicalism, Pentecostals and Mennonites must guard against such patriotic and nationalistic proclivities. In spite of counter-cultural origins, Pentecostals and Mennonites are not immune to this temptation.[23]

## Pentecostal and Mennonite Primitivism

Grant Wacker writes: "The genius of the Pentecostal movement lay in its ability to hold two seemingly incompatible impulses in productive tension," namely primitivism and pragmatism.[24] For Wacker, primitivism does not refer to a primitive faith or praxis but rather a return to an original plan, to first and fundamental ideals.[25] Pentecostals strive not only to capture "lightning in a bottle" but to keep it there decade after decade.[26] The notion of primitivism resonates with Pentecostal attraction to Acts—a constant desire to recreate and continue the apostolic church. William Seymour, presumably chief editor of the Azusa Street Paper, *The Apostolic Faith*, introduces the inaugural newsletter in September 1906 with the headline, "Pentecost Has Come" and follows with a lead article entitled, "Los Angeles Being Visited by a Revival of Bible Salvation and Pentecost as Recorded in the Book of Acts." Approximately seventy years later, the refrain remains the same. In the *Pentecostal Testimony,* the official organ of the Pentecostal

York: Farrar, Straus, and Giroux, 2003).

23. Russell Spittler first suggests "the evangelicalization of the Assemblies of God" ("A Celebration of Sovereignty," *Agora* 5 [summer 1981] 13–14) aptly cited by Gary B. McGee, "'More Than Evangelical': The Challenge of the Evolving Identity of the Assemblies of God" in *Church, Identity, and Change: Theology and Denominational Structures in Unsettled Times,* edited by David A. Roozen and James Nieman, 35–44 (Grand Rapids: Eerdmans, 2005). McGee also points to the two way nature of this encounter. While Pentecostals continue in the process of "evangelicalization," Evangelicals (and broader Christianity) are also experiencing a parallel "pentecostalization" (41). On the Mennonite side, see Paul M. Lederach, *A Third Way: Conversations about Anabaptist/Mennonite Faith* (Scottdale: Herald, 1980); Bruce Guenther, "Living With the Virus: The Enigma of Evangelicalism Among Mennonites in Canada" in *Aspects of Evangelical Experience,* edited by George Rawlyk, 223–40 (Montreal: McGill-Queens University Press, 1997); David L. Weaver-Zercher, "A Modest (Though Not Particularly Humble) Claim for Scholarship in the Anabaptist Tradition" in Jacobsen & Jacobsen, *Scholarship,* 103–17.

24. Wacker, *Heaven Below*, 10.

25. Ibid., 12.

26. Ibid., 10. Wacker cites Wheaton College sociologist James Mathisen (Personal Conversation, March 1993). Mathisen suggests this idea is central to most religious movements and Wacker utilizes it for Pentecostal identity.

342 PENTECOSTALS AND NONVIOLENCE

Assemblies of Canada, Karel Marek entitled his article "Acts Chapter 29" with a subtitle: "In case you hadn't noticed recently there are only 28 chapters recorded in the Book of Acts in your Bible."[27] His opening paragraph begins with a vintage Pentecostal exhortation: "I've frequently heard of churches with a desire to 'write' Acts chapter 29. Is it not the dream of every preacher? Is this not what the world needs to see?"[28] From the first generation to the current generation, Pentecostals continue passionate pursuit and extension of first century Christianity.

This restitution of the New Testament church also resonates with Mennonites. According to Franklin H. Littell, Anabaptists see the early church as the age of heroes and strive to gather and disciple a true church based upon the apostolic pattern. Littell envisions continuity in order "to relive in studied fashion" the New Testament in all of its phases.[29] More poignantly, C. Henry Smith asserts "the whole movement was an attempt to reproduce as literally as possible the primitive apostolic church in its original purity and simplicity and restore Christianity."[30]

At the same time, as Roland Bainton notes, "If there is no accommodation [to culture], Christianity is unintelligible and cannot spread."[31] Indeed, Pentecostals and Mennonites must wrestle with the tension between primitivism and acculturation. While proponents of both traditions strive to live as disciples and pilgrims, as strangers in the values of the world, the temptation to forego this ethos looms large with the ensuing result: "If there is too much accommodation it will spread, but no longer be Christianity."[32] When healthy, these traditions find the foundation for their respective counter-cultural and primitivistic worldviews in their reading of the Scriptures.

## Interpretation of the Scriptures

According to Charismatic Catholic Peter Hocken, "Pentecostalism represents a protest for Spirit against a powerless and largely cerebral

27. Karel Marek, "Acts 29," *Pentecostal Testimony* 70 (1989) 24–25.

28. Ibid.

29. Franklin H. Littell, *The Anabaptist View of the Church* (Hartford: American Society of Church History, 1952) 50.

30. C. Henry Smith, *The Story of the Mennonites*, 3rd ed., revised and enlarged by Cornelius Krahn (Newton, Mennonite Publication Office, 1950) 21.

31. Roland H. Bainton, "The Enduring Witness," *Mennonite Life* 9 (1954) 89.

32. Ibid.

Protestantism, in which attachment to the Word was not evidently ac-companied by the vitality of the Spirit."[33] This statement rings true for Pentecostals and Mennonites. Their hermeneutical approaches animate their respective pursuit of primitivism. While both traditions embrace with Evangelicals the call to conversion, Mennonites and Pentecostals share a unique methodological approach based upon a similar reading of the Scriptures.

Interpretative method among Mennonites furthers the develop-ments founded by the Reformers. Mennonites lament the establishment of any church unable to produce spiritual and moral development of its followers. They cultivate an alternative to the actualization of Christianity as mere regeneration, holiness, and love as realized in the realm of intel-lect and doctrinal belief. Speaking about the Scriptures, Kenneth Davis asserts: Anabaptists "were not primarily concerned about theories of inspiration and inerrancy. Rather they accepted it as an authentic reflec-tion of Jesus and asked what it would mean to obey it."[34] The Mennonite refrain *Nachfolge Christi* calls for a radical discipleship, namely, a faith that mirrors the life of Christ. In the words of Hans Deck, "no man can know Christ unless he follows after him in life." [35] Similarly, Yoder in-sists, "the Christian life is not a matter of rules, definable once for all and for everyone, but of constantly living under the leading of God. The Bible's prohibitions show us the minimum, not the maximum level of obedience."[36] Rigorous exegesis does not merely posture the believer for intellectual assent to the gospel but also for a transformed life.

Pentecostals and Mennonites may not share the same transforma-tional language, but they walk by way of a shared biblical methodology. Consider Pentecostal theologian Terry L. Cross:

> While Pentecostals may share many theological tenets in com-mon with other Christians, we have experienced God in ways others do not confess. Rather than viewing theology as a descrip-

33. Peter Hocken, *The Glory and the Shame: Reflections on the Twentieth Century Outpouring of the Spirit* (Guildford, Surrey, UK: Eagle, 1994) 156. See also Harvey Cox, *Fire from Heaven: The Rise of Pentecostal Spirituality and the Reshaping of Religion in the Twenty-First Century* (Reading, MA: Addison-Wesley, 1995).

34. Kenneth R. Davis, "The Origins of Anabaptism: Ascetic and Charismatic Elements Exemplifying Continuity and Discontinuity," in *The Origins and Characteristics of Anabaptism* , edited by M. Liehard, 37 (Hague: Martinus Nijhoff, 1977) 37.

35. See Nation, *Yoder*, 26.

36. Yoder, "The Respectable Worldliness," *Christian Living* (January 1995) 48.

tion of our distinctives, we need to understand the all-encompassing difference which [is] our experience of God through His
Spirit. . . . We may be evangelical in that we hold to the common
truths of the faith handed down for generations, but we are not
just evangelicals who speak in tongues! We are a people invaded
by the Spirit, knocked off our horses as was Saul (Acts 9); therefore, we cannot think, live, or write as if this experience of the
living God were peripheral.[37]

Cross remarks elsewhere:

Theology, therefore, can no longer be left out in the deep freeze
of the intellectual life, pretending that emotions and experience
have no impact on its work. Theology is a deeply passionate and
experiential way of knowing; certainly Pentecostals carry no
shame in this.[38]

At the beginning of this new century, Pentecostals may now be experiencing their most positive turning point for a sustainable interpretative
method due to the recent migration of literary/narrative criticism from
the humanities into biblical studies. In fact, possibly more than any other
contemporary tradition, Pentecostals may now articulate a technical exegetical method utilized informally since the origin of the movement at
the turn of the twentieth century. Pentecostals have long been aware that
the power of the Holy Spirit is unleashed through orality—in witnessing,
telling, and hearing the stories of God's mighty love and actions—that is
not possible through mere theological argument.[39]

37. Terry L. Cross, "The Rich Feast of Theology," *JPT* 16 (2000) 33–34.

38. Cross, "A Proposal to Break the Ice: What Can Pentecostal Theology Offer
Evangelical Theology?" *JPT* 18 (2002) 44–73.

39. Consider the following correspondence between Michael Dowd and Assemblies
of God scholar Jerry Camery-Hoggart (Personal letter, July 23, 1985) cited in Dowd,
"Contours of a Narrative Pentecostal Theology and Practice" (*Society for Pentecostal
Studies Seminar Paper*, 1985) 16.

Pentecostals have been doing narrative theology for years although without the
added dimension of critical self-reflection. Hence there is a critical need for hermeneutical theorizing along these lines. And narrative theology as it is developing outside of Pentecostalism may often provide helpful vocabulary and criteria
of evaluation as we become self-conscious about what we have for so long done
naturally. . . . With the discovery of narrative theology we are suddenly on the cutting edge of the contemporary theological scene (July 23, 1985).

Accordingly, Pentecostals, like Mennonites, counterbalance a prop-ositional theology and hermeneutic with one that is more experiential, imaginative, story-based, and Spirit-led. While Pentecostals continue to draw insight from historical-critical approaches, these tools offer only pre-interpretive work. Pentecostals find the charge of the Christian story and of individual biblical stories not primarily in dissection, but in their ability to grab attention, capture the imagination, and so draw in and change the reader. By drawing upon the emerging narrative method-ologies, Pentecostals proclaim that propositional truth cannot report the whole truth. Narrative approaches to Scripture create expectations for future encounters with God, helping the believing community transform God's "Great Story" into "our story."[40]

Finally, the apparent triumph of literary analysis does not leave Pentecostals immune to challenges from other academic or ecclesial communities. Pentecostal Paul Elbert, for example, in his dialogue with members of the Evangelical Theological Society, observes that:

> Historicity, not narrative theology and pneumatology, has domi-nated Evangelical scholarship in Acts. And this is, of course, a proper and important enterprise. But if it becomes an exclusive vision, the interpretation of Paul (dispensational and otherwise) can unduly overshadow the Christian tradition, description, and practice as portrayed by Luke.[41]

In a footnote to this quotation Elbert makes a bold observation concern-ing the practical implications for Evangelical conclusions: "We believe that the events of Acts happened, we just don't want them to happen to us." While conservative Evangelicals fight alongside Pentecostals in de-fense of the historical reliability of the Lukan narratives, as Pentecostals read the Scriptures, the expectation persists that these same events ought to occur among contemporary Christians. In sum, as counter-cultural primitivists, both Pentecostals and Mennonites demand transformation based upon the rigorous teachings of the Scriptures.

---

40. See John Goldingay, "Biblical Story and the Way It Shapes Our Story," *JEPTA* 17 (1997) 6.

41. Paul Elbert, "Pentecostal/Charismatic Themes in Luke-Acts at the Evangelical Theological Society: The Battle of Interpretative Method" *JPT* 12.2 (2004) 207.

*Interpretation—Who is Jesus?*

The narrative-based theology of Mennonites and Pentecostals leads naturally to Christology, the foundation of all Christian theology. Pentecostals and Mennonites, however, differ from other traditions by their care to correlate Jesus' death and resurrection with his life and teaching. For example, whereas Evangelicals declare the necessity of confession to Jesus as savior, they do not place the same emphasis upon Jesus' stated ideals and the embodiment of his life.[42] Yoder captures this distinction:

> Jesus was not just a moralist whose teachings had some political implications; he was not primarily a teacher of spirituality whose public ministry was unfortunately seen in a political light; he was not just a sacrificial lamb preparing for his immolation, or a God-Man whose divine status calls us to disregard his humanity. Jesus was, in his divinely mandated prophethood, priesthood, and kingship, the bearer of a new possibility of human, social, and therefore political relationships. His baptism is the inauguration and his cross is the culmination of that new regime in which his disciples are called to share.[43]

So also J. Denny Weaver stresses the ethical implications of the Jesus story: "[the] narrative identifies Jesus in a way that makes discipleship an inherent dimension of identifying with Jesus."[44] Yoder continues, "servanthood replaces dominion, forgiveness absorbs hostility. Thus—and only thus—are we bound by New Testament thought to 'be like Jesus.'"[45]

Similarly, Pentecostals look to Jesus not only as the sacrificial savior but as the consummate miracle worker, healer, and exorcist. Early Pentecostals confessed Jesus as "Savior, Baptizer, Healer, and Soon Coming King"; Jesus was the subject of their faith and the master to be

42. See Chris K. Huebner, "Mennonites and Narrative Theology: The Case of John Howard Yoder," *The Conrad Grebel Review* 16 (1998) 15–38.

43. Yoder, *Politics*, 52. He cites the contrary position of Reinhold Niebuhr: "The Good News of the Gospel is not the law that we ought to love one another. The good news . . . is that there is a resource of divine mercy." Yoder follows with a summary of such a position: "Jesus did not come to teach a way of life; most of his guidance is not original. His role is that of Savior, and for us to need a Savior presupposes that we do not live according to his stated ideal" (18).

44. J. Denny Weaver, "Narrative Theology in an Anabaptist-Mennonite Context," *The Conrad Grebel Review* 12 (1994) 172–73.

45. Yoder, *Politics*, 131.

followed and obeyed.[46] Thus, Pentecostals seeking a model for the life of the Spirit begin with the life of Jesus, the paradigmatic man of the Spirit. As Luke describes the Spirit-led apostles in the book of Acts, so also contemporary Pentecostals seek power not from within themselves but from the Spirit of God, the same Spirit whom Jesus himself received from the Father and now pours out upon his followers (Acts 2:33). In short, the life of the Spirit mirrors the life of Jesus (Acts 1:1). As Pentecostals desire to continue Jesus' signs and wonders, the kingdom of God is manifest and God's love is poured out through human agency. Note this passion as expressed by way of hymnody among the early Pentecostals. The following favorites reflect the normativity of Jesus' life:

> To be like Jesus, to be like Jesus! My desire—to be like Him!
> All thru life's journey from earth to glory, My desire—to be like Him.

And

> Breathe on me Breath of God, fill me with life anew,
> That I may love what Thou dost love, And do what Thou wouldst do.[47]

The words of these songs assert that the meaning of the incarnation is lost if a fusion of Jesus' life and teaching is not normative. Again, while Jesus as Lord and Savior was and is the most precious insight of the Reformation, for Mennonites and Pentecostals he is more. Jesus' life and teaching serve as the model for the transformation of the individual believer and society.

## Nationalism and Pacifism

Unsurprisingly, Mennonite ideals point clearly to the rejection of nationalism. As noted above, a primary distinctive of Mennonite identity refuses the nationalistic pursuits of the Magisterial Reformers. Yoder represents such a position with his refutation of the Constantinian shift that resulted in a fusion of the church with the ruling political regime of the day. So while the sixteenth century Reformers called for radical challeng-

46. Aimee Semple McPherson founded the (International) Church of the Foursquare Gospel upon these cardinal doctrines descriptive of Jesus. Pentecostal bodies such as the Church of God in Christ and Church of God (Cleveland, TN) hold to a fivefold gospel that includes Jesus as Sanctifier.

47. Words by Edwin Hatch and Thomas Chisholm (1897) respectively. Others favorites include: "O To Be Like Thee" and "I Want to Be Like Jesus" by Thomas Chisholm.

es to Roman Catholicism, they failed to disengage themselves from the predominant nationalism of the time. Instead, the Reformers remained entangled in the various quests for power through rising nation states. According to the Anabaptists, the complexities of Reformation national-ism resulted in the marginalization of Jesus' call to radical discipleship. Mennonites challenge the inability of the Reformers to separate church and state with an alternative church that resists the temptation to run the world and make history turn out right, and instead endeavor to live faithfully as witnesses in and to the world.[48]

While the earliest Pentecostals rejected nationalism based primar-ily upon their pacifist ideals, a number of leading figures addressed the underlying issue of allegiance to a nation. When referring passionately to Scriptures such as Matt 22:21 and Phil 3:20, early leaders associated na-tionalism with abomination, prostitution, and fanaticism.[49] Furthermore, the strong restoration impulse of early Pentecostals made allegiance to a nation superfluous. Hymns like "This World is not My Home" and "I'll Fly Away" express the incompatibility of eschatological urgency and al-legiance to nation.

However, as the years pass, many Pentecostals begin to entertain na-tionalist tendencies. According to numerous scholars, such Pentecostal leanings may be linked to a hasty marriage to Evangelicalism. Several Pentecostal denominations joined the newly formed National Association of Evangelicals in 1940.[50] The nationalist tendencies of Evangelicals cer-tainly influence Pentecostals with increasing escalation. Consider the words of early NAE president Harold John Ockenga at the first constitu-tional convention:

> I believe that the United States of America has been assigned a destiny comparable to that of ancient Israel which was favored, preserved, endowed, guided, and used by God. Historically, God has prepared this nation . . . as no government except Israel has

48. A. James Reimer, "Mennonites, Christ and Culture: The Yoder Legacy," *Conrad Grebel Review* 12 (1994) 13.

49. See James Bennett, "Nationalism," in *The New International Dictionary of Pentecostal and Charismatic Christianity*, edited by Stanley Burgess, 327 (New York: Routledge, 2006) 327.

50. On the pros and cons of Pentecostal alliances with Evangelicals see Cecil M. Robeck, "National Association of Evangelicals," in *The New International Dictionary of Pentecostal and Charismatic Movements*, edited by Stanley M. Burgess (Grand Rapids: Zondervan, 2002) 922–25.

ever been . . . and with an enlightenment in the minds of the
average citizen which is the climax of social development.[51]

The cumulative effects of a waning eschatological urgency, the lure of acceptance by the Evangelical communities, and the loss of pacifist roots
make an overzealous nationalism attractive. Today, while the vision of
Pentecostals varies only slightly from their forebears, loyalty to a nation
rests upon the individual conscience of the believer. However, while the
church speaks officially of citizenship in heaven, an underlying current of
nationalistic fervor continues to increase.[52]

The shared pacifist heritage of Mennonites and Pentecostals flows
out of a rejection of nationalism. While the rich pacifist heritage of
Mennonites is well known, many (including Pentecostals) are often surprised to learn of the pacifist roots of Pentecostalism.[53] Pacifism remains
the primary distinctive of the Anabaptist vision. The ethic of love and
nonresistance invites complete abandonment of all warfare, strife, violence, and the taking of human life. As people of the book, Mennonites
look again to the life and teaching of Jesus Christ. Jesus conquers principalities and powers and launches the new kingdom of God, but not
according to the majority expectations of his day. Jesus incarnates the
paradigmatic message of peace, love, and nonresistance.

Early Pentecostals embrace pacifism in conjunction with primitivism, "a moral sign of a restored New Testament apostolic church."[54]
Participation in war runs contrary to the teaching of Jesus and Spirit-led
evangelism. Azusa Street participant Frank Bartleman insists: "converting men by the power of the Gospel and later killing these same converts,

51. Edith Blumhofer, *The Assemblies of God: A Chapter in the Story of American Pentecostalism*, vol. 2 (Springfield: Gospel, 1989) 30. Blumhofers cites from this letter by Ben Hardin, "United We Stand: NAE Constitutional Convention Report," from the Herbert J. Taylor papers at the Billy Graham Center Archives (see Blumhofer, 210 n. 35 and 215 n.53).

52. Note the similar tone of Yoder, "if we were to make sense of North American Mennonitism, it would have to become more Anabaptist, more radical, more self-critical, less mainstream Evangelical, less institution centered" (in Nation, *Yoder*, 20).

53. I suggest the temptation and unfortunate reality of Pentecostal amnesia. Pentecostals tend to focus upon the current work of the Spirit. The events of yesterday constitute old news.

54. Murray Dempster, "Pacifism in Pentecostalism: The Case of the Assemblies of God," in *Proclaim Peace: Christian Pacifism from Unexpected Quarters*, edited by T. F. Schabach and R. T. Hughes (Chicago: University of Illinois Press, 1997) 35.

across some imaginary boundary line is unthinkable."[55] The Assemblies of God adopted a pacifist position in 1917, three years after the founding of the fellowship in 1914, only to shift its position to individual conscience in 1967.[56] According to Joel Shuman, the 1967 decision was a "grievous error" and "inconsistent with the theological vision of the tradition."[57] Paul Alexander chronicled the rise of nationalism and militarism in the Assemblies of God over the course of the twentieth century.[58] But all may not be lost, for the minority voices of pacifism continue to beseech adherents. While Pentecostals have all but abandoned pacifism, the revised statement retains a small window of opportunity. Pacifists continue to issue a prophetic call for a community of radical Pentecostals to return to their pacifist heritage.[59]

In sum, my experience with numerous Mennonites also points to an undercurrent of nationalism and loss of pacifism not unlike that among the Pentecostals.[60] In a world of increasing nationalism, whether in a time of war or peace, the challenge of Christians scattered among the nations of the world is to live as the one body of Christ and to pledge allegiance not to one nation under God, but to one church under God, members united to Christ and each other through the power of the Holy Spirit. Pentecostals and Mennonites must continue to provide rigorous theological instruction that reaches the ecclesial mass of their respective traditions. Furthermore, intentional dialogue between Mennonites and Pentecostals should inspire not only ongoing passion for their respective heritages but also enlarge the conversation in other Christian circles.

55. Frank Bartleman, *Christian Citizenship* (Los Angeles: Author, 1922).

56. For a historical trajectory of pacifism in the Assemblies of God (and other Pentecostal bodies), see Jay Beaman, *Pentecostal Pacifism: The Origins, Development and Rejection of Pacific Belief Among the Pentecostals* (Hillsboro, KS: Center for Mennonite Brethren Studies, 1989) and Paul Alexander, *Peace to War: Shifting Allegiances in the Assemblies of God* (Telford, PA: Cascadia, 2009).

57. Shuman, "Pentecost and the End of Patriotism," 70–71.

58. Paul Alexander, *Peace to War: Shifting Allegiances in the Assemblies of God* (Telford, PA: Cascadia, 2009).

59. See Pentecostals & Charismatics for Peace & Justice (www.pcpj.org).

60. I recall the following responses to pacifism with several Mennonite friends: "Oh, we don't talk about it much" or "We are not defined by it anymore." This resonates with a passionate appeal given by plenary speaker Ronald Sider at the Evangelical Mennonite Conference Convention 2006 in Winnipeg. In a session entitled "Rethinking Pacifism in a Dangerous World," Sider implored delegates and guests to renew their commitment to pacifism.

## OUTLOOK: PROPHETIC AND POSTMODERNISM

I am optimistic concerning the future of the Mennonite and Pentecostal traditions. The emergence of postmodernism, while frightening for some, furnishes unquestionable opportunities. Christians searching for an authentic living faith should find Pentecostal and Mennonite passion for living like Jesus attractive. Charismatic encounter with the Spirit alongside prophetic peace and social justice finds continuity with the living Jesus as a tangible embodiment of his journey. Tradition, when healthy, facilitates authentic community through shared purpose and experience. Given a new generation of Christians longing for connection to ancient faith, primitivistic impulses should provide a link not only between the apostolic church and contemporary communities but also between their respective histories. Pentecostals and Mennonites suffering from historical amnesia must identify with a great cloud of witnesses—their stories of the past—thereby identifying with a truly inter-generational Christian community. These same factors also place Mennonites and Pentecostals in a solid position for significant societal impact. When evangelistic efforts move beyond a cerebral internalized gospel and moral rhetoric, the living Jesus stands not only as the center of a creed, but also as the model for a transformed life and society. As the life and teaching of Jesus proves central to our respective traditions, so also our common vision and witness should reflect the kind of love for one another envisioned by Jesus. Our churches and our world deserve the counter-cultural voices of all Menno-costals!

# 17

## "Thank You and Please"

### *An Address to Mennonite Church USA, July 4, 2007*[1]

#### Paul Alexander

When I was a kid growing up on a farm in Kansas I would sprinkle bird-seed in the snow in the dead of winter, hide in the garage with my pellet gun, and pick off snowbirds and sparrows one by one as they came to eat. They'd all fly away when I shot, but then they'd come back. And I'd shoot another one.

On the journey from being a good Christian boy who snipes birds to being a man who supports sniping people as one of many legitimate violent things that good Christians who love their country could do for Jesus, something happened to me that radically changed me and altered the course of my life. And it has involved you Mennonites.

So thank you for this invitation to say thank you. All of you here tonight are going to have to bear the brunt of my overly enthusiastic and demonstrative praise of your faithfulness in living as best as you can like Jesus wants us to live, and in helping other people learn do it too. People

---

1. This is a slightly edited version of the address I delivered at the Mennonite Church USA biennial convention in San Jose, CA on July 4, 2007.

352

like me, who didn't know much about this particular way of following Jesus. Thank you.

Last October when I got the invitation to speak tonight, I read it, thought about it, and then I bawled like a baby. I turned out the lights in my office, laid face down on the floor, and prayed. And I knew immediately, right then, what I was supposed to say to you tonight. I wept, and snotted, and I prayed, and I just laid there in the dark silence and listened. I knew, I knew what I needed to say.

My message is very simple. I'm just a simple Pentecostal farm boy from Kansas so I only have two points. First, I need to say Thank You, to do that I need to tell a little of my story, my testimony, and I hope and pray that I can say it well enough to do you justice. Second, I need to say Please. Please keep being, continue to be, the people that God is calling, and leading, and empowering, you to be. Please.

Thank you, first, and then Please. Just like Paul said it in Ephesians.

## THANK YOU

Ephesians 1:15–23 says,

> Ever since I heard about your faithfulness to the Lord Jesus and your love for all the saints, I have not stopped giving thanks for you, remembering you in my prayers. I keep asking that the God of our Lord Jesus Christ, the glorious father, may give you (and me) the Spirit of wisdom and revelation, so that you (and I and all of us) may know him even better.

Just like Paul thanked God for the faithfulness of the Ephesians, I thank God for you. Because I'm not supposed to be here tonight, I'm supposed to be a wealthy, powerful, congressman voting *against* immigrants, voting *for* increased military spending in Iraq, and *for* an invasion of Iran. But my Pentecostal pacifist heritage and you crazy Mennonites got in my way.

I was born and reared in Kansas by Assemblies of God (that means Pentecostal) parents who prayed for me almost every night of my life. My dad would come up to my room, kneel next to my bed, and weep as he prayed for me and my brother, our family, our church, the pastor, the missionaries, the world. . . . The essence of his theological and practical advice for me, that he has repeated repeatedly my entire life, is "Seek Jesus." Can everybody here say "seek Jesus"? That's not bad advice.

I went to church at least three times a week. I did not swim with girls, nor attend movies, nor wear shorts, nor dance. I was a member of the Junior National Rifle Association and I had a large assortment of weapons.

I told racist jokes, most of which I learned from the leaders of the boys group at my Assembly of God church, and many of which I still remember though I really wish I could forget them. I loved Jesus with all my heart and began speaking in tongues when I was twelve. I loved playing war and took all my toy guns in a big brown paper bag to "show and tell" in Kindergarten. I loved BB gun and smoke bomb fights, and I did lots of hunting. I once killed three deer in less than one minute, this was legal because I had a three-deer-tag, but I also poached. My parents had a copy of *Foxe's Book of Martyrs*, and I grew up reading it. I went on church missions trips to Guatemala and Venezuela when I was 15 and 16.

I wrote a high school English paper explaining why burning the U.S. flag should be illegal. I went to church camp and youth conventions like this one every summer. As a teenager I read Josh McDowell's *Why Wait? What You Need To Know About the Teen Sexuality Crisis.*

In college, I was a youth ministry/business major my first month, but changed to Cross Cultural Missions because I felt called to Muslims (this was 1990). I started listening to Rush Limbaugh and that became my favorite three hours of each weekday. I enjoyed the 100-hour-war with Iraq in January, 1991 and as a freshman cheered as the bombs dropped, singing along to "bomb, bomb, bomb . . . bomb, bomb Iraq." But I was so concerned with Americans needing to be saved that a friend and I talked about whether it would be worth an American military defeat to turn Americans back to God, and we concluded that it would be. If a military defeat would result in millions of people getting saved then it's worth it since salvation is more important than anything else. That was a stretch for me as a nationalistic militaristic American, but Jesus mattered.

While attending a Pentecostal seminary, right after Bill Clinton was elected president, to make a little extra money I tried to sell t-shirts that said, "Don't blame me, I didn't vote for the dope smoking, draft dodging, womanizing, governor of a backwater state."

After seminary I taught at my alma mater for a year and then started PhD work at Baylor. I had purchased my first rental home the year before so that I could become a millionaire, and I borrowed $50,000, put it in the stock market and started day trading while studying theology and ethics. One day in the student lounge I was talking about day trading and another student said, "what about the business practices of the companies you buy and sell, do you know if they're just?" I said, "I don't even know the names of the companies, I'm trading based on charts, that stuff doesn't matter." I then left the lounge because I was embarrassed and was trying to figure out what in the world he was talking about . . . justice, business, not buying a stock because of unjust practices. It just didn't compute for me. I was 24. Everybody out there under the age of 24 who understands unjust business practices like sweatshops and not paying a living wage, and that that stuff matters to Jesus and should matter to us, raise your hand. Thank you.

Then three things happened together over the next couple of years. First, I lost my faith that there was a God. I mean, really, ultimate revelation through this little people group on the backside of a desert that's supposed to be truer than anybody else's truth? I'm sorry, but how stupid is that. Miracles, healing, the rapture . . . I saw it all clearly for what it was—baloney (that's my Midwestern Pentecostal way of cussing). But the big one was this suffering world and suffering people, a loving and all powerful God that could fix it and make it better but doesn't? The compassion of my wife was so great that I began to think that if God loved the world half as much as Deborah loved the people in it then God would fix it, because Deborah sure would if she had the power.

Marlon Millner, an African-American friend of mine, and I were swapping testimonies one time and at this point he said, "Yeah, you white people and your loss of faith in graduate school. That doesn't happen to black folk because we don't quit going to church like you do." He's right, I quit going to church and separated from my community because it was painful going to a Pentecostal church while doing a PhD in theology. I learned to be embarrassed about being a Pentecostal and I completely quit identifying myself as one. But more seriously I guess; I had to quit believing in God.

Second, while I was experiencing this faith crisis I discovered something that blew me away. Many early Pentecostals were pacifists. Let me say that again. Most early Pentecostals—the movement that has grown in the last century to include almost six hundred million people around the world—were nonviolent, anti-war, conscientious objectors.

Please indulge me for a minute, and let me read the voices of some of these early Pentecostals (you all have your *Martyrs Mirror*). This stuff, and all of *you*, completely changed my life. The Assemblies of God, The

Church of God in Christ, and many other Pentecostals said things like this:

> WHEREAS the Scriptures have always been accepted and interpreted by our churches as prohibiting Christians from shedding blood or taking human life;
>
> THEREFORE we, as a body of Christians, while purposing to fulfill all the obligations of loyal citizenship, are nevertheless constrained to declare we cannot conscientiously participate in war and armed resistance which involves the actual destruction of human life, since this is contrary to our view of the clear teachings of the inspired Word of God, which is the sole basis of our faith.[2]

> The nation, the voters, the church members, could stop this [war] if they would insist upon it . . . [but] we are willing to receive these millions of blood money. We had better pluck out the stars from our flag and instate dollar marks in their place.[3]

> Patriotism has been fanned into a flame. The religious passion has been invoked, and the national gods called upon for defense in each case. What blasphemy![4]

> We have killed off about all of our American Indians. What we have not killed outright we have starved. . . . Will not God deal in judgment with such a nation as this? We have stolen the land from the North American Indians. . . . Our wrong to the black people was avenged in blood. What will the next be?[5]

> National pride, like every other form of pride, is abomination in the sight of God. And pride of race must be one of the all things that pass away when one becomes a new creature in Christ Jesus. . . . When seen from the heavenly viewpoint, how the present conflict is illumined. The policy of our God is plainly declared in the Word, 'Peace on earth, good will toward men.'[6]

---

2. "The Pentecostal Movement and the Conscription Law," *The Weekly Evangel*, 4 August 1917, 6. I provide an analysis of this statement later in this article.

3. Frank Bartleman, "The European War," *The Weekly Evangel*, 10 July 1915, 3. Bartleman wrote the best selling and possibly definitive account of the Azusa Street Revival in Los Angeles, California (led by the son of former slaves, William Seymour) ,the birthplace of the Pentecostal movement.

4. Ibid.

5. Ibid., 2.

6. Ibid.

That last quote challenged my nationalism, my racism, and my pro-war opinions in one paragraph. Those were my Pentecostal ancestors—and there are thousands more quotes, sermons, lives, jail terms, conscientious objectors, and martyrs to go along with these. Dave Allen, a 26-year-old Pentecostal in Alabama was beaten and shot to death by two police officers in his home, in front of his wife, because he would not fight in World War I. His murder was reported in a Pentecostal magazine in 1918

> Brother Allen was in the second draft and was called for in October. Knowing that his Bible church opposed war, he felt he could not kill. . . . He carried his Bible with him everywhere he went. . . . We feel he might be classed among the martyrs. We extend to his wife and parents our heartfelt sympathy. God's grace will be sufficient. Keep pressing on . . . I am looking for the time to come when many will have to seal our testimony with our blood."

And then I found out that my grandfather was a Pentecostal conscientious objector during World War II, and my wife's grandfather was a Pentecostal noncombatant—along with many other Assemblies of God members.

The story of Assemblies of God pacifism, increasing nationalism, and militarism had never been thoroughly researched and told, and it intrigued and challenged me so I wrote my dissertation on it. Most early Pentecostal denominations had official pacifist statements, the Assemblies of God didn't change their position until 1967 (forty years ago this summer), the Church of God in Christ still has their statement on the books (that's a 5.5 million member predominantly African American denomination).

So the early Pentecostal denominations are Historic Peace Churches, during World War II the Assemblies of God was listed as the third largest peace church in America! Just most of them lost their peace witness after a couple of generations. I want them to be Living Peace Churches.

Third, while simultaneously losing my faith in God and finding out that my Pentecostal ancestors were lily-livered anti-American yellow-bellied pacifists, I took a class with John Howard Yoder. This was in the summer of 1997, six months before he passed away. I have to confess something for the first time here—I didn't know who he was. I was told I should take his class; all I knew was that he had written *The Politics of Jesus* (which I hadn't read). I was the one at the far end of the table thinking, "what, you mean you don't just shoot 'em?" And here's one of the biggest regrets of my life—I cut the last class to go to Florida on vacation.

But I finished my coursework, went back again to my undergraduate alma mater to teach, and wrote my dissertation on a hundred years of Pentecostals, war, and nation.[7] I also kept buying real estate and trading stocks so that I could get rich. I was serving Mammon rather than God, but I was thinking and reading and when I finished the dissertation I was thoroughly convinced that the witness of the early Pentecostals regarding the priority of our kingdom of God citizenship, nonviolence, and justice was right on track.

Along the way I read loads and loads of John Howard Yoder. Reading passionate first generation Pentecostal voices proclaiming Jesus' gospel of enemy love alongside Yoder . . . what was a fourth generation Pentecostal, whose Dad always told him to "seek Jesus," to do? I had no response, I couldn't argue against it.

Reading Mennonites helped me believe in God again, because of Jesus. Jesus kind of, well, saved me. I didn't necessarily believe everything I believed before, but I could hesitatingly and carefully follow this Jesus of Nazareth who was a bit different from the Christianity I was used to, but it wasn't that far of a stretch, I just had to change my identity. I had to become first and foremost a *Christ*-ian rather than an *Americ*-an. Changing allegiances from one nation, like America for instance, to the kingdom of God, is painful, and hard. It hurt to the core of my being. I described it once as "identity shattering and character transforming." But it was also liberating and freeing.

So as a 27-year-old Pentecostal pacifist (I still winced at both those words though) I started looking around for others to talk to, learn from, get resources from. I needed help.

So when I found the Mennonite Central Committee I thought I was in heaven. I ordered almost everything they had that was free or less than a dollar, and a lot of other things that I just had to have, my first order was around $240. A few days later I got boxes of material in the mail. I read it and handed it out and used it in my college classes and my local church where I was a Sunday School teacher. There was a brochure on Soap—a

---

7. "An Analysis of the Emergence and Decline of Pacifism in the History of the Assemblies of God," PhD diss., Baylor University, 2000. Later revised, expanded, and published as *Peace to War: Shifting Allegiances in the Assemblies of God* (Telford, PA: Cascadia, 2009).

little kid holding a bar of soap and smiling. I thought that was so cool. Wow! The Mennonites hand out soap! I got the conflict transformation handbook in Spanish. I don't speak Spanish.

And I love the videos! Did you know that Mennonites loan videos and other stuff for *free*? I had never heard of such a thing. No profit. All I had to do was email and ask for a couple and they'd show up in the mail! This is crazy! You Mennonites helped me learn that I'm first of all a citizen in the kingdom of God, that my view of money is supposed to be more like those Christians in Acts 2 and 4 (sharing what you have), and that I love my enemies rather than kill them.

I figured out ways to show free Mennonite videos in just about all my classes—there has to be a way to show *Affluenza* in my Greek classes.[8] Hmmm, "affluenza" sounds kind of like a Greek word. . . .

And the posters! I love the Franciscan Blessing one. I still have it on my office door.

> May God bless you with Discomfort
>> at easy answers, half-truths, and superficial relationships,
>> so that you may live deep within your heart.
> May God bless you with Anger
>> at injustice, oppression, and exploitation of people,
>> so that you may work for justice, freedom, and peace.
> May God bless you with Tears
>> to shed for those who suffer from pain, rejection, starvation, and war,
>> so that you may reach out your hand to comfort them and turn your pain to joy.
> May God bless you with enough Foolishness
>> to believe that you can make a difference in this world,
>> so that you can DO what others claim cannot be done.

MCC, the Peace and Justice Support Network, MCUSA, your existence helped me realize that we can follow Jesus in the twenty-first century. *I* needed all that you had to offer, and so did my university, my church, my denomination, my family. Thank you.

So I kept ordering books, posters, videos, pamphlets, manuals, and magnets for our refrigerator (I love the one that says "Anti-racism—A Christian Value," it's at home on our refrigerator right now). Do you understand how cool that is? Your stuff is also what I gave family members

---

8. Produced by Oregon Public Broadcasting, http://www.pbs.org/kcts/affluenza.

and friends for Christmas and birthdays. I ordered *Parent Trek* for my sister-in-law, and then discovered the concept of "simplicity" and ordered about ten books on that. Then I read the books and realized that I shouldn't have ordered ten books on simplicity, there they were on my shelf, ten books on simplicity. That really happened. Because *I don't know what I'm doing.*

I then found a Baptist Peace Fellowship, an Orthodox Peace Fellowship, a Disciples Peace Fellowship; but I couldn't find any organization devoted to sustaining and encouraging peacemaking and working for justice for Pentecostals and Charismatics (and there are about 14,000 denominations).

So as a very wet behind the ears pacifist, in July 2001 I wrote and presented, "Spirit Empowered Peacemaking: Toward a Pentecostal Peace Fellowship." I quoted a lot of early Pentecostals, but I got scared, because other than my grandfathers and those few that I myself had taught at Southwestern, I was not aware of having ever met another Pentecostal pacifist. So I read Yoder's *The Original Revolution*[9] one more time just to make sure I wasn't crazy. My goal in the paper and for the Pentecostal Peace Fellowship was simple, and limited. I knew the value of keeping a goal manageable, not too big, small enough to be able to be accomplished: I simply wanted to help every single one of the 600,000,000 Charismatics and Pentecostals in the world to reclaim their nonviolent, peacemaking heritage and be Jesus Shaped Holy Spirit Empowered peacemakers. That's all.

Then seven weeks later September 11 happened.

September 11, 2001, was the day I came out of the closet as an inexperienced newly born citizen of the kingdom of God, as a Christian pacifist. It was a tragic day, I'm sure you remember it. Tragic events preceded it and tragic events have followed it, but that day revealed our truest and deepest allegiances. Everyone has their own 9/11 story, here's mine.

I was teaching a systematic theology class and then Greek I. We prayed together—we actually wept and "cried out" and interceded, that's what Pentecostals do—and I felt very strongly like I should go talk to the president of the university because I could see the tide of nationalism and violence rising and I wanted to try to calm it before chapel began at 11:00 am (central time)—about four hours after the first tower was hit.

---

9. John Howard Yoder, *The Original Revolution* (Eugene, OR: Wipf & Stock, 1998).

I quietly told the president as we briskly walked across campus toward the auditorium, "we have to remember who we are, we're followers of Jesus, we have to remember who we are. A lot of people will be saying a lot of things that are hateful, we have to remember who we are."

The first hour and a half of chapel was prayer and a lot of apocalyptic, end-times, prophecy fulfillment talk. It involved the Middle East, the rapture, Israel, Armageddon, tribulation, the anti-Christ, the United States, patriotism, war, and Muslims. And where ten years before I would have been saying "amen," this time I was squirming in my seat and feeling a very definite, what we Pentecostals call a "leading of the Holy Spirit" to address the students and faculty, there were about 1,300 people present. I avoided this prompting and ignored it and tried to talk myself out of it for a long time. I shifted in my seat and prayed. I put my head in my hands and prayed. But I finally went up and asked the president if I could speak, and he handed me the microphone.

I sat down in the middle of the stage, crossed my legs, and spoke very quietly, doing the best I could in that context (you'll hear me talking about my own sins, which I also saw as the sins of my church).

> I love you guys. I have a dream . . . and a vision, and a purpose. And it's to tell the truth, amen? Just to tell the truth. We just want to follow Jesus faithfully, that's what we want to do. And I just want to point out, in all humbleness, in fact, I'm going to have to sit down to say this, because you have to take me for who I am, in all humility—we have participated in some sins. We have talked about confession [today], and that's a good thing, but we need to know what to confess. . . .

> What we can do in this time is examine ourselves, there's going to be a lot of picking the speck out of other people's eyes but maybe we could use this as a time to pick the beam out of our eyes, amen? To critique ourselves, to let God speak to us and see 'who are we to be as faithful followers of Jesus?' That we can be who we are supposed to be in all situations, in a time of mourning, human mourning, this is a human tragedy, beyond an American tragedy, this is a human tragedy.

> So I just pray and I want you to pray that you will examine your understanding of the church, your understanding of your allegiances and your loyalties, what are the purposes and visions and dreams that we have, that they are good, that they are in line

with what God wants us to be. And that we can confess some sin that the church has participated in . . . arrogance, liking power, liking control . . . it's fun to dominate, it's nice, you get what you want, and I'm not sure that's how Jesus led the church. So if we can critique ourselves even in those things. . . .

Now let me quote the President [of the university] . . . "revival begins with confession." It's true. You have your personal sins, but there are also social sins like racism that we participate in. There's no room for this in our body, amen? Because we are a chosen people, a holy nation, a royal priesthood. That's who we are first and foremost.

I fought against saying this, and I've said it very softly, but I know that God had this for us this morning, and that things said here are appropriate. And we won't say that God caused this to happen by no means, no, but retaliation for retaliation for retaliation for retaliation, that happens in the world, right? If someone hits you, you hit them back. Eye for eye, tooth for tooth. What people have thought they're doing is they're taking the eye of America because they think America has taken their eye, America has taken their tooth. And now they're taking our tooth, and that is the system of when you get it, you give it back. What did Jesus call us to do? When someone takes your eye, what do you do? You forgive them, right? We won't take this into what will happen now, but I'll tell you what will happen. Now America will respond, and that will be responded to, and that system of escalating violence will continue. . . . This is what happens, the "why" the World Trade Center and the Pentagon were bombed is because they're seen as the symbols of what makes America what it is—we expand ourselves economically and militarily so they attack the economic and military centers. It's an attack on that, ok? As Christians, we say, "Yes, that's what happens. We reap what we sow. We hit, we get hit back." Look, it's written to the largest scale it's ever been written. And now what do we do? We be faithful followers of Jesus, let's confess our participation in it and let God move us forward to being the faithful followers of Jesus.

I spent all my "capital" that day, it was gone, I was broke. That was my revealing myself as a pacifist at my alma mater in front of all the people who had educated me and loved me and hired me, and there were faculty who didn't talk to me for years and some who tried to get me fired. My dean, the retired Colonel, took my favorite class away from me, Scripture and Ethics, for three semesters and told me it was a scheduling mistake. I didn't die, or get tortured, or get fired, so it wasn't really that bad.

The following fall Marlon Millner wrote a Pentecostal letter to President Bush asking him not to invade Iraq.[10] I and many others signed it.

I got in a lot of trouble for doing this. I got to talk to the president of the university and the executive leadership of the Assemblies of God. In fact, the Board of Regents of the university passed a resolution to "Express concern regarding any faculty member taking a public stand in opposition to the war situation currently facing America."[11] That's a resolution I would have agreed with a few years before, but now it was directed at me.

The peace fellowship slowly began to grow and we started selling books and resources at Pentecostal conferences. I went through the Herald Press catalog with a blue highlighter, grinning and circling, and ordered two or three of at least fifty different titles, thinking, "Pentecostals just have to read this stuff!"

Time does not permit me to tell you the many peacemaking attempts and mistakes I've made the last few years. They include several of the students, staff, and faculty trying to get the university to fix the slums they owned and rented to Latinos across the street from the college.

This is probably already very clear, but I want to make sure. I do not know what I am doing. Becoming a first generation Pentecostal Anabaptist type, peacemaking, conflict creating, out loud talking radical . . . it's hard, frustrating, great, wonderful, and painful, and it can be confusing.

I tried for four years to get my university to honor Dr. Martin Luther King Jr. by closing the school on MLK Day or at least recognizing the day with an official event. Neither ever happened. I made a clumsy immature mistake and wrote a letter to the editor of the local paper about MLK Day and said that I wished the university would observe MLK Day.

I was reprimanded rather severely for this. I shared my concerns and encouraged the administration to read some of my articles if they had not. They did. I think one of the ones they read was "'The War Church is a Harlot Church:' Pacifism, Nationalism, and Militarism in American Pentecostalism."

10. This letter appears as chapter seven of this book.

11. "Summary of Interaction with Dr. Paul Alexander Concerning His Involvement in a Petition Against the United States Initiation of a War with Iraq." Personal files of the author.

A few weeks later my new dean, an old friend whom I've known since I was eighteen years old, told me that the president is "over here" and that I am "over there" and neither of us is going to change. . . .

So at the age of thirty-three, after nine years of serving my alma mater, I was set free. Thankfully, I had applied for the position at Azusa Pacific University several months before because Deborah and I were already feeling a "release" and a good friend there was encouraging me to apply.

So how does all this relate to you Mennonites? So what? That's simple—it's your fault that I got fired. Just kidding. I didn't get fired; I just didn't have my full time faculty contract renewed.

This relates to you because you are, in my limited experience, awesome followers of Jesus, and even though you know all kinds of faults and shortcomings about yourselves (and I'm learning them), you follow Jesus extremely well. And you encourage others of us, you show us how, and, by the power of the Holy Spirit, you make it possible. Thank you. Thank you. Thank you.

## And Now for My Second Point—Please

After saying "thank you," in Ephesians 4:1 Paul said "I urge you (all y'all) to please live a life worthy of the calling you (all y'all) have received." This is the conference theme (live the call!), but from me personally, on behalf of all the other Christians in the world *and* all those who aren't Christians—it's a plea, a request, an appeal, an encouragement to keep on doing what you're so good at. Even when you don't think you're very good at it. And if you do think you're really good at it, work on the humility thing, but I praise the Lord that you're confident. I want you to be encouraged and strengthened, please keep living the beautiful and inspirational call that you have received.

Deborah and I have been messily born again into Jesus' way, and we have been around a lot of messy births in the last few years. Birth is messy, and when people abandon their old allegiances, and nationalisms, and patriotisms, and violences, and prejudices, and hatreds, and arrogances, and self-righteousnesses and try to live new lives shaped by Jesus, it's challenging and messy, and we don't know how to do it because we haven't seen it done. So thank you for helping us do it, and please, please, please don't stop. We all need you.

I also want to encourage each of you personally. You may not struggle with your faith, or with questioning God, or with the worth and value of your church. Many of you may not need what I'm saying now, but some of you might. I was absolutely certain that there was a God, that Jesus was Lord, and that I knew how best to live for God. Then came gnawing doubt followed by complete uncertainty. If you have questions or if things aren't making sense, talk with somebody about it. You can talk with me, I might not have the answers but I'll listen. We are in this for the long haul and we need each other. If you're in darkness and you can't see your way ahead, I wish I could infuse in you my love for Jesus that I have found once again. But we can share our light with each other when some of our lights dim. I want you to have faith and hope in the God who is clearly revealed in Christ Jesus.

For the youth, I don't know if you like your local church, or don't like it, or what your relationship with God is. Please don't leave Jesus; please don't leave your church. You have a great church that has problems like all churches. My awareness of the need of the world, of other Christians, for your witness and faithfulness is not to put too much of a burden on you. It's connected to an excitement and hope and power of what God is doing in the world, in this century, through all of us. I'm not being needy and whiny, "please don't leave, please don't leave." I'm saying that what you have is powerful and life changing and world rocking, that's why scripture talks about boldness, and strength, and power in witness along with suffering, and tragedy, and weakness. The two go together. This is not a pathetic whine, it's an awareness that what you have is the most powerful force in the world; it's a war cry, a battle cry, and we defeat the enemy through our own suffering love.

Live your faith. It's okay. Invite people to your church. This gospel we live, we claim it's real, and if it is real then it's worth sharing. The stories I've just shared show that I really don't know what I'm doing most of the time; I say and do dumb things a lot. There's a lot of bumbling and tripping and falling and getting back up along the way.

So this is my Please. The resources that bless the world come from your *lives*—your lives of faithfulness to Jesus. Christian Peacemaker Teams (CPT), Mennonite Disaster Relief, Mennonite Mutual Aid, the things you do and participate in are amazing. I know it may be hard for you to realize, but free videos for me to use in my church rocked my world. And led me along the path toward being part of a CPT trip and encouraging others to participate as well, and now we're working with Palestinian Pentecostals to bring their perspective of the situation to American Pentecostals. But long term lives of faithfulness in difficult areas of the world, whether among bulldozed homes in Palestine or with the families of assassinated pastors in Central America, you Mennonites embody the kind of faithfulness to Jesus that I aspire to.

The first time I went to a Mennonite church for worship, Sunday School consisted of a woman from Clergy and Laity United for Economic Justice talking about the plight of the hotel workers near the Los Angeles International Airport. At the end of the education hour she asked if any of us would participate in a direct action of Holy Obedience (civil disobedience) and be arrested in front of the hotels and go to jail in order to bring more attention to their needs and address the injustice.

I want to encourage you and ask you to please talk about your faith with others. You often hear in Pentecostal circles that it doesn't matter how high you jump, but how straight you walk when your feet hit the ground. But I want to say to you that you are walking straight, your feet are on the ground, and it is wonderful, you are living it out. But it's okay to share it, to talk about it with your friends and neighbors. Invite people to fellowship and church, be bold as you live the call. It involves conversation as well as just doing it. The world needs you. It's really weird for me to say this because to Pentecostals I would say, maybe we could talk a little less and live Jesus' way a little more. A little less talking and little more action, but for you I feel like I should say "keep on with the action, the world needs it, but talk about it even more." I want the world to hear what you have to say about Jesus.

There are so many things I admire about you and the resources that just flow from you. One of my favorites is the pledge of allegiance to Jesus, written by June Alliman Yoder and Nelson Kraybill, that thing is so cool. I saw it and thought, wow, what a great idea! It's stuck on our computer monitor at home in the room where Nathan and Kharese have school.

I pledge allegiance to Jesus Christ,
and to God's kingdom for which he died--
one Spirit-led people the world over,
indivisible,
with love and justice for all.

I can say *that* pledge. Please keep coming up with resources like this. It seems that great stuff like this just flows from you all. That's how I feel when I'm around Mennonites—all these great ideas, and actions, and practices. It's so inspiring.

The church and the world needs you. I need you. The body of Jesus globally needs MCUSA, this hurting world needs you, please keep being who and what you are.

So I just want to say thank you. Thank you for not pledging your allegiance to the nations, so that when Deborah and I and Nathan and Kharese are trying to pledge *all* of our loyalty to Jesus, you're here to help us know how to do that. Thank you. Please keep being non-nationalistic citizens of God's transnational, global kingdom. I have no words of wisdom or insight, please just persevere—live your article twenty-three.

> We believe that the church is God's "holy nation," called to give full allegiance to Christ its head and to witness to all nations about God's saving love. The church . . . gives its allegiance to God alone. As citizens of God's kingdom, we trust in the power of God's love for our defense. The church knows no geographical boundaries and needs no violence for its protection. The only Christian nation is the church of Jesus Christ, made up of people from every tribe and nation, called to witness to God's glory. . . . Because we confess that Jesus Christ has been exalted as Lord of lords, we recognize no other authority's claims as ultimate.

Thank you for being discipled that way, for discipling each other, and for helping to disciple the rest of the church. First Peter 2:9 says that, "You are a chosen race, a royal priesthood, a holy nation, a people for God's possession, so that you can *proclaim the praises of the one who called you out of darkness into his marvelous light!*" You live your faith so well. You embody it, you *be* it, you do it.

So I pray for you and humbly implore you to please, in the power of the Holy Spirit, keep talking about and living faithfully the gospel of Jesus Christ. Thank you.

# Bibliography of Resources for Further Study

## Compiled by Brian K. Pipkin

Ackley, Heather Ann. "Dynamics of Ministry Training and Ministry Opportunities for Charismatic Women: Socio-historical Perspective of Wesleyan, Pentecostal, and Holiness Women in Ministry in the Nineteenth and Twentieth Century U.S." *Cyberjournal for Pentecostal-Charismatic Research* [Journal on-line] 15 (February 2006).

Adams, Michael K. "Hope in the Midst of Hurt: Towards a Pentecostal Theology of Suffering." Paper Presented at The Society for Pentecostal Studies, 1996.

Akinsanya, Gbolahan. "Transcending Ethnic Barriers: Pentecostalism in the Nigerian Context." *Pneuma* 1 (1999).

Alexander, Estrelda Y. "What Doth the Lord Require?: Toward a Pentecostal Theology of Social Justice." *Paper presented at The Society for Pentecostal Studies,* 1996.

————. *The Women of Azusa Street.* Cleveland, OH: Pathway, 2005.

Alexander, Stewart C., and Sherry S. DuPree. *The Silent Spokesman: Bishop Robert Clarence Lawson Founder of the Church of Our Lord Jesus Christ of the Apostolic Faith, Inc. New York City.* Displays for Schools, 1995.

Alexander, Paul. "Bearing Witness: A Challenge to Christian Zionism." *The Christian Century* (January 2007) 9.

————. "Christianity as Civil Religion." In *The Encyclopedia of Christian Civilization,* edited by George T. Kurian. Oxford, UK: Blackwell, 2008.

————. "Historical and Contemporary Pentecostal Critiques of Nationalism." Paper presented at the 34th Society for Pentecostal Studies, 2003.

————. "Historical and Theological Origins of Assemblies of God Pacifism." *Quaker Theology* 7.12 (2005–2006) 35–76.

————. "Just Peacemaking." In *The Encyclopedia of Christian Civilization,* edited by George T. Kurian. Oxford, UK: Blackwell, 2008.

————. "Justice." In *Dictionary of Everyday Theology and Culture.* Colorado Springs: NavPress, 2009.

————. "Magic Seeds of Peace in Palestine." Editorial for *Pax Pneuma: The Journal of the Pentecostal Charismatic Peace Fellowship* 1 (Summer 2005).

369

———. "Nationalism and Ethnicity." In *The Encyclopedia of Christian Civilization*, edited by George T. Kurian. Oxford, UK: Blackwell, 2008.

———. "Pacifism and Peace." In *Encyclopedia of Pentecostal and Charismatic Christianity*, edited by Stanley M. Burgess. Great Barrington, MA: Routledge, 2006.

———. "Peace, Power, and Pentecost: A Pentecostal Word for the Rest of the Church." Paper presented at The Ekklesia Project Gathering, Chicago, IL, 2001.

———. *Peace to War: Shifting Allegiances in the Assemblies of God*. Telford, PA: Cascadia, 2009.

———. "Pentecostal Charismatic Peace Fellowship." In *Encyclopedia of Pentecostal and Charismatic Christianity*, edited by Stanley M. Burgess. Great Barrington, MA: Routledge, 2006.

———. "A Pentecostal Protest/imony about Justice, anti-Theodicy, and HIV/AIDS in Africa." Paper presented at The Society for Pentecostal Studies, Duke University Divinity School, Durham, NC (March 7, 2008).

———. *Pentecostals and Peacemaking: Recovering our Authentic Heritage for Twenty-First Century Faithfulness*. Pentecostals, Peacemaking, and Social Justice 5. Eugene, OR: Pickwick, 2009.

———. "Prophecy." In *Dictionary of Everyday Theology and Culture*. Colorado Springs: NavPress, 2009.

———. "Spirit Empowered Peacemaking: Toward a Pentecostal Charismatic Peace Fellowship." *Journal of the European Pentecostal Theological Association* 22 (2002) 78–102.

———. "Speaking in the Tongues of Nonviolence: American Pentecostals, Nationalism, and Peacemaking." *Evangelical Review of Society and Politics: An Interdisciplinary Journal for the Christian Analysis of Social and Political Issues* 1.2 (2007) 1–19.

———. "Talk it Out, Reduce Nukes: A Theological Case for International Cooperation." *Theology News and Notes* 55.3 (2008).

———. "Toward Particular Declarations of Human Gifts: A Christian Reflection on Religions, Stories, and Untold Suffering." *Religion of Human Rights* 3.3 (2008) 235–47.

———. "Voting With Our Lives." In *Electing Not to Vote*, edited by Ted Lewis. Eugene, OR: Cascade, 2008.

———. "Who Makes All Those Race Cards?" *Pax Pneuma* 5.2 (2009) 4–6.

Althouse, Peter. "Canadian Pentecostal Pacifism." *Eastern Journal of Practical Theology* 4 (1990) 32–43.

———. "The Ideology of Power in Early American Pentecostalism." Paper presented at The Society for Pentecostal Studies, 1993.

———. "Left Behind—Fact or Fiction: Ecumenical Dilemmas of the Fundamentalist Millenarian Tensions within Pentecostalism." *Journal of Pentecostal Theology* 13.2 (2005) 187–207.

Alvarez, Carmelo E. "Latin American Pentecostals: Ecumenical and Evangelical." *Pneuma* 9 (1987) 91–95.

Alvarsson, Jan-Åke. "Conversion to Pentecostalism among Ethnic Minorities." *Swedish Missiological Themes/Svensk Missions Tidskrift* 87.3 (1999) 359–88.

Amos, Barbara M. "Race, Gender, and Justice." *Pneuma* 18 (1996) 132–35.

———. "The Radical Reconciliation Dialogue Held in Memphis, Tennessee in October 1994." Paper presented to The Society for Pentecostal Studies, 1996.

Anderson, Allan. "The Dubious Legacy of Charles Parham: Racism and Cultural Insensitivities Among Pentecostals." *Pneuma* 27 (2005) 51–64.

———. "Global Pentecostalism in the New Millenium." In *Pentecostals After a Century: Global Perspectives on a Movement in Transition*, edited by Allan Anderson and Hollenweger. Sheffield: Sheffield Academic, 1999.

———. "The Gospel and Culture in Pentecostal Missions in the Third World." *Missionalia* 27.2 (1999) 220–30.

———. "Pentecostals and Apartheid in South Africa during Ninety Years 1908–1998." *Cyberjournal for Pentecostal-Charismatic Research* [Journal on-line], vol. 9, February 2001; Internet.

———. "Signs and Blunders: Pentecostal Mission Issues at 'Home and Abroad' in the Twentieth Century." *Pneuma* 1 (2000).

———. *Spreading Fires: The Missionary Nature of Early Pentecostalism*. New York: Orbis, 2007.

Anderson, Robert M. *Vision of the Disinherited: The Making of American Pentecostalism*. New York: Oxford University Press, 1979.

*The Apostolic Church: Its Principles and Practices*. Gradford, UK: Apostolic, 1961.

Archer, Kenneth J. *A Pentecostal Hermeneutic for the Twenty-first Century: Spirit, Scripture and Community*. New York: Continuum, 2004.

———. "Pentecostal Babblings: The Narrative Hermeneutic of the Marginalized." *Pneuma* 1, (1998).

Attanasi, Katy. "Following Jesus as Global Citizens (Curriculum)." *Pax Pneuma* 5 (2009) 62–80.

Baer, Hans A. "The Socio-Religious Development of the Church of God in Christ." In *African Americans in the South: Issues of Race, Class, and Gender*, edited by Hans A. Baer and Yvonne Jones, 111–22. Southern Anthropological Society Proceedings 25. Athens: University of Georgia Press, 1992.

Bare Sr., Harold L. "The Evolution of Leadership in a Sacred Bureaucracy: A Socio-Historical Study of the Church of God." *Paper presented at the The Society for Pentecostal Studies*, 1997.

Bartleman, Frank. *Christian Citizenship*. Los Angeles: Author, 1922.

———. "Christian Preparedness." *Word and Work* (ca. 1916) 114.

———. "The European War." *The Weekly Evangel* (July 10, 1915) 3.

———. "War and the Christian." *Word and Work* (ca. 1915) 83.

———. "What Will the Harvest Be?" *The Weekly Evangel* (August 7, 1915) 1.

Baskett, Thomas A. "The Coming Postmodern Reformation: Toward a Creative Synthesis of Reformed and Pentecostal Theologies." *Pneuma* 1 (1999).

Beaman, Jay. "Pacifism Among the Early Pentecostals: Conflicts Within and Without." In *Proclaim Peace: Christian Pacifism From Unexpected Quarters*, edited by Theron Schlabach and Richard Hughes. Urbana: University of Illinois Press, 1997.

———. "Pacifism and the World View of Early Pentecostalism." Paper presented at The Society for Pentecostal Studies, 1983.

———. "Pacifism and the World View of Early Pentecostalism." In *Pastoral Problems in the Pentecostal-Charismatic Movement*, edited by H. D. Hunter, 1983.

———. *Pentecostal Pacifism: The Origins, Development and Rejection of Pacific Belief Among the Pentecostals*. Hillsboro, KS: Center for Mennonite Brethren Studies, 1989.

———. "Pentecostal Pacifism: The Origin, Development, and Rejection of Pacific Belief among Pentecostals." MDiv thesis, North American Baptist Seminary, 1982.

Bell, E. N. "Questions and Answers." *The Weekly Evangel* (August 25, 1917) 9.

Benvenuti, Sheri. "Pentecostal Racial Reconciliation: Let Justice Roll Down." *Pneuma* 1 (1999).

Benvenuti, Sherilyn. "Anointed, Gifted and Called: Pentecostal Women in Ministry." *Pneuma* 17 (1995) 229–35.

Best, Felton O. "Loosing the Women: African-American Woman and Leadership in the Pentecostal Church, 1890-Present." Paper presented at The Society for Pentecostal Studies, 1994.

Betancourt, Esdras. "Hispanic Pentecostals: History and Mission." Paper presented at The Society for Pentecostal Studies, 1993.

Bloch-Hoell, Nils. *The Pentecostal Movement: It's Origin, Development, and Distinctive Character*. New York: Humanities, 1964.

Blumhofer, Edith L. *Aimee Simple McPherson: Everybody's Sister*. Grand Rapids: Eerdmans, 1993.

————. *The Assemblies of God: A Chapter in the Story of American Pentecostalism*, vol. 1 (to 1941). Springfield, MO: Gospel, 1989.

————. "Reflections on the Source of Aimee Semple McPherson's Voice." *Pneuma* 17 (1995) 21–24.

————. *Restoring the Faith: The Assemblies of God, Pentecostalism, and American Culture*. Illinois: University of Illinois Press, 1993.

————. "Women in American Pentecostalism." *Pneuma* 17 (1995) 19–20.

Bomann, Rebecca P. *Faith in the Barrios: The Pentecostal Poor in Bogotá*. Boulder, CO: Rienner, 1999.

Bonino, José M. *Faces of Latin American Protestantism*. Grand Rapids: Eerdmans, 1997.

Booth-Clibborn, Arthur. *Blood Against Blood*. New York: Cook, 1914.

Booth-Clibborn, Samuel H. "The Christian and War." *Weekly Evangel* (April 1914).

————. *Should a Christian Fight? An Appeal to Christian Young Men of All Nations*. Swengal, PA: Bible Truth Depot, circa 1917–1918.

Brumback, Carl. *Suddenly From Heaven: A History of the Assemblies of God*. Springfield, MO: Gospel, 1961.

Bueno, Ronald N. "Listening to the Margins: Re-historicizing Pentecostal Experiences and Identities." In *The Globalization of Pentecostalism: A Religion Made to Travel*, edited by Murray Dempster, Bryon D. Klaus, and Douglas Petersen. Oxford: Regnum, 1999.

Bundy, David. "The Ecumenical Quest of Pentecostalism." *Cyberjournal for Pentecostal-Charismatic Research* [Journal on-line], vol. 5 (February 1999).

————. "Pentecostalism as a Global Phenomenon: A Review Essay of Walter Hollenweger's Pentecostalism: Origins and Developments Worldwide." *Pneuma* 21.2 (1999) 289–303.

Burgess, Stanley M., and Gary B. McGee. *Dictionary of Pentecostal and Charismatic Movements*. Grand Rapids: Zondervan, 1988.

Butler, Anthea. "Gender, Race, and Healing in the Holiness/Pentecostal Traditions: Intersections and Trajectories." *Pneuma*, 1998.

————. "Katrina and Its Aftermath." *Pax Pneuma* [Journal on-line] (Winter 2005–2006). Online: www.pcpf.org.

————. "Walls of Division: Racism's Role in Pentecostal History." Paper presented at The Society for Pentecostal Studies, 1994.

————. *Women in the Church of God in Christ: Making a Sanctified World*. Chapel Hill: University of North Carolina Press, 2007.

Cartwright, Desmond W. "Your Daughters Shall Prophesy: The Contribution of Women in Early Pentecostalism." Paper presented at The Society for Pentecostal Studies, 1985.

Casey, Michael. "Pentecostal Pacifism: The Origin, Development, and Rejection of Pacific Belief among the Pentecostals. *Mennonite Life* 46.2 (1991) 25–26.

Castellani, Vincent. "Sanctification: Toward a Theology of Pentecostal Social Ethics." *Paper presented at The Society for Pentecostal Studies, 1997.*

Cerillo, Augustus Jr., in Roland A. Wells. "Moving Up: Some Consequences of the New A/G Social Status." *Agora* 1 (Winter 1978) 8–11.

———. *The Wars of America: Christian Views.* Grand Rapids: Eerdmans, 1981.

Cerillo, Augustus, and Murray Dempster. *Salt and Light: Evangelical Political Thought in Modern America.* Grand Rapids: Baker, 1989.

Chan, S. "Asian Pentecostalism, Social Concern and the Ethics of Conformism." *Transformation* 11 (1994) 32.

Chesnut, R. Andrew. *Born Again in Brazil: The Pentecostal Boom and the Pathogens of Poverty.* London: Rutgers University Press, 1997.

Christenson, Larry. *A Charismatic Approach to Social Action.* Minneapolis: Bethany Fellowship, 1974.

Chung, Paul, "Calvin and the Holy Spirit: A Reconsideration in Light of Spirituality and Social Ethics." *The Society for Pentecostal Studies* 24 (2002) 40–55.

Clark, Matthew. "Pentecost and Politics." Paper presented at The Society for Pentecostal Studies, 1988.

Cleary, Edward L. "Introduction: Pentecostals, Prominence and Politics." In *Power, Politics and Pentecostals in Latin America*, edited by Cleary, Edward, Stewart-Gambino, W. Hannah. Boulder: Westview, 1997.

Clemmons, Ithiel. "True Koinonia: Pentecostal Hopes and Historical Realities." *Pneuma* 4 (1982) 46–56.

Collins Christian T. *From the Margins: A Celebration of the Theological Work of Donald W. Dayton.* Eugene, OR: Pickwick, 2007.

Comblin, Jose. *The Holy Spirit and Liberation.* New York: Orbis, 1989.

Conn, Charles W. *A History of the Church of God.* Cleveland: Pathway, 1977.

Cox, Harvey. *Fire from Heaven: The Rise of Pentecostal Spirituality and the Reshaping of Religion in the 21st Century.* Cambridge, MA: Da Capo, 2001.

Crews, Mickey. *The Church of God: A Social History.* Knoxville: University of Tennessee Press, 1990.

Daneel, Inus. *Quest for Belonging.* Gweru, Zimbabwe: Mambo, 1987.

Daniels, David D. "Afro-American Worship: A Source for Pentecostal Theology." Paper presented at the Society for Pentecostal Studies, 1985.

———. "Dialogue between Black and Hispanic Pentecostal Scholars: A Report and Some Personal Observations." *Pneuma* 17.2 (1995) 219–28.

Dart, John. "Debunking Some Pentecostal Stereotypes." *The Christian Century* (October 31, 2006) 12.

David Rees, Thomas. "The Holy Spirit is Color Blind." *CAM* 27.3 (1974) 3–5.

Dayton, Donald. "Pentecostal/Charismatic Renewal and Social Change: A Western Perspective." *Transformations* 5 (1988) 7–13.

———. "Pentecostal–Charismatic Renewal and Social Change." *Transformation* 5.4 (1988) 7–13.

———. "Theological Roots of Pentecostalism." *Journal of the Society for Pentecostal Studies* 2 (1980) 3–21.

De Kock, Wynand J. "Pentecostal Power for a Pentecostal Task: Empowerment through Engagement in South African Context." *Journal of Pentecostal Theology* 16 (2000) 102–16.

de Leon, Victor. *The Silent Pentecostals.* Taylors, SC: Faith, 1979.

Dearman, Marion. "Christ and Conformity: A Study of Pentecostal Values." *Journal for the Scientific Study of Religion* (1974) 437–53.

Dempster, Murray W. "Christian Social Concern in Pentecostal Perspective: Reformulating Pentecostal Eschatology." *Journal of Pentecostal Theology* 2 (1993) 53–66.

———. "Church, Mission, and Social Concern: The Changing Global Face of Classical Pentecostalism." *Transformation* 11 (1994) 1–33.

———. "'Crossing Borders': Arguments Used By Early American Pentecostals In Support of the Global Character of Pacifism." *EPTA Bulletin: Journal of the European Pentecostal Theological Association* 10.2 (1991) 63–88.

———. "Dialogue: Learning the Art of Listening and Experiencing the Power of Engagement." *Pneuma* 17.2 (1995) 159–61.

———. "Eschatology, Spirit Baptism, and Inclusiveness: An Exploration into the Hallmarks of a Pentecostal Social Ethic." In *Fresh Perspectives on Pentecostal Eschatologies,* edited by Peter F. Althouse and Robert C. Waddell, 155–88. Eugene, OR: Pickwick, 2010.

———. "Evangelism and Social Concern, and the Kingdom of God." In *Called and Empowered: Global Mission in Pentecostal Perspective,* edited by Murray W. Dempster, Bryon D. Klaus and Douglas Petersen. Peabody, MA: Hendrickson, 1991.

———. "Feedback: Women and Pentecostalism." *Pneuma* 17.2 (1995) 229–52.

———. "Jay Beaman, *Pentecostal Pacifism: The Origins, Development and Rejection of Pacific Belief Among the Pentecostals.* Hillsboro, KS: Center for Mennonite Brethren Studies, 1989. Reviewed by Murray W. Dempster." *Pneuma* 11 (1989) 60–64.

———. "A Pentecostal Approach to Evangelization and Social Concern." *Transformation: An International Evangelical Dialogue on Mission and Ethics* 16 (1999) 41–73.

———. "Pentecostal Social Concern and the Biblical Mandate of Social Justice." *Pneuma* 9.2 (1997) 129–53.

———. "Pacifism in Pentecostalism: The Case of the Assemblies of God." In *Fragmentation of the Church and its Unity in Peacemaking,* edited by Jeffrey Gros and John D. Rempel. Grand Rapids: Eerdmans, 2001.

———. "Pacifism in Pentecostalism: The Case of the Assemblies of God." In *Proclaim Peace: Voices of Christian Pacifism from Unexpected Sources,* edited Theron F. Schlabach and Richard T. Hughes, 31–57. Champaign, IL: University of Illinois Press.

———. "Pacifism as a Divisive Issue in the Pentecostal Tradition." A Consultation on "The Fragmentation of the Church and its Unity in Peacemaking," sponsored by the Faith and Order Working Group of the National Council of Churches/USA and by the Joan B. Kroc Institute for International Peace Studies at Notre Dame, held at the University of Notre Dame, Notre Dame, Indiana, June 13–17, 1995.

———. "Peacetime Draft Registration and Pentecostal Moral Conscience." *Agora* 3 (1980) 2–3.

———. "Pentecostal Social Concern and the Biblical Mandate of Social Justice." *Pneuma* 9 (1987) 129–53.

————. "Pentecostal and Charismatic Scholars Call for End to Apartheid." *Transformation* 9 (1992) 32–33.

————. "Pentecostal Social Concern and the Biblical Mandate of Social Justice." *Pneuma* 9 (1987) 129–53.

————. "Pentecostals in Dialogue." *Pneuma* 17.2 (1995) 159–228.

————. "Reassessing the Moral Rhetoric of Early American Pentecostal Pacifism." *Crux: A Quarterly Journal of Christian Thought and Opinion* 26 (March 1990) 23–36.

————. "Responding to the Changing Official Position on Abortion within the Assemblies of God, USA." Paper presented at The Society for Pentecostal Studies, 1993.

————. "Scholars at the Sixth Conference of Pentecostal and Charismatic Research in Europe Declare Solidarity in Ending Apartheid in South Africa." *Transformation: An International Dialogue on Evangelical Social Ethics* 9 (1992) 32–33.

————. "Social Concern in the Context of Jesus' Kingdom, Mission, and Ministry." *Transformation*: An International Dialogue on Mission and Ethics 16 (1999) 43–53. Reprinted under the title changed by the editors, "A Theology of the Kingdom—A Pentecostal Contribution." In *Mission as Transformation: A Theology of the Whole Gospel*, edited Vinay Samuel and Chris Sugden. Irvine, CA: Regnum, 1999.

————. "The Church's Moral Witness: A Study of Glossolalia in Luke's Theology of Acts." *Paraclete* 23 (1989) 1–7.

————. "The Structure of a Christian Ethic Informed by Pentecostal Experience: Soundings in the Moral Significance of Glossolalia." In *The Spirit and Spirituality: Essays in Honor of Russell P. Spittler*, edited by Wonsuk Ma and Robert P. Menzies. New York: T. & T. Clark, 2004.

Dirksen, Murl. "Pentecostal Healing as a Transitional Stage to Modernization of Health System." Paper presented at The Society for Pentecostal Studies, 1986.

Dodson, Michael. "Pentecostals, Politics and Public Space in Latin America." In *Power, Politics, and Pentecostals in Latin America*, edited by Edward L. Cleary and Hannah W. Stewart-Gambino. Boulder, CO: Westview, 1997.

Dowie, Alexander J. *A Voice from Zion: Sermons and Addresses by the Rev. John Alexander Dowie*. 5 vols. Chicago: Zion, 1902.

DuPree, Sherry. "Documenting Religious Activity in Non-Religious and Religious Depositories With Emphasis on Black Pentecostalism." Paper presented at The Society for Pentecostal Studies, 1987.

Dusing, Michael. "Toward a Pentecostal Theology of Physical Suffering." Paper presented at The Society for Pentecostal Studies, 1996.

Dyck, Henry. "L'Esprit du Seigneur Est Sur Moi?: A Brief Analysis of the Social Ethics of the Pentecostal Assemblies of Canada (PAOC)." Paper presented at The Society for Pentecostal Studies, 1996.

Elinson, Howard. "The Implications of Pentecostal Religion for Intellectualism, Politics, and Race Relations." *The American Journal of Sociology* 70.4 (1965) 403–15.

Espinosa, G. "Black Theology." In *International Dictionary of Pentecostal and Charismatic Movements*, edited by Stanley M. Burgess and Eduard M. Van Der Maas, 428–32. Grand Rapids: Zondervan, 2003.

Gaxiola, Adoniram. "Experience of Latin American Pentecostalism and Ecclesial Base Communities." *The Society for Pentecostal Studies* 13.2 (1991) 167–74.

Fahey, Sheila. *Charismatic Social Action: Reflection/Resource Manual*. New York: Paulist, 1977.

Faupel, David W. *The American Pentecostal Movement: A Bibliographical Essay.* Wilmore, KY: Asbury Theological Seminary, 1972.

Fee, Gordon. "The Kingdom of God and the Church's Global Missions." In *Called and Empowered: Global Mission in Pentecostal Perspective*, edited by Murray Dempster, Bryon D. Klaus, and Douglas Petersen. Peabody: Hendrickson, 1991.

Fields, Rebecca. "A White Girl's Reflection on Dr. King." *Pax Pneuma* (2005–2006). Online: www.pcpf.org.

Flora, Cornelia Butler. "Social Dislocation and Pentecostalism: A Multivariate Analysis." *Sociological Analysis* 34 (1973) 296–304.

Flores, Daniel F. "Guerrilla Christianity: Towards Recovering an Apocalyptic Paradigm for Spirit-filled Ministry." *Cyberjournal for Pentecostal-Charismatic Research* 11 (2002).

Flower, Roswell J. "What Will the Harvest Be? Article in Last Week's Evangel Receiving Just Criticism." *Weekly Evangel* 14 (1915) 2.

Ford, J. Massyngberde. "The Social and Political Implications of the Miraculous in Acts." *Faces of Renewal: Studies in Honor of Stanley M. Horton*, edited by Paul Elbert. Peabody, MA: Hendrickson, 1989.

Franklin, Robert Michael. *Another Day's Journey: Black Churches Confronting the American Crisis.* Minneapolis: Augsburg Fortress, 1997.

———. *Crisis in the Village: Restoring Hope in African American Communities.* Minneapolis: Augsburg Fortress, 2007.

———. *Liberating Visions: Human Fulfillment and Social Justice in African American Thought.* Minneapolis: Augsburg Fortress, 1989.

Freston, Paul. *Evangelicals and Politics in Asia, Africa and Latin America.* Cambridge: Cambridge University Press, 2001.

———. "Pentecostals in Latin America: Local Dynamism, Global Significance and Uncertain Future." A paper presented at the conference Twenty Years and More: Research into Minority Religions, New Religious Movements and "the New Spirituality," organized by CESNUR (Center for Studies on New Religions) and INFORM (Information Network Focus on Religious Movements) London: School of Economics (April 2008) 16–20.

Froats, Janenne, and Jennifer E. Kerslake. "Black and White: A Gray Area in the Assemblies of God." *Evangel Lance* (February 21, 1992) 4–6.

Frodsham, Stanley H. "Our Heavenly Citizenship." *Word and Witness* 12 (1915) 3.

Gabourel, Eric. "Loyalty and Perseverance: The Bible Is Just As It Is And We Should Follow It Close." *Pax Pneuma.* 2007–2008. Online: www.pcpf.org.

Gabriel, Andrew K. "Pneumatological Perspectives for a Theology of Nature: The Holy Spirit in Relation to Ecology and Technology." *Journal of Pentecostal Theology* 15.2 (2007) 195–212.

Garner, Mike. "U.S. Complicity for the Sex Industry in the Philippines." *Pax Pneuma* 5.2 (2009) 18–21.

Gaxiola, Adoniram. "Poverty as a Meeting and Parting Place: Similarities and Contrasts in the Experiences of Latin American Pentecostalisms and Ecclesial Base Communities." *Pneuma* 13.2 (1991) 167–74.

Gaxiola-Gaxiola, M. J. "Latin America Pentecostalism: A Mosaic within a Mosaic." *Pneuma* 13.2 (1991).

Gee, Donald. "Conscience." *Pentecostal Evangel* 13 (1938) 1.

———. "Conscientious Objection." *Pentecostal Evangel* 4 (1940) 4.

———. "Conscientious Objection." *Pentecostal Evangel* 15 (1930) 2–3.

———. "War, the Bible, and the Christian." *Pentecostal Evangel* 15 (1930) 2–3.

————. "War, the Bible, and the Christian." *Pentecostal Evangel* 8 (1930) 6–7.

Georgianna, Sharon Linzey. "The American Assemblies of God: Spiritual Emphasis and Social Activism." In *Faces of Renewal*, edited by Paul Elbert. Peabody, MA: Hendrickson, 1989.

Gerloff, Roswith I. H. "The Holy Spirit and the African Disapora. Spiritual, Cultural and Social Roots of Black Pentecostal Churches." Society for Pentecostal Studies Conference, Mattersey, England, July 1995.

Gernet, Maxine O'Dell. "Pentecost Confronts Abuse." *Journal of Pentecostal Theology* 17 (2000) 117–30.

Gingles, Dallas J. "Divorce as Christian Practice." *Pax Pnuema* 5 (2009) 34–45.

Glifford, Paul. *Christianity and Politics in Doe's Liberia*. Cambridge: Cambridge University Press, 1993.

Groff, James R., Jr. *Fields White Unto Harvest: Charles F. Parham and the Missionary Origins of Pentecostalism*. Fayetteville: University of Arkansas Press, 1988.

Gros, Jeffrey. "Toward a Dialogue of Conversion: The Pentecostal, Evangelical and Conciliar Movements." *Pneuma* 17.2 (1995) 192–94.

Hall, David. "A Church of God in Christ Conscientious Objection Principle." *Pax Pneuma*. (Summer 2005). Online: www.pcpf.org.

————. "Elements of Peace and Conflict from a Pentecostal Perspective." Paper presented at The Society for Pentecostal Studies (2011).

Harder, Kathleen. "The Expanding Politicization of the World Pentecostal Movement." Paper presented at The Society For Pentecostal Studies 1992.

Hardesty, Nancy A. "Holiness is Power: The Pentecostal Argument for Women's Ministry." Paper presented at The Society of Pentecostal Studies 1983.

Harris, John. "Palestinian Pentecostals in the West Bank: Following Jesus and Working for Peace." *Pax Pneuma* (Winter 2007–2008). Online: www.pcpf.org.

Harris, Rebecca. "Does God Engage in Rape? Rape as a Military Motif in the Prophets." *Pax Pneuma* 5.2 (2009) 7–17.

Haughey, John C. "Proselytism as an Ethical Issue." *Pneuma* 1 (1998).

Hittenberger, Jeffrey S. "Globalization, Marketization, and the Mission of Pentecostal Higher Education in Africa." *Pneuma* 26.2 (2004) 182–215.

Hocken, P. D. "Ethics in the Classical Pentecostal Tradition." In *International Dictionary of Pentecostal and Charismatic Movements*, edited by Stanley M. Burgess and Eduard M. Van Der Maas, 605–10. (Grand Rapids: Zondervan, 2003).

Hollenweger, W. H. "Pentecostalism and Black Power." *Theology Today* 30.3 (1973) 228–38.

Hollenweger, Walter J. "Black Pentecostal Concept." *Concept Journal* 30 (1970) 27–28.

————. "The Challenge of Reconciliation." *The Journal of the European Pentecostal Theological Association* 19 (1999) 5–16.

————. "An Introduction to Pentecostalisms." *Journal of Beliefs & Values* 25.2 (2004).

————. "Pentecost Between Black and White: Five Case Studies on Pentecost and Politics." Belfast, Ireland: *Christian Journals Limited* (1974) 13–32.

————. *Pentecostalism: Origins and Developments Worldwide*. Peabody, MA: Hendrickson, 1997.

————. "The Pentecostal Elites and the Pentecostal Poor: A Missed Dialogue?" *Charismatic Christianity as a Global Culture*, edited by Karla O. Poewe. Columbia: University of South Carolina Press, 1994.

————. *The Pentecostals*. Peabody, MA: Hendrickson, 1988.

Holmes, Barbara. "That All May Hear: Towards a Spirit-Led Cultural Critique." *Pneuma* 1 (1999).

Holmes, Pamela. "An Educational Encounter: A Pentecostal Considers the Work of Elisabeth Schüssler Fiorenza." Paper presented at The Society for Pentecostal Studies, 2001.

Howard N. Kenyon. "An Analysis of Ethical Issues in the History of the Assemblies of God." PhD diss., Baylor University, 1988, 42–176.

———. "Black Ministers in the Assemblies of God." *Assemblies of God Heritage* 7 (1987) 10–13, 20.

Hudson, N., and K. Warrington. "Cohabitation and the Church." *Journal of the European Pentecostal Theological Association* 13 (1994) 63–73.

Hunter, Harold. "A. J. Tomlinson's Journey Toward Racial Reconciliation." *History and Heritage* (Winter/Spring 2003) 5–7, 10.

———. "A Journey Toward Racial Reconciliation: Race Mixing in the Church of God of Prophecy." *Refleks - med karismatisk kristendom i focus* 3–1 (2004) 19–43.

———. "Some Ethical Implications of Pentecostal Eschatology." *Journal for the European Pentecostal Theological Society* 22 (2002) 45–55.

Jackson, Mary Elizabeth Jones. "The Role of Women in Ministry in the Assemblies of God." PhD diss., University of Texas at Arlington, 1997.

Jacobsen, Douglas. *Thinking in the Spirit: The Theologies of the Early Pentecostal Movement.* Bloomington: University of Indiana Press, 2003.

———. "We Cannot Make a Difference between Flesh for We are Brethren: The Anti-Racist Theology of Bishop R. C. Lawson." Paper presented at The Society for Pentecostal Studies, 2001.

Jenkins, Philip. *The Next Christendom: The Coming of Global Christianity.* 2nd ed. New York: Oxford University Press, 2007

Jewett, Paul K. "The Ordination of Women." Paper presented at The Society for Pentecostal Studies, 1983.

Johns, Cheryl Bridges. "The Adolescence of Pentecostalism: In Search for a Legitimate Sectarian Identity." Paper presented at The Society for Pentecostal Studies, 1993.

———. "Affective Conscientization: A Pentecostal Response to Paul Freire." Paper presented at The Society for Pentecostal Studies, 1991.

———. "Finding Faith in the Margins." *Other Side* 34.6 (1998) 14–19.

———. "Finding Faith in the Margins: Pentecostalism, Social margins as Resources for Contemporary Theology." *Other Side* 34 (1998).

———. "From the Margins to the Center: The Public Presence of Pentecostalism." *Theological Education* 38 (2001).

———. "The Holy Spirit: Meeting God in the Margins." *Living Pulpit* 5 (1996) 26-7.

———. "The Meaning of Pentecost for Theological Education." *Ministerial Formation* 87 (1999) 42.

———. "Meeting God in the Margins: Ministry Among Modernity's Refugees." *Papers of the Henry Luce III Fellows in Theology* 3 (1999) 7–31.

———. "Pentecostalism as Public Religion: Response to Harvey Cox." *Paper presented in Pentecostalism and Mission in the 21st Century Study Group,* 2001.

———. *Pentecostal Formation: A Pedagogy Among the Oppressed.* UK: Sheffield Academic, 1993. Jose, Costa Rica: Editorial Departamento Ecumenico de Investigaciones, 1992.

———. "Pentecostal Spirituality and the Conscientization of Women." In *All Together in One Place: Selected Papers from Brighton.* Sheffield, UK: Sheffield Academic, 1993.

————. "The Pentecostal Vision for Christian Unity." In *Pilgrims on the Sawdust Trail: Evangelical Ecumenism an the Quest for Christian Identity*, edited by Timothy George. Grand Rapids: Baker Academic, 2004.

————. "Pentecostals and the Praxis of Liberation: A Proposal for Subversive Theological Education." *Transformation* 11 (1994) 11.

————. "Religious and Ethical Reflections on Climate Change." Paper presented at Caring For Creation: Ethical Responses to Climate Change Conference, Mercer University, 2009.

————. "The Sanctity of Life: More than a Slogan." *Church of God Evangel* (January 2009).

————. "When East Meets West and North Meets South." Paper presented at the Global Christian Forum, Nairobi, Kenya, 2007.

————. "Women in Ministry." *The Pentecostal Minister* 7 (1987).

Jones, Charles E. *Black Holiness: A Guide to the Study of Black Participants in Wesleyan Perfectionist and Glossolalic Pentecostal Movements.* Metuchen: Scarecrow, 1987.

————. "The 'Color Line' Washed Away in the Blood? In the Holiness Church, Azusa Street and Afterward." *Pneuma* 1 (1998).

Jones, Lawrence Neale. "The Black Pentecostal." In *The Charismatic Movement*, edited by Michael P. Hamilton. Grand Rapids: Eerdmans, 1975.

Kalu, Ogbu U. "The Third Response: Pentecostalism and the Reconstruction of Christian Experience in Africa, 1970–1995." Journal *of African Christian Thought* 1.2 (1998) 3–16.

Kärkkäinen, Veli-Matti. "Are Pentecostals Oblivious to Social Justice?" *Missiology* 29.4 (2001) 417–31.

————. "Deification and a Pneumatological Concept of Grace: Unprecedented Convergences Between Orthodox, Lutheran, and Pentecostal-Holiness Soteriologies." *Pneuma* 1 (1999).

————. "Spirit, Reconciliation and Healing in the Community: Missiological Insights from Pentecostals." *International Review of Mission* 94.372 (2005) 43–50.

————. "Spirituality as a Resource for Social Justice: Reflections from the Catholic-Pentecostal Dialogue." *Asian Journal of Pentecostal Studies* 6 (2003) 83–96.

Kay, William. "A woman's place is on her knees: the pastor's view of the role of women in Assemblies of God." *Journal of the European Pentecostal Theological Association* 18 (1999) 64–75.

————. "British Assemblies of God: The War Years." *Pneuma* 11 (1989).

Keener, Craig S. *Paul, Women and Wives: Marriage and Women's Ministry in the Letters of Paul.* Peabody, MA: Hendrickson, 1992.

Kendrick, Klaude. *The Promise Fulfilled: A History of the Modern Pentecostal Movement.* Springfield, MO: Gospel, 1961.

Kenyon, Howard. "An Analysis of Ethical Issues in the History of the Assemblies of God." PhD diss., Baylor University, 1988.

Kircher, Leon G. "The History of the Organizational Development and Ministry to the Military by the Assemblies of God December 1941–December 1979." Springfield, MO: Assemblies of God Theological Seminary, 1979.

Kornweibel, Theodore, Jr. *Bishop C. H. Mason and the Church of God in Christ During World War I: The Perils of Conscientious Objection.* Southern Studies Institute of Northwestern State University, 1987.

————. "Race and Conscientious Objection in World War I: The Story of the Church of God in Christ." In *Proclaim Peace: Christian Pacifism from Unexpected Quarters,* edited by Theron F. Schlabach and Richard T. Hughes. University of Illinois Press, 1997.

Kung, Lap-Yan. "Globalization and Ecumenism: A Search for Human Solidarity, with Reference to Pentecostalism/Charismaticism in Hong Kong." *Cyberjournal for Pentecostal-Charismatic Research* 12 (2003).

Kuzmič, Peter. "Pentecostals Respond to Marxism." In *Called and Empowered: Global Mission in Pentecostal Perspective*, edited by Murray Dempster, Bryon Klaus and Douglas Petersen. Peabody: Hendrickson, 1991.

Lawson, Robert Clarence and Arthur M. Anderson. *For the Defense of the Gospel: The Writings of Bishop R. C. Lawson*. New York: Church of our Lord Christ of the Apostolic Faith, 1971.

Lederle, Henry. "Pentecostals and Ecumenical Theological Education." *Ministerial Formation* 80 (1998) 46.

Leoh, Vincent. "Toward Pentecostal Social Ethics." *Journal of Asian Missions* 7 (2005) 39–62.

Lewis, Paul W. "A Pneumatological Approach to Virtue Ethics." Paper presented at The Society for Pentecostal Studies, 1992.

———. "Toward a Pentecostal Epistemology: The Role of Experience in Pentecostal Hermeneutics." *Pneuma* 1 (1998).

Liias, Jurgen W. "Charismatic Power or Military Service." *Christian Century* 100 (1983) 1110–113.

Lorentzen, Lois Ann and Rosalina Mira. "El milagro está en casa: Gender and Private/Public Empowerment in a Migrant Pentecostal Church." *Latin American Perspectives* (2005) 32, 57.

Lovett, Leonard. "Black Holiness Pentecostalism." In *Dictionary of Pentecostal and Charismatic Movements*, edited by Stanley M. Burgess and Gary B. McGee, 76–84. Grand Rapids: Zondervan, 1988.

———. "Black Holiness-Pentecostals: Implications for Ethics and Social Transformation." PhD diss., Emory University, 1979.

———. "Black Origins of the Pentecostal Movement." In *Aspects of Pentecostal-Charismatic Origins*, edited by Vinson Synan, 123–42. Plainfield, NJ: Logos, 1975.

———. "Black Theology." In *Dictionary of Pentecostal and Charismatic Movements*, ed. Stanley M. Burgess and Gary B. McGee, 84–86. Grand Rapids: Zondervan, 1988.

———. "Liberation: A Dual Edged Sword." *Pneuma* 9 (1987) 155–72.

———. *Opening the Front Door of Your Church*. Bakersfield: Pneuma, 1993.

———. "The Present: The Problem of Racism in the Contemporary Pentecostal Movement." *Cyberjournal for Pentecostal-Charismatic Research* 14 (May, 2005).

———. "Racism and Reconciliation." *Charisma* 18.9 (1993) 14–15

Lozano, Felipe Emmanuel Agredano. "The Apostolic Assembly at the Crossroads: The Politics of Gender." Paper presented at The Society of Pentecostal Studies, 1994.

Ma, Wonsuk. "When the Poor are Fired Up: The Role of Pneumatology in Pentecostal-Charismatic Mission." *Cyberjournal for Pentecostal-Charismatic Research* 15 (February, 2006).

Macchia, Frank D. "From Azusa to Memphis: Evaluation the Racial Reconciliation Dialogue among Pentecostals." *Pneuma* 17.2 (1995) 203–18.

———. "I Belong to Christ: A Pentecostal Reflection on Paul's Passion for Unity." *Pneuma* 25 (2003) 1–6.

———. "Praying for the Terrorists." *Pneuma* 23 (2001) 193–96.

———. "Roundtable: Racial Reconciliation." *Pneuma*, 18 (1996) 113–40.

————. *Spirituality and Social Liberation: The Message of the Blumhardts in the Light of Wuerttemberg Pietism, with Implications for Pentecostal Theology.*" Basel, Switzerland: University of Basel, 1990.

————. "Terrorists, Security, and the Risk of Peace: Toward a Moral Vision." *Pneuma* 26 (2004) 13.

MacRobert, Iain. *Black Pentecostalism: Its Origins, Functions and Theology with Special Reference to a Midland Borough.* Edinburgh: St. Andrew's, 1993.

————. *The Black Roots and White Racism of Early Pentecostalism in the USA,* New York: St. Martin's, 1988.

Mason, Elsie W. "Bishop C.H. Manson, Church of God in Christ." In *Afro-American Religious History: A Documentary Witness,* edited by Milton C. Sernett, 286. Durham, NC: Duke University Press, 1985.

McCafferty, Burton. "Is European War Justifiable?" *The Christian Evangel* (December 12, 1914) 1–2.

————. "Should Christians Go To War?" *The Christian Evangel* (January 16, 1915) 1.

Mariz, Cecilia. *Coping with Poverty: Pentecostals and Christian Base Communities in Brazil.* Philadelphia: Temple University Press, 1994.

Marshall-Fratani, Ruth. "Mediating the Global and Local in Nigerian Pentecostalism." *Journal of Religion in Africa* 28.3 (1998) 278–315.

May, Daniel Jordan. "Unbelted Every Soldier: A Brief Note on Pre-Montanist Tertullian's Pacifism." *Pax Pneuma* (Summer 2008).

McDonnell, Kilian. *The Charismatic Renewal and Ecumenism.* New York: Paulist, 1978.

McGee, Gary B. "Pentecostal Missiology: Moving Beyond Triumphalism to Face the Issues." *Pneuma* 16.2 (1994) 275–82.

————. *This Gospel Shall be Preached. Vol 2, A History and Theology of Assemblies of God Foreign Missions since 1959.* Springfield, MO: Gospel, 1989.

McLean, Mark D. "A Pentecostal Perspective on Theodicy." *Pneuma* 1 (1998).

Melander, Veronica. "New Pentecostalism Challenges Old Liberation Theology?" *Swedish Missiological Themes/ Svensk Missions Tidskrift* 87.3 (1999) 341–58.

Menzies, William. *Anointed to Serve: The Story of the Assemblies of God.* Springfield, MO: Gospel, 1971.

————. "Defending the Faith: How the Assemblies of God Responded to Four Challenges to its Beliefs and Practices." *Assemblies of God Heritage* 27 (2007) 48–52.

Menzies, William, and Stanley Horton. *Bible Doctrines.* Springfield, MO: Gospel, 1993.

Miller, Albert G. "Pentecostalism as a Social Movement: Beyond the Theory of Deprivation." *Journal of Pentecostal Theology* 9 (1996) 97–114.

Miller, Donald E., and Tetsunao Yamamori. *Global Pentecostalism: The New Face of Christian Social Engagement.* Berkley: University of California Press, 2007.

Milner, Marlon. "Ancestral Spirits and African-American Apostolicism: Revisiting the Origins, Developments, and Future of Black Apostolic Identity in Light of Afrocenntric Philosophy." Paper presented at The Society for Pentecostal Studies, 2001.

————. "Send Judah First: A Pentecostal Perspective on Peace." Letter to President George Bush, 3 March 2003. Online: www.pcpj.org.

Mills, Robert A. "Musical Prayers: Reflection on the African Roots of Pentecostal Music." *Journal of Pentecostal Theology* 12 (1998) 109–26.

*Minutes of the General Council of the Assemblies of God, 1916.*

*Minutes of the General Council of the Assemblies of God, 1967.*

Mittelstadt, Martin William. "Finding Peace: A Personal and Vocational Narrative." In *The Spirit Leads us to Jesus: Peace and Justice Testimonies of Pentecostal and Charismatic Christians*. Eugene, OR: Wipf & Stock, 2010. [**AQ: not in our list**]

———. "My Life as a Mennocostal: A Personal and Theological Narrative." *Theodidaktos: Journal for EMC Theology and Education* 3.2 (2008) 10–17.

———. "Spirit and Peace in Luke-Acts: Possibilities for Pentecostal/Anabaptist Dialogue." Paper Presented at The Society for Pentecostal Studies, Eugene Bible College, Eugene, OR, 2009.

Mittlestadt, Martin William, and Geoffrey W. Sutton. *Forgiveness, Reconciliation, and Restoration: Multidisciplinary Studies from a Pentecostal Perspective*. Pentecostals, Peacemaking, and Social Justice 3. Eugene, OR: Pickwick, 2010.

Moltmann, Jürgen. "Pentecost and the Theology of Life." In *Pentecostal Movements as an Ecumenical Challenge*, edited by Jürgen Moltmann and Karl-Josef Kuschel, Concilium Series. Maryknoll: Orbis, 1996.

Moon, Jesse K. *War and the Christian*. Springfield, MO: by the author, 1988.

Moore, Rickie D. "Walter Brueggemann: Prophet to the Critical Establishment and Sage to Pentecostals at the Margin." *Pneuma* 1 (1998).

Mouw, Richard J. "Life in the Spirit in an Unjust World." *Pneuma* 9 (1987) 109–28.

Nathan, Ronald A. "Pentecostalism and Ethnic and Racial Diversity." *Cyberjournal for Pentecostal-Charismatic Research* [Journal on-line]. Vol. 5 February, 1999.

Nelson, Douglas J. "The Black Face of Church Renewal: The Meaning of a Charismatic Explosion, 1901–1985." In *Faces of Renewal: Studies in Honor of Stanley M. Horton*, edited by Paul Elbert. Peabody, MA: Hendrickson, 1989.

Nelson, Douglas. "For Such a Time as This: The Story of Bishop William J. Seymour." PhD diss., University of Birmingham, 1981.

Nichol, John Thomas. *Pentecostalism*. New York: Harper & Row, 1966.

Owen, Philip Clifford. "The Ecumenical Nature of Charismatic Renewal: A Study of Anglican and Roman Catholic Charismatic Renewal in England." PhD diss., University of Birmingham, 2007.

Parham, Charles Fox. *The Life of Charles F. Parham: Founder of the Apostolic Faith Movement*, compiled by his wife [Sarah Parham]. New York: Garland, 1985.

Paris, Arthur E. Black *Pentecostalism: Southern Religion in an Urban World*. Amherst, MA: University of Massachusetts Press, 1982.

Paul, George H. "The Religious Frontier in Oklahoma: Dan T. Muse and the Pentecostal Holiness Church." PhD diss., University of Oklahoma, 1965.

"The Pentecostal Movement and the Conscription Law." *Weekly Evangel* (August 4, 1917) 6.

Petersen, Douglas. "The Kingdom of God and the Hermeneutical Circle: Pentecostal Praxis in the Third World." In *Called and Empowered: Global Mission in Pentecostal Perspective*, edited by Murray Dempster, Bryon D. Klaus, and Douglas Petersen. Peabody: Hendrickson, 1991.

———. "Latin American Pentecostalism: Social Capital, Networks, and Politics." *Pneuma* 26.2 (2004) 293–306.

———. *Not by Might Nor by Power: A Pentecostal Theology of Social Concern in Latin America*. Oxford UK: Begnum, 1996.

———. "Toward a Latin American Pentecostal Political Praxis." Paper presented at The Society for Pentecostal Studies, 1996.

Plüss, Jean-Daniel. "Globalization of Pentecostalism or Globalization of Individualism? A European Perspective." In *The Globalization of Pentecostalism: A Religion Made to Travel,* edited by Murray Dempster, Byron D. Klaus, and Douglas Petersen. Oxford: Regnum Books, 1999.

Pipkin, Brian K. "Church of God in Christ Endorses Human Rights in the Hague." *Pax Pneuma* 5 (Spring 2009) 5–10.

———. "The Foursquare Conscientious Objector: Jesus' Role in Shaping a Christian Response to War and Peace in the Early Literature of the International Church of the Foursquare Gospel from 1917 to 1943." MAR thesis, Azusa Pacific University, December 2009.

———. "Pentecostal Conscientious Objectors in World War II." In *Peace to War: Shifting Allegiances in the Assemblies of God,* edited by Paul Alexander, 352–57. Telford, PA: Cascadia, 2008.

Poewe, Karla. "Links and Parallels between Black and White Charismatic Churches in South Africa and the States: Potential for Cultural Transformation." *Pneuma* 10.2 (1988) 141–58.

———. "The Nature, Globality and History of Charismatic Christianity." In *Charismatic Christianity as a Global Culture,* edited by Karla Poewe. Columbia: University of South Carolina Press, 1994.

———. "Rethinking the Relationship of Anthropology to Science and Religion." In *Charismatic Christianity as a Global Culture,* edited by Karla Poewe. Columbia: University of South Carolina Press, 1994.

Price, Lynne. *Theology Out of Place: A Theological Biography of Walter J. Hollenweger.* New York: Sheffield Academic Press, 2002.

Pruitt, Richard. "Java and Justice: Journeys in Pentecostal Missions Educattion." *Pneuma* 30 (2008) 164–65.

Quebedeaux, Richard. *The New Charismatics II.* New York: Harper & Row, 1983.

Ramirez, Daniel. "Pentecostal Praxis: An Analysis of the Experience of Latino Immigrants in the Apostolic Assembly Churches of the United States." Paper presented at The Society for Pentecostal Studies, 1991.

Raven, Charles Earle. *Theological Basis of Christian Pacifism.* Nyack, NY: Fellowship, 1951.

Reid, Robert G. "Savior and Lord in the Lukan Birth Narrative: A Challenge to Caesar?" *Pax Pneuma* 5 (Spring 2009) 46–61.

Richie, Tony. "Pentecostal Spirituality Politically Applied." *Pax Pneuma* 5 (Spring 2009) 28–33.

———. "The Unity of the Spirit: Are Pentecostals Inherently Ecumenists and Inclusivists?" *The Journal of the European Pentecostal Theological Association* 26 (2006) 21–35.

Roebuck, David G. "Big Brother and the Lady Evangelist: The Masculinization of Evangelism in the Church of God." Paper presented at The Society for Pentecostal Studies, 1996.

———. "From Extraordinary Call to Spirit Baptism: Phoebe Palmer's Use of Pentecostal Language to Justify Women in Ministry." Paper presented at The Society for Pentecostal Studies, 1988.

———. "Go and Tell my Brothers:" The Waning of Women's Voices in American Pentecostalism." Paper presented at The Society for Pentecostal Studies, 1990.

Robeck, Cecil M. *The Azusa Street Mission and Revival.* Nashville: Nelson, 2006.

———. "David du Plessis and the Challenge of Dialogue." *Pneuma* 9 (Spring 1987) 14.

———. "Pentecostals and Social Ethics." *Pneuma* 9 (Fall 1987) 103–7.

———. "Pentecostals and Ecumenism in a Pluralistic World." In *The Globalization of Pentecostalism: A Religion Made to Travel*, edited by Murray Dempster, Byron D. Klaus, and Douglas Petersen. Oxford: Regnum, 1999.

———. "Pentecostals and Social Ethics." *Pneuma* 9.2 (1987) 103–7.

———. "Pentecostals and the Apostolic Faith: Implications for Ecumenism." *Pneuma* 9 (1987) 61–68.

———. "Racial Reconciliation at Memphis: Some Personal Reflections." *Pneuma* 18 (Spring 1996) 135–40.

———. "The Social Concern of Early American Pentecostalism," in *Pentecost, Mission, and Ecumenism: Essays on Intercultural Theology*. Studies in the Intercultural History of Christianity 75. Frankfurt am Main: Peter Lang, 1992, 97–106.

———. "Southern Religion with a Latin Accent." *Pneuma* 13.2 (1991).

———. *Witness to Pentecost: The Life of Frank Bartleman*. New York: Garland, 1985.

Robert, Dana L. "Shifting Southward: Global Christianity since 1945." *International Bulletin of Missionary Research* 24.2 (2000) 50–58.

Robins, Roger. "A Chronology of Peace: Attitudes Toward War and Peace in the Assemblies of God: 1914–1918." *Pneuma* 6 (Spring 1984) 3–25.

———. "Our Forgotten Heritage: A Look at Early Pentecostal Pacifism." *Assemblies of God Heritage* 6 (Winter 1986–1987) 3–5.

Robinson, James. "Arthur Booth-Clibborn: Pentecostal Patriarch." *Journal of the European Pentecostal Theological Association* 21 (2001) 68–90.

Rodriquez, Darío López. "And Jesus Gave Him to His Mother: When the Fragile Encounter the God of Life." *Pax Pneuma* (Winter 2007–2008). Online: www.pcpf.org.

———. "From Alternative Religion to Established Religion: The Deconstruction of the 'Subversive Memory' of the Church of God." *Pax Pneuma* 5.2 (Fall 2009) 54–63.

———. "The Liberating Mission of Jesus: A Reading of the Gospel of Luke in Missiological Key." *Transformation* 14 (1997) 23–30.

———. "Pentecostal Identity, Diversity, and Public Witness: A Critical Review of Allan Anderson's An Introduction to Pentecostalism." *Journal of Pentecostal Theology* 16 (2007) 51–57.

Roebuck, David. "Perfect Liberty to Preach the Gospel: Women Ministers in the Church of God." *Pneuma* 17 (1995) 25–32.

Rutherford, Brinton. "The Historical Development of 'Forgiveness' and 'Reconciliation' in the Ecumenical Ministry of David Du Plessis." Paper presented at The Society for Pentecostal Studies, 1999.

Sanders, Cheryl. "Afrocentric and Womanist Approaches to Theological Education." *Ministerial Formation* 93 (April 2001) 7–12.

———. "And Still We Rise: An Introduction to Black Liberation Theology." *Journal of Church and State* 39.3 (1997) 599.

———. "Democracy Matters: Winning the Fight Against Imperialism." *Christian Century* 122.14 (2005) 35–37.

———. "Hope and Empathy: Toward an Ethic of Black Empowerment." *Journal of Religious Thought* 52–53.2 (1996) 1–17.

———. "How We Do Church: Worship, Empowerment and Racial Identity." In *Gospel in Black and White: Theological Resources for Racial Reconciliation*, edited by Dennis L. Okholm. Downers Grove, IL: InterVarsity, 1997.

———. "Kingdom Beyond Color: Re-Examining the Phenomenon of Racism." *Pneuma* 27 (2005) 202–4.

————. "Resistance, Rebellion, and Reform: The Collegiate Gospel Choir Movement in the United States." *Journal of the Interdenominational Theological Center* 27 (1999–2000) 199–211.

————. "Themes of Exile and Empowerment in the Million Man March." In *Black Religion After the Million Man March*, edited by Garth Kasimu Baker-Fletcher. Maryknoll, NY: Orbis, 1998.

————. "Tribal Talk: Black Theology, Hermeneutics, and African American Ways of Telling the Story." *Modern Theology* 17.2 (2001) 256–58.

Sandidge, Jerry L. "Roman Catholic/Pentecostal Dialogue: A Contribution to Christian Unity." *Pneuma* 7 (1985) 41–60.

Santiago-Vendrell, Angel. "From Religious Sect to Prophetic Movement: A Missiological Interpretation of Pentecostalism in Brazil in Dialogue with M. Richard Shaull." *Pax Pneuma* 5.2 (Fall 2009) 38–47.

Satyavrata, Ivan M. "Contextual Perspectives on Pentecostalism as a Global Culture: A South Asian View." In *The Globalization of Pentecostalism: A Religion Made to Travel*, edited by Murray Dempster, Bryon D. Klaus, and Douglas Petersen. Oxford: Regnum, 1999.

Self, Charles E. "Conscientization, Conversion and Convergence: Reflections on Base Communities and Emerging Pentecostalism in Latin America." *Pneuma* 14 (1992) 59–72.

Sepúlveda, Juan. "The Challenge for Theological Education from a Pentecostal Staindpoint." *Ministerial Formation* 87 (1999) 29–30.

————. "Pentecostalism and Liberation Theology: Two Manifestations of the Work of the Spirit for the Renewal of the Church." In *All Together in One Place: Theological Papers from the Brighton Conference on World Evangelization*, edited by Harold Hunter and P. D. Hocken. Sheffield: Sheffield Academic Press, 1993.

————. "Pentecostal Theology in the Context of the Struggle of Life." In *Faith Born in the Struggle for Life: A Rereading of Protestant Faith in Latin America Today*, edited by Dow Kirkpatrick. Grand Rapids: Eerdmans, 1988.

————. "To Overcome the Fear of Syncretism: A Latin American Perspective." In *Mission Matters*, edited by L. Price, J. Sepúlveda, and G. Smith. Frankfurt: Peter Lang, 1997.

Sheppard, Gerald T. "Pentecostals, Globalization, and Postmodern Hermeneutics: Implications for the Politics of Scriptural Interpretation." In *The Globalization of Pentecostalism: A Religion Made to Travel*, edited by Murray Dempster, Bryon D. Klaus, and Douglas Petersen. Oxford: Regnum, 1999.

Sheppard, Jerry W. "Attitudes of Pentecostals toward Civil Rights, Civil Liberties and Welfare Issues." Paper presented at The Society for Pentecostal Studies, 1990.

Shively, Jordan. "Consumerism in Light of the Poor." *Pax Pneuma* (Summer 2005). Online: www.pcpf.org.

Shuman, Joel. "Pentecost and the End of Patriotism: A Call for the Restoration of Pacifism among Pentecostal Christians." *Journal of Pentecostal Theology* 9 (1996) 70–96.

————. "The Priority of Love: Christian Charity and Social Justice." *Modern Theology* 20.4 (2004) 618–20.

————. "Same-sex Marriage? A Christian Analysis." *Christian Century* 121.13 (2004) 38–39.

————. "Theological Bioethics: Participation, Justice, and Change. *Modern Theology* 24.3 (2008) 508–10.

Smidt, Corwin. "Praise the Lord Politics: A Comparative Analysis of the Social Characteristics and Political Views of American Evangelical and Charismatic Christians." *Sociological Analysis* 50 (Spring 1989) 53–72.

Smilde, David A. "Gender Relations and Social change in Latin American Evangelicalism." In *Coming of Age: Protestantism in Contemporary Latin America*, edited by Daniel R. Miller. Washington: University Press of America, 1994.

Smith, Calvin L. "Book Review of Whose Land? Whose Promise?" Review of *Whose Land? Whose Promise? What Christians Are Not Being Told About Israel and the Palestinians*, by Gary M. Burge, Cleveland, OH: Pilgrim, 2003.

———. "Revolution, Revival and Religious Conflict in Sandinista Nicaragua." *Exchange* 36.2 (2007) 226–28.

———. "Revolutionaries and Revivalists: Pentecostal Eschatology, Politics, and the Nicaraguan Revolution." *Pneuma* 30 (2008).

Smith, Dennis. "Coming of Age: A Reflection on Pentecostals, Politics, and Popular Religion in Guatemala." *Pneuma* 13.2 (1991).

Smith, James K. A. "Private Religion, Public Injustice? A Levinasian Critique of Pentecostal Worship." *Pneuma* 2 (2000).

Snell, Jeffrey T. "Beyond the Individual and into the World: A Call to Participation in the Larger Purposes of the Spirit on the Basis of Pentecostal Theology." *Pneuma* 14 (1992) 43–57.

Solivan, Samuel. "The Reconciliation Dialogue of Oct. 17–19, 1994, Memphis Tennessee: A Hispanic/Latino Pentecostal Response." Paper presented at The Society for Pentecostal Studies, 1996.

———. *The Spirit, Pathos and Liberation: Toward a Hispanic Pentecostal Theology.* Sheffield, UK: Sheffield Academic Press, 1999.

Spellman, Robert C. "Issues of Consensus and Controversy Within and Amongst Mainline Black Pentecostal Church Organizations." Paper presented at The Society for Pentecostal Studies, 1990.

Stanley, John E. "Liberation as a Focal Image for New Testament Ethics: A Response to Richard B. Hays." *Pneuma* 2 (1998).

Stephenson, Lisa P. "Religious Symbols and Ecclesial Practices: Women's Full Humanity and Their Status within the Church." *Pax Pneuma* 5.2 (Fall 2009) 48–53.

Stewart, Alexander C. "From Immigration to Migration: The Influence of African Caribbean Americans and West Indians on the American Pentecostal Movement." *Pneuma* 2 (1998).

Stoll, David. *Is Latin America Turning Protestant? The Politics of Evangelical Growth.* University of California Press, 1991.

Story, Lyle J. "Finishing the Story of Peace: A Biblical Study on 2 Kings 6:8–23." *Pax Pneuma* 5.2 (Fall 2009) 35–37.

———. "The Spirit-Filled Servant's Agenda of 'Becoming the Neighbor." *Pax Pneuma* 5 (Spring 2009) 21–27.

Stronstad, Roger. "Affirming Diversity: God's People as a Community of Prophets." *Pneuma* 17 (1995) 145–57.

Suico, Joseph. "Pentecostalism and Social Change." *Asian Journal of Pentecostal Studies*. 8.2 (July 2005) 195–213.

———. "Pentecostalism: Towards A Movement of Social Transformation in the Philippines." *Journal of Asian Mission* 1 (1999) 7–19.

Sunrmond, Jean-Jacques. "Christ King: A Charismatic Appeal for an Ecological Lifestyle." *Pneuma* 10 (Spring 1988) 26–35.

Sutton, Matthew. *Aimee Semple McPherson and the Resurrection of Christian America*. London: Harvard University Press, 2007.

Syan, Vinson. "The Future: A Strategy for Reconciliation." *Cyberjournal for Pentecostal-Charismatic Research* [Journal on-line] 14 (May 2005).

———. *The Holiness-Pentecostal Movement in the United States*. Grand Rapids: Eerdmans, 1971.

———. *The Old-Time Power*. Franklin Springs, GA: Advocate, 1973.

Taylor, Aaron. *Alone With a Jihadist: A Biblical Response to Holy War*. Manchester, CT: Foghorn, 2009.

———. "How a Radical Jihadist Led Me To Jesus." *Pax Pneuma* (Summer 2008). Online: www.pcpf.org.

Thomas, Christopher. "Women in the Church: An Experiment in Pentecostal Hermeneutics." *Evangelical Review of Theology* 20 (1996) 220–32.

Thompson, H. Paul, Jr. "On Account of Conditions that Seem Unalterable: A Proposal about Race Relations in the Church of God (Cleveland, TN) 1909–1929." *Pneuma* 25.2 (2003) 240–64.

Tinney, James S. "William J. Seymour; Father of Modern-Day Pentecostalism." *The Journal of the Interdenominational Theological Center* 4 (1976) 34–44

Villafañe, Eldin. *Beyond Cheap Grace: A Call to Radical Discipleship, Incarnation, and Justice*. Grand Rapids: Eerdmans, 2006.

———. *The Liberating Spirit: Toward an Hispanic American Pentecostal Social Ethic*. Grand Rapids: Eerdmans, 1993.

———. "Pentecostal Call to Social Spirituality: Confronting Evil in Urban Society." Paper presented at The Society for Pentecostal Studies, 1990.

———. "The Politics of the Spirit: Reflections on a Theology of Social Transformation for the Twenty-First Century." *Pneuma* 18.2 (1996) 161–70.

Vinson Synan. *The Holiness Pentecostal Movement in the United States*. Grand Rapids: Eerdmans, 1971.

Volf, Miroslav. *Exclusion and Embrace: A Theological Exploration of Identity, Otherness and Reconciliation*. Nashville: Abingdon, 1996.

———. "Human Work, Divine Spirit and New Creation: Towards a Pneumatological Understanding of Work." *Pneuma* 9.2 (1996) 173–93.

———. "Materiality of Salvation: An Investigation in the Soteriologies of Liberation and Pentecostal Theologies." *Journal of Ecumenical Studies* 26.3 (1989).

———. *Work in the Spirit: Toward a Theology of Work*. Eugene, OR: Wipf & Stock, 2001.

Vondey, Wolfgang. "Christian Amnesia: Who in the World Are Pentecostals?" *Pneuma* 2 (2000).

Wacker, Grant. *Heaven Below*. Cambridge: Harvard, 2001.

Wainwright, Geoffrey. "The One Hope of Your Calling? The Ecumenical and Pentecostal Movements after a Century." *Pneuma* 25 (2003) 7–28.

Waldrop, Richard E. "The Social Consciousness and Involvement of the Full Gospel Church of God in Guatemala." *Cyberjournal for Pentecostal-Charismatic Research* [Journal on-line] 2 (July 1997).

Walsh, Arlene M. Sánchez. "Building as Multicultural Church: Historical Perspectives." Paper presented at the Wilson Institute for Pentecostal Studies, Vanguard University, 2000.

———. "Christian Coalition," "Pat Robertson." In *Encyclopedia of Modern Christian Politics*. Greenwood, 2006.

————. "Does it Matter that 11 a.m. Sunday is the Most Segregated Hour in the U.S.?" Paper presented at the UIC Sociology Department, Race and Ethnicity Conference, 2001.

————. "Future of Latino Pentecostalism." In *The Future of Pentecostalism*, edited by Edmund Rybarcyzk. Lexington, 2007.

————. "Holy Ghost Set-up: Victory Outreach and the Search for Latino/a Pentecostal Identity." *Pneuma* 2 (1998).

————. "Intersections for Ecumenical Discussion Among Latino Catholics and Pentecostals." Paper presented at the Catholic Theological Union, ACTHUS Conference, 2001.

————. "Latino Evangelicals: Rediscovering a Religious Heritage." Paper presented at the Wesleyan/Pentecostal Consultation Conference, Kansas City, 2004.

————. "Latino Pentecostal Identity: A Roundtable Discussion of New Books." Paper presented at The Society for Pentecostal Studies, 2004.

————. *Latino Pentecostal Identity: Evangelical Faith, Society, and Self.* New York: Columbia University Press, 2003.

————. "Latino Protestant Ministry in Los Angeles." Paper presented at the Center for Religion and Civic Culture, University of Southern California, 2000.

————. "Mexican Americans." In *Latino Religion in the United States*, edited by Hector Avalos, (2004).

————. "Popular Culture and the Making of La Vina Christian Fellowship." Paper presented at The Society for Pentecostal Studies, 2000.

————. "Slipping into Darkness: Victory Outreach, the Vineyard, and the Creation of a Latino Evangelical Youth Culture." In *Gen-X Religion*, edited by Donald E. Miller and Richard Flory. Routledge, 2000.

————. "Underground Fire: Creating a Latino Evangelical Youth Culture." *Pneuma* 2 (2000).

————. "World Apart: Multicultural Evangelical Youth Culture." Paper presented at The Society for Pentecostal Studies, 2004.

Wenk, Matthias. "The Creative Power of the Prophetic Dialogue." *Pnuema* 26 (Spring 2004) 118–29.

————. "The Holy Spirit as Transforming Power within a Society: Pneumatological Spirituality and its Political—Social Relevance for Western Europe." *Journal of Pentecostal Theology* 11 (2002) 130–42.

Wessels, G Francois. "Charismatic Christian Congregations and Social Justice—A South African Perspective." *Missionalia* 25.3 (1999) 360–74.

————. "A Pentecostal Response to Violence in the Book of Nahum." Paper presented at The Society for Pentecostal Studies, 2001.

West, Russell W. "Fighting Racism's Giants in Saul's Armor: An Interpretative Critique of the Pentecostal Leadership's Quest for Racial Unity." *Pneuma* 2 (1999).

Wilkinson, Michael. "The Migration of Pentecostals to North America: A Case Study of Ethnic Congregations in Canada." *Pneuma* 2 (1999).

Williams, David T. "Kenotic Warfare: Christian Action against Aggression." *Evangel* 25.3 (2007) 80–86.

Williamson, Rick L. "Female/Male Pairs in Luke: Gender Balance in Proclaiming the Word of God." *Pneuma* 2 (1998).

Wilson, Bryan. "Role Conflicts and Status Contradictions of the Pentecostal Minister." *American Journal of Sociology* 64 (1959) 494–504.

Wilson, Dwight. "Pacifism." In *Dictionary of Pentecostal and Charismatic Movements*, edited by Stanley M. Burgess, and Gary B. McGee. Grand Rapids: Zondervan, 1988.

Wilson, Everett. "Latin American Pentecostals: Their Potential for Ecumenical Dialogue." *Pneuma* 9 (1987) 85–90.

———. *Strategy of the Spirit: J. Philip Hogan and the Growth of the Assemblies of God Worldwide 1960–1990*. Oxford: Regnum, 1997.

Wimber, John. *Beyond Intolerance*. Anaheim, CA: Vineyard Ministries, 1996.

Yoder, John Howard. *Christian Attitudes to War, Peace, and Revolution: A Companion to Bainton*. Elkhart, IN: Co-Op Bookstore, 1983.

———. Foreword to *Pentecostal Pacifism*, by Jay Beaman. Hillsboro, KS: Center for Mennonite Brethren Studies, 1989.

———. *When War is Unjust*. Maryknoll: Orbis, 1996.

Yong, Amos. "Beyond the Liberal-Conservative Divide: An Appreciative Rejoinder to Allan Anderson." *Journal of Pentecostal Theology* 16 (2007) 103–11.

———. "Creation Ex Nihilo for an Intra-Pentecostal Dispute." *Pneuma* 19 (Spring 1997) 81–107.

———. *Discerning the Spirit(s): A Pentecostal-Charismatic Contribution to Christian Theology of Religions*. Journal of Pentecostal Theology Supplement Series 20. Sheffield: Sheffield Academic Press, 2000.

———. "Guests, Hosts, and the Holy Ghost: Pneumatological Theology and Christian Practices in a World of Many Faiths." In *Lord and Giver of Life: Perspectives on Constructive Pneumatology*, edited by David H. Jensen. (Louisville: Westminster John Knox, 2008) 71–86.

———. "Justice Deprived, Justice Demanded: Afropentecostalisms and the Task of World Pentecostal Theology Today." *Journal of Pentecostal Theology* 15 (2006) 127–47.

———. "Not Knowing Where the Wind Blows: On Envisioning a Pentecostal-Charismatic Theology of Religions." *Journal of Pentecostal Theology* 14 (1999) 81–112.

———. "Salvation, Society, and the Spirit: Pentecostal Contextualization and Political Theology from Cleveland to Birmingham, from Springfield to Seoul. *Pax Pneuma* 5.2 (Fall 2009) 22–34.

———. *The Spirit Poured Out on All Flesh: Pentecostalism and the Possibilities of Global Theology*. Grand Rapids: Baker Academic, 2005.

———. "What Empire? Which Multitude? Pentecostalism & Social Liberation in North America & Sub-Saharan Africa." In *Evangelicals and Empire: Christian Alternatives to the Political Status Quo*, edited by Bruce Ellis Benson and Peter Goodwin Heltzel, 237–51. Grand Rapids: Brazos, 2008.

———. "Whither Asian American Evangelical Theology? What Asian? Which American? Whose Evangelion?" *Evangelical Review of Theology* 32 (2008) 22–37.

www.ingramcontent.com/pod-product-compliance
Lightning Source LLC
Chambersburg PA
CBHW072042020426
42334CB00017B/1365